"The study of the covenants and their role in Reformed theology has, at least since the nineteenth-century work of Heppe, commanded a large swath of scholarly writing. Academics have weighed in on such varied arguments as the significance of the number of the covenants, the active participants in biblical covenants, and the centrality of those covenants in any given system. Rarely does such a lengthy conversation find a new, helpful partner, but Robert Wainwright has proved to be that rare exception. His masterly examination of the discussions of covenant in the primary sources and in their historical context not only clarifies the development of this theological trajectory, but also sheds light on the broader project of English Reform. Wainwright's work must now take its rightful place in the canon of English Reformation studies."

—**Jonathan W. Arnold**, Associate Professor of Church History and Historical Theology, Director of Research Doctoral Studies, Southwestern Baptist Theological Seminary

"The clarity of its analysis and the richness of its evidence make Robert Wainwright's book an excellent guide to the early English Reformers' encounter with the theology of Zurich and Basel, Strasbourg and Geneva."

—**Steven Gunn**, Professor of Early Modern History, Merton College, University of Oxford

"Focusing on the concept of covenant as a marker of Swiss influence on English theology during the early Reformation period, Robert Wainwright offers a timely, scholarly, and persuasive reassertion of the Reformed character of the English Reformation. His study not only provides welcome discussion of several significant but neglected voices within early English Protestantism, but also explores the distinctive character of early Reformed covenant theology more widely. *Early Reformation Covenant Theology* will consequently be very welcome to anyone interested in the development of Reformed Protestantism, whether in England or elsewhere."

—**Stephen Hampton**, Dean and Senior Tutor, Peterhouse, University of Cambridge

"Rob Wainwright has written a path-breaking study of covenant theology in early Tudor England. He shows how vital Swiss influence was in the construction of evangelical identities, and argues powerfully that the Reformed theologians of Zurich and Strasbourg have been underestimated, that of Luther overstressed. The book will be essential reading for all those engaged in the study of the early Reformation."
—**Felicity M. Heal**, FBA, Emeritus Fellow and Lecturer in History, Jesus College, University of Oxford

"Robert Wainwright's monograph *Early Reformation Covenant Theology* rides the crest of a wave of an innovative reinterpretation of the English Reformation. More than likely to set the cat among the pigeons, Wainwright challenges the widely held assumption of the 'exceptional' or 'peculiar' character of England's Reformation that has long constituted an axiom of English Reformation historiography, both traditional and revisionist. Yet as Wainwright persuasively shows, this narrative of English exceptionalism has obscured the profound influence of Swiss Reformed theology on English Protestant thought dating from the 1520s and flowering during the reign of Edward VI. The reception of Continental Reformed divinity, especially of Huldrych Zwingli, Heinrich Bullinger, John Calvin, and Peter Martyr Vermigli, exerted a decisive influence on the shape of the Elizabethan Settlement. Wainwright cogently demonstrates that the 'Zurich Connection' in particular played a key role in defining the course of the Reformation in England."
—**Torrance Kirby**, FRHistS, Professor of Ecclesiastical History, Graduate Programme Director, McGill University

"Robert Wainwright's meticulous study of covenantal thinking in the early English Reformation is a model for how the history of theology and the history of religious movements can be fruitfully integrated. It should also be required reading for anyone who still thinks that the Reformation in England had little to do with the currents of reform elsewhere in sixteenth-century Europe."
—**Peter Marshall**, FBA, Department of History, University of Warwick

"*Reformation Covenant Theology* is well researched and well composed. In particular, Wainwright's work shines a light on a previously murky question—namely, the extent to which Continental Reformed work was influencing the English church in that first generation of the Reformation. I think this book will pave the way for future, very fruitful studies, capitalizing on the author's efforts. Highly recommended."

—**Benjamin R. Merkle**, President, New Saint Andrews College

"In this important contribution to Reformation scholarship, Robert Wainwright explores the influence of the Swiss Reformation—particularly as it took shape in Zurich—on the early English Reformers, specifically William Tyndale, Miles Coverdale, John Hooper, and John Bradford. Examining covenant theology and the theology of the sacraments, Wainwright argues for the significance of the European dimension of the English Reformation and particularly for the early influence of the emerging Reformed tradition. Wainwright's careful reading of the writings of the Continental Reformers (Huldrych Zwingli, Heinrich Bullinger, and Jean Calvin) alongside those of the English Reformers (Tyndale, Coverdale, Hooper, and Bradford) shows similarities and lines of influence in a way that has not been done before. Wainwright argues convincingly for a strong and direct influence of Reformed theology on the theology of the early English Reformation. Although Wainwright's is not a new argument, the evidence that he adduces here makes possible a deeper understanding of the English Reformation's indebtedness to the Reformed strand of the Continental Reformation."

—**Charlotte Methuen**, Professor of Ecclesiastical History, University of Glasgow

Early Reformation Covenant Theology

Reformed Academic Dissertations

A Series

Series Editor
John J. Hughes

Early Reformation Covenant Theology

English Reception of Swiss Reformed Thought, 1520–1555

Robert J. D. Wainwright

P U B L I S H I N G
P.O. BOX 817 • PHILLIPSBURG • NEW JERSEY 08865-0817

© 2020 by Robert J. D. Wainwright

All rights reserved. No part of this book may be reproduced, stored in a retrieval system, or transmitted in any form or by any means—electronic, mechanical, photocopy, recording, or otherwise—except for brief quotations for the purpose of review or comment, without the prior permission of the publisher, P&R Publishing Company, P.O. Box 817, Phillipsburg, New Jersey 08865-0817.

Scripture quotations are taken from the New Revised Standard Version Bible (NRSV). Copyright © 1989 by the National Council of the Churches of Christ in the United States of America. Used by permission. All rights reserved.

Early Reformation Covenant Theology: English Reception of Swiss Reformed Thought 1520–1555, Robert J. D. Wainwright, B.A., University of Durham, England, M.A., M.St., D.Phil., University of Oxford, England, 2011, for the degree of D.Phil. Co-supervisors: Charlotte Methuen, Professor of Church History, University of Glasgow; Susan Brigden, Emeritus Fellow, Lincoln College, Oxford.

Printed in the United States of America

ISBN: 978-1-62995-700-5

For Robin,
in quo dolus non est

Ite et vos in vineam meam, et quod iustum fuerit dabo vobis.
S. Matthew xx. 4

Contents

Series Introduction   ix
Foreword by Diarmaid MacCulloch   xi
Acknowledgments   xiii
Abbreviations   xv

1. Introduction   1
   Covenant and the Reformed Tradition
   Covenant and Late Medieval Scholasticism
   Exception and Reception
   Covenant and the English Reformers
2. Reformed Theology in England   42
   Henry VIII
   Reformed Evangelicalism, 1520–47
   Early Evangelicalism in the Low Countries
   Lollardy
   Humanism
   Reformed Evangelicalism, 1547–55
3. Swiss Concepts of Covenant   113
   Huldrych Zwingli
   Heinrich Bullinger
   John Calvin
4. English Concepts of Covenant   146
   William Tyndale
   Miles Coverdale

Contents

  John Hooper
  John Bradford

5. Swiss Sacramental Theology 222
  Huldrych Zwingli
  Heinrich Bullinger
  John Calvin

6. English Sacramental Theology 264
  William Tyndale
  Miles Coverdale
  John Hooper
  John Bradford

7. Imprecisely Reformed 331

 Bibliography 351
  Manuscripts
  Printed Primary Sources
  Secondary Literature
  Unpublished Dissertations
 Index of Scripture 391
 Index of Subjects and Names 393

Series Introduction

P&R Publishing has a long and distinguished history of publishing carefully selected, high-value theological books in the Reformed tradition. Many theological books begin as dissertations, but many dissertations are worthy of publication in their own right. Realizing this, P&R has launched the Reformed Academic Dissertation (RAD) program to publish top-tier dissertations (Ph.D., Th.D., D.Min., and Th.M.) that advance biblical and theological scholarship by making distinctive contributions in the areas of theology, ethics, biblical studies, apologetics, and counseling.

Dissertations in the RAD series are curated, which means that they are carefully selected, on the basis of strong recommendations by the authors' supervisors and examiners and by our internal readers, to be part of our collection. Each selected dissertation will provide clear, fresh, and engaging insights about significant theological issues.

A number of theological institutions have partnered with us to recommend dissertations that they believe worthy of publication in the RAD series. Not only does this provide increased visibility for participating institutions, it also makes outstanding dissertations available to a broad range of readers while helping to introduce promising authors to the publishing world.

We look forward to seeing the RAD program grow into a large collection of curated dissertations that will help to advance Reformed scholarship and learning.

John J. Hughes
Series Editor

Foreword

The insularity of the English, so evident in national events of the last three years, takes at least some of its force from the insular history of the English Reformation created by one historical tradition in the Church of England. On this view, the theology and devotional practice of the English Reformation owed nothing of importance to unfortunate events over the English Channel from 1517, which merely signified that it was time for Anglicanism to present a more native form of Western Christianity, without interference from the Bishop of Rome. Happily, such distortion of reality has largely disappeared from the thinking of those who actually study the course of events in the sixteenth and seventeenth centuries; we now see how the English Reformation represented the outer waves of events in mainland Europe, and in particular how it reflected the struggles of English Reformation theologians to work out what a Protestant Reformation meant. They made choices out of what was on offer in the various different aisles of the Reformation supermarket, and they did so from early days with an informed eye and with distinctive long-term results. Even though here as elsewhere, Martin Luther's stance against the Pope mightily impressed those drawn to Reformation, England was destined like its neighbour Scotland to move away from what turned into a specific Protestant identity called 'Lutheranism,' towards the theologians of central Europe who became convinced that Luther had seen only part of the truth.

Robert Wainwright's study of this process is a forensic demonstration not merely of 'the strange death of Lutheran England,' but of the positive English turn towards what in the course of the sixteenth

Foreword

century gained an identity as Reformed Protestantism. He explores the theme of reciprocal covenant pioneered by Huldrych Zwingli and much further expounded by his successor Heinrich Bullinger; he shows how early this theme entered English discussion, as William Tyndale brooded on its implications for understanding the Christian message, and influenced Miles Coverdale to follow suit in their enterprises of biblical translation and exposition. Might such theologians have supposed that the arch-opponent of justification by faith and chief enemy of Luther, King Henry VIII, could be drawn to this moralist theme and thence to an understanding of Protestantism? If so, their hopes were to be disappointed, as King Henry chose to cast a hostile eye on Swiss eucharistic theology instead. Yet the long-term implications of covenant in English theological construction effortlessly outlived the much-married monarch. A sure-footed and expert guide, Robert Wainwright gives us the resources to set out on that English Reformed Protestant journey.

Diarmaid MacCulloch
Professor of the History of the Church
University of Oxford

Acknowledgments

The research that forms the basis of this monograph was funded by the Arts and Humanities Research Council between 2008 and 2011. I could not have asked for better allies in my supervisors Susan Brigden and Charlotte Methuen who proffered thorough advice with enormous patience and generosity on my every visit to Lincoln and to Keble. I am further indebted to Felicity Heal and Peter Marshall for their examination and recommendation to publish. I was, then, immediately preoccupied with Schools and ordination, but once in parish Paul Helm kindly encouraged me to revise the thesis for publication with P&R. I am grateful to John Hughes for accepting it into the Reformed Academic Dissertations series and for the help given throughout the process.

Many scholars in Oxford and further afield have given freely of their advice and stimulating discussion, among them Diarmaid MacCulloch, Christopher Haigh, Sarah Mortimer, Sarah Apetrei, Steve Gunn, Glyn Redworth, the late Chris Brooks, Peter Stephens, Torrance Kirby, Ian Hazlett, the late David Loades, Philip Johnston, Eric Descheemaeker, Lydia Schumacher, Brian Leftow, and the librarians at the Bodleian. At Christ Church I was glad of the friendship and expertise of numerous fellow students, especially my housemate Mario Paganini. I am gratefully indebted to Patrick and Lydia Gilday and Nick and Sally Welsh for their extraordinary support through Finals and much else besides.

My cousin Simon Burton first suggested covenant theology to me as a subject for a Master's thesis. He has been a friend and intellectual companion all my life. Tony Jones provoked the initial

Acknowledgments

questions for which I sought answers. I continue to reap the benefit of those foundational conversations with Tom Underhill, Kirsty and Matthew Pringle, Katherine Totton, Joanna Deadman, Phil Keen, and with Robin Ham, to whom this book is dedicated, whom I trust more than myself. His steady consistency from the first day until now has helped me to see what covenant faithfulness looks like. To my parents Nick and Meg and sisters Iley and Lydia, for their constancy in the greatest virtue, my love and deepest thanks. Iley has written her own book on 'the covenant theology' which promises to be much more fun.

Robert J. D. Wainwright
Oriel College, Oxford
Charles, King and Martyr, 2019

Abbreviations

AM	John Foxe, *Acts and Monuments*, The Unabridged Acts and Monuments Online
ARG	*Archiv für Reformationsgeschichte*
BQ	*The Baptist Quarterly*
CH	*Church History*
CO	*Ioannis Calvini opera quae supersunt omnia*, edited by G. Baum, E. Cunitz, and E. Reuss, 59 vols.
CR	*Corpus Reformatorum*, edited by K. Bretschneider *et al.*, 101 vols. vol. 1–28: Philip Melanchthon, *Opera quae supersunt omnia*. vol. 29–87: *CO* vol. 88–101: *HZSW*
CUP	Cambridge University Press
CLRC	*Courtenay Library of Reformation Classics*
EHR	*The English Historical Review*
ETL	*Ephemerides Theologicae Louvanienses*
HJ	*Historical Journal*
HTR	*Harvard Theological Review*
HUP	Harvard University Press
HZW	*Huldrych Zwingli: Writings*, edited by E. J. Furcha and H. W. Pipkin, 2 vols.
HZSW	*Huldreich Zwinglis Sämtliche Werke*, edited by E. Egli and G. Finsler, 14 vols.

Abbreviations

JBS	*Journal of British Studies*
JEH	*Journal of Ecclesiastical History*
JTS	*Journal of Theological Studies*
LCC	*The Library of Christian Classics*
LP	*Letters and papers, foreign and domestic, of the reign of Henry VIII, 1509–1547*, edited by J. S. Brewer, J. Gairdner and R. H. Brodie, 21 vols. Citations refer to volume number then document number, e.g., *LP*, iv/2. #4396 is volume 4, part 2, document number 4396.
LW	*Luther's Works*, edited by J. Pelikan, H. Lehmann, *et al.*, 55 vols.
LWHZ	*The Latin Works of Huldreich Zwingli*, edited by S. M. Jackson, 3 vols. vol. 1. (1912); vol. 2. edited by W. J. Hinke (1922), repr. *On Providence and other essays* (1983); vol. 3. edited by C. N. Heller (1929), repr. *Commentary on True and False Religion* (1981).
ODNB	*Oxford Dictionary of National Biography*
OED	*Oxford English Dictionary*
OER	*Oxford Encyclopaedia of the Reformation*
OL	*Original Letters Relative to the English Reformation*, edited by H. Robinson, 2 vols. with continuous pagination.
OUP	Oxford University Press
PBA	*Proceedings of the British Academy*
PP	*Past and Present*
PS	The Parker Society
RQ	*Renaissance Quarterly*
RRR	*Reformation and Renaissance Review*

Abbreviations

RSTC	Revised Short Title Catalogue
SCJ	*Sixteenth Century Journal*
SJT	*Scottish Journal of Theology*
TBGAS	*Transactions of the Bristol and Gloucestershire Archaeological Society*
TRHS	*Transactions of the Royal Historical Society*
TRP	*Tudor Royal Proclamations*, edited by P. Hughes and J. Larkin, 3 vols. Citations refer to volume number then document number, e.g., *TRP*, i. #30 is volume 1, document number 30.
TVZ	Theologischer Verlag Zürich
WTJ	*Westminster Theological Journal*
YUP	Yale University Press
ZL	*The Zurich Letters, comprising the correspondence of several English bishops and others, with some of the Helvetian Reformers, during the early part of the reign of Queen Elizabeth*, edited by H. Robinson, 2 vols.

1

Introduction

> *The entire sum of piety consists in these very brief main points of the covenant. Indeed, it is evident that nothing else was handed down to the saints of all ages, throughout the entire Scripture, other than what is included in these main points of the covenant.*
> —*Heinrich Bullinger (1534)*[1]

In 1534 Heinrich Bullinger (1504–75) identified the divine covenant as the summary principle of the Christian faith. Bullinger was the *Antistes*—overseer or bishop—of Zürich where the concept of covenant had been a current of theological inquiry for over a decade. It had been deployed there in local controversy, yet its significance extended to the reforms sweeping through the Swiss Confederation and Europe more generally. In the Bible God's arrangement with the patriarch Abraham and his descendants defined the mechanics of salvation according to a divine promise; theologians had been reflecting on that covenant agreement for centuries. During the Reformation, however, covenant theology

---

[1] Heinrich Bullinger, *A Brief Exposition of the One and Eternal Testament or Covenant of God, 1534*, trans. C. S. McCoy and J. W. Baker, in *Fountainhead of Federalism* (Louisville, KY: Westminster John Knox Press, 1991), 112.

received a distinct formulation from the reformers of Zürich and Geneva which made it a signature of Swiss Reformed influence further afield.[2] For them the covenant was the key to the interpretation of Holy Scripture and essential to a right understanding of salvation and the sacraments. It became a particular mark of Swiss influence on English reformers during the reigns of King Henry VIII and King Edward VI. This examination of Reformation covenant theology focuses our attention on the core intellectual tenet of Reformed theology and identity in the period.

Covenant theology was conceptualised in different ways during the Reformation. Scholars have advanced a number of interpretations of the positions taken by continental reformers and, in turn, the reception of continental theology in England has generated extensive historiographical debate. This means that an approach to English reception of the Swiss concept of covenant needs to be established for the period from the 1520s to the 1550s. Although the formal process of confessionalisation did not begin until the 1560s, it is not anachronistic to think in terms of confessional trajectories in preceding decades.[3] Several distinct flavours of Reformation theology were being articulated and disseminated from the 1520s onwards. The leading centre of Reformed theology during the 1520s was the city of Zürich under the spiritual oversight of Huldrych Zwingli (1484–1531), who was succeeded by Bullinger in 1531. Strassburg was another important locus from 1523 until Martin Bucer (1491–1551) was forced to flee to England in the wake of the Augsburg Interim (1548). Only from the late 1540s

---

[2] For convenience the adjective 'Swiss' will be used here to include Geneva even though the Republic of Geneva was not a member of the Swiss Confederation.

[3] Erika Rummel, *The Confessionalisation of Humanism in Reformation Germany* (Oxford: OUP, 2000), 4. On the beginning of Reformed confessionalisation in c.1565 see Richard Muller, "Reformed Theology between 1600 and 1800," in *The Oxford Handbook of Early Modern Theology, 1600–1800*, eds. U. Lehner, R. Muller and A. G. Roeber (New York: OUP, 2016), 173–74.

Introduction

did Geneva begin to assume pre-eminence, although John Calvin (1509–64) had been gaining influence since the 1530s.

The Reformed trajectory can be distinguished from other patterns of Reformation by its 'eminently ethical' understanding of redemption.[4] Those who adopted this approach understood 'reformation' as rejuvenation of the divine order by way of personal and communal renewal. For this reason Heiko Oberman argued that the medieval and Reformed traditions are together distinguished from the thought of Martin Luther (1483–1546) for whom 'reformation' involved a rejection of humanity's very attempt to renew itself.[5] The Reformed trajectory was, nonetheless, united with other patterns of Reformation in the 'normative centring' of the power for, and object of, moral rectitude around the *sola* formulae: *sola gratia*, *sola fide*, *solus Christus*.[6]

At the source of the Lutheran and Reformed trajectories lie two interpretations of the biblical use of the concept of covenant. The relationship established by God with Abraham and his descendants is described in Genesis 15 and 17 by the Hebrew word *berît*, which was translated *diathēkē* in the Greek Septuagint (c.275–c.100

---

[4] Theodore Bozeman, *The Precisianist Strain: Disciplinary Religion and Antinomian Backlash in Puritanism to 1638* (Chapel Hill, NC and London: University of North Carolina Press, 2004), 17, 77–79; Marshall Knappen, *Tudor Puritanism: a chapter in the history of idealism* (Gloucester, MA: Peter Smith, 1963), 48–49. On the continuity between medieval and Reformation priorities see Heiko Oberman, *The Dawn of the Reformation: Essays in Late Medieval and Early Reformation Thought* (Edinburgh: T&T Clark, 1986), 18–38.

[5] Heiko Oberman, *Forerunners of the Reformation: The Shape of Late Medieval Thought* (New York: Holt, Rinehart and Winston, 1966), 9–10, 20; see also Christine Christ-von Wedel, *Erasmus of Rotterdam: advocate of a new Christianity* (Toronto & London: University of Toronto Press, 2013), 13. For an example of 'reformation' used in the sense of efforts towards renewal see John Strype, *Ecclesiastical Memorials, relating chiefly to religion, and the Reformation of it*, 3 vols. (Oxford: OUP, 1822), i/1, 72.

[6] Berndt Hamm, *The Reformation of Faith in the Context of Late Medieval Theology and Piety*, trans. H. Heron, G. Wiedermann and J. Frymire (Leiden & Boston: Brill, 2004), 20, 43.

Introduction

b.c.). The Latin Vulgate (a.d. c.380–c.405) rendered the term as *pactum* (pact) or *foedus* (league or covenant). These terms could denote a unilateral promise of salvation made by God to Abraham which was passively received. Alternatively, they might refer to a bilateral or reciprocal agreement between God and Abraham in which both parties undertook certain obligations pertaining to salvation. The continuance of the agreement might be subject to the fulfilment of conditions by one or both parties, and sanctions might be imposed if either party defaulted on their obligations.[7] By the early sixteenth century the systematic use of this terminology had been conflated by biblical exegetes such that *pactum* and *foedus* could be used in the sense of a 'last will and testament.'[8] While *testamentum* usually connoted the unilateral concept as God's unconditional promise or bequest, the bilateral (or mutual) and conditional concept of covenant was still a possible reading.

The covenant concept was significant at an early stage in Luther's theology. He increasingly defined it in terms of a testator's

---

[7] For biblical scholarship see: Klaus Baltzer, *The Covenant Formulary in Old Testament, Jewish and Early Christian Writings*, trans. D. Green (Oxford: Basil Blackwell, 1971); E. P. Sanders, "The covenant as a soteriological category in the nature of salvation in Palestinian and Hellenistic Judaism," in *Jews, Greeks and Christians: Religious Culture in Late Antiquity*, eds. R. Hamerton-Kelly and R. Scroggs (Leiden: Brill, 1976), 39–42; Ernest Nicholson, *God and His People: Covenant and Theology in the Old Testament* (Oxford: OUP, 1986), 97; Staffan Olofsson, *The LXX Version: a guide to the translation technique of the Septuagint* (Stockholm: Almqvist & Wiksell, 1990), 7; Menahem Haran, "The Běrît 'Covenant': its nature and ceremonial background," in *Tehillah Le-Moshe: Biblical and Judaic Studies in honour of Moshe Greenberg*, eds. M. Cogan, B. Eichler, and J. Tigay (Winona Lake, IN: Eisenbrauns, 1997), 205–8; Emanuel Tov, *The Greek and Hebrew Bible: Collected Essays on the Septuagint* (Leiden & Boston: Brill, 1999), 92–93, 261–62; Georg Walser, *The Greek of the Ancient Synagogue: an investigation on the Greek of the Septuagint, Pseudepigrapha and the New Testament* (Stockholm: Almqvist & Wiksell, 2001), 169.

[8] Heiko Oberman, *The Reformation: Roots and Ramifications*, trans. A. Gow (Edinburgh: T&T Clark, 1994), 108; Leonard Trinterud, "The Origins of Puritanism," *CH* 20, 1 (1951): 43; see also Derk Visser, "Covenant," in *OER*, ed. H. J. Hillerbrand (New York and Oxford: OUP, 1996), 1:442–45.

unilateral bequest to his heirs: God had promised Abraham and his descendants that they would inherit righteousness. In 1519 he drew a distinction between a covenant and a testament: 'He who stays alive makes a covenant; he who is about to die makes a testament.'[9] In 1520 he discussed the testament in the context of the Eucharist, leaving no room for mutual participation or for conditions to be imposed on humanity.[10] Christ, in his humanity, had made a last will and testament. Human beings were entirely passive in receiving the inheritance of salvation unilaterally bequeathed by Christ's death.[11] Meanwhile early Swiss Reformed theologians were interpreting the covenant in reciprocal terms.

Covenant and the Reformed Tradition

Modern scholarly reflection on Reformation covenant theology has suffered from its attachment to the study of post-Reformation federal theology.[12] In 1939 Perry Miller downplayed its significance by asserting that the concept of covenant had 'not been known, or at least not emphasised' until New England Puritans introduced

---

[9] Martin Luther, *Lectures on Galatians* [1519 and 1535], ed. J. Pelikan, *LW* (Saint Louis, MO: Concordia, 1964), 27:268.

[10] Martin Luther, *The Babylonian Captivity of the Church* [1520], trans. A. Steinhauser, *LW* (Philadelphia: Fortress Press, 1959), 36:38.

[11] On Luther's view see: Kenneth Hagen, "From Testament to Covenant in the Early Sixteenth Century," *SCJ* 3, 1 (1972): 8–15; Alister McGrath, *Luther's Theology of the Cross: Martin Luther's Theological Breakthrough* (Oxford: Blackwell, 1985), 85–92.

[12] Andrew Woolsey's literature survey reveals the overwhelming scholarly preoccupation with federal theology and Puritanism: Andrew Woolsey, *Unity and Continuity in Covenantal Thought: A Study of the Reformed Tradition to the Westminster Assembly* (Grand Rapids, MI: Reformation Heritage Books, 2012), ch. 3 and 4. See the predominantly Anglo-American bibliography in Visser, "Covenant," 445. There are few German-language studies of the early Reformation concept. See the bibliography in J. F. Gerhard Goeters, "Föderaltheologie," in *Theologische Realenzyklopädie*, eds. H. Balz et al. (Berlin & New York: Walter de Gruyter, 1983), 11:251–52.

it during the first half of the seventeenth century. In his view the Puritans saw the covenant as a 'legitimate extension' of Reformed theology establishing 'the submerged grounds for moral obedience and for an assurance of salvation.'[13] Miller's assertion of the late appearance of the conditional covenant—and only in New England at that—provoked a hunt for continental European precedents.[14] The self-conscious excavation of 'the origins of Puritanism' which ensued insinuated an anachronistic agenda into the interpretation of the Reformation concept of covenant. The assumption that the conditional elements of federal theology were inconsistent with Calvin's legacy encouraged the identification of alternative Reformed well-springs.[15] In 1951 Leonard Trinterud published a seminal article on the origins of Puritanism claiming that the unconditional 'testament' attributed to Geneva was only one version of the concept. He suggested that a conditional 'law-covenant' was the 'organising principle of the entire Rhineland reformation movement,' by which he meant principally Zürich, Basle, and Strassburg.[16]

Trinterud's bifurcation of the Reformed tradition was maintained by a number of scholars including Jens Møller in 1963, Richard Greaves in 1968, Michael McGiffert in 1982, and Robert Letham in 1983.[17] In 1980 Trinterud's thesis was definitively restated

---

[13] Perry Miller, *The New England Mind: The Seventeenth Century*, 2nd ed. (New York and London: Macmillan, 1954), 366–67, 374; see also Perry Miller, *Errand into the Wilderness* (London and Cambridge, MA: HUP, 1956), 82–89.

[14] Miller, *New England Mind*, 398.

[15] Important statements of the discontinuity thesis include Basil Hall, "Calvin against the Calvinists," in *John Calvin: a collection of distinguished essays*, ed. G. Duffield (Grand Rapids, MI: Eerdmans, 1966), 19–37; R. T. Kendall, *Calvin and English Calvinism to 1649* (Oxford: OUP, 1979).

[16] Trinterud, "Origins," 41, 45, 56.

[17] Jens Møller, "The Beginnings of Puritan Covenant Theology," *JEH* 14 (1963): 47–50; Richard Greaves, "The Origins and Early Development of English Covenant Thought," *The Historian* 31, 1 (1968): 21–35; Michael McGiffert, "Grace and Works: The Rise and Division of Covenant Divinity in Elizabethan Puritanism," *HTR* 75, 4 (1982): 472; Robert Letham, "The Foedus Operum: some factors accounting for its development," *SCJ* 14, 4 (1983):

Introduction

and expanded in a monograph by Wayne Baker entitled *Heinrich Bullinger and the Covenant: The Other Reformed Tradition*. Baker claimed that Bullinger represented the alternative bilateral approach to Calvin's predestinarian unilateral testament.[18] In 1990 David Weir tried to refine Baker's conclusions by arguing that post-Reformation federal theology was designed to 'bridge both worlds: that of the unilateral covenant and that of the bilateral covenant.'[19] However in 1991 Baker, together with Charles McCoy, argued that Bullinger had initiated a Federalist Reformed tradition which ought to be distinguished from the Calvinist Reformed tradition.[20]

This dichotomisation of bilateral and conditional versus unilateral and unconditional covenants tended to involve a subjective judgment on conditionality. For Miller conditionality was a positive comfort and moralistic counterweight to absolute predestinarianism whereas later accounts accused the reciprocal concept of upholding legalism at the expense of grace and election. According to those who subscribed to the view that conditionality entailed legalism the radical predestinarianism of Calvinist orthodoxy 'paralysed' the conditional covenant idea in federal theology.[21]

Since the 1980s there have been several notable critiques of Trinterud's dual-tradition thesis. In 1983 Lyle Bierma argued that all early Reformed expressions of the concept of covenant should be considered together.[22] He demonstrated in 1990 that the conditional

---

457–67. McGiffert accepts the dichotomy with the qualification that it went unacknowledged in the early Reformation.

[18] J. Wayne Baker, *Heinrich Bullinger and the Covenant: The Other Reformed Tradition* (Athens, OH: Ohio University Press, 1980).

[19] David Weir, *The Origins of the Federal Theology in Sixteenth-Century Reformation Thought* (Oxford: OUP, 1990), 32.

[20] J. Wayne Baker and Charles McCoy, *Fountainhead of Federalism: Heinrich Bullinger and the Covenantal Tradition* (Louisville, KY: Westminster John Knox Press, 1991), 24.

[21] E.g., Baker, *Other Reformed Tradition*, 204–15.

[22] Lyle Bierma, "Federal Theology in the Sixteenth Century: Two Traditions?" *WTJ* 45 (1983): 304–21.

concept was not necessarily opposed to double predestinarianism, thereby undermining a basic assumption of the unilateral-bilateral dichotomy.[23] In 2001 Peter Lillback suggested close associations between Calvin's understanding of covenant and those of other Swiss theologians.[24] In 2002 Cornelis Venema queried Baker's view of Bullinger as the founder of a second Reformed tradition, arguing that Bullinger's and Calvin's doctrines of predestination were not responsible for two different concepts of covenant.[25] Then in 2012 Andrew Woolsey inverted the dual-tradition thesis by presenting Reformed covenant thought as a continuous and unified movement from the early Reformation to the seventeenth century.[26]

These critiques form part of a more fundamental assault led by Richard Muller on the thesis of discontinuity between Reformation and post-Reformation Reformed theology.[27] In two volumes published in 2000 and 2003 discussing the foundation and development of the Reformed tradition Muller rejected the view that unilateral and bilateral conceptions were 'mutually exclusive and held by different thinkers, to the point that the unilateral definition belongs to a more "predestinarian" approach and the bilateral definition to an approach that verges on synergism in its emphasis on human responsibility.'[28]

---

[23] Lyle Bierma, "The Role of Covenant Theology in Early Reformed Orthodoxy," *SCJ* 21, 3 (1990): 456.

[24] Peter Lillback, *The Binding of God: Calvin's Role in the Development of Covenant Theology* (Grand Rapids, MI: Baker Academic, 2001), 306.

[25] Cornelis Venema, *Heinrich Bullinger and the Doctrine of Predestination: Author Of 'The Other Reformed Tradition'?* (Grand Rapids, MI: Baker Academic, 2002), 111–12.

[26] Woolsey, *Unity and Continuity*.

[27] E.g., Richard Muller, *Christ and the Decree: Christology and Predestination in Reformed Theology from Calvin to Perkins* (Grand Rapids: Baker, 1986); Ulrich Lehner, Richard Muller and A. G. Roeber, 'Introduction' in Lehner, Muller and Roeber, eds., *Oxford Handbook of Early Modern Theology*, 3–4. On this debate see Carl Trueman, "Calvin and Reformed Orthodoxy," in *The Calvin Handbook*, ed. H. Selderhuis (Grand Rapids and Cambridge: Eerdmans, 2009), 474–76.

[28] Richard Muller, *The Unaccommodated Calvin: Studies in the Foundation*

Introduction

Bullinger's bilateral conception did not preclude a Reformed predestinarianism, nor did Calvin's predestinarianism prevent him from developing themes of mutuality in his commentaries and sermons.[29] Reformed writers utilised both definitions of covenant and all of them upheld the monergistic soteriology of their confession. Predestination and covenant were neither in opposition nor in tension: in 2016 Muller helpfully clarified that 'covenant is a doctrine that primarily explicates the personal and corporate dimensions of salvation in the historical economy of salvation—predestination is a doctrine that defines the purpose from a different perspective, being primarily concerned with divine intentions and ends and with the issues of eternity and time, decree and execution.'[30]

The essential lesson of recent research is that theological diversity amongst Reformed theologians should not be misconstrued as indicative of multiple Reformed traditions. Muller has argued for the recognition of 'a single but variegated Reformed tradition, bounded by a series of fairly uniform confessional concerns but quite diverse in patterns of formulation.'[31] This implies the unity of the Reformed identity, not only between Reformation and post-Reformation Reformed theologians, but also between contemporaries like Bullinger and Calvin who nonetheless placed different theological emphases.[32] Whilst the severance of any necessary link

---

of a Theological Tradition (Oxford: OUP, 2000); Richard Muller, *After Calvin: Studies in the Development of a Theological Tradition* (Oxford: OUP, 2003), citations at 9, 99.

[29] Muller, *Unaccommodated Calvin*, 183.

[30] Muller, "Reformed Theology between 1600 and 1800," 175–76. See also Muller, *After Calvin*, 12–13, 99; Dewey Wallace, *Puritans and Predestination: Grace in English Protestant Theology, 1525–1695* (Chapel Hill, NC: University of North Carolina Press, 1982), 10.

[31] Muller, *After Calvin*, 7–9.

[32] Ibid., 85–86; see also John Whitgift, *The Works of John Whitgift, D.D.*, ed. J. Ayre, PS (Cambridge: CUP, 1851–53), 1:436; Knappen, *Tudor Puritanism*, 78; C. M. Dent, *Protestant Reformers in Elizabethan Oxford* (Oxford: OUP, 1983), 1.

between predestinarianism and a unilateral concept of covenant exposes an untenable model, this does not imply that all Reformed theologians expounded mutuality between God and humanity to the same degree. The unilateral concept of covenant was assumed in one form or another by everyone but only some took the further step of formulating reciprocal features, and these were not necessarily detrimental to the priority of divine grace. Trinterud and Baker were mistaken in their belief that covenant theology divided the theologians of Zürich and Geneva.

Woolsey's emphasis on the coherence and unity of the early Swiss concept of covenant strongly encourages study of its reception by early English evangelicals. His valuable analysis of Johannes Œcolampadius of Basle (1482–1531), Zwingli and Bullinger improves on all previous work and he complements Lillback with his own extensive account of Calvin's covenant theology. Although his study, like many others, approaches the Reformation from the direction of Puritanism and the Westminster Assembly, and while the historiographical survey prepares the reader to think again in these terms, he rightly looks to medieval covenant thought as the immediate context of the early Reformed concept. Only occasionally does his interest in the origins of federal theology obtrude into his otherwise compelling analysis of the early Swiss reformers.[33] Their influence on early English Reformed theology is arguably the more promising place to explore the impact of their covenant thought than in the new directions it took later in the century.

Seeing that the early Swiss reformers formulated reciprocal concepts of covenant that constituted a unifying characteristic of Swiss Reformed theology, the line of Reformed theological diversity

---

[33] Woolsey, *Unity and Continuity*. For example he asks the question of Calvin's concept, 'What more is needed to constitute a covenant of works arrangement?' Ibid., 282. The emphasis on the unity between Reformation and post-Reformation Reformed theology is a helpful corrective providing that early Reformed covenant theology is not assimilated into post-Reformation categories.

ought now to be drawn between the Swiss on the one hand and the Germans on the other. The theologians of Strassburg are to be considered alongside the Lutherans. Martin Bucer developed a concept of covenant without significant mutual or conditional elements, which is important insofar as he was in a position to exert major influence in England especially in his final years at Cambridge.

Bucer's concept of covenant came close to Luther's position albeit with idiosyncratic ambiguity. Although Nicholas Thompson suggests that 'Bucer treated *testamentum* as a synonym for *foedus*' and, to a greater extent than Luther, 'emphasised the human side of the covenant,'[34] his bilateral themes should not be unduly emphasised; they are concentrated in his early work and have primary reference to the sacraments rather than to salvation.[35] In *Grund und Ursach* [*Basic Principles*] (1524) he wrote that 'Christians renew their spiritual and everlasting covenant and testament in the Lord with holy food and drink,'[36] but Thompson explains that, for Bucer, the Christian offers 'nothing other than the obedience of faith' in the sense of patristic eucharistic sacrifice.[37] In *Epistola Apologetica* [*Apologetical Letter*] (1529) the sacraments are called 'a symbol and token of the covenant which God has made with us [by which] we are reminded of those things which it befits God to do for us and us, in turn, to do for God.'[38] While Luther placed sacrament and sacrifice in opposition, Bucer preserved the sacrificial element of 'grateful response' from humanity.[39] This was 'the Godward and human dimension of any "ceremony" appointed to seal God's covenant,'[40] rather than a

---

[34] Nicholas Thompson, *Eucharistic Sacrifice and Patristic Tradition in the Theology of Martin Bucer, 1534–1546* (Leiden & Boston: Brill, 2005), 105.

[35] Bucer also compared covenant renewal with oaths of citizenship and discipline: Amy Nelson Burnett, *The Yoke of Christ: Martin Bucer and Christian Discipline* (Kirksville, MO: SCJ Publishers, 1994), 213, 218.

[36] Quoted in Thompson, *Eucharistic Sacrifice*, 115.

[37] Ibid.

[38] Quoted in Ibid., 118.

[39] Ibid., 120.

[40] Ibid., 285.

developed reciprocal feature of the covenant itself. Kenneth Hagen has noted that in another of Bucer's early works, *Ennarationes in evangelia* [*Explanations of the Gospels*] (1527), the *verum et aeternum Dei foedus* is defined as God's promise, requiring nothing of believers.[41] The unilateral sense is clearly pronounced in Bucer's mature writings. In *De Regno Christi* [*Of Christ's Reign*] (1551) *foedus* is understood as unilateral adoption: '*sollenique foederis divini, id est adoptionis in filios pactione, et sanctione*' (and a solemn pact and sanction of divine treaty, that is, of adoption as sons).[42] Peter Stephens' study of Bucer finds an overwhelming tendency towards understanding the covenant as God's promise of forgiveness.[43] Hence Luther's and Bucer's formulations must both be distinguished from those of the reformers of Zürich and Geneva.

Covenant and Late Medieval Scholasticism

Reformation covenant theology is more logically approached by way of late medieval thought than by working backwards from post-Reformation developments. The early reformers were products of their medieval intellectual heritage and they are best understood in that context.[44] Late medieval scholastic theology is remarkable for

---

[41] Hagen, "Testament to Covenant," 22–23. This also appears to be the sense of Bucer's *Apology concerning Christ's Supper* (1526) in *Commonplaces of Martin Bucer*, ed. D. F. Wright (Abingdon: Sutton Courtenay Press, 1972), 323.

[42] Quoted in Møller, "Beginnings," 54. My translation. See also the different applications of *testamentum* and *foedus* in Martin Bucer, *Confession on the Eucharist* (1550), in Wright, ed., *Commonplaces*, 397.

[43] W. P. Stephens, *The Holy Spirit in the Theology of Martin Bucer* (Cambridge: CUP, 1970), 109–11, 115, 218, 246, 249, 265–66.

[44] See especially Heiko Oberman, *The Harvest of Medieval Theology: Gabriel Biel and late medieval Nominalism* (Cambridge, MA: HUP, 1963) and Alister McGrath, *The Intellectual Origins of the European Reformation* (Oxford: Basil Blackwell, 1987). See further Martin Greschat, "Der Bundesgedanke in der Theologie des späten Mittelalters," *Zeitschrift für Kirchengeschichte* 81 (1970): 44–63; Berndt Hamm, *Promissio, Pactum, Ordinatio: freiheit und selbstbinding Gottes in der scholastischen gnadenlehre* (Tübingen: Mohr, 1977); Woolsey, *Unity*

its presuppositional and doctrinal diversity generated in large part by the philosophical controversy between the realist and non-realist epistemologies of the *via antiqua* and the *via moderna*.

In the twelfth and thirteenth centuries a broad consensus developed that salvation necessitated an ontological change in humanity. Theologians of what came to be known as the *via antiqua*, such as Thomas Aquinas (1225–74) and Peter Aureole (c.1280–1322), held that the formal cause of justification was a created or infused habit of grace or charity. This consensus began to collapse when Franciscan theologians like Duns Scotus (c.1266–1308), in seeking to uphold God's freedom as well as his reliability, suggested that the created order was determined not by the very nature of reality but was contingent on the ordained will of God (*potentia Dei ordinata*). The only constraints on God are self-imposed but he is faithful to his own sovereign decisions. For William of Ockham (1285–1347) one of the soteriological implications of this was that created habits, rather than being absolutely necessary *ex natura rei*, were only *de facto* necessary in that God had ordained to accept them as the immediate cause of justification.[45]

The heterogeneous movement initiated by Ockham known as the *via moderna* sought to negate the philosophical turn of the early thirteenth century.[46] It had in common a rejection of meta-categories in theology and an emphasis on scriptural revelation over against

---

and Continuity, 194–200; Muller, "Reformed Theology between 1600 and 1800," 168. The same issues highlighted by Paul Helm's critique of McGrath's study are discussed by Oberman: Paul Helm, *John Calvin's Ideas* (Oxford: OUP, 2004), 321–23; Oberman, *Harvest*, 100–103. See also Alister McGrath, *Iustitia Dei: a history of the Christian Doctrine of Justification*, 3rd ed. (Cambridge: CUP, 2005), 153–54.

[45] McGrath, *Intellectual Origins*, 18–29, 76–78; Oberman, *Dawn*, 27; Ulrich Leinsle, *Introduction to Scholastic Theology*, trans. M. Miller (Washington, DC: The Catholic University of America Press, 2010), 226.

[46] I am grateful to Lydia Schumacher for discussion of the early Franciscans, the *Summa Halensis* (1236–45), and 'grey areas' in scholastic theology before the thirteenth century.

natural theology. This undermined the ontological foundations for habitual grace. While early medieval theologians had spoken of God as having an obligation (*obligatio* or *debitum*) to bestow grace on humans who do what is in them (*facit quod in se est*), the *moderni* drew on emerging economic and political ideas about covenants or contracts to posit a divine covenant (*pactio divina*) that guaranteed the reliability of God's ordained will, not least with regard to salvation.[47] God would not deny grace to the *humiles* (humble or meek) and promises to justify those who do their best. Grace was now conceived as a dimension of God's disposition towards humanity and emphasis fell on the personal nature of the relationship.[48] The efficacy of the sacraments depended on the covenant which guaranteed that God would bestow grace whenever a sacrament was received.[49]

Humanity's reciprocal action in procuring grace was defined in terms of love for God. The Tübingen theologian Gabriel Biel (c.1420/25–95) explained the condition of *quod in se est* as being '*declinare…a malo et facere bonum*' (to decline from evil and to do good).[50] The medieval conception of the Church as the 'guardian of morality' encouraged such a legal emphasis.[51] Biel referred to Christ as *legislator*, more than *salvator, noster* and taught that humans have the innate power to love God for God's own sake.[52] This allowed the condition for justification to be understood as being the same under both the Old and the New Testament but, as McGrath has emphasised, to be discussed without necessary reference to Christ.[53]

---

[47] McGrath, *Theology of the Cross*, 86–87. On medieval contract theory see Woolsey, *Unity and Continuity*, 185–94.

[48] McGrath, *Intellectual Origins*, 79; Oberman, *Dawn*, 28–29.

[49] Bryan Spinks, *Early and Medieval Rituals and Theologies of Baptism: from the New Testament to the Council of Trent* (Farnham: Ashgate, 2006), 147–48.

[50] Gabriel Biel, quoted in McGrath, *Intellectual Origins*, 79.

[51] Heiko Oberman, *Forerunners*, 5; John Bossy, "Moral Arithmetic: Seven Sins into Ten Commandments," in *Conscience and Casuistry in Early Modern Europe*, ed. E. Leites (Cambridge: CUP, 1988), 215–17.

[52] Oberman, *Harvest*, 117.

[53] Alister McGrath, "*Homo Assumptus*? A study in the Christology of the *Via*

Following Ockham, theologians of the *via moderna* considered the meritorious value of human love to be worth whatever God accepted it to be. While it might be of little intrinsic value it could still merit justification. The wisdom governing divine *iusticia*, both as Decalogue and as Gospel, was beyond human comprehension—and for that reason it might appear arbitrary—yet it was utterly reliable and consistent in accordance with the *pactum Dei*.[54] The fulfilment of its conditions elicited saving grace.[55]

Indications of Luther's impending break from medieval covenant theology can be observed in his *Dictata super Psalterium* (1513–15) where the exegetical tendency to conflate *pactum* and *testamentum* placed him at odds with the *moderni*.[56] He distinguished a 'new rule of Christ' unknown under the old covenant, the difference being that the new covenant cannot be cancelled by human sin. God still promises grace to the *humiles* but it is applied only when they acknowledge their extreme humiliation before God as the place where grace operates.[57] He rejected Biel's interpretation of 'seek and you shall find' (Luke 11:9) in terms of *facere quod in se est*, 'as if those words meant that it is in our power to seek and to convert ourselves, when it says in Psalm 13 [14.2] that no-one understands or seeks God!'[58] Instead he fundamentally altered the terms of the discussion:

Moderna with particular reference to William of Ockham," *ETL* 60 (1984): 283–97.

[54] McGrath, *Intellectual Origins*, 79–81; McGrath, *Theology of the Cross*, 60; Oberman, *Harvest*, 98.

[55] Oberman, *Harvest*, 133, 140–41, 153, 161–62; Oberman, *Forerunners*, 168; John Farthing, *Thomas Aquinas and Gabriel Biel: interpretations of St. Thomas Aquinas in German Nominalism on the eve of the Reformation* (Durham, NC and London: Duke University Press, 1988), 162–64; see also Olli-Pekka Vainio, *Justification and Participation in Christ: the development of the Lutheran doctrine of justification from Luther to the Formula of Concord (1580)* (Leiden & Boston: Brill, 2008), 29.

[56] Hamm, *Promissio*, 377–90.

[57] Oberman, *The Reformation*, 100–101.

[58] Luther's marginalia to Gabriel Biel's *Collectorium in quattuor libros sententiarum* and *Sacri canonis missae expositio*, quoted in Oberman, *The Reformation*, 107.

human action consisted not in meeting any minimal requirement but in confessing that salvation can only be found *extra nos*.

The humility with which believers respond to the covenant is not, for Luther, a saving virtue but the necessary result of faith, a recognition of their total poverty and wretchedness. In his Romans lectures of 1515–16 faith became the sole condition for justification, no longer a human act but a divine gift. The condition is fulfilled entirely by God, making the covenant unconditional on humanity's part. Consequently the legal nature of the *testamentum* became not a means of regulating Christian conduct but a requirement upon God to deliver that which he has graciously promised. His transition from a bilateral to a unilateral concept of covenant becomes apparent after 1516 in his increasing emphasis on *sola fide* as opposed to *sola gratia* as *pactum* recedes behind *promissio* and *evangelium* in his thought.[59]

Although Luther believed that the covenant theology of the *via moderna* was repeating the error of Pelagius, Biel was part of what Berndt Hamm describes as 'the late-medieval endeavour to transfer the weight of salvation from the side of the spiritual quality and activity of mankind to the side of God's gracious, saving mercy.'[60] Divine *concursus* in humanity's 'natural' ability to do anything was assumed in the teaching that sinners are able to prepare themselves for the reception of justifying grace by loving God for his own sake above all else. Biel laid stress on the inadequacy of human merit and the need for divine assistance.[61] *Facere quod in se est* was not conceived as a means of earning salvation through personal effort but an insistence on a minimal level of penitence in response to God's initiative, which was a standard feature of the Western Christian tradition. Oberman explains that 'to desire God's help is doing one's very best.'[62] '*By the generally accepted standards of the time,*'

---

[59] McGrath, *Theology of the Cross*, 130–32; Hamm, *Reformation of Faith*, 99–100; Oberman, *The Reformation*, 113–14.
[60] Hamm, *Reformation of Faith*, 119.
[61] Oberman, *Harvest*, 140–41, 156, 175.
[62] Ibid., 133.

insists McGrath, 'and *by his own definition of Pelagianism*, Biel's doctrine of justification is not only not Pelagian, but is actually strongly anti-Pelagian.'[63]

At the turn of the sixteenth century devotional writers were stressing God's readiness to exercise compassion in the face of human inability. If there was a christological lacuna in the schools partial compensation was offered in the pulpits. Luther's mentor Johannes von Staupitz (c.1460–1524) based the Christian life on the *sola misericordia* and *sola gratia* of God and the *solus Christus* of the Passion. It was only conjoined with Christ's sufferings that any human merit was possible.[64] In Nuremberg Stephan Fridolin (1430–98) preached Christ's Passion as being 'the middle point, the centre, the most central town in the region of our hope.'[65] The Strassburg cathedral preacher Johannes Geiler von Kayserberg (1445–1510) settled on *facere quod in se est* to express a self-doubting reliance upon the mediation of Christ, Mary and the saints. Love for God was most meritorious when it discounted its own merit.[66] In the decades preceding the Reformation the twelfth-century emphasis on a severe *Christus iudex* had shifted strongly towards a humble figure suffering on the Cross in order to effect salvation, if only sinners would accept his help and demonstrate corresponding repentance by living in imitation of him.[67]

Facere quod in se est was understood to be a flexible condition gratuitously measured to the ability of the individual sinner. Oberman makes the important point that 'Biel's concern is to provide

---

[63] McGrath, *Theology of the Cross*, 62. His emphasis. Oberman concludes that Biel's doctrine of justification is 'at once *sola gratia* and *solis operibus*' and '*essentially Pelagian*' (his emphasis) but, as McGrath points out, the canons of the Council of Carthage (417–18) were still the standard of orthodoxy, however unequal they were to the intellectual demands made of them by medieval scholastics: Oberman, *Harvest*, 176–77; McGrath, *Theology of the Cross*, 11–12.

[64] Hamm, *Reformation of Faith*, 12, 118–20.

[65] Stephan Fridolin, quoted in Ibid., 13.

[66] Hamm, *Reformation of Faith*, 81–82.

[67] Ibid., 32–33.

Introduction

a way to justification within reach of the average Christian.'[68] For Johannes von Paltz (1445–1511), Luther's colleague at Erfurt, even attrition—*doleo quod non doleo* (I grieve that I do not grieve)—was sufficient: 'offer to the one who was offered for you, because he so willed it, as much as you have: at least a good will (*bonam saltem voluntatem*) and, by virtue of his sacrifice, have confidence that you will be saved!'[69] The range of opinion as to whether this minimal offering elicited grace or responded to it was what disturbed Luther. Jared Wicks notes that in Staupitz's treatment of the thief on the cross (Luke 23:39–43) 'the thief makes no self-disposing good effort of searching and doing what he could, but instead confesses his own sin and acknowledges Jesus as righteous.' By contrast, Paltz adduced the thief as evidence that conversion could begin with natural human effort to which God's responds with grace.[70] As Hamm remarks, 'two preachers within the same order, who shared the same tradition, could also share intentions and an emphasis on mercy while articulating them in two very different ways.'[71] Perhaps even worse in Luther's mind was never being sure that one had really done *quod in se est* and, consequently, whether one merited justification. The *imitatio Christi*, as the standard of love at which he was expected to aim, did not offer enough certainty about his own salvation.[72]

Not everyone shared Luther's misgivings. The major pastoral problem in Geiler's long experience as a preacher, far from any lack of assurance, was presumption:

> God has made a covenant [*pactum*] with us. Come then, the devil says, sin bravely, for however great your sins may be,

---

[68] Oberman, *Harvest*, 157.

[69] Johannes von Paltz, quoted in Hamm, *Reformation of Faith*, 93–94.

[70] Jared Wicks, "Johann von Staupitz under Pauline Inspiration," in *A Companion to Paul in the Reformation*, ed. R. Holder (Leiden & Boston: Brill, 2009), 321n, 325.

[71] Hamm, *Reformation of Faith*, 42.

[72] McGrath, *Theology of the Cross*, 110–11.

> God's mercy is still greater. [...] The whole world in our time is so corrupt that it is quite dangerous to preach about God's mercy. For where there is one who despairs there are one hundred, nay one thousand, and ten times one hundred thousand overconfident people; and yet they are all mistaken.[73]

Geiler is undoubtedly liable to the charge that Christ's Passion is a necessary but not sufficient condition for salvation, but in his mind he was able to offer complete assurance to those who despaired of their ability to do *quod in se est*: 'for God's mercy is so great that he would never condemn a person laid with all the sins of the world who felt the pain that he had, in committing them, arrogantly offended so good a lord, his God, and firmly resolved to refrain [from such sins] in the future.'[74] The promise of grace within the context of covenant relationship was what invigorated spiritual and social renewal. Far from being contradictory, most people experienced the dual focus on justice and mercy as being positively complementary. They could look for signs of grace in their own lives, like the subjective experience of peace and joy or the desire to receive the sacraments, and thereby make reasonable conjectures about their standing before God.[75] The parallels with post-Reformation Puritanism should not surprise us: the same intellectual and cultural currents flowed from late-medieval covenant theology through the Reformation.

Early Reformed theologians recast the principle that God does not ask anything from humans beyond their capability within a radically gracious economy which excluded human merit altogether.[76]

---

[73] Johannes Geiler von Kayserberg, quoted in Hamm, *Reformation of Faith*, 74.
[74] Ibid., 79.
[75] Leinsle, *Scholastic Theology*, 240.
[76] Hamm, *Reformation of Faith*, 102; Heiko Oberman, *Masters of the Reformation: the emergence of a new intellectual climate in Europe*, trans. D. Martin (Cambridge: CUP, 1981), 278; see also Alister McGrath, "Justification and the Reformation: the significance of the doctrine of justification by faith to sixteenth century urban communities," *ARG* 81 (1990): 13–17.

This fundamental break between late-medieval and Reformation theology did not exclude logical development and continuity of thought. There had already been a significant body of pastoral theology expounding minimal requirements for salvation (*sola misericordia, sola crux, sola caritas, sola humilitas, sola spes, sola contritio,* etc.) and these were further concentrated on 'the singular and one-sided efficacy of God's role in man's salvation' (*solus Christus, sola gratia, sola scriptura,* etc.). Hamm maintains that the Late Middle Ages and the Reformation were 'bound together by complex combinations of theological, pastoral, social and political trends which produced both a culture of mercy and release and a culture of regulation and discipline.'[77] Reformed theologians were able to hold together salvation *sola gratia* and the requirement for godliness without resorting to Luther's radical solifidianism to maintain the distinction.[78] They were as comfortable as their predecessors had been with seamless conceptual links between righteousness, faith, and sanctification under the auspices of covenant relationship according to the law of love.[79]

Exception and Reception

Serious attempts to study the English Reformation against the patterns of the Reformation on the continent have been made only since the end of the twentieth century. The venture incites debate even before specific theological concepts can be invoked and some clarity must be established before we may proceed to measure the intellectual currents which flowed across the Channel. A review of historiographical interpretations of the period from the 1520s to the 1550s reveals an almost unswerving assessment of England as an exception from continental patterns of Reformation, being characterised by political rather than theological change.

---

[77] Hamm, *Reformation of Faith*, 21, 43, 45, 126–27.
[78] Ibid., 150–51.
[79] See Oberman, *Forerunners*, 39–40; Letham, "Foedus Operum," 462; Hamm, *Reformation of Faith*, 152, 195.

Introduction

In 1825 Samuel Maitland questioned the trustworthiness of histories bequeathed by members and admirers of the 'puritan sect,' amongst whom he counted the likes of John Foxe (1516/17–87), Thomas Fuller (1593–1667), Gilbert Burnet (1643–1715) and John Strype (1643–1737).[80] In reacting against their allegedly unreliable accounts of the Reformation, nineteenth-century historians distanced the English experience from the populist doctrinal upheaval on the continent, stressing instead the reluctance of the English people to embrace reform, the avarice of the rulers who imposed it, and the apparently minimal effect reform had upon doctrine.[81]

Charles Smyth, writing in 1926, explained the Henrician Reformation as a diplomatic necessity, while 'the Edwardine Reformation was a dangerous and an unpopular experiment' whose 'alien influences [. . .] left the whole country seething with [. . .] heretics and sectaries of every description.' 'In the end,' wrote Smyth patriotically, 'it was not Protestantism that converted England from Catholicism, but the Spanish Match.'[82] The story told by Norman Sykes in 1938 of a thoroughly constitutional Reformation of the *Ecclesia Anglicana* reached its apogée during the Second World War with Maurice Powicke's epithetical 'act of state'. Thomas Cranmer (1489–1556), maintained Powicke, 'was always the primate, the English theologian [. . .] seeking a settlement suited to English needs.'[83]

The rehabilitation of the religious character of the English Reformation began after the Second World War. In 1947 Gordon Rupp ventured the suggestion that 'the English Reformation is not

---

[80] S. R. Maitland, *Essays on Subjects Connected with the Reformation in England* (London: Francis and John Rivington, 1849), 1, 22.

[81] See the survey by Patrick Collinson, "The Fog in the Channel Clears: The Rediscovery of the Continental Dimension to the British Reformations," in *The Reception of Continental Reformation in Britain*, ed. P. Ha and P. Collinson, *PBA*, Vol. 164 (Oxford: OUP, 2010), xxvii-xxxvii.

[82] Charles Smyth, *Cranmer and the Reformation under Edward VI* (Cambridge: CUP, 1926), 2–3, 6.

[83] Norman Sykes, *The Crisis of the Reformation* (London: Geoffrey Bles, 1938), 77–95; F. M. Powicke, *The Reformation in England* (London: OUP, 1941), 1, 82.

Introduction

wholly to be explained in terms of that conspiracy by which a lustful monarch and predatory gentry combined to plunder the Church and rend the unity of Christendom. It had, after all, something to do with the beliefs of Christian men.'[84] Rupp also countenanced recognition of some continental influence:

> We shall be wise if we refuse to imitate those historians who loved to glorify some imaginary and splendid isolation of the English Church, as though there was something inherently disreputable in borrowing from abroad [. . .]. Nevertheless, facts are facts, and it will be our business to note that even where our Reformers set their faces most steadfastly towards Wittenberg, Strasbourg or Zürich, their caps were tilted after an English fashion.[85]

In 1948 Maynard Smith seemed to have heeded Rupp's pleas in dividing his attention equally between 'The Political Reformation' and 'The Religious Reformation,' but he retained English insularity. 'The great majority of quiet respectable folk had no desire for change,' he wrote, and the small minority whose humanism Luther did catalyse 'cared very little for Lutheran teaching.'[86] In 1950 T. M. Parker observed that the resemblances between England and the continent were 'closer than are sometimes admitted' but this concession does not appear to have inspired deeper examination of continental influence.[87]

Between the 1950s and the 1970s interpretations were divided on the nature of the English Reformation yet its insularity continued

---

[84] E. G. Rupp, *Studies in the Making of the English Protestant Tradition (Mainly in the Reign of Henry VIII)* (Cambridge: CUP, 1949), xi.

[85] Ibid., 47–48.

[86] H. Maynard Smith, *Henry VIII and the Reformation* (London: Macmillan & Co, 1948), 356, 361–62, cf. 251–62.

[87] T. M. Parker, *The English Reformation to 1558* (London: OUP, 1950), vii, cf. 27–28.

to be generally affirmed.⁸⁸ Historians with very different perspectives, such as Clifford Dugmore, Owen Chadwick and Geoffrey Elton, maintained the uniquely political nature of the English Reformation.⁸⁹ Meanwhile research in local archives encouraged others to emphasise popular enthusiasm for reform originating, not on the continent, but in continuity and exchange with native, medieval traditions of dissent, specifically Lollardy. This approach was adopted not only by Geoffrey Dickens, but also by the medieval historian Margaret Aston.⁹⁰ In 1964 Dickens acknowledged that continental doctrines had exacerbated existing native conflicts but this was lost beneath the fact that, 'if the English clergy were perturbed in 1536 by any doctrines save those of neo-Lollardy, they made extremely little of the fact.'⁹¹ In the 1980s a number of different scholars, including

---

⁸⁸ Although Harry Porter noted numerous continental connections, he made no concerted attempt to integrate the English experience into continental patterns: H. C. Porter, *Reformation and Reaction in Tudor Cambridge* (Cambridge: CUP, 1958).

⁸⁹ Clifford Dugmore, *The Mass and the English Reformers* (London: Macmillan, 1958), vii, 24–25, 58; Owen Chadwick, *The Reformation* (Harmondsworth: Penguin, 1964), 97; G. R. Elton, *Reform and Reformation: England 1509–1558* (London: Edward Arnold, 1977). See also G. R. Elton, *The Tudor Revolution in Government* (Cambridge: CUP, 1953); G. R. Elton, *England under the Tudors* (London: Methuen, 1955); G. R. Elton, *Policy and Police: The Enforcement of the Reformation in the Age of Thomas Cromwell* (Cambridge: CUP, 1972).

⁹⁰ E.g., A. G. Dickens, *Lollards and Protestants in the Diocese of York, 1509–1558* (Oxford: OUP, 1959); A. G. Dickens, "Heresy and the Origins of English Protestantism," in *Britain and The Netherlands: Anglo-Dutch Historical Conference 1962*, ed. J. S. Bromley and E. H. Kossmann (Utrecht & Amsterdam: J. B. Walters, 1964), 2:47–66; Margaret Aston, "Lollardy and the Reformation: Survival or Revival?" *History* 49 (1964): 149–70. These amplified an earlier estimation of sixteenth-century Lollardy by James Gairdner, *Lollardy and the Reformation: A Historical Survey*, 4 vols. (London: Macmillan, 1908–13). A related approach recognised the continental context of English humanist sympathies but not of English dogma. Reform was attributed to the humanist endeavour. See James McConica, *English Humanists and Reformation Politics under Henry VIII and Edward VI* (Oxford: OUP, 1965); Maria Dowling, *Humanism in the Age of Henry VIII* (London: Croom Helm, 1986).

⁹¹ A. G. Dickens, *The English Reformation*, 1st ed. (London: B. T. Batsford,

INTRODUCTION

Aston, Dickens, Susan Brigden, John Davis and Anne Hudson, came to similar conclusions about popular support for Reformation and its continuities with Lollardy.[92] In 1989 however the second edition of Dickens' *The English Reformation* anticipated a new awareness of 'the powerful European forces' exerted on Henrician England.[93]

From the mid-1970s revisionist historians began to reinvigorate the old interpretation of Reformation as slow and politically-driven.[94] Nevertheless, the exceptional nature of the English experience persisted in revisionist arguments, whatever the extent of their scepticism as to the popularity of reform. In 1984 Jack Scarisbrick argued that 'the peculiar character of the English Reformation' was that its initiation, in the form of the Royal Supremacy and monastic dissolutions, 'officially owed nothing and in practice little to Protestantism.'[95] In 1992 Eamon Duffy's elegiac account

---

1964), 37, 69, 81.

[92] Susan Brigden, "Youth and the English Reformation," *PP* 95 (1982); John Davis, *Heresy and Reformation in the South-East of England, 1520–1559* (London: Royal Historical Society, 1983); Margaret Aston, *Lollards and Reformers: Images and Literacy in Late Medieval England* (London: Hambledon Press, 1984); A. G. Dickens, "The Early Expansion of Protestantism in England 1520–1558," *ARG* 78 (1987): 187–222; Anne Hudson, *The Premature Reformation: Wycliffite Texts and Lollard History* (Oxford: OUP, 1988); Susan Brigden, *London and the Reformation* (Oxford: OUP, 1989); Margaret Aston, "Iconoclasm at Rickmansworth, 1522: Troubles of Churchwardens," *JEH* 40, 4 (1989): 524–52. The possibility of a debt to Lollardy continues to be mooted: e.g., Diarmaid MacCulloch, "Sixteenth-century English Protestantism and the Continent," in *Sister Reformations: the Reformation in Germany and in England: symposium on the occasion of the 450th anniversary of the Elizabethan Settlement, September 23rd-26th, 2009*, ed. D. Wendebourg (Tübingen: Mohr Siebeck, 2010), 5–6, 14.

[93] A. G. Dickens, *The English Reformation*, 2nd ed. (London: B. T. Batsford, 1989), 22. Dickens' analysis, like many contemporary studies, lacked great theological acuity. His observation reflected his own largely derivative studies of the German Reformation, e.g., A. G. Dickens, *The German Nation and Martin Luther* (London: Edward Arnold, 1974).

[94] See the collected essays in Christopher Haigh, ed., *The English Reformation Revised* (Cambridge: CUP, 1987).

[95] J. J. Scarisbrick, *The Reformation and the English People* (Oxford: Basil Blackwell, 1984), 61.

INTRODUCTION

of England's religious world before 'the stripping of the altars' proceeded without attempting any substantial engagement with the Reformation on the continent at all.⁹⁶ In 1993 Christopher Haigh scorned the assumption that 'what happened in England was simply a local manifestation of the wider European movement,' stating that 'English Reformations' 'did not follow any general Continental pattern.' Although he recognised that there was borrowing from and coincidence with the continental Reformation, he insisted that 'English Reformations' were 'different'.⁹⁷ In 2005 George Bernard demonstrated no more concern for the continent in his account of reform driven by the Crown than Duffy had thirteen years earlier.⁹⁸

Students of continental history have shown a greater willingness to see England as one scene on the European stage. In 1991 Euan Cameron stated that 'Europe's offshore islands [. . .] were as readily exposed to the ideas of the Reformation as anywhere on the Continent.'⁹⁹ In 2002 Philip Benedict specifically censured early Tudor revisionists for displaying 'a much more limited awareness of the larger world of European Reformation scholarship and its implications for their topic.'¹⁰⁰ Benedict's criticism broaches one explanation for English exceptionalism: the relatively short supply of Anglophone scholarship of the European Reformation until the latter half of the twentieth century.¹⁰¹ The first useful studies of

---

⁹⁶ Eamon Duffy, *The Stripping of the Altars: Traditional Religion in England c.1400–c.1580* (New Haven & London: YUP, 1992).

⁹⁷ Christopher Haigh, *English Reformations: Religion, Politics, and Society under the Tudors* (Oxford: OUP, 1993), 12–13, cf. 340.

⁹⁸ G. W. Bernard, *The King's Reformation: Henry VIII and the remaking of the English Church* (New Haven & London: YUP, 2005).

⁹⁹ Euan Cameron, *The European Reformation* (Oxford: OUP, 1991), 280; cf. the opposite impression given by G. R. Elton, *Reformation Europe 1517–1559* (London: Collins, 1963), 122–23.

¹⁰⁰ Philip Benedict, *Christ's Churches Purely Reformed: a social history of Calvinism* (New Haven & London: YUP, 2002), 232.

¹⁰¹ See the surveys by Patrick Collinson, "The Reformation," in *A Century of Theological and Religious Studies in Britain*, ed. E. Nicholson, The British Academy (Oxford: OUP, 2003), esp. 191–95; Thomas Brady, "From Revolution to

INTRODUCTION

Luther in English were pioneered by Roland Bainton in 1950 and Rupp in 1953.[102] The non-Lutheran Reformations trailed behind. Calvin studies were aided by the translation of François Wendel's French-language study in 1963 and the publication of T. H. L. Parker's English-language biography in 1975.[103] The first satisfactory study of Zwingli in English was by George Potter in 1976 and only in 2002 was a complete history of the Swiss Reformation published in English by Bruce Gordon.[104] Gordon's contribution, followed in 2009 by an impressive biography of Calvin, is the product of a growing awareness of the importance of continental influence on England.[105]

Most historians, as this survey suggests, have concentrated on political and devotional change. Felicity Heal, who in 2003 produced an integrated account of the Reformation across Britain and Ireland, suggests that this concentration encourages national studies. 'Historians of doctrine and ideas have found it easiest to transcend fixed boundaries,' she writes. 'But when the reception of these ideas and their assimilation into the political mainstream is at issue, national historians have a tendency to revert to claims of local exceptionalism.'[106]

The confluence of historiography emphasising the popularity of reform with revisionist historiography produced a post-revisionist

---

the Long Reformation: Writings in English on the German Reformation, 1970–2005," *ARG* 100 (2009): 48–64.

[102] Roland Bainton, *Here I Stand: a life of Martin Luther* (New York: Abingdon Press, 1950); E. G. Rupp, *The Righteousness of God: Luther Studies* (London: Hodder and Stoughton, 1953).

[103] François Wendel, *Calvin: the origins and development of his religious thought*, trans. P. Mairet (London: Collins, 1963); T. H. L. Parker, *John Calvin: a biography* (London: J. M. Dent & Sons, 1975).

[104] G. R. Potter, *Ulrich Zwingli 1484–1531* (Cambridge: CUP, 1976); Bruce Gordon, *The Swiss Reformation* (Manchester & New York: Manchester University Press, 2002).

[105] Bruce Gordon, *Calvin* (New Haven & London: YUP, 2009).

[106] Felicity Heal, *Reformation in Britain and Ireland* (Oxford: OUP, 2003), 6–7.

INTRODUCTION

equilibrium around the turn of the century. Post-revisionism has had several effects. First, scholarly attention has shifted decidedly to the late sixteenth century when reform was inculcated on a national scale. Second, early Reformation studies have turned to the 'popular piety' or 'popular politics' of the majority of people who had been alienated from traditional religion but were yet to embrace new beliefs.[107] Third, a few historians have tackled 'the highly complex and multifaceted processes through which an English Protestant movement was formed and sustained, and a distinctive Protestant identity created.'[108] It is amongst this latter group that the capability of intellectual history to transcend national boundaries has, at least in part, been realised.

Students of England's debt to continental reform have often worked with intellectual history or historical theology. In 1992 Diarmaid MacCulloch claimed that 'to chronicle the theological story of the English Reformation is largely to chronicle the shifting influences from the Continent, and English assimilation of them or reaction against them.'[109] Since then more scholars have begun

---

[107] E.g., Beat Kümin, *The Shaping of a Community: the Rise and Reformation of the English Parish c.1400–1560* (Aldershot: Scolar, 1996); Caroline Litzenberger, *The English Reformation and the Laity: Gloucestershire, 1540–1580* (Cambridge: CUP, 1997); Christopher Marsh, *Popular Religion in Sixteenth-Century England: Holding Their Peace* (Basingstoke: Macmillan, 1998); Ethan Shagan, *Popular Politics and the English Reformation* (Cambridge: CUP, 2003).

[108] The best example is Peter Marshall and Alec Ryrie, eds., *The Beginnings of English Protestantism* (Cambridge: CUP, 2002), quotation at 12–13.

[109] Diarmaid MacCulloch, "England," in *The Early Reformation in Europe*, ed. A. Pettegree (Cambridge: CUP, 1992), 169. MacCulloch's subsequent work has repeatedly highlighted continental influences, e.g., Diarmaid MacCulloch, "Henry VIII and the Reform of the Church," in *The Reign of Henry VIII: politics, policy and piety*, ed. D. MacCulloch (Basingstoke: Macmillan, 1995), 186; Diarmaid MacCulloch, *Thomas Cranmer: a life* (New Haven & London: YUP, 1996), 173; Diarmaid MacCulloch, *Tudor Church Militant: Edward VI and the Protestant Reformation* (London: Allen Lane, 1999), 170f; Diarmaid MacCulloch, "Heinrich Bullinger and the English-Speaking World," in *Heinrich Bullinger: Life—Thought—Influence: International Congress Heinrich Bullinger 2004*, eds. E. Campi and P. Opitz (Zurich: TVZ, 2007), 2:891–934; Diarmaid

to discuss continental influence so that, by 2007, Peter Marshall could claim 'that the Reformation in these islands possesses not just a "European context" in which it can be helpfully viewed, but a European *dimension* from which it cannot meaningfully be separated.'[110] Interest in this European 'dimension' led to a British Academy symposium held in 2007 being devoted to the subject of British reception of the continental Reformation. Numerous papers were concerned with the reception of ideas.[111]

A survey of these studies is suggestive of the progress that has been made. In 1994 Carl Trueman demonstrated that the radicalisation of the early English reformers was 'Luther's legacy' in spite of their modifications to Luther's theology.[112] In 1999 Richard Rex surveyed the early impact of continental theology at Cambridge.[113] Rory McEntegart argued in 2002 for the sincerity of English interest in the theological aspects of negotiations with the Lutheran princes during the 1530s.[114] Alec Ryrie's important study of Henrician reformers in 2003 suggested identifications with Lutheranism,[115] and in 2009 a symposium was convened in Berlin to examine the relationship between the 'Sister Reformations' in England and the

---

MacCulloch, "Sixteenth-century English Protestantism," 1–14; Diarmaid MacCulloch, *Thomas Cromwell: A Life* (London: Allen Lane, 2018).

[110] Peter Marshall, "Religious Exiles and the Tudor State," in *Discipline and Diversity*, eds. K. Cooper and J. Gregory, Ecclesiastical History Society (Woodbridge: Boydell Press, 2007), 283.

[111] Patrick Collinson and Polly Ha, eds., *The Reception of the Continental Reformation in Britain*, PBA Vol. 164 (Oxford: OUP, 2010).

[112] Carl Trueman, *Luther's Legacy: Salvation and English Reformers, 1525–1556* (Oxford: OUP, 1994), 6.

[113] Richard Rex, "The Early Impact of Reformation Theology at Cambridge University, 1521–1547," *RRR* 2 (1999): 38–71.

[114] Rory McEntegart, *Henry VIII, the League of Schmalkalden and the English Reformation* (Woodbridge: Royal Historical Society, 2002), 6–7.

[115] Alec Ryrie, *The Gospel and Henry VIII: evangelicals in the early English Reformation* (Cambridge: CUP, 2003), 145. See also Alec Ryrie, *The Age of Reformation: the Tudor and Stewart realms 1485–1603* (Abingdon: Routledge, 2017), 130–31.

Holy Roman Empire, particularly, that is, in Wittenberg.¹¹⁶ These have all been valuable correctives to English exceptionalism but it is apparent that most of them have concentrated upon specifically German Lutheran influence. This in spite of MacCulloch's assessment that the 'nearest relative' of the English Reformation was 'a string of Reformations which stretched from Martin Bucer's Strassburg to Heinrich Bullinger's Zürich.'¹¹⁷

Loss of institutional unity in western Christendom contributed to a crisis of identity which, besides its social and political expressions, was fundamentally religious. Marshall's proposal that 'we should see the English Reformation primarily as a crucible of religious identity formation' begins to deal with the sense of dislocation that ensued after the collapse of the late-medieval Church.¹¹⁸ The crisis was not only religious, but theological; it demanded reassessment, not only of the individual's relationship to the Church and to the state, but also of the way in which he related to God. It is impossible to understand religious identities properly without appreciating the context of theological discourse in which they operated.¹¹⁹

Luther may have led the vanguard of the revolt against papal authority but his self-identification with *bona fide* Christianity did

---

¹¹⁶ Dorothea Wendebourg, ed., *Sister Reformations: the Reformation in Germany and in England: symposium on the occasion of the 450th anniversary of the Elizabethan Settlement, September 23rd-26th, 2009* (Tübingen: Mohr Siebeck, 2010), ix.

¹¹⁷ MacCulloch, "Sixteenth-century English Protestantism," in Ibid., 3. Woolsey's exploration of Reformed influence covers post-Reformation Puritans and Presbyterians: Woolsey, *Unity and Continuity*, ch. 16–19.

¹¹⁸ Peter Marshall, "(Re)Defining the English Reformation," *JBS* 48, 3 (2009): 583–84; see also Susan Brigden, *New Worlds, Lost Worlds: the rule of the Tudors 1485–1603* (London: Penguin, 2000), x.

¹¹⁹ On the implications of theology for all aspects of the human condition see Porter, *Cambridge*, 277; see also Robert Kolb, *Luther's Heirs Define His Legacy: studies on Lutheran confessionalisation* (Aldershot: Variorum, 1996), x. An example of a study of religious identity which marginalises doctrinal factors is Lucy Wooding, *Rethinking Catholicism in Reformation England* (Oxford: OUP, 2000), 3, 14.

not win universal recognition from those who abandoned Rome. One such sceptic was the bishop of Winchester, Stephen Gardiner (1483–1555), who complained in 1541, 'You have not abolished the authority of Rome throughout the world, but you have appropriated it to yourselves, and transferred it to Wittenberg.'[120] Gardiner was addressing Lutherans, yet for some time—certainly since the late 1520s—Luther had been one among several leading reformers, and the cities of Zürich and Strassburg had emerged as alternative models to Wittenberg of what was authentic and evangelical Christianity. The radical reformer Melchior Hoffman even predicted that in 1533 Strassburg would be instated as the New Jerusalem.[121] Cameron has described Luther as 'a leader who did not provide all the answers; an icon who commanded immense respect but could not be followed word for word.'[122] The enormous market for Luther's publications did not necessarily represent informed or uncritical support.[123] His belief in justification by faith alone and his concomitant attack on the meritorious value of human works for salvation were touchstones of Reformation theology, but they were assimilated by some who retained greater emphasis on morality and obedience. Although ethical priorities might arise for a number of different reasons, in some cases it was the reciprocal concept of covenant that contributed powerfully to their formation. Conversely, the reciprocal covenant might be developed as a response to accusations of antinomianism against evangelical doctrine.

The Henrician Reformation saw dalliances with continental Lutheranism but doctrinally it is better to speak of an 'Anglo-Lutheran

[120] Stephen Gardiner, *Contemptum humanae legis* [1541], in Pierre Janelle, ed., *Obedience in Church and State: three political tracts by Stephen Gardiner* (Cambridge: CUP, 1930), 209.

[121] Diarmaid MacCulloch, *Reformation: Europe's House Divided 1490–1700* (London: Penguin, 2004), 188.

[122] Euan Cameron, "The Search for Luther's Place in the Reformation," *JEH* 45, 3 (1994): 485.

[123] Lee Wandel, *The Eucharist in the Reformation: incarnation and liturgy* (Cambridge: CUP, 2006), 107–9.

moment rather than a 'movement.'[124] It is difficult to name individual English theologians who were authentically Lutheran. Even Robert Barnes (1495–1540), a friend and student of Luther's at Wittenberg, can be seen to have exhibited 'important areas of difference' on the Law amongst other doctrines.[125] It is highly significant that the vast majority of Luther's works which were translated into English during the early Reformation did not concern his doctrine of justification.[126] Those reformers who embraced salvation *sola gratia* were not necessarily committed to Luther's assessment of the human condition in terms of forensic guilt. Many of them, including Cranmer, framed it in terms of moral disease.[127] The effect was detrimental to the progress of radical solifidianism in English evangelicalism.[128]

The scholarly focus on Lutheran influence in the early English Reformation can be unhelpful in encouraging us to think of the theology of the period in terms of a mild, proto-Anglican *via media*. More radical individuals are necessarily cast as proto-Puritans. Inadequate attention to continental influences other than Lutheranism during Henry VIII's reign needs to be redressed. This was when

[124] Ryrie, *Gospel*, 145; see also Carl Trueman and Carrie Euler, "The Reception of Martin Luther in Sixteenth- and Seventeenth-Century England," in *The Reception of Continental Reformation in Britain*, ed. P. Ha and P. Collinson, *PBA*, Vol. 164 (Oxford: OUP, 2010), 63; Heal, *Reformation*, 315; G. R. Elton, "England and the Continent in the Sixteenth Century," in *Reform and Reformation: England and the Continent c.1500–c.1750*, ed. D. Baker (Oxford: Blackwell, 1979), 11; McGrath, *Iustitia Dei*, 258.

[125] Trueman, *Luther's Legacy*, 196–97; see also Trueman and Euler, "Reception of Luther," 65–67.

[126] Carrie Euler, "Does Faith Translate? Tudor Translations of Martin Luther and the Doctrine of Justification by Faith," *ARG* 101 (2010): 80. Bozeman asks of the Bibles produced by Coverdale, Rogers, and Cranmer in the 1530s, 'what reader of their prefaces reasonably could infer that justification by faith only is its definitive message?' Bozeman, *Precisianist Strain*, 22.

[127] Bozeman, *Precisianist Strain*, 19; see also Wallace, *Puritans and Predestination*, 9; Knappen, *Tudor Puritanism*, 1–102.

[128] The progress of solifidian ideas is explored, and somewhat overstated, by D. Broughton Knox, *The Doctrine of Faith in the Reign of Henry VIII* (London: James Clarke & Co., 1961), esp. 1–78.

the 'Zürich connection' first began: the term was used by Torrance Kirby in 2007 to describe the profound influence that operated after Bullinger and Peter Martyr Vermigli (1499–1562) became the 'chief architects' of Edward VI's Church.[129] Carrie Euler's monograph of 2006 is by far the most detailed discussion of the reception of the Zürich tradition in Henrician England. She begins in 1531 and analyses the process of transmission with special attention to the history of the book, pastoral theology, and to polemic aimed at Catholic material piety and Anabaptism, footnoting the debate about covenant theology.[130] Ryan Reeves' work in 2014 reveals the connection between Swiss Reformed political thought and English evangelical attitudes to civil authority.[131] Further scrutiny and deeper theological analysis will be required for some time yet, but there is good reason to believe that Reformed theology made a contribution to the English Reformation from its earliest years.

The Edwardian links deserve further exploration as well, for they anticipate the influence on Elizabethan religion exerted by Bullinger and Vermigli through networks established during the Marian Exile and via their publications.[132] After his return to England from exile in 1559, John Jewel wrote wistfully, 'O Zurich! O Zurich! how much oftener do I now think of thee than ever I thought of England when I was at Zurich!'[133] The prevalence of continentally-inspired Reformed theology in the Elizabethan Church of England was so

[129] Torrance Kirby, *The Zurich Connection and Tudor Political Theology* (Leiden & Boston: Brill, 2007), 3, 5.

[130] Carrie Euler, *Couriers of the Gospel: England and Zürich 1531–1558* (Zurich: TVZ, 2006), 32n.

[131] Ryan Reeves, *English Evangelicals and Tudor Obedience, c.1527–1570* (Leiden & Boston: Brill, 2014); Ryan Reeves, "'Ye Gods': Political Obedience from Tyndale to Cromwell, c.1528–1540," *ARG* 105, 1 (2014): 230–56.

[132] Kirby, *Zurich Connection*, 23; Diarmaid MacCulloch, "The Myth of the English Reformation," *JBS* 30, 1 (1991): 14; Benedict, *Christ's Churches*, 232, 244–45; Joan O'Donovan, *Theology of Law and Authority in the English Reformation* (Grand Rapids: Eerdmans, 2004), 91–127.

[133] Jewel to Peter Martyr, undated, *ZL*, 1:23.

great that Kirby has called it a 'flowering' of Zürich theology. Zürich certainly excelled Geneva as the point of reference.

This contribution towards understanding Swiss Reformed influence on English theology from the 1520s to the 1550s focuses on the soteriology and sacramental theology associated with the covenant concept. Quentin Skinner stipulates that some very demanding conditions should be met before 'influence' can be ascribed: he requires (1) that there should be 'genuine similarity between the doctrines of *A* and *B*,' (2) 'that *B* could not have found the relevant doctrine in any writer other than *A*,' (3) 'that the probability of the similarity being random should be very low.'[134] Here 'influence' will be used less stringently as a form of reception. It is 'a question of tendencies, in part unconscious,' as Gottfried Locher makes clear: 'We should not expect an exact copy of the Zurich reformation. But when one or more of the aforementioned characteristics is seen to strive to take effect in programmatic form, then we may think in terms of relationship, repetition, or influence.'[135]

Covenant and the English Reformers

The seventeenth century has acted as a scholarly base camp for explorations of sixteenth-century Reformation covenant theology. Research has been preoccupied with its significance for post-Reformation federal theology and the presenting task has been to grapple with continental formulations of the covenant within the Reformed tradition. Little interest has hitherto been shown in the development of the concept in England, but research into continental concepts of covenant has now progressed sufficiently to warrant extension of the investigation to the English Reformation. In addition, the recent historiography of the English Reformation

---

[134] Quentin Skinner, "Meaning and Understanding in the History of Ideas," *History and Theory* 8, 1 (1969): 26.

[135] Gottfried Locher, *Zwingli's Thought: New Perspectives* (Leiden: Brill, 1981), 342–43.

encourages exploration of English concepts of covenant as part of a process of religious identity formation in the context of continental influences. The reciprocal concept of covenant can be used to illustrate the influence of Swiss Reformed theology on certain English reformers.

The lack of any concentrated analysis of the concept of covenant in early English Reformation theology has permitted the assumption that it became significant only in the late sixteenth century. The most detailed account to date appeared in 2004 as a preliminary chapter to Theodore Bozeman's study of post-Reformation Puritanism. The chapter is valuable because it avoids the anachronisms of Trinterud and his followers. Bozeman claims that the majority of early English reformers 'either expressed no special interest in the covenant idea or expounded it, with [John] Bradford [1510–55], in noncontractual or unilateral terms.' Cranmer was typical in this respect; his writings exhibit no special appreciation of the covenant even *à propos* his reading of Swiss sacramental theology. Bozeman does, nevertheless, identify several early reformers as exponents of the reciprocal concept: Miles Coverdale (1488–1569), George Joye (1490/95–1553), William Tyndale (c.1491–1536), John Bale (1495–1563), John Hooper (1495/1500–1555), Thomas Becon (1512/13–67) and Edmund Allen (1510s–59).[136]

The covenant was a significant feature of English Reformed theology. The concepts articulated by Zwingli, Bullinger and Calvin provide a basis for a systematic investigation of the concepts belonging to Tyndale, Coverdale and Hooper as three of those reformers rightly identified by Bozeman as espousing reciprocal themes. Bradford's concept of covenant will also be examined here for the sake of comparison and in order to determine the reasons for variety within the English Reformed tradition. These four reformers were fairly representative of educated English reformism between the 1520s and 1550s: Tyndale and Hooper were Oxford men while Coverdale

---

[136] Bozeman, *Precisianist Strain*, 24.

and Bradford studied at Cambridge; Tyndale and Coverdale were Bible translators; Tyndale, Coverdale and Hooper experienced exile, Bradford did not; Coverdale and Hooper became bishops; Tyndale, Hooper and Bradford were martyred, Coverdale died an old man.

Of the early English reformers Tyndale has received by far the most scholarly attention after Cranmer himself. James Mozley's landmark biography of 1937, complemented by Stanley Greenslade's essay of 1938, had enduring value; they were succeeded in 1994 by David Daniell's biography with a literary bent.[137] The tenor of interpretation was set in 1948 when Maynard Smith called Tyndale 'an austere Puritan.'[138] Trinterud added theological credence to this in 1951 and 1962 with his remarks on the legal nature of Tyndale's conditional covenant motif.[139] In 1961 Broughton Knox, echoed by Møller in 1963, accused Tyndale of 'overthrowing the whole basis of the Reformation' on the grounds that he attached God's promises to the fulfilment of conditions.[140] This interpretation was enshrined in 1964 in William Clebsch's conclusion that, while Tyndale's soteriology had been solifidian in the 1520s, in 1530 he adopted a 'bifocal theology of gospel and law' involving 'a twin justification, by faith before God and by works before men.'[141] By 1532, wrote Clebsch, 'Tyndale had revised his theology radically around the controlling notion of covenant, understood as a moralistic contract between God and man.'[142] This became the standard interpretation and was

---

[137] J. F. Mozley, *William Tyndale* (London: SPCK, 1937); S. L. Greenslade, *The Work of William Tindale* (London & Glasgow: Blackie and Son, 1938); David Daniell, *William Tyndale: a biography* (New Haven & London: YUP, 1994).

[138] Smith, *Henry VIII*, 280.

[139] Trinterud, "Origins," 39, 55; Leonard Trinterud, "A Reappraisal of William Tyndale's Debt to Martin Luther," *CH* 31 (1962): 39.

[140] Knox, *Doctrine of Faith*, 6; Møller, "Beginnings," 51–52.

[141] William Clebsch, *England's Earliest Protestants, 1525–1535* (Westport, CT: Greenwood Press, 1964), 137–204, quotations at 155, 171.

[142] Ibid., 180. Clebsch locates Tyndale within Trinterud's thesis at 191 and 199.

accepted in 1968 by Greaves who aligned Tyndale with Zwingli and Œcolampadius.[143]

Clebsch's thesis was broadly accepted by Charles Williams in 1969 and by McGiffert in his article of 1981 dealing with Tyndale's concept of covenant. McGiffert addressed the specifically soteriological question of whether Tyndale saw works as efficacious and concluded that he was not really legalistic.[144] He then assented to Trinterud's thesis, reinforcing the view that Tyndale had little influence on later covenant theology.[145] In 1994 Trueman reiterated McGiffert's denial of the contractual soteriology of Tyndale's concept. He claimed that it better resembled a familial relationship and that Tyndale had confined conditionality to an ethical imperative for Christians.[146] Trueman's more novel contribution was to argue that there had been no fundamental revision of Tyndale's soteriology in 1530–32.[147] However, although Trueman helpfully demonstrated Tyndale's early ethical emphases, he was so concerned to exonerate Tyndale of legalism that he allowed conditionality to have no bearing whatsoever on justification.[148] In 1996 Patrick Collinson judged that analysis of Tyndale had been 'vitiated' by the agenda seeking the origins of Puritanism.[149] This appears to be true of all previous

---

[143] Greaves, "Origins," 26–27.

[144] C. H. Williams, *William Tyndale* (London: Thomas Nelson & Sons, 1969), 133–34; Michael McGiffert, "William Tyndale's Conception of Covenant," *JEH* 32 (1981): 174–80.

[145] McGiffert, "Tyndale," 181–84.

[146] Trueman, *Luther's Legacy*, 108–19; Carl Trueman, "Early English Evangelicals: Three Examples," in *Sister Reformations: the Reformation in Germany and in England: symposium on the occasion of the 450th anniversary of the Elizabethan Settlement, September 23rd-26th, 2009*, ed. D. Wendebourg (Tübingen: Mohr Siebeck, 2010), 21.

[147] Trueman, *Luther's Legacy*, 101–8.

[148] Ibid., esp. 100–101. On Tyndale's doctrine of justification see Robert Wainwright, "William Tyndale on Covenant and Justification," *RRR* 13, 3 (2011): 353–72.

[149] Patrick Collinson, "William Tyndale and the Course of the English Reformation," *Reformation* 1 (1996): 86. E.g., Trinterud, "Origins," 39–45; Møller,

Introduction

studies save Trueman's. Another impediment has been the absence of any systematic survey of the concept of covenant throughout Tyndale's works.[150] Thus Arne Dembek could still suggest in 2010 that the concept had not emerged as Tyndale's theological '*Leitmotiv*' until as late as 1533.[151] In 2014 Reeves demonstrated that Tyndale was accessing Swiss Reformed writings no later than 1527/28.[152]

The scarcity of interest shown in Coverdale—as opposed to Coverdale's translations—is surprising.[153] Almost nothing has been written by historians since Maynard Smith in 1948 and Mozley in 1953, both of whom devoted more print to his Bible translations than to the man himself or to his theology.[154] The only other

---

"Beginnings," 51–54; Greaves, "Origins," 26–28.

[150] Ralph Werrell recognises the centrality of Tyndale's concept of covenant but he makes anachronistic and implausible claims about it: Ralph Werrell, *The Theology of William Tyndale* (Cambridge: James Clarke & Co., 2006); Ralph Werrell, "Sin and Salvation in William Tyndale's Theology," in *Sin and Salvation in Reformation England*, ed. J. Willis (Farnham: Ashgate, 2015), 23–38. Werrell seeks to dismiss the influence of continental theology on Tyndale: Ralph Werrell, *The Roots of William Tyndale's Theology* (Cambridge: James Clarke & Co., 2013), 48–61. See also Ralph Werrell, *The Blood of Christ in the Theology of William Tyndale* (Cambridge: James Clarke & Co., 2015).

[151] Arne Dembek, *William Tyndale (1491–1536): Reformatorische Theologie als kontextuelle Schriftauslegung* (Tübingen: Mohr Siebeck, 2010), 201, 234, 373.

[152] Reeves, "Ye Gods," 243. Reeves is concerned with Tyndale's political thought. On Tyndale's view of civil authority and ecclesiastical polity see Brad Pardue, *Printing, Power, and Piety: appeals to the public during the early years of the English Reformation* (Leiden & Boston: Brill, 2012) and Karl Gunther, *Reformation Unbound: Protestant Visions of Reform in England, 1525–1590* (Cambridge: CUP, 2014), 20–31.

[153] On Coverdale's translation work see, e.g., Jamie Ferguson, "Miles Coverdale and the Claims of Paraphrase," in *Psalms in the Early Modern World*, eds. L. Austern, K. McBride and D. Orvis (Farnham: Ashgate, 2011), 137–54; Micheline White, "Women's Hymns in Mid-Sixteenth Century England: Elisabeth Cruciger, Miles Coverdale, and Lady Elizabeth Tyrwhit," *ANQ* 24, 1–2 (2011): 21–32.

[154] Maynard Smith, *Henry VIII*, 326–35; J. F. Mozley, *Coverdale and His Bibles* (London: Lutterworth, 1953).

significant studies, both from 1982, were Esther Hildebrandt's dissertation, which recounted Coverdale's exile abroad, and Celia Hughes' analysis of several episodes of his life.[155] There have been no assessments of his concept of covenant aside from Trinterud's comment that Coverdale's Bible translations were, in his view, 'indifferent' to it.[156]

Hooper has attracted rather more attention than Coverdale but usually for his participation in the Vestment Controversy rather than his theology. In 1951 Trinterud claimed Hooper as an exponent of the 'covenant, or federal, school of thought.'[157] Morris West followed with three articles in 1954 and 1955 assessing Hooper's contribution to Puritanism. The first of these suggested that the covenant provided a framework for Hooper's theology,[158] a view vociferously contradicted by Møller in 1963.[159] In 1968 Greaves took a single sentence to note the significance of conditionality in Hooper's understanding of the Decalogue,[160] but J. H. Primus supported West in claiming that Hooper's 'concept of authority rooted in the covenant' was the basis for most of his 'Puritan traits'.[161] A *via media* was ploughed in 1992 by E. W. Hunt: although West had probably claimed too much, the covenant was 'by no means peripheral' to Hooper's thought.[162] In 1994 Trueman acknowledged

---

[155] Esther Hildebrandt, "A Study of the English Protestant Exiles in Northern Switzerland and Strasbourg 1539–47, and Their Role in the English Reformation," PhD diss. (University of Durham, 1982), 56–63, 154–57, 222–25; Celia Hughes, "Coverdale's Alter Ego," *Bulletin of the John Rylands Library* 65, 1 (1982): 100–124.

[156] Trinterud, "Origins," 44.

[157] Ibid.

[158] W. M. S. West, "John Hooper and the Origins of Puritanism [1]," *BQ* 15, 8 (1954): 356–59.

[159] Møller, "Beginnings," 56.

[160] Greaves, "Origins," 27.

[161] J. H. Primus, "The Role of the Covenant Doctrine in the Puritanism of John Hooper," *Dutch Review of Church History* 48, 2 (1968): 184.

[162] E. W. Hunt, *The Life and Times of John Hooper (c.1500–1555) Bishop of Gloucester* (Lampeter: Edwin Mellen Press, 1992), 241.

in passing that Hooper had articulated a 'bilateral' concept of 'contract' which took effect only after reconciliation to God.[163] John Franke's dissertation in 1996 recognised the foundational significance of a conditional 'notion of a contract' to Hooper's theology but his analysis of it was limited in scope.[164] In 2003 Andries Raath and Shaun de Freitas identified Hooper as the link between Bullinger's federalism and Puritanism, implicitly fortifying Trinterud's and Baker's positions.[165] Alison Dalton's dissertation of 2008 explored influences on Hooper, placing him definitively in the Swiss camp, but she did not undertake extensive theological investigation.[166] David Newcombe's biography of 2009 took up Møller's denial of the significance of Hooper's concept but failed to provide supporting evidence from Hooper's writings.[167] A more satisfactory assessment is undoubtedly needed.

Historians often cite Bradford but without any extended analysis. His reforming career was brief and ended prematurely, yet the wealth of his writing deserves exploration. For Trinterud he was an emergent Puritan, apparently undeserving of further comment.[168] For Møller he participated in the formation of what would become Puritan covenant theology.[169] The most accomplished study remains Philip Johnston's 1963 dissertation which excelled both biographically and

---

[163] Trueman, *Luther's Legacy*, 230, 241.

[164] John Franke, "The Religious Thought of John Hooper," DPhil diss. (University of Oxford, 1996), 113–23. Franke does not discuss the contract in relation to Hooper's sacramental theology.

[165] Andries Raath and Shaun de Freitas, "From Heinrich Bullinger to Puritanism: John Hooper's Theology and the Office of Magistracy," *SJT* 56, 2 (2003): 208–30.

[166] Alison Dalton, "John Hooper and His Networks: a study of change in Reformation England," DPhil diss. (University of Oxford, 2008). I am grateful to Dr Dalton for supplying me with a copy of her thesis.

[167] D. G. Newcombe, *John Hooper: Tudor Bishop and Martyr* (Oxford: Davenant Press, 2009), 42.

[168] Trinterud, "Origins," 38.

[169] Møller, "Beginnings," 56.

theologically;[170] his examiner Gordon Rupp delivered a commemorative sermon on Bradford that same year, and in 1964 Marcus Loane published a brief biography.[171] In 1968 Greaves described Bradford as reflecting Calvin's concept of covenant, thereby allocating him to the Calvinist, as opposed to Rhenish, tradition in Trinterud's model.[172] In 1975 Haigh's study of Lancashire included mention of Bradford, who was a native of that county, and in 1983 Hughes contributed a useful overview of Bradford's life and writings.[173] Andrew Penny's study in 1990 of the mid-Tudor predestinarian controversy concerned Bradford's doctrine of election, a theme which Trueman treated at greater length in 1994.[174] Subsequently Megan Wheeler in 2006 and Michael Graham and Gretchen Minton in 2013 treated Bradford as a prisoner under Mary Tudor and in 2015 Alastair Minnis published on his doctrine of the Resurrection.[175] A clear evaluation of the covenant in Bradford's thought has never been attempted before and the importance of Bucer to his theological development makes for illuminating comparison.

---

[170] P. F. Johnston, "The Life of John Bradford, the Manchester Martyr, c.1510–1555," BLitt diss. (University of Oxford, 1963).

[171] E. G. Rupp, "John Bradford, Martyr. ob. 1 July, 1555," *The London Quarterly and Holborn Review*, 6th series, 32 (1963): 50–55; Marcus Loane, *Pioneers of the Reformation in England* (London: The Church Book Room Press, 1964), 137–78.

[172] Greaves, "Origins," 28; see also Kendall, *Calvin*, 43–44.

[173] Christopher Haigh, *Reformation and Resistance in Tudor Lancashire* (Cambridge: CUP, 1975); Celia Hughes, "Two Sixteenth-Century Northern Protestants: John Bradford and William Turner," *Bulletin of the John Rylands Library* 66, 1 (1983): 104–21.

[174] D. A. Penny, *Freewill or Predestination: the battle over saving grace in mid-Tudor England* (Woodbridge: Royal Historical Society, 1990); Trueman, *Luther's Legacy*, 243–88.

[175] Megan Wheeler, "Protestants, Prisoners and the Marian Persecution," DPhil diss. (University of Oxford, 2006); Alastair Minnis, "The Restoration of All Things: John Bradford's Refutation of Aquinas on Animal Resurrection," *Journal of Medieval and Early Modern Studies* 45, 2 (2015): 323–42; Michael Graham and Gretchen Minton, "The Word as as an Artifact of Remembrance," *Reformation* 18, 1 (2013): 64–83.

Introduction

This investigation of the concept of covenant as a marker of Swiss influence on English Reformed theology begins in chapter two with a discussion of the complex question of religious and theological identity. Consideration is given to the problems which pertain to analysis of developing and competing theological opinions in England, and evidence for Reformed theology under Henry VIII and Edward VI is surveyed. Chapters three and four introduce the reciprocal covenant as a characteristic of the Reformed tradition and use it to indicate English reception of Swiss theology. The writings of each of the reformers selected are examined with attention given to attendant views on justification, sanctification and predestination when these elucidate distinctively Reformed characteristics. This reception model is developed further in chapters five and six through a similarly structured study of the concept's impression upon sacramental theology. Sacramental controversy emerged at an early stage of the Reformation with acute relevance to covenant theology in both the Swiss and English discourses.

2

Reformed Theology in England

To the third article as touching Swingli & others, he thinck-
eth that they hold the same doctrine, that Luther doth, how
be it he supposeth they vary in some poyntes.[1]
—Articles laid to Richard Bayfield, 1531

It was Richard Bayfield's responsibility as chamberlain of the Abbey of Bury St Edmunds to see to it that visitors were 'well entertained,' but when Robert Barnes came to stay it was Bayfield who 'delighted much' in the conversation. Barnes and his companions from the London Brickmakers gave him two copies of the New Testament, one in Latin and one newly-released in English by the exile William Tyndale. So enthused was Bayfield by his reading that he was gagged, stocked and imprisoned in the abbot's gaol for several months until Barnes took him off to Cambridge. Barnes himself was arrested in early 1526 and Bayfield fled overseas. There he became Tyndale's agent, smuggling books by Martin Luther, 'diuers others of his dampnable sect, & of Œcolampadius the great heretike, and diuerse other heretikes' like Huldrych Zwingli. His illicit shipments

---

[1] John Foxe, *AM* [1563] (Sheffield: HRI Online Publications, 2011), 3:538, http://www.johnfoxe.org.

to England in 1530–31 landed him in the Tower and he was burnt at Smithfield as a suspected sacramentary.[2]

Bayfield is noteworthy not only for the number of reformers whose books he sold but also for his inability to distinguish between their different theological positions. When the bishop of London asked him 'whether Zwinglius was of Luther's sect, he answered, that he neuer spake wyth him. Being asked whether Zwinglius was a Catholike, he answered, that he could not tel,' but he did acknowledge 'that the common fame hathe bene within these ii. or iii. yeares, that Œcolampadius and Zwinglius be heretickes, also that suche as leane to Martyne Luther be heretickes.' Bayfield, however, had 'red no heresies' in these books but rather 'iudged they were good, and of the true faith.' Significantly he could not articulate the difference between Luther's teaching and that of Zwingli.[3]

The fracturing of Latin Christendom in the sixteenth century was a matter of countless individuals being forced to reconsider, reinvent and redefine their religious identities in response to the changing theological and devotional landscape, and to face the often-heated consequences of doing so. Bayfield's problem of definition has only augmented with the centuries and historians ought to proceed with caution. Following Anne Overell, we do well to avoid the fallacious notion that 'European influence on England came in orderly, separate waves, first Lutheran and later Swiss, then Calvinist, with Mary Tudor's Spanish and Italian advisers washed up in 1554 to provide a brief papalist interlude.'[4] In reality English engagement with the continent was far more complex, perhaps especially with regard to theology, which had a profound and too often under-appreciated impact on religious identity formation. All

---

[2] Ibid., 3:536–40. Foxe incorrectly suggests that Bayfield was given Tyndale's *The Parable of the Wicked Mammon* and *The Obedience of a Christian Man* when Barnes visited Bury but these were not published until 1528.

[3] Ibid.

[4] Anne Overell, *Italian Reform and English Reformations, c.1535–c.1585* (Aldershot: Ashgate, 2008), 3.

religious commitments have doctrinal content to a greater or lesser degree and it was often doctrinal convictions that gave rise to the most serious conflict. Bruce Gordon rightly acknowleges that 'theology and historical identity were the very things for which each side was prepared to put the other to death.'[5]

The growth of reforming activity across Europe from the 1490s faltered abruptly in the 1520s when renewal movements were tainted by association, fairly or otherwise, with Martin Luther. Nowadays the Lutheran character of reformism in the 1520s and 1530s cannot be assumed and is often contested. The broader characterisation 'evangelical' has instead gained consensus,[6] although it does not stand for reforming inclinations of every kind. 'We should avoid the hindsight that forces all evangelicals in these early confused days of the Reformation into a seamless web of solidarity,' writes Diarmaid MacCulloch.[7]

The word 'evangelical' is derived from the Greek word meaning 'gospel,' to which all Christians lay claim. During the Reformation, however, the term 'gospeller' was applied pejoratively in

---

[5] Bruce Gordon with Luca Baschera and Christian Moser, "Emulating the Past and Creating the Present: Reformation and the Use of Historical and Theological Models in Zurich in the Sixteenth Century," in *Following Zwingli: Applying the Past in Reformation Zurich*, eds. L. Baschera, B. Gordon and C. Moser (Farnham: Ashgate, 2014), 10.

[6] Basil Hall, "The Early Rise and Gradual Decline of Lutheranism in England (1520–1600)," in *Reform and Reformation: England and the Continent c.1500–c.1750*, ed. D. Baker (Oxford: Blackwell, 1979); Carl Trueman, *Luther's Legacy: Salvation and English Reformers, 1525–1556* (Oxford: OUP, 1994), 75–80; Diarmaid MacCulloch, *Thomas Cranmer: a life* (New Haven & London: YUP, 1996), 2; Richard Rex, "The Early Impact of Reformation Theology at Cambridge University, 1521–1547," *RRR* 2 (1999): 40n, 52–43; Nicholas Tyacke, *Aspects of English Protestantism c.1530–1700* (Manchester & New York: Manchester University Press, 2001), 43; Alec Ryrie, *The Gospel and Henry VIII: evangelicals in the early English Reformation* (Cambridge: CUP, 2003), xv–xvi.

[7] Diarmaid MacCulloch, *Thomas Cromwell: A Life* (London: Allen Lane, 2018), 120.

England to those questioning the authority of the Church in preference for Scripture. In 1531 William Barlowe censured those 'most rifest and most busy to prate of the Gospell,' 'these new Gospellers [...] whych be raylers & gesters, vycyous lyuers & fals hypocrrytes without any conscyence.'[8] In this light 'evangelical' reformers are appropriately defined relative to Catholic reformers who remained loyal to traditional ecclesiastical authorities. There are cases which challenge strict parameters, such as the Meaux Circle in France,[9] Anne Boleyn in England,[10] Italy's *spirituali*,[11] and the peripatetic Erasmus of Rotterdam.[12] Theirs was the acute experience of moderation, perhaps contradiction, and indecision.[13] Admittedly Barlowe

---

[8] William Barlowe, *Dialogue on the Lutheran Factions*, ed. A. McLean, *CLRC*, Vol. 15 (Appleford: Sutton Courtenay Press, 1981), 116–20.

[9] Jonathan Reid, "France," in *The Reformation World*, ed. A. Pettegree (London & New York: Routledge, 2000), 212–16; Bruce Gordon, *Calvin* (New Haven & London: YUP, 2009), 193–94.

[10] Eric Ives, *Anne Boleyn* (Oxford: Basil Blackwell, 1986), 313–28; James Carley, "'Her Moost Lovyng and Fryndely Brother Sendeth Gretyng': Anne Boleyn's manuscripts and their sources," in *Illuminating the Book: makers and interpreters*, ed. M. Brown and S. McKendrick (London: British Library, 1998), 270–72. See Felicity Heal, *Reformation in Britain and Ireland* (Oxford: OUP, 2003), 251–52.

[11] Exemplary among the *spirituali*, Gasparo Contarini emphasised faith but not solifidianism, seeking renewal within the Roman Church. Contrasts with Luther are made in Dermot Fenlon, *Heresy and Obedience in Tridentine Italy: Cardinal Pole and the Counter Reformation* (Cambridge: CUP, 1972), 9, 17–18; see also Stephen Bowd, *Reform Before the Reformation: Vincenzo Querini and the Religious Renaissance in Italy* (Leiden: Brill, 2002), 218. The reformism of the *spirituali* was possible in the closing years of pre-Tridentine plurality but the perplexities involved ('not abandoning the doctrine of the Church, but believing in it more than in our wits,' said Contarini, quoted in Fenlon, *Heresy*, 65) were irreconcilable for some, like Peter Martyr Vermigli, Bernardino Ochino, and the more radical wing of Italian reformism in the 1540s and 1550s. See Bruce Gordon, "Italy," in *The Reformation World*, ed. A. Pettegree (London and New York: Routledge, 2000), 285–92.

[12] Christine Christ-von Wedel, *Erasmus of Rotterdam: advocate of a new Christianity* (Toronto & London: University of Toronto Press, 2013), 4, 6–7, 10.

[13] See J. B. Ross, "Gasparo Contarini and his friends," *Studies in the*

allowed that a 'very few' gospellers simply wanted vernacular Scripture, but this minority deserves separate classification. The theological priorities of different individuals were nuanced and it does not help to relax the referential remits of taxonomy to embrace liminal figures.

In the Low Countries traditionalists classified all dissidents as *'lutheriaenen'* because Wittenberg was held responsible for all kinds of nonconformity whether or not offenders had much in common with Luther's theology. In practice the Habsburg authorities were tackling Sacramentarian heresies (the denial of sacramental grace and of the corporal presence of Christ in the Eucharist) which were not naturally Lutheran.[14] Similar examples are found in Spain, where the mystic *alumbrados* (illuminists) were dubbed Lutheran,[15] and in France, where dissenters of any kind were classified in this way.[16] In Zürich Huldrych Zwingli complained in 1523 that

> all teaching of Christ, regardless of who on earth proclaims it, is called Lutheran. Though a person may not even have read Luther's teachings and kept himself strictly to the word of God, they dare, nonetheless, to denounce him as Lutheran. This has happened to me.[17]

Renaissance 17 (1970): 217, 225.

[14] Alastair Duke, *Reformation and Revolt in the Low Countries* (London & Ronceverte: Hambledon Press, 1990), 15, 19; Joke Spaans, "Reform in the Low Countries," in *A Companion to the Reformation World*, ed. R. Po-Chia Hsia (Oxford: Blackwell, 2004), 119–20.

[15] David Coleman, "Spain," in *The Reformation World*, ed. A. Pettegree (London & New York: Routledge, 2000), 300–301.

[16] Reid, "France," 212.

[17] Huldrych Zwingli, *Exposition and Basis of the Conclusions or Articles* [July 1523], *HZW*, 1:116. See also Huldrych Zwingli, "On Baptism [May 1525]," in *Zwingli and Bullinger: Selected Translations*, ed. G. Bromiley, *LCC*, Vol. 24 (Philadelphia: Westminster Press, 1953), 173. For an example of Zwingli drawing on Luther's Ninety-Five Theses see Huldrych Zwingli, *Erläuterungen zur Genesis* [March 1527], *CR*, 100:107.

With such misnomers occurring across Europe, it is reasonable to assume that English 'Lutheranism' was composed of competing theological commitments.

There are numerous hazards to negotiate in discerning different types of evangelical within the reformist *milieux*. Attempts to identify early reformers with confessional groupings are problematic for two elementary reasons. Firstly, confessionalisation did not begin until the end of the 1550s. Indeed, the Marburg Colloquy of 1529, far from exposing confessional distinctions, achieved consensus on fourteen of the fifteen points discussed.[18] The labels traditionally applied—'Protestant,' 'Catholic,' 'Lutheran,' 'Zwinglian,' 'Calvinist,' 'sacramentarian,' 'Anglican,' 'papist'—are often anachronistic and usually lack precision in the English context. They could also be polemical and pejorative. In Zürich Zwingli rejected 'sacramentarian' as a 'term of reproach' and sought to redirect it against his opponents.[19] Henry VIII complained in 1545 of his subjects' name-calling because 'the one calleth the other Hereticke and Anabaptist, and he calleth hym again, Papist, Ypocrite and Pharisey.' Some were 'to[o] styff in their old Mumpsimus, other be to[o] busy and curious in their newe Sumpsimus.'[20] Other examples include the contemporary use of 'new learning' to smear evangelicalism with the taint of novelty,[21] the mysterious 'known men,' and the 'Christian brethren'.[22]

---

[18] *The Marburg Colloquy and the Marburg Articles*, trans. M. Lehmann, *LW*, Vol. 38 (Philadelphia: Fortress Press, 1971), 85–89.

[19] Huldrych Zwingli, *Friendly Exegesis, That Is, Exposition of the Matter of the Eucharist to Martin Luther* [February 1527], *HZW*, 2:246.

[20] Quoted in Peter Marshall, "Mumpsimus and Sumpsimus: The Intellectual Origins of a Henrician *Bon Mot*," *JEH* 52, 3 (2001), 512.

[21] Richard Rex, "The New Learning," *JEH* 4, 1 (1993): 26–44; e.g., Heinrich Bullinger, *The Olde Fayth, an euydent probation out of the Holy Scripture, that the Christen Fayth (which is the right true, old & undoubted faith, hath endured sens the beginnyng of the worlde)*, trans. M. Coverdale (Antwerp?: Thomas Vautroullier, 1541; RSTC 4070.5), *3r.

[22] E. G. Rupp, *Studies in the Making of the English Protestant Tradition (Mainly in the Reign of Henry VIII)* (Cambridge: CUP, 1949), 6–14.

To use confessional labels in the 1520s, 30s and 40s is, to some extent, an uncomfortable historiographical convenience; the true complexity of the situation must be kept in sight. Gury Schneider-Ludorff advocates a 'pluriform' interpretative model 'that heightens awareness of the simultaneous coexistence of a variety of positions, coalitions, and delimitations in dialogue with each other.' She argues that in territories (as opposed to cities) 'it was possible to tolerate the co-existence of the various groups for longer without any major political repercussions.'[23] This resonates fairly well with the *de facto* situation in England where, according to Peter Marshall, 'a fair amount of popular confessionalisation preceded, accompanied, and sometimes opposed fitful attempts at state confessionalisation.'[24]

A second problem with confessional labels is that identification according to a checklist of conscious doctrinal and devotional characteristics fails to take account of the amorphous and idiosyncratic nature of personal religious affections.[25] Not only are religious identities more than the sum of their doctrinal parts, but confessional categories impose chimerical structures on complex and diverse paradigms. The reasons for, and experiences of, conversion are difficult to analyse. How did converts perceive their transition with regard to the contested nature of the Church? What were the repercussions for their participation in official religion?[26] Thomas Bilney was

---

[23] Gury Schneider-Ludorff, "Philipp of Hesse as an example of Princely Reformation: a contribution to Reformation Studies," *RRR* 8, 3 (2006): 312.

[24] Peter Marshall, "(Re)Defining the English Reformation," *JBS* 48, 3 (2009): 584.

[25] The fictional aspect of autobiography is explored in Stephen Greenblatt, *Renaissance Self-Fashioning: from More to Shakespeare* (Chicago & London: University of Chicago Press, 1980).

[26] See Peter Marshall, "Evangelical Conversion in the Reign of Henry VIII," in *The Beginnings of English Protestantism*, ed. P. Marshall and A. Ryrie (Cambridge: CUP, 2002), 14–37. The same issues are discussed for the late and post-Reformation eras in Michael Questier, *Conversion, Politics and Religion in England, 1580–1625* (Cambridge: CUP, 1996), 2–4. Contemporaries would have struggled to articulate their own personal experiences, writes Anne Ferry, *The "Inward" Language: Sonnets of Wyatt, Sidney, Shakespeare, Donne* (Chicago

one who struggled to perceive the implications of his conversion reading Erasmus' *Novum Testamentum*.[27] A further difficulty is the evolutionary nature of these identities, exemplified by Thomas Hitton, a Maidstone preacher burnt in 1530, whom Sir Thomas More described as a Lutheran who had subsequently progressed to the Reformed opinions of Zwingli and Œcolampadius.[28]

In attempting to delineate divisions between shifting identities we stretch our retrospective vantage to its limits; as Brian Cummings points out, 'often the protagonists themselves could hardly quantify what the differences were. Indeed, in the effort to locate difference, a writer might deviate all too quickly into his own sense of contradiction'[29]—witness Richard Bayfield. Marshall advises that identities should be understood 'as social personae fundamentally constituted by and through forms of engagement and self-representation, very often polemical and political ones.' This incorporates 'the extent to which the religious situation at the time was fluid and indeterminate,'[30] a state of flux that encouraged individuals into a penumbra in which their theological commitments could be obscured.

Some sense may be made of the internal contradictions of contemporary identities by the simple observation that these believers did not have as-yet-non-existent confessional parameters in mind. Their categories were drawn from the past, not the future.

& London: University of Chicago Press, 1983), 40–42.

[27] John Davis, "The Trials of Thomas Bylney and the English Reformation," *HJ* 24, 4 (1981): 775, 777–78, 781, 787–88; see also Marshall Knappen, "William Tyndale—First English Puritan," *CH* 5 (1936): 211; Patrick Collinson, "William Tyndale and the Course of the English Reformation," *Reformation* 1 (1996): 76.

[28] John Davis, *Heresy and Reformation in the South-East of England, 1520–1559* (London: Royal Historical Society, 1983), 80.

[29] Brian Cummings, *The Literary Culture of the Reformation: grammar and grace* (Oxford: OUP, 2002), 13.

[30] Peter Marshall, *Religious Identities in Henry VIII's England* (Aldershot: Ashgate, 2006), vi, 4.

Archbishop William Temple reflected on historical Christian experience that 'as we look forwards, we peer into darkness, and none can say with certainty what course the true progress of the future should follow. But as we look back, the truth is marked by beacon-lights, which are the lives of saints and pioneers.'[31] The atavistic biblicism of the evangelicals, determined to comprehend their lives in terms of the scriptural narrative, and their concern to stand in the succession of the true Church—in whatever way they defined it against the late-medieval Church—evidences such an approach to their situation.[32] Luther, for his own part, had honed his theology gradually through a series of breakthroughs in his interpretation of Scripture.[33] He may have been a salutary guide to others seeking to define authority *sola scriptura*, but it ought not to be assumed that individuals' adoption of Reformed theological conclusions had first necessitated their passage through Lutheranism.

From this viewpoint the divisions within evangelicalism begin to collapse. Consider these words of the Elizabethan ecclesiastic John Jewel: 'As for those persons whom they upon spite call Zwinglians and Lutherans, in very deed they of both sides be Christians and good friends and brethren. They vary not betwixt themselves upon the principles and foundations of our religion.'[34] Given this perspective, Gordon Rupp observed well that English evangelicals 'were not

---

[31] William Temple, *Readings in St John's Gospel* (London: Macmillan, 1939), 8.

[32] Biblicism is eminently expressed in the *Exhortation to the reading of scripture* in Thomas Cranmer, *Certayne Sermons, or Homelies appoynted by the Kynges Maiestie* (London: Rychard Grafton, 1547; RSTC 13640), A3v-B4v. An example of drawing inspiration from past believers is John Bale, *A Brefe Chronycle concernynge the examinacyon and death of the blessed martyr of Christ Syr Iohan Oldecastell the Lorde Cobham* (Antwerp: 1544; RSTC 1276). See Graeme Murdock, "The Importance of Being Josiah: an image of Calvinist identity," *SCJ* 29, 4 (1998); J. S. Coolidge, *The Pauline Renaissance in England: Puritanism and the Bible* (Oxford: OUP, 1970).

[33] Heiko Oberman, *Luther: Man between God and the Devil* (New Haven & London: YUP, 1989), 165–66.

[34] John Jewel, *The Works of John Jewel, Bishop of Salisbury*, ed. J. Ayre, PS, Vol. 1 (Cambridge: CUP, 1845), 69–70.

concerned to avoid or seek to learn from Wittenberg or Geneva or Canterbury, but with the faith once for all delivered to the saints.'[35] There was consciousness of catholicity even if the term itself was contested.[36] There were those, especially within the Reformed camp like Martin Bucer and Thomas Cranmer, who exerted themselves in a quest to unite the various evangelical identities in opposition to Rome.[37]

Although a sensible degree of deconstruction is helpful, we must resist the epistemic agnosticism that disallows 'true' historical judgment of 'reality'.[38] While theological identities lacked uniform coherence between individuals, there is the opposing risk of rejecting essential identity traits altogether. Christopher Haigh's term 'English Reformations' tends to obscure the fundamental parity of the Reformation as expressed in different places over time,[39] and a general tendency to deal only in terms of 'Catholicisms' or 'Lutheranisms' goes too far. Of course there was development, but a certain essentialism is required to prevent *reductio ad absurdum*. Brad Gregory has attacked the 'hermeneutic of suspicion' which breeds excessively tentative classifications of identity. For example, he condemns inverted commas around such terms as 'heretic' and 'superstition,' 'as though their contentiousness compels subjectivi-

---

[35] Rupp, *Studies*, xiv-xv.

[36] Peter Marshall, "Is the Pope a Catholic? Henry VIII and the Semantics of Schism," in *Catholics and the 'Protestant Nation': religious politics and identity in early modern England*, ed. E. Shagan (Manchester: Manchester University Press, 2005); Diarmaid MacCulloch, "Calvin: Fifth Latin Doctor of the Church?" in *Calvin and His Influence, 1509–2009*, eds. I. Backus and P. Benedict (Oxford and New York: OUP, 2011).

[37] Luc Racaut and Alec Ryrie, "Introduction: Between Coercion and Persuasion," in *Moderate Voices in the European Reformation*, eds. L. Racaut and A. Ryrie (Aldershot: Ashgate, 2005), 7–8.

[38] E.g., Hayden White, *The Content of the Form: narrative discourse and historical representation* (London & Baltimore: John Hopkins University Press, 1987), 27, 36–27, 44.

[39] Christopher Haigh, *English Reformations: Religion, Politics, and Society under the Tudors* (Oxford: OUP, 1993).

sation—implying that Protestants were not *really* heretics, Catholics were not *really* superstitious.'[40] Relativistic nominalism becomes otiose in making an art of stating the obvious. It can also risk becoming 'crassly functionalist' in its presentation of profound religious feelings and theological convictions.[41]

The studies in the chapters hereafter require close-reading of theological texts. Here it must be remembered that the application of theological identity labels requires precision because divisions could be so slight as to hang on parts of speech.[42] Specific doctrinal views may be assigned a particular label, but to identify a whole person with a dogmatic label without necessary qualification is foolhardy. In England no one reformer bequeathed a personalised 'ism,' which suggested to Patrick Collinson that the English Reformation had considerable success in exalting scriptural authority.[43] We must at least contemplate a correct, if unconstructive, category of individual-ism, and, having acknowledged that ideal, may settle for a more pragmatic approach. The remainder of this chapter will seek to establish constructive grounds for the discussion of Reformed theology in England.

Henry VIII

Henry VIII's own theological convictions largely determined the kind of Reformation that was officially advanced in England. This is important because it defined the context in which Reformed theological commitments amongst his subjects emerged or, indeed, were concealed. Ever since the duke of Saxony concluded that 'he

---

[40] Brad Gregory, *Salvation at Stake: Christian martyrdom in early modern Europe* (London & Cambridge, MA: HUP, 1999), 13.

[41] On confessional allegiances among historians see Marshall, "(Re)Defining," 571–74.

[42] Cummings, *Literary Culture*, 63–64, 214–16, 228–31.

[43] Patrick Collinson, "England," in *The Reformation in National Context*, eds. B. Scribner, R. Porter, and M. Teich (Cambridge: CUP, 1994), 86.

understands little of religion,'[44] historians have variously described Henry as: 'a Catholic—only a Catholic of sorts, but a Catholic nonetheless';[45] 'never a Lutheran; indeed, in some matters he was intransigently conservative';[46] a 'moderate reformist';[47] 'a man whose theological outlook came to resemble a magpie's nest';[48] 'as committed in 1547 as he had been in 1509 to maintaining religious uniformity.'[49]

When the *Assertio Septem Sacramentorum* against Luther was published in the name of Henry VIII in 1521, no one could have predicted the extent to which its purported author would allow Reformation to proceed in his realm after 1529. Rory McEntegart points out that the composition of the *Assertio* gave Henry the opportunity to consider Luther's theology in detail, meaning that 'even at this early stage in the reign's history of theological disputation, his own religious position was being framed and shaped in terms of how it stood in relation to the new learning.'[50] He was able to engage intelligently with complex theological ideas and to distinguish between different opinions. It was not merely his enduring personal antipathy towards the Wittenberg reformer that makes it

[44] John Frederick of Saxony to Philip of Hesse, 13 July 1536, quoted in Rory McEntegart, *Henry VIII, the League of Schmalkalden and the English Reformation* (Woodbridge: Royal Historical Society, 2002), 75.

[45] Christopher Haigh, "Henry VIII and the German Reformation," in *Religion und Politik in Deutschland und Grossbritannien*, eds. R. Bonney, F. Bosbach, and T. Brockmann (Munich: K. G. Saur, 2001), 40.

[46] J. J. Scarisbrick, *Henry VIII*, 2nd ed. (New Haven & London: YUP, 1997), 399.

[47] Lucy Wooding, *Henry VIII* (London & New York: Routledge, 2009), 186.

[48] Diarmaid MacCulloch, "The Religion of Henry VIII," in *Henry VIII: a European Court in England*, ed. D. Starkey (London: Collins & Brown, 1991), 160.

[49] Richard Rex, *Henry VIII and the English Reformation*, 2nd ed. (Basingstoke: Palgrave Macmillan, 2006), 107.

[50] Rory McEntegart, "Henry VIII and the German Lutherans: a reassessment," in *Sister Reformations: the Reformation in Germany and in England: symposium on the occasion of the 450th anniversary of the Elizabethan Settlement, September 23rd-26th, 2009*, ed. D. Wendebourg (Tübingen: Mohr Siebeck, 2010), 37.

fanciful to label Henry's taste in reform 'Lutheran'.[51] The intellectual influence of German Lutheran theologians on the English king—as on his subjects—was consistently shallow.[52]

Henry's first positive encounter with the continental Reformation came in the person of a Swiss reformer visiting England in 1531, but Simon Grynaeus made no lasting impression, even though his Swiss colleagues approved the king's decision to divorce Katherine of Aragon.[53] 'Henry could be politely appreciative when continental reformers later sent him their works to augment his impressive library,' writes MacCulloch, 'but there is no evidence that their writings directly affected his thinking.'[54] In 1538 Henry expressed a wish to have a book presented by Heinrich Bullinger translated into English, but his single annotation was to declare one argument irrelevant.[55]

Consideration of Henry's humanist sympathies must anticipate discussion of humanism itself. In September 1527 he wrote to Desiderius Erasmus:

> Now, seeing the unwearied labours which you have suffered in the cause of Christianity, I am desirous of succouring your pious efforts, for I have myself felt for some years the same desire of restoring the faith and religion of Christ to its pristine dignity, and repelling the impious attacks of the heretics, that the Word of God may run on purely and freely.[56]

---

[51] *LP*, vii. #232.

[52] See MacCulloch, "Sixteenth-century English Protestantism," in Dorothea Wendebourg, ed., *Sister Reformations: the Reformation in Germany and in England: symposium on the occasion of the 450th anniversary of the Elizabethan Settlement, September 23rd-26th, 2009* (Tübingen: Mohr Siebeck, 2010), 4–5.

[53] Bruce Gordon, *The Swiss Reformation* (Manchester & New York: Manchester University Press, 2002), 299.

[54] Diarmaid MacCulloch, "Henry VIII and the Reform of the Church," in *The Reign of Henry VIII: politics, policy and piety*, ed. D. MacCulloch (Basingstoke: Macmillan, 1995), 162.

[55] *LP*, xiii/2. #373.

[56] *LP*, iv/2. #3438.

These sentiments seemed to bear fruit in the attack on absenteeism and superstitions to do with relics, shrines and miracles,[57] and in vernacular translations, including the Decalogue, Creed and Bible in 1538.[58] In the 1530s and 1540s some reforms could be seen as no more than typically Erasmian, including the regulation of feast days and Sundays, aiming to discipline religious expression.[59]

Henry's notion of 'pristine dignity' soon considerably surpassed the Erasmian ideal. He was prepared to disown the papacy, dissolve the monasteries and have images defaced. Purgatory was damned to vague impotence,[60] while confirmation, ordination and extreme unction were downgraded as sacraments. Nevertheless, he insisted on matrimony as a sacrament,[61] and refused to deny the pragmatic value of auricular confession, clerical celibacy, private masses and communion in one kind.[62] Moreover, he consistently held to the doctrine of Christ's Real Presence in the Mass by means of transubstantiation and never embraced the doctrine of justification *sola fide*. A humanist programme inadequately describes the powerful, multifarious and largely irreconcilable religious affections and theological convictions which the king harboured.[63] How is this unique blend to be explained?

A keen awareness of divine providence characterised much of Henry's life. As the 'godly prince,' his kingship was an inviolable divine commission to which the English Church was obliged to

---

[57] *Iniunctions gyuen by the auctoritie of the Kynges Highnes to the clergie* (London: Thomas Berthelet, 1536; RSTC 10084.7).

[58] *Iniunctions for the clerge* (London: Thomas Berthelet, 1538; RSTC 10086).

[59] Rex, *Henry VIII*, 76.

[60] *Articles devised by the Kynges Highnes Maiestie* [Ten Articles] (London: Thomas Berthelet, 1536; RSTC 10033.2), D3r-v.

[61] Diarmaid MacCulloch, *Thomas Cranmer: a life* (New Haven & London: YUP, 1996), 212.

[62] Ibid., 219–21.

[63] Wooding's concentration on Erasmian humanism cannot explain Henry's theological position. Her analysis of his theology lacks precision: Wooding, *Henry VIII*, 188, 251.

yield. He aspired to the rôle of *Fidei Defensor* long before the pope bestowed the title and he retained it even after his break with Rome. Indeed, he always assumed the rôle of a Catholic king, not least for its ideological value, as Marshall writes, but equally because of his theological self-image.[64] His idiosyncratic notion of catholicity still defended a universal faith but substituted the universality of God's commissioning of princes for a singular papal authority.

Henry's personal struggles were also attributed to God's providence, or judgment. It was his marriages—annulling his first to Katherine of Aragon, condemning Anne Boleyn, grieving over Jane Seymour, smarting from Katherine Howard's infidelity—that particularly provoked Henry to theological reflection, seeking divine solace when events escaped his jurisdiction.[65] The 'King's Great Matter' was an act of atonement conceived as an attempt to right his original offence against God's prohibition against marrying his brother's wife which had resulted in childlessness (Leviticus 18:16; 20:21) or, in his case, lack of male issue. Stephen Gardiner's *De Vera Obedientia* (1535) made the case for the king's conscientious obedience to divine law which was, suggests Richard Rex, 'the principle which underlies many of the apparently unrelated initiatives of his Reformation.'[66] The possibility of a *volte-face* after Katherine and Anne were both dead was not even entertained, even for the sake of the political security that reconciliation with Rome might have restored. Henry became irrevocably convinced of his responsibility before God for the English Church.[67]

There is no question as to Henry's devoted piety, demonstrated

---

[64] Marshall, "Is the Pope a Catholic?" 29.

[65] Virginia Murphy, "The Literature and Propaganda of Henry VIII's First Divorce," *The Reign of Henry VIII: politics, policy and piety*, ed. D. MacCulloch (Basingstoke: Macmillan, 1995), 148; Pamela Tudor-Craig, "Henry VIII and King David," in *Early Tudor England: proceedings of the 1987 Harlaxton Symposium*, ed. D. Williams (Woodbridge: Boydell Press, 1989), 194.

[66] Rex, *Henry VIII*, 16.

[67] Alec Ryrie, *The Age of Reformation: the Tudor and Stewart realms 1485–1603* (Abingdon: Routledge, 2017), 118.

not least in the activities of hearing divine service, alms-giving and so forth, but it was Henry who accommodated God. His personal Psalter reveals his self-identification with the biblical King David, functioning as an archetype of Christ. Indeed, he assumed Christ's preeminent position on the title-page of the Great Bible (1539), in contrast to the Coverdale Bible (1535). Consequently God's foes were also the king's and, more conveniently, *vice versa*.[68] His relationship with the Almighty was 'all-important, and the chief guarantee of his kingship.'[69] Arguably this reciprocity, 'by the grace of God,' explains the king's religious fervour. Beneath the rituals of religious observance were claims to authority, both secular and spiritual.

The 1530s, though fraught with challenges for the historian, are a most informative decade in attempting to comprehend the problem of religious identity in the Reformation. From the charge of *praemunire* against the clergy in 1531 to the Act of Supremacy in 1534 and the Act against the authority of Rome in 1536, this decade saw the subordination of the English Church to the Crown as the authority of the Supreme Head emerged in lieu of the supreme pontiff. This lends weight to J. J. Scarisbrick's belief that 'if there is any single thread to [Henry's] theological evolution it is his anti-clericalism,'[70] but it can be cast more constructively.

As Henry VIII's princely identity was refashioned,[71] so was his religious identity, making it impossible to distil the political ideology from Henry's theological interests. Obedience to the Royal Supremacy itself became the effective end of his theology,[72] not least because 'he believed, passionately and sincerely, that God has entrusted him with the Church of England, and that he would eventually be

---

[68] Tudor-Craig, "David," 183–205.
[69] Wooding, *Henry VIII*, 57.
[70] Scarisbrick, *Henry VIII*, 417.
[71] See Kevin Sharpe, *Selling the Tudor Monarchy: authority and image in sixteenth-century England* (New Haven & London: YUP, 2009), 84–87.
[72] Marshall, *Religious Identities*, 13; see also Alec Ryrie, "Divine Kingship and Royal Theology in Henry VIII's Reformation," *Reformation* 7 (2002).

answerable for the purity of its faith.'[73] In May 1538 John Forest, an Observant Franciscan and confessor to the late Queen Katherine, was executed at Smithfield for heresy with these verses affixed to the gallows:

> And Forest the Frier
> That obstinate lier
> That wilfully shalbe dead
> In his contumacy
> The gospell do deny
> The king to be supreame head.[74]

Later, in December, a letter from Thomas, Lord Wentworth to Thomas Cromwell (1485–1540) equated the 'word of God' with obedience: Thomas Becon was described as 'a true preacher of the word of God, a great setter forth of the king's most just and lawful title of supremacy.'[75] Perhaps there was no more perspicuous statement than Richard Sampson's *'Verbum Dei est, obedire Regi, non Episcopo Romano.'*[76] Reformist theologies of obedience did not so much create as give credibility to the Supremacy. In Henry's mind at least, justification by faith alone threatened to overturn this imperative by removing the need for charity and penance. He perceived in it the same potential for instability and licentiousness as the cheap grace he detested in Roman absolution and purgation. This is evidenced by one of his annotations on the Bishops' Book (1537), a convoluted text in which some readers found the doctrine of justification *sola*

---

[73] David Loades, *Henry VIII: court, church and conflict* (Kew: The National Archives, 2007), 184.

[74] Foxe, *AM* [1563], 3:628. On Forest's case see Peter Marshall, "Papist as Heretic: the burning of John Forest, 1538," *HJ* 41, 2 (1998): esp. 360.

[75] Quoted in Richard Rex, "The Crisis of Obedience: God's Word and Henry's Reformation," *HJ* 39, 4 (1996): 890.

[76] John Strype, *Ecclesiastical Memorials, relating chiefly to religion, and the Reformation of it*, 3 vols. (Oxford: OUP, 1822), i/2:175.

fide.⁷⁷ Henry clarified that, alongside the receipt of Christ's benefits by faith, there was a conditional caveat: 'I doing my duty.'⁷⁸ The prospect of antinomianism threatened confidence in the religious infrastructure over which he sought Supremacy.⁷⁹

A particularly incisive approach towards revealing the king's religious outlook is taken by McEntegart's study of Anglo-Schmalkaldic relations. It facilitates comparison of religious identities as they interacted directly in theologically-charged political dialogue. Henry's overtures to the German states were indiscriminate on religious grounds until a major policy shift occurred in late 1533. On 2 December Henry notified his ambassador in Paris of plans to send emissaries 'to the princes of Germany and others, to join ourselves in amity with them.' In light of 'the Pope's ungodly determination against us' the advance targeted the Protestant states: 'considering the injuries we have received, have required us no longer to endure these attempts of the Pope, but to find some remedy for

---

[77] Stephen Gardiner wrote later that the Bishops' Book resembled 'a common storehouse, where every man layd uppe in storre suche ware as he lyked, and could tell where to fynde to serve his purpose': Gardiner to Cranmer, July 1547, *The Letters of Stephen Gardiner*, ed. J. A. Muller (Cambridge: CUP, 1933), 351. Broughton Knox incorrectly insists that the text was solifidian: D. Broughton Knox, *The Doctrine of Faith in the Reign of Henry VIII* (London:James Clarke & Co., 1961), 160–61, 166. Certain passages could easily be mistaken to imply solifidianism and the king apparently thought that they did, but detailed analysis reveals that the salvation deserved only by Christ's passion and death is received by means of a life lived in faith and charity, not faith alone: Charles Lloyd, ed., *Formularies of faith put forth by authority in the reign of Henry VIII* (Oxford: OUP, 1825), 35–36, 47. Far from positively expounding solifidianism, the Bishops' Book contains some strikingly reactionary statements on justification, e.g., Ibid., 58.

[78] See the corrections in Thomas Cranmer, *Miscellaneous Writings and Letters of Thomas Cranmer, Archbishop of Canterbury, Martyr, 1556*, ed. J. Cox, PS (Cambridge: CUP, 1846), 89.

[79] Central government depended on local ties of 'goodwill and service' to exercise control, writes Helen Speight, "'The Politics of Good Governance': Thomas Cromwell and the government of the south-west of England," *HJ* 37, 3 (1994): 632–33.

them by a total abolition of his authority, and in so doing obtain the advice and assistance of the Princes aforesaid.'[80] The king's diplomatic policies were being harmonised with his anti-papal legislation in the Reformation Parliament.

Two particular considerations emerge from McEntegart's study as motivating Henry's interest in the Schmalkaldic League. Firstly, the potential repercussions of a General Council were a mutual and consistent concern for Henry and the German Protestants throughout the 1530s, making them natural allies.[81] In the 1530s the Schmalkaldic princes alone could offer the requisite military strength and, in the case of marriage alliances, noble connections. The Swiss Reformed city states possessed no comparable potency or sanguinity. Secondly, the expulsion of papal authority in England created a state of doctrinal uncertainty which the king, as Supreme Head, sought to resolve. In August 1534, three months before the Supremacy Act, the king initiated plans for 'how the false heresies which the bishop of Rome hath taught the people should be brought out of their conscience and hearts.' These included 'pamphlets against the doctrines of celibacy of the clergy, honouring of images and prayers for the dead to be printed before Parliament begins.'[82] Philip Melanchthon's moderate reputation made him an attractive consultant to Henry, and requests that he visit England became a regular feature of negotiations from 1534 onwards.[83] Thus there should be no doubt that Reformation was as central as political necessity to Henry's interest in the Schmalkaldic League.

It is important to emphasise Henry's consistent interest in theological discussion. On 15 December 1535 Bishop Edward Foxe told the League diet that 'the King, being devoted to the Gospel, is desirous of receiving an embassy from the princes and states of

---

[80] *LP*, vi. #1491.
[81] McEntegart, *Schmalkalden*, 33–37.
[82] *LP*, vii. #1043.
[83] McEntegart, *Schmalkalden*, 45–46; John Schofield, *Philip Melanchthon and the English Reformation* (Aldershot: Ashgate, 2006), 118.

Germany that he may be informed as to the state of religion, and receive advice as to what to reform in England in matters relating to faith and religion.'[84] He did not want so much to replace Rome with Wittenberg as to employ Lutheran expertise in fashioning his own religious settlement.[85] This was exemplified in his appointment of men of diverse opinion to the discussion committee in June 1538; the Lutheran delegates received neither a wholly favourable nor wholly critical hearing. Moreover, during his progress of autumn 1538, the king showed himself capable of engaging with the theological questions personally, even if at other times he could be an inept, impatient and shocking theologian.[86]

McEntegart explains that Henry abandoned hopes of accommodation in May 1539, finally proceeding with the Six Articles on 28 June only when he 'was persuaded that the Germans had no further interest in theological negotiation.'[87] A mere three months later he was interested, in spite of differences on a few points of doctrine, in renewing negotiations on the basis of common enmity towards 'the bishop of Rome, his unholy superstitions and his self aggrandised power.'[88] Although Henry had never been prepared to swallow the Augsburg Confession as it stood, his candour about this discounts political manipulation of the League. Further evidence of his consistent theological concern is that the impetus for negotiation was never the prospect of Franco-Imperial crusade and that negotiations persisted long after the *rigmarôle* of his divorce abated on Katherine of Aragon's death in January 1536.[89] All this is not to suggest that the king was pushing a coherent and personal vision for Reformation. George Bernard's argument that Henry pursued a

---

[84] *LP*, ix. #979.
[85] McEntegart, *Schmalkalden*, 48, 63.
[86] Ibid., 108, 118–27; Scarisbrick, *Henry VIII*, 404–5.
[87] McEntegart, *Schmalkalden*, 156, 166.
[88] Christopher Mont to John Frederick of Saxony and Philip of Hesse, September 1539 (Mont's commission was dated 15 August), quoted in Ibid., 173.
[89] Ibid., 64.

'middle way' with 'clear and definitive religious purposes' is unpersuasive.[90] Although the king wanted his own religious settlement, that does not mean that he knew what he wanted his ultimate settlement to be.

If obedience is seen as Henry VIII's maxim,[91] it is important to emphasise that the official Henrician statements of justification were never Lutheran in the proper sense. Between 1536 and 1543 the Ten Articles, enforced by the Injunctions of 1536 and 1538, were the only fully authorised statement regarding justification. They went only so far as to base justification on Christ's merits alone: it was

> not as though our contrition or faith, or any works proceeding thereof, can worthily merit or deserve to attain the said justification; for only the mercy and grace of the Father, promised freely unto us for his Son's sake, Jesus Christ, and the merits of his blood and passion, be the only sufficient and worthy causes thereof.[92]

The articles rejected the Lutheran position of the Augsburg Confession: justification was not apprehended by faith alone but 'by contrition, and faythe ioyned with charitie.'[93] In 1543 the King's Book essentially restored the Roman understanding of justification

---

[90] G. W. Bernard, "The Making of Religious Policy, 1533–1546: Henry VIII and the search for the middle way," *HJ* 41, 2 (1998): 333; G. W. Bernard, *The King's Reformation: Henry VIII and the remaking of the English Church* (New Haven & London: YUP, 2005), 240–43. Bernard's view is adopted without substantial qualification by Wooding, *Henry VIII*, 225, 250–51.

[91] On popular responses of deference and obedience, see Heal, *Reformation*, 221–25.

[92] Lloyd, ed., *Formularies*, xxvi.

[93] Ibid. See also a statement of Catholic orthodoxy by Johann Eck, "The *Confutatio Pontificia*: in reference to the matters presented [. . .] pertaining to the Christian Orthodox Faith [. . .] 3 August 1530," in *The Augsburg Confession: a collection of sources*, ed. J. Reu, trans. J. Mattes and J. Bodensieck (Chicago, IL: Wartburg Publishing House, 1930), 350–52.

which had been used *de facto* prior to 1536.[94] These were the official contexts in which theological identities developed: Reformed evangelicals had every reason to be discreet; it was prudent to show obedience to the king, but the kingdom's theological position never seemed settled and might always change again.

Reformed Evangelicalism, 1520–47

On the 27 July 1534 the fellows of Oriel College, Oxford gathered in the chapel and subscribed to the Royal Supremacy, apparently without exception. 'What they really thought,' writes Jeremy Catto, 'is not, of course, recorded. [. . .] Doubtless the overriding consideration for most of them, whatever their sympathies, was to survive.'[95] In light of official religious policy it is no wonder that Englishmen throughout the land were reluctant to nail their colours to any one mast. Identities had not only to be veiled but adaptable too. Conversion of an individual, or a country, could be a gradual process. Reformed theological identity need not rest on mature doctrinal convictions. Sacramentarianism was often the ultimate rather than initial step and other Reformed traits might long precede it, such as the harmonisation of law and Gospel and a disapproval of images.[96] Still, Cranmer complained in 1538 'that error of the sacrament of the altar was so greatly spread abroad in this realm, and daily increasing more and more.'[97] The universities and the city of London, where Susan Brigden recognises that religious choices were 'demanded most immediately,' deserve the greatest attention.[98]

---

[94] *The King's Book, or a Necessary Doctrine and Erudition for Any Christian Man* [1543], Church Historical Society (London: SPCK, 1932), 9, 39, 152–53, 158–59.

[95] Jeremy Catto, "Oriel in Renaissance Oxford, 1479–1574," in *Oriel College: a history*, ed. J. Catto (Oxford: OUP, 2013), 82–83.

[96] On taxonomies of reform, see Heal, *Reformation*, 243–53.

[97] Cranmer to Cromwell, 22 June 1538, Thomas Cranmer, *The Remains of Thomas Cranmer, D.D.*, ed. H. Jenkyns, 4 vols. (Oxford: OUP, 1833), 1:249.

[98] Susan Brigden, *London and the Reformation* (Oxford: OUP, 1989), 2.

'England was not a quiet place for a man with a conscience,' Rupp observed. 'London during the Six Articles, the West in the time of Edward VI, all England in the time of Mary, these were places where men did not prudently noise abroad their secret thoughts.'[99] 'Dissimulation was the key to success,' writes Steven Gunn.[100] Religion involved political risk and acquiescence to official policy, policy which individuals hoped to accelerate, redirect or reverse without transgressing the limits of obedience to Henry VIII. Lying, mental reservation and equivocation (ambiguity calculated to precipitate misperception) were Nicodemite strategies commonly employed by reformers.[101] The pressure could be overwhelming: after his recantation, Robert Wisdom lamented 'his frailty and fearful weakness, whereby he for fear of death fell to this impiety [. . .] and desireth all faithful Christians to forgive him that offence.'[102] Under circumstances requiring 'hair-trigger sensitivity to the limits of royal tolerance and curiosity'[103] outward personae are fickle indicators of theological commitment.

Obedience to the royal will could be uncomfortable for people of any religious persuasion.[104] Cuthbert Tunstall, Edmund Bonner and Stephen Gardiner reverted to Roman allegiance under Mary Tudor, so due caution should be observed in ascribing more heartfelt approval of Henry VIII's policies to evangelicals. Thomas Becon's instruction to evangelicals to obey the ruler 'wythoute ony dissimulacion or Hypocrysy' seems ironic in light of his equivocal recantation

---

[99] Rupp, *Studies*, xv-xvi.

[100] Steven Gunn, "The Structures of Politics in Early Tudor England," *TRHS* 6th series, v (1995): 68.

[101] Susan Wabuda, "Equivocation and Recantation During the English Reformation: The 'Subtle Shadows' of Dr Edward Crome," *JEH* 44, 2 (1993).

[102] Quoted in Sherwin Bailey, "Robert Wisdom under Persecution, 1541–43," *JEH* 2 (1951): 186.

[103] Marshall, *Religious Identities*, 8.

[104] There were some who sincerely shared Henry VIII's vision of 'Catholic reform': Alec Ryrie, "Paths Not Taken in the British Reformations," *HJ* 52, 1 (2009): 18–20.

in 1543. Apparently he felt he had discharged his 'duety to obey.'[105] Scarisbrick suggests that 'authentic Protestantism looked for a prince who would serve true religion, not one who would take upon himself the role of an autocratic *summus episcopus*.'[106] On the other hand, Cranmer was unswervingly persuaded that the Supremacy was the best means of constructing a godly realm. More cunning evangelicals anticipated the potential for legitimisation by their self-association with loyalty to the Crown.[107] Either way, this was the environment in which the king's subjects fashioned their religious identities. In the words of Sir Thomas Wyatt, charged with treason in 1541, 'all powers namely absolute ar[e] so[re] roodes when theie fall into evell mens handes, and yet I saye their ar[e] to be obeyed by expres lawe of god.'[108]

Persecution of evangelicals by the English government began on 12 May 1521 when Cardinal Wolsey presided over the denunciation of Luther's opinions at Paul's Cross. Many of Luther's books were already available for burning on that occasion.[109] Persecution intensified after 1525 as the threat seemed to grow and it yields evidence of the circulation of Reformed opinions. Against the Swiss position, Johannes Fabri, the vicar-general of Constance, who was visiting London, composed a riposte to Œcolampadius

---

[105] Thomas Becon, *A Pleasaunt Newe Nosegaye Full of Many Godly and Swete Floures* (London: Iohn Mayler for Iohn Gough, 1543; RSTC 1743), I2v.

[106] Scarisbrick, *Henry VIII*, 397.

[107] Diarmaid MacCulloch, "Archbishop Cranmer: concord and tolerance in a changing Church," in *Tolerance and Intolerance in the European Reformation*, eds. O. Grell and B. Scribner (Cambridge: CUP, 1996), 200–201; Alec Ryrie, "The Problem of Legitimacy and Precedent in English Protestantism, 1539–47," in *Protestant History and Identity in Sixteenth-Century Europe*, ed. B. Gordon, Vol. 1 (Aldershot: Ashgate, 1996), 81–82; Ethan Shagan, "Clement Armstrong and the Godly Commonwealth: radical religion in early Tudor England," in *The Beginnings of English Protestantism*, eds. P. Marshall and A. Ryrie (Cambridge: CUP, 2002), 61–62.

[108] Quoted in Susan Brigden, "'The Shadow That You Know': Sir Thomas Wyatt and Sir Francis Bryan at Court and in Embassy," *HJ* 39 (1996): 12.

[109] *LP*, iii/1. #1274.

dated 1 April 1527 in which he praised English orthodoxy, simultaneously making Œcolampadius' condemnation of the cult of saints available in English.[110] Bishop John Fisher of Rochester, the chancellor of the University of Cambridge, also published a formidable defence against Œcolampadius in 1527. Fisher had corresponded with the anti-evangelical controversialist Johannes Cochlaeus about him in 1526.[111] It is significant that Fisher, as a leading defender of orthodoxy, bothered to include a Swiss reformer in his campaign; presumably Œcolampadius' views had spread far enough to concern Fisher. In 1531 Barlowe's *Dialogue* made available an outline of the eucharistic positions of Œcolampadius, Zwingli and Andreas Karlstädt.[112] When Cranmer examined John Frith in June 1533, he supposed Œcolampadius to be the source of Frith's Sacramentarianism.[113] It was still felt necessary to publish against Frith's teaching in 1536, indicating its persistent popularity.[114] Œcolampadius was even condemned in the Pontefract Articles of the conservative Pilgrimage of Grace in 1536.[115] Reformed theology had gained a significant enough profile to be attacked by traditionalists, and their refutations inadvertently raised its profile and promoted its dissemination.

Censorship and controls on book imports were first introduced in early 1529, with severe restrictions being placed on continental

---

[110] On Œcolampadius in Basle, see Amy Nelson Burnett, *Teaching the Reformation: ministers and their message in Basel, 1529–1629* (Oxford: OUP, 2006), 26–27.

[111] Richard Rex, "The English Campaign against Luther in the 1520s," *TRHS* 5th series, 39 (1989): 96, 99, 101, 104.

[112] Barlowe, *Dialogue*, 52–54; see also Henry Gold's condemnation of Karlstädt in 1534: *LP*, vii. #523.

[113] *LP*, vi. #661.

[114] William Clebsch, *England's Earliest Protestants, 1525–1535* (Westport, CT: Greenwood Press, 1964), 130.

[115] Bruce Gordon, *The Swiss Reformation* (Manchester & New York: Manchester University Press, 2002), 299. Œcolampadius was singled out among the Swiss reformers, appearing in a list that also names Luther, Melanchthon and Bucer.

imports in 1534.[116] These reveal which books were thought to be in circulation. Earlier, in October 1524, when Bishop Tunstall took informal steps against book imports from Germany, he was specifically concerned with Luther's errors.[117] By the late 1520s Wittenberg writers were already outnumbered by alternatives,[118] and Swiss Reformed texts became available in England fairly soon after their first publications. Six different titles were published in English by Zürich authors alone before the end of Henry's reign.[119]

As early as 1526 an unspecified book of Zwingli's against Anabaptists was forbidden by Archbishop Warham,[120] and four Hanse merchants in London admitted to propagating works by Karlstädt as well as by Luther.[121] The 1529 proclamation proscribed fifteen books, including two by the Sacramentarian William Roye, four by William Tyndale, and Miles Coverdale's translation of Bullinger's *Christen state of matrimonye*.[122] Tunstall's prohibition of 1530 listed Zwingli's *Refutation of the Tricks of the Catabaptists* (1527), and soon the bishops also proscribed Zwingli's *Education of Youth* (1523), *Commentary on True and False Religion* (1525), *Original Sin* (1526), *Friendly Exegesis of the Eucharist* (1527), *On Providence* (1530), and six other titles—both commentaries and letters—including his other writings on the Eucharist.[123] John Foxe also specified ten titles by Œcolampadius, including eucharistic treatises and, significantly, his

---

[116] Lotte Hellinga, "The Bookshop of the World: books and their makers as agents of cultural exchange," in *The Bookshop of the World: the role of the Low Countries in the book-trade 1473–1941*, ed. L. Hellinga ('t Goy-Houten: Hes and De Graaf, 2001), 24.

[117] Brigden, *London*, 157.

[118] E. G. Rupp, "The Battle of the Books," in *Reformation in Principle and Practice: essays in honour of A. G. Dickens*, ed. P. Brooks (London: Scolar Press, 1980), 18.

[119] Carrie Euler, *Couriers of the Gospel: England and Zürich 1531–1558* (Zurich: TVZ, 2006), 114.

[120] Gordon, *Swiss Reformation*, 299.

[121] *LP*, iv/1. #1962.

[122] *TRP*, i. #122.

[123] Foxe, *AM* [1563], 3:502–4.

commentary on Isaiah (1525), which contained extensive teaching on the covenant.[124]

George Joye's *The Souper of the Lord* (1533) was a summary and translation of Zwingli's *On the Lord's Supper* (1526). Joye preserved a strict Zwinglianism,[125] adding to the availability of Reformed eucharistic doctrine in England. His *Subversion of More* (1534) held the Old and New Testaments together with a concept of covenant characteristic of Zürich theology.[126] In 1543 Joye was also responsible for a translation of Zwingli's *Ratio Fidei* [*Account of the Faith*] (1530) which was published successively in Antwerp then London, although ostensibly in 'Ziiryk'.[127] Carrie Euler points out that this falsification means that readers were expected to be familiar with the reputation of cities like Zürich and Basle as centres of evangelical reform.[128]

---

[124] Ibid. On Œcolampadius' Isaiah commentary see Peter Lillback, *The Binding of God: Calvin's Role in the Development of Covenant Theology* (Grand Rapids, MI: Baker Academic, 2001), 83–87; Andrew Woolsey, *Unity and Continuity in Covenantal Thought: A Study of the Reformed Tradition to the Westminster Assembly* (Grand Rapids, MI: Reformation Heritage Books, 2012), 210–11. See also the list of books confiscated from Bayfield in 1531. Among the authors were Zwingli, Œcolampadius, Bucer and Capito: John Fines, ed., *A Biographical Register of Early English Protestants and Others Opposed to the Roman Catholic Church, 1525–1558*, Vol. 1 (Abingdon: Sutton Courtenay Press, 1981), unpaginated.

[125] George Joye, *The Souper of the Lorde [. . .] the declaracion of the later parte of the .6. ca. of S. Johan [. . .] wheryn incidently M. Moris letter agenst Johan Frythe is confuted* (Antwerp: Niclas Twonson [N. Hill?], 1533; RSTC 24468). On the authorship of the treatise, previously ascribed to Tyndale, see: W. D. J. Cargill Thompson, "Who wrote 'The Supper of the Lord'?" *HTR* 53 (1960); William Clebsch, "More evidence that George Joye wrote the Souper of the Lorde," *HTR* 55 (1962); see also Clebsch, *Earliest Protestants*, 216–18.

[126] George Joye, *The Subuersion of Moris False Foundacion* (Emden [Antwerp]: Jacob Aurick [G. von der Haghen], 1534; RSTC 14829).

[127] Huldrych Zwingli, *The Rekening and Declaracion of the Faith and Beleif of Huldrik Zwingly Bisshoppe of Ziiryk the cheif town of Heluetia, sent to Charles V*, trans. G. Joye (Antwerp: Widow of C. Ruremund, 1543; RSTC 26138); see also RSTC 26138.5.

[128] Euler, *Couriers*, 115.

William Tolwin, rector of St Antholin in London, was apprehended with a satchel containing eighteen heterodox books in 1541. These included Lutheran and Lollard texts, but of particular interest is Zwingli's *On Providence* 'whych,' wrote John Bale in his account of 1543, 'that most notable clarke Huldricus Zuinglius wrote at the instaunt request of the ryght worshypfull lorde Phylypp the Landgraue of Hesse.'[129] Anabaptism was represented by Balthasar Hubmaier's *Catechysme of Pacimontanus* showing, in Brigden's opinion, that extreme brands of reformism might be 'spread by association with more moderate reform.'[130]

By the 1540s texts by Bullinger were available in translation, usually under another name. Whether or not English followers knew the identity of Swiss reformers is superfluous to the spread of their theology. The first English translation of a Zürich text was his commentary on 2 Thessalonians published in 1538.[131] His *Christen state of matrimonye*, first prohibited in 1529 and valued for its covert evangelicalism, was republished in Antwerp in 1541, with another three editions printed in London by 1547 under the sponsorship of Thomas Becon.[132] Its popularity may have stemmed from its being purchased as a wedding gift.[133] More significant was Coverdale's translation in 1541 of Bullinger's *The Old Fayth* (1537).[134] The covenant was axiomatic to this fundamental work of theology which sold well because of its practical content.[135]

The influence of Zwingli's Zürich Bible (1531) is to be found in English Bible translation through the mediation of Coverdale.

---

[129] John Bale, *Yet a Course at the Romyshe Foxe* (Antwerp: Olyuer Iacobson [A. Goinus], 1543; RSTC 1309), 46v-57v, esp. 50r-v.

[130] Brigden, *London*, 337.

[131] MacCulloch, *Cromwell*, 461.

[132] Heinrich Bullinger, *The Christen State of Matrimonye*, trans. M. Coverdale (Antwerp: M. Crom, 1541; RSTC 4045); see also RSTC 4046-58; MacCulloch, 'Bullinger,' 911.

[133] Ryrie, *Gospel*, 126.

[134] Bullinger, *The Olde Fayth*.

[135] Euler, *Couriers*, 117.

Coverdale's translation from Latin and German probably used the Zürich edition rather than Luther's: the Psalms were a direct translation from Zwingli's; order and style were identical; even the same woodcuts were used.[136] Similarly Joye's English Psalter of 1534 was made from a Latin version of Zwingli's German Psalter.[137] Evangelical literature and vernacular Bibles were purchased and read by a wide range of people. Brad Pardue cites examples that include singers, husbandmen, leather sellers and lawyers, besides priests and monks.[138] These books were not unaffordable either. The average price of Tyndale's New Testament was *2s 2d*, meaning that even an unskilled labourer could buy one with six days' wages.[139]

London was among the most likely entrances for continental ideas into England by virtue of its mercantile community. Most of the foreigners resident in London were 'Dutch,' whether from the Hanseatic cities or the Low Countries.[140] Among them were many of England's most significant printers whose business interests straddled the Channel, making for an easy flow of published material. For example Reinar Wolfe, one of Cranmer's preferred printers, settled in London from Strassburg in 1533. He had annual dealings with Zürich's leading publisher Christoph Froschauer via the Frankfurt book fair.[141] Several incidents suggest that more extreme, Sacramentarian versions of reformism were available in the City by the early to mid-1520s. In 1522, under examination by Cardinal Wolsey's commissioners, Adam Dolveyn, a 'Dutchman,'

---

[136] Gordon, *Swiss Reformation*, 300. For Tyndale's influence on Coverdale's Bible, see Clebsch, *Earliest Protestants*, 193.

[137] George Joye, *Dauids Psalter, diligently and faithfully translated by George Ioye* (Antwerp: Maryne Emperowr, 1534; RSTC 2372).

[138] Brad Pardue, *Printing, Power, and Piety: appeals to the public during the early years of the English Reformation* (Leiden & Boston: Brill, 2012), 78.

[139] Ibid., 82.

[140] Brigden, *London*, 136. See Andrew Pettegree, *Foreign Protestant Communities in Sixteenth-Century London* (Oxford: OUP, 1986), 12–22.

[141] David Davis, *Seeing Faith, Printing Pictures: Religious Identity during the English Reformation* (Leiden & Boston: Brill, 2013), 34–36.

admitted responsibility for the publication of a book containing notes by Cornelisz Hoen, whose sacramental theology was to influence Zwingli.[142] A refutation of Karlstädt's opinions by Luther was among the books brought to London in 1526 by the Hanse merchants already cited.[143] An Anabaptist cell exposed in 1532 included at least two 'Flemings,' one of whom was 'the bishop and reader to the Anabaptists.' Their books, estimated to number over three hundred, had been imported.[144]

An underground network of 'Christian brethren' was formed at an early stage in London, though it extended further afield.[145] Perhaps numbering only a few hundred in the late 1520s, it made a greater impact than its size might suggest. The Christian brethren relied on mutual support, financial contributions and dissimulation to further their common cause. It was they who sponsored the publication of Sacramentarian literature, including perhaps William Roye's translation *A Brefe Dialog bitwene a Christen father and his stobborne Sonne* (1527), the first 'Zwinglian' book in English.[146] Widely used in Strassburg, writes William Clebsch, *A Brefe Dialog* presented 'a highly spiritualistic interpretation of New Testament religion, after the fashion of Zwingli and his exaggerators.'[147] The original author was not, in fact, Zwingli but Wolfgang Capito, a leading reformer in Strassburg.[148]

---

[142] Pettegree, *Foreign Protestant Communities*, 19.

[143] *LP*, iv/1. #1962.

[144] *LP*, Addenda i/1. #809.

[145] The term 'Christian brethren,' referring to evangelicals generally, was sometimes used interchangeably with the term 'known men,' which usually denoted Lollards. Rupp refuses the conclusion that all the early evangelicals therefore had Lollard connections. Rather, the Christian brethren encompassed 'all who shared in the cause of the Reform, and especially the making of books': Rupp, *Studies*, 8.

[146] Brigden, *London*, 110, 124–15, 189–91.

[147] Clebsch, *Earliest Protestants*, 233.

[148] Anthea Hume, "William Roye's 'Brefe Dialogue' (1527): an English version of a Strassburg catechism," *HTR* 60 (1967): 307–8.

Some members of the Christian brethren, including 'Sir George Parker, Pathmere, Mershall [William Marshall?], preestes, Tho[ma]s. Keyle, mercer, Shreve [John Sheriff], surgeon and barber,' held 'that the Sacrament of the Altar after the consecration is nother body nor blood but remaineth bread and wine.'[149] Parker was claiming in 1531 'that they had already 2,000 books out against the blessed Sacrament in the Commons' hands.'[150] This particular statement was not certainly Sacramentarian—Parker himself drew on both Lutheranism and Sacramentarianism—but radical opinions were acceptable within the brethren:[151] in 1531 John Tewkesbury, a London leather sealer, was executed for his belief that the sacrament 'is not the very body of Christe in fleshe & bloude as it was borne of the virgin Mary.'[152] In 1532 James Bainham said that 'Christes body is not chewed with teeth, but receiued by faith.'[153] During Frith's imprisonment in the Tower, a royal chaplain named Dr Currein complained that Sacramentarianism was thriving due to Frith's writings.[154] 'One Andrewe, a tailor of London' was condemned with Frith in 1533 'for the self-same opinion.'[155]

Investigations in 1540 under the Six Articles exposed many such heretics. The presence of Reformed theology at this juncture deserves greater recognition than it is usually assigned. Thomas Cappes, a chaplain, believed 'that the blessed sacrament of the altar was but a memory and a remembrance of the Lord's death'; Richard White said 'that he did not think that Christ was in the sacrament of the altar within the "sepulture" b[ut in] heaven above.' To Henry Bird the sacrament was 'no better than a piece of bread,' while Thomas

---

[149] *LP*, Addenda i/1. #752.
[150] Ibid.
[151] Brigden, *London*, 401.
[152] Foxe, *AM* [1563], 3:452. Although Luther could technically agree by distinguishing the resurrected body of Christ, this was undoubtedly not Tewkesbury's intended meaning.
[153] Foxe, *AM* [1563], 3:550.
[154] Clebsch, *Earliest Protestants*, 103.
[155] *LP*, vi. #661.

Trentham called it 'a very good thing but it was not as men took it, very God.' Ralph Bylby, a draper, and Christopher Dray, a plumber, likewise denied the physical presence of Christ.[156] The brethren were unable to save the sacramentary John Porter from martyrdom in 1542; Porter had spoken his mind at Calais in 1539 and worried Bishop Bonner by drawing crowds to St Paul's in 1541.[157]

The brethren counted some eminent figures among their number, like Thomas Keyle. He was joined in the Mercers' Company by the leading brethren George Robinson, Robert Packington (associated with Thomas Cromwell's evangelical agent Stephen Vaughan and murdered by conservatives in 1536),[158] Augustine Packington (who craftily funded Tyndale's work by buying up New Testaments for burning, financed by Tunstall, in 1530)[159] and Henry Brinklow. In 1542 Brinklow recommended Frith's writings on the sacrament to his readers and prayed for the reformation of the Eucharist in line with the cities of Zürich, Basle and Strassburg.[160] Francis Denham, admitted to the Middle Temple in 1524, translated for the brethren, amongst other books, Francis Lambert's *De Causis Excæcationis* and had purchased Lambert's *Commentarii de Prophetia* in Paris sometime between 1526 and his arrest in 1528.[161] Richard Hilles did penance for his evangelicalism whilst he was an apprentice to a merchant taylor of London Bridge in 1532; when this Zwinglian enthusiast eventually initiated correspondence with Bullinger from Strassburg in August 1540, he began by remarking 'how greatly I have always desired to write to you.'[162]

---

[156] *LP*, Addenda i/2. #1463.

[157] Muriel St. Clare Byrne, ed., *The Lisle Letters*, 6 vols. (Chicago & London: University of Chicago Press, 1981), v. #1515a; Brigden, *London*, 333, 339.

[158] On Robert Packington, see Marshall, *Religious Identities*, 61–79.

[159] David Daniell, *William Tyndale: a biography* (New Haven & London: YUP, 1994), 196–97.

[160] Brigden, *London*, 182, 187n; Alec Ryrie, "The Strange Death of Lutheran England," *JEH* 53, 1 (2002): 75.

[161] *LP*, iv/2. #4396; Brigden, *London*, 116.

[162] *LP*, vi. #99; *OL*, 196; Susan Brigden, "Thomas Cromwell and the

A number of the brethren were active in the book trade, such as the bookbinders John Birt and Michael Lobley and the book agent John Tyndale, who was active even after his abjuration in 1530.[163] John Gough supplied the books trafficked by Thomas Garrett in 1528.[164] Gough had been converted by reading the New Testament sometime before 1525 and in 1532 he supplied the unidentifiable *Confession of the citie of Geneva* to an Anabaptist sect. He was not himself an Anabaptist—certainly not in his mature views—but he did exhibit many Reformed characteristics, such as his iconoclasm.[165] In 1538 the stationer Richard Reynolds, apparently a Sacramentarian, was reported as thinking 'the Mass was nought, and the memento was bawdery, and after the consecration it was an idolatry.'[166] In January 1540 John Mayler, printer, grocer, and partner of Gough in the 1540s, called 'the blessed sacrament of the altar the baken god.'[167] Clearly some book traders were exposed to and adopted Reformed opinions.

An intriguing twist in the early progress of Reformation was the prohibition in 1534 of discussion regarding the veneration of images, foreshadowing an official policy against images. Pamphlets were ordered against the 'honouring of images' and parliamentary bills were drawn up 'prohibiting, on a penalty of 10*l*., all offerings to images.'[168] This resembled Swiss priorities, bearing little relation to Lutheranism. In 1537 the Bishops' Book adopted the 'Zürich numbering' of the Decalogue (first used by Leo Jud in 1527) emphasising the prohibition of graven images. This had already been done 'from below' in Joye's primer of 1530 and William Marshall's of

---

'Brethren,'" in *Law and Government under the Tudors*, ed. C. Cross, D. Loades, and J. Scarisbrick (Cambridge: CUP, 1988), 36.

[163] Brigden, *London*, 190–91, 300.

[164] *LP*, iv/2. #4004.

[165] Alec Ryrie, "Gough, John (d.1543/4)," *ODNB* (Oxford: OUP, 2004); MacCulloch, *Cromwell*, 288.

[166] Quoted in Brigden, *London*, 275.

[167] *LP*, Addenda i/2. #1463.

[168] *LP*, vii. #1043.

1535.[169] The same year Marshall published a translation of Bucer's *Treatise declaring and showing that images are not to be suffered in churches*, thereby winning official approval.[170] 1538 saw popular attacks as well as officially organised iconoclasm.[171] In May the famous rood at St Margaret Pattens was dismantled by thirty vigilantes led by Gough. His presence, and that of some Flemings, suggests to Brigden that their inspiration was 'Zwinglianism and Anabaptism [. . .] spreading in the capital among a few zealots' as distinct from native iconoclastic traditions;[172] yet iconoclasm was a campaign that had captured the royal imagination too. Publications attacking images always remained permissible, like Grafton's *Glasse for housholders* in 1542.[173]

In London, then, there were opinions concurrent with the Swiss position circulating from the mid-1520s. The numbers involved were undoubtedly small: only six percent of London wills in the 1530s expressed solifidian tenets.[174] Reformed believers would represent only a portion of these, but they might be less inclined to emphasise faith alone anyway. The point is that these ideas were available and were exerting themselves disproportionately to the number of adherents.

Traditionally Cambridge has been identified as the spring of educated reformism, although the White Horse Inn is now considered

---

[169] Margaret Aston, *England's Iconoclasts: laws against images*, Vol. 1 (Oxford: OUP, 1988), 203–10, 239–41, 381; MacCulloch, *Cranmer*, 192.

[170] Martin Bucer, *A treatise declaring and showing that images are not to be suffered in churches*, trans. W. Marshall ([title page missing]: 1535; RSTC 24238); William Underwood, "Thomas Cromwell and William Marshall's Protestant books," *HJ* 47, 3 (2004): 526–28.

[171] On the nuances of Reformed attitudes to imagery see Davis, *Printed Images*, 47–54.

[172] Brigden, *London*, 289–91. On popular iconoclasm in Zürich see Lee Wandel, *Voracious Idols and Violent Hands: Iconoclasm in Reformation Zurich, Strasbourg, and Basel* (Cambridge: CUP, 1995), 61–101.

[173] Ryrie, *Gospel*, 43, 126–27; Anon., *A Glasse for Housholders* (London: Richard Grafton, 1542; RSTC 11917), A6v-7r.

[174] Thirteen percent of wills were unequivocally evangelical in the 1540s: Brigden, *London*, 382–84.

something of a wild goose.[175] The university was undoubtedly the leading centre for the discussion of reformist ideas but enthusiasts should not simply be labelled Lutheran. Tunstall's examination of Thomas Forman in 1528 suggests that the sometime president of Queens' College and rector of All Hallows,' Honey Lane in London had not adopted Luther's sacramental theology, so simply labelling him a Lutheran exaggerates the clarity of his identity.[176] There were clearly multiple influences on reformist identity even if certain features were Lutheran. Thomas Bilney and Hugh Latimer exhibited predominantly Lollard characteristics, for example, and the general impact of Erasmian humanism cannot be ignored.[177] By the 1540s, however, evangelicalism was the 'leading contender for Cambridge's religious identity.'[178] Cambridge evangelicalism need not have been pre-eminently Reformed for there to have been Reformed influences on some students. When William Turner (1509/10–68), Fellow of Pembroke College, published *The Hunting and Finding out of the Romish Fox* (1543) he had only recently returned from Zürich where he began a lifelong commitment to Reformed doctrine.[179] Calvin's ideas were available in Albert Pighius' *De libero hominis arbitrio et divina gratia*, published in 1542, which attacked Luther and Calvin on the subject of original sin and predestination. Roger Ascham of St John's College reported that the question was being debated in 1545.[180]

---

[175] See Porter, *Cambridge*, 41–73; Winthrop Hudson, *The Cambridge Connection and the Elizabethan Settlement of 1559* (Durham, NC: Duke University Press, 1980), 46–60.

[176] Rex, "Early Impact," 58.

[177] Stuart Dunnan, "The Preaching of Hugh Latimer: a reappraisal," DPhil diss. (University of Oxford, 1991), 56, 101; James McConica, *English Humanists and Reformation Politics under Henry VIII and Edward VI* (Oxford: OUP, 1965).

[178] Ryrie, *Gospel*, 183.

[179] Whitney Jones, "Turner, William (1509–10–1568)," *ODNB* (Oxford: OUP, 2004).

[180] Tyacke, *Aspects*, 43.

Until Edward VI's reign Lutheran books were more popular in Cambridge than those of Zwingli, Œcolampadius or John Calvin, although Bullinger and Bucer enjoyed a greater popularity than other Reformed writers.[181] Among the Reformed authors whose works were translated into English in the late 1530s were Bucer, Bullinger, Capito and Calvin, who was just commencing his career.[182] Of ninety-nine books owned by Cambridge testators between 1535 and 1547, forty-six were of Reformed authorship. Twenty of these were by Zwingli, Bullinger and Calvin,[183] representing a significant fifth of the market. If allowance is made for the high concentration of works by Luther in one particular library belonging to Oliver Ainsworth, then nearly a quarter of the sample can be assigned to these three Swiss reformers.[184]

The University of Oxford deserves greater recognition for reformism than has been traditionally conferred, its then governors having sorely and successfully exerted themselves in protecting its reputation for orthodoxy.[185] In 1528 John London, the Warden of New College, complained about the Cambridge dons recruited for Wolsey's new Cardinal College, most of whom were evangelicals known to Cromwell.[186] In 1534 the Provost of Oriel, Thomas Ware, was reported to say that 'the principal sacrifice of the Church of God was the sacrifice of thanksgiving. This was his answere when I

---

[181] Rex, "Early Impact," 62–63.

[182] Richard Rex, "The Role of English Humanists in the Reformation up to 1559," in *The Education of a Christian Society: Humanism and Reformation in Britain and the Netherlands*, eds. N. Amos, A. Pettegree and H. van Nierop (Aldershot: Ashgate, 1999), 24.

[183] See Elizabeth Leedham-Green, *Books in Cambridge Inventories: Book Lists from Vice-Chancellor's Court Probate Inventories in the Tudor and Stuart Periods*, 2 vols. (Cambridge: CUP, 1986), 2:160–63, 172–80, 813–14.

[184] Ibid., 1:82; see also Ryrie, *Gospel*, 172.

[185] Craig D'Alton, "The Suppression of Lutheran Heretics in England, 1526–1529," *JEH* 54, 2 (2003): 248–52; see also Rex, *Henry VIII*, 113; Ryrie, *Gospel*, 170–78.

[186] MacCulloch, *Cromwell*, 65.

demanded of him what could be said for the sacrifice of the Masse.'[187] By 1535 fellows at Magdalen College were expressing evangelical enthusiasm about the visitors' replacement of scholastic methods and introduction of a Greek lecture.[188]

According to Charlotte Methuen a significant proportion of the supporters of humanist educational approaches in Oxford in the early 1520s were inspired by German evangelical theology.[189] There was an appetite for reformist literature: in 1520 a dozen of Luther's books were sold by John Dorne;[190] in 1528 Thomas Garrett (Forman's curate at Honey Lane and, before his execution in 1540, chaplain to Cranmer) was caught trafficking books to Oxford where he had 'distributed many books among the scholars.'[191] Garrett stocked over a hundred titles including texts by Zwingli and Œcolampadius. Sometimes he sold fifty copies, and he operated a discreet lending service.[192] Probably a majority of these books were Lutheran but considering the wide circulation of such works in London a selection of Reformed works could easily have been conveyed.[193]

The years 1536 and 1537 witnessed an exchange programme with Zürich involving a coterie of eight young men from Oxford: Nicholas Partridge, John Butler, William Woodroffe, Nicholas Eliot, William

---

[187] Quoted in Catto, "Oriel in Renaissance Oxford," 83.

[188] MacCulloch, *Cromwell*, 367.

[189] Charlotte Methuen, "Oxford: Reading Scripture in the University," in *A Companion to Peter Martyr Vermigli*, eds. T. Kirby, E. Campi, and F. James (Leiden & Boston: Brill, 2009), 78.

[190] David Loades, "Books and the English Reformation prior to 1558," in *The Reformation and the Book*, ed. J. Gilmont (Aldershot: Ashgate, 1998), 266; S. L. Greenslade, "The Faculty of Theology," *The History of the University of Oxford*, ed. J. McConica (Oxford: OUP, 1986), 3:314.

[191] *LP*, iv/2. #3962; see also Marshall Knappen, *Tudor Puritanism: a chapter in the history of idealism* (Gloucester, MA: Peter Smith, 1963), 24.

[192] John Fines, ed., *A Biographical Register of Early English Protestants and Others Opposed to the Roman Catholic Church, 1525–1558*, Vol. 2 (typescript: 1985), G3.

[193] See also Jennifer Loach, "Reformation Controversies," in *The History of the University of Oxford*, ed. J. McConica (Oxford: OUP, 1986), 3:364.

Peterson (the brother of an Oxford man), John Finch, Bartholomew Traheron and one other.[194] Bullinger took a personal interest, meeting them to discuss Isaiah, supplying them with notes from Theodore Bibliander's lectures (delivered between 1533 and 1538), and encouraging other Swiss reformers to cultivate links with England.[195] In 1537 Rudolph Gwalther, Bullinger's adopted son and Zürich's future *Antistes*, visited Cranmer at Lambeth and proceeded to Oxford with Partridge and Woodroffe as his guides. He praised Magdalen for its humanist—and by implication evangelical—sympathies,[196] and made many friends, including John Parkhurst, Fellow of Merton College, who later became the Elizabethan bishop of Norwich and Bullinger's voice in England. Gwalther recalled that Parkhurst had begun to profess 'pure faith in Christ' at that time; he broke the Lent fast two years later in something akin to the Zürich sausage-eating of 1522.[197] The exchanges 'remained a spectacularly successful initiative,' emphasises MacCulloch; 'the alumni of Zürich kept alive the Switzerland-Strasbourg-England circuit, and showed the way for others to join it, with major consequences for the Church of Edward VI.' If Cranmer did not maintain links with Bullinger, he did with Bullinger's English devotees,[198] and there was a direct link between them and the exiles that fled to Zürich in the wake of the Six Articles.[199]

[194] See Euler, *Couriers*, 59–65; MacCulloch, *Cromwell*, 366–71; Gilbert Burnet, *The History of the Reformation of the Church of England*, 6 vols. (London: Baynes and Son, 1825), iii/1:204–5; George Gorham, ed., *Gleanings of a few scattered ears, during the period of the Reformation in England* (London: Bell and Daldy, 1857), 17–18.

[195] Gordon, *Swiss Reformation*, 300; Euler, *Couriers*, 60–61; Esther Hildebrandt, "A Study of the English Protestant Exiles in Northern Switzerland and Strasbourg 1539–47, and Their Role in the English Reformation," PhD diss. (University of Durham, 1982), 20–22.

[196] Tyacke, *Aspects*, 26.

[197] Ralph Houlbrooke, "Parkhurst, John (1511?-1575)," *ODNB* (Oxford: OUP, 2004); Gordon, *Swiss Reformation*, 304.

[198] MacCulloch, *Cranmer*, 177, 184–75, MacCulloch, *Cromwell*, 369–70; see also *OL*, 614–15, 627–28.

[199] Hildebrandt, "Protestant Exiles," 22–23.

It is highly significant that Cromwell rather than Cranmer was the sponsor of the Zürich exchange. Although it was both proper and politic that Cranmer should be the more visible and Cromwell the more covert, all the exchange students were closely connected with Cromwell's inner circle.[200] Scholars have puzzled over the minister's cryptic religious identity. Bernard concludes that Cromwell was simply a mouthpiece for the king,[201] yet one wonders if contemporaries like William Gray were really qualified to vouch for Cromwell's orthodoxy.[202] His determination to believe even as the king believed, in light of our discussion of Henry's religious policy, raises the possibility that he officially forbade more extreme opinions than he might personally have found admissible.[203] McEntegart comments on Cromwell's 'insidious methods of working within the government.'[204] The Oxford-Zürich exchange had no strategic value nor could it ever have gained royal approval. As MacCulloch writes, 'No cynical, "secular-minded" politician would have taken such risks.'[205]

MacCulloch's research confirms analyses of Cromwell that point in the direction of Zürich. This cosmopolitan individual was already advanced among theologically-curious laymen in obtaining in 1517 Erasmus's Latin New Testament.[206] In the 1520s his friends and associates included both Lollards and evangelicals of varying hues, but Cromwell was pragmatic in attaching himself to those with power to effect change: 'a consciously Nicodemite outlook might explain the apparently stark contradiction between Cromwell's developing evangelicalism and his loyal service to that most

---

[200] MacCulloch, *Cromwell*, 211, 368–69.

[201] Bernard, *King's Reformation*, 521.

[202] William Gray, *A balade agaynst malycyous sclaunderers* (London: Iohn Gough, 1540; RSTC 1323.5).

[203] R. G. Merriman, ed., *Life and Letters of Thomas Cromwell*, 2 vols. (Oxford: OUP, 1902), 1:279; Gunn, "Structures," 69, 86.

[204] McEntegart, *Schmalkalden*, 191.

[205] MacCulloch, *Cromwell*, 371.

[206] Ibid., 34.

grandiose of late medieval English churchmen, Thomas Wolsey.'[207] This is what put him in a position to recruit evangelical dons for the cardinal's new college in Oxford. Brigden rightly detects his fear that Sacramentarian 'radicalism would prejudice the evangelical cause and threaten the free passage of the Word.'[208] That Cromwell would take action against his friends for the sake of long-term Reformation was evident in his arrest of Barnes and others after Robert Packington's funeral in November 1536.[209] Far from looking like a radical, Cromwell sought to be inconspicuous as he played the long game: to guide England in a Reformed direction under the nose of an unsympathetic monarch. A salutary comparison might be drawn with Philip of Hesse who, in spite of his own eucharistic beliefs approximating to Zwingli's, chose to align Hesse with Wittenberg for political reasons. His policies nonetheless 'enabled various positions to co-exist.'[210]

Cromwell's sponsorship and protection of his evangelical clients is telling of his sympathies.[211] The Sacramentarian Coverdale had 'wasted no time in becoming one of Cromwell's protégés' in 1526,[212] while the iconophobic lawyer William Marshall was quickly ushered into Cromwell's circle.[213] The translations published by Marshall between 1534 and 1535 were paid for by Cromwell and included works by Bucer and Zwingli's friend and disciple Joachim Vadian.[214] In 1531 Cromwell secured 'denization' for Chrisopher Mont as a permanent resident in England. Mont was a native of Cologne and a Reformed evangelical in touch with Bullinger and Bucer. He remained in Cromwell's service, joining all seven English embassies

[207] Ibid., 72.
[208] Brigden, *London*, 298; see also MacCulloch, "Concord and Tolerance," 206.
[209] Brigden, *London*, 253.
[210] Schneider-Ludorff, "Philipp of Hesse," 307–10.
[211] Underwood, "Thomas Cromwell," 536.
[212] Davis, *Heresy*, 70.
[213] Brigden, *London*, 289.
[214] Underwood, "Thomas Cromwell," 519–21.

to the Schmalkaldic League.[215] In 1534 Cromwell licensed the publication of the French Sacramentarian Antoine de Marcourt's *Boke of Marchaunts*,[216] and in 1535 the first English vernacular Bible based on Tyndale's text. 'The King probably never realised,' remarks MacCulloch, 'that Cromwell was manipulating his power as Supreme Head to promulgate a translation inspired by the man he had grown to hate.'[217]

On 8 October 1535 Cranmer suggested appointments to Cromwell for Calais's 'instruction in the word of God.'[218] Cromwell's support certainly perpetrated heterodoxy there beyond his official licence. In correspondence with Lord Lisle about heresy in Calais he omitted to define true doctrine and regarded the 'sacramentary' label as far from straightforward. He wrote with meaning: 'it is sore to note any man for a Sacramentary unless he that shall be the author of the infamy know well what a Sacramentary is.'[219] Presumably Cromwell thought he did know.

If Cromwell's theology had become Reformed it would explain how he could so easily be portrayed by his enemies as a Sacramentarian in 1540.[220] There is no doubt he understood the distinction between Lutheran and Reformed views.[221] This way of understanding Cromwell admits both his description of John Lambert to Wyatt

---

[215] MacCulloch, *Cromwell*, 142–43.

[216] Torrance Kirby, "Wholesale or Retail? Antoine de Marcourt's *The Boke of Marchauntes* and Tudor political theology," *Renaissance and Reformation* 28, 2 (2004): 48.

[217] MacCulloch, *Cromwell*, 363.

[218] *LP*, ix. #561.

[219] Byrne, ed., *Lisle Letters*, 526 and #1429.

[220] MacCulloch, *Cromwell*, 524–25; MacCulloch, "Bullinger," 900–901; MacCulloch, "Sixteenth-century English Protestantism," 6; see also Burnet, *Reformation*, iii/1:215. Underwood seeks to distinguish between the denial of the corporal presence and the denial of the sacrificial nature of the Mass, suggesting that Cromwell was accused of the latter: Underwood, "Thomas Cromwell," 537.

[221] MacCulloch, *Cromwell*, 365.

on 28 November 1539 as a 'miserable heretic sacramentary'[222] and Foxe's account that 'it is reported of many that Cromewel desired him of forgiuenes for that he had done.'[223] From the scaffold on 28 July 1540 he insisted that he died 'in the Catholicke faithe,' yet significantly he also confessed to past heterodoxy:

> I dye in the Catholicke faithe not doubting of any article of my faithe, no, nor doubting of any Sacramentes of the churche for many hathe slaunder me that I haue bene a bearer of them & that I haue mayntayned evell opinions, yet all were not slaunders for as god hathe instruct so hathe the divell seduced, yet beare me recorde that I dye in the catholike faythe of holy churche.[224]

MacCulloch ventures that Cromwell may actually have been 'Zürich's best friend in Henry's England' in ways that often amounted to 'deception of his prince.'[225]

Reformed theological opinions extended into Henry VIII's own household.[226] In December 1527 Richard Foster, yeoman usher at court, abjured his belief that 'a priest could not consecrate the body of Christ.'[227] There is no indication that Anne Boleyn, with her French links and humanist encouragement of Bible reading, promoted specifically Reformed ideas as the preeminent court evangelical from, and perhaps before, her royal marriage in 1533 until 1536.[228]

---

[222] Quoted in Brigden, *London*, 298.
[223] Foxe, *AM* [1563], 3:625.
[224] Parker Library, Cambridge: CCCC MS. 168, fo. 209r.
[225] MacCulloch, "Sixteenth-century English Protestantism," 7; MacCulloch, *Cromwell*, 524.
[226] On the evangelical environment of the court see Heal, *Reformation*, 227–32.
[227] Quoted in Brigden, *London*, 127.
[228] See also Maria Dowling, "Anne Boleyn and Reform," *JEH* 35, 1 (1984): 30–46. The Placards Affair in Paris in 1534 involved the denunciation of the sacrifice of the Mass but it was not representative of French evangelicalism.

Nevertheless, in 1529 she commended Tyndale's treatise *The Obedience of a Christian Man* (1528) to the king.[229] She also patronised significant evangelical clergy, including Hugh Latimer and Nicholas Shaxton, but they had not then progressed in a Reformed direction.[230] Rather it was Cromwell who bequeathed a more radical strain of evangelicalism to the king's household.

In the 1540s there were numerous evangelicals in the privy chamber, some of whom held Reformed opinions. Thomas Sternhold was certainly associated with the sacramentary Anthony Pearson executed in 1543. John Lascells, who in 1538 had defended his 'heresy' as 'orthodox and perfectly Christian,' provided the evidence which destroyed Katherine Howard in 1541. He died for his Sacramentarianism in 1546, along with Anne Askew, one of Katherine Parr's ladies-in-waiting.[231] The king intervened to rescue George Blage from the stake in July 1546. Although he was an incorrigible sacramentary, he was also Henry's favoured 'pig'.[232]

Susan James believes that by 1544 Henry's last queen espoused a developed 'evangelical Lutheranism and the radical fringes of Calvinism' (though the term 'Calvinism' is rather anachronistic for this period).[233] Bullinger's Oxford disciple Parkhurst composed an epigram in that year praising her surpassing virtues; he soon became her chaplain.[234] Janel Mueller's analysis of her *Psalms or Prayers* (1544) indicates that she drew on the versions by Bucer and Zwingli for her

---

Marguerite de Navarre was quick to distance herself from it. See Gordon, *Calvin*, 40–41.

[229] Ives, *Boleyn*, 161–63.

[230] MacCulloch, "Reform of the Church," 168.

[231] Ryrie, *Gospel*, 48, 202; John Lascells to James Prestwich, 1538, quoted in Susan Brigden and Nigel Wilson, "New Learning and Broken Friendship," *EHR* 112 (1997): 403.

[232] Ryrie, *Gospel*, 56; Brigden, *London*, 375.

[233] Susan James, *Kateryn Parr: the making of a queen* (Aldershot: Ashgate, 1999), 198–213.

[234] Janel Mueller, ed., *Katherine Parr: Complete Works and Correspondence* (Chicago & London: University of Chicago Press, 2011), 74.

translation.[235] Her secretary, Walter Bucler, stayed in Strassburg in 1545 with Hilles, who was committed to Zürich theology.[236]

There were others who might be suspected of concealing Reformed beliefs. Being so closely located to a hostile monarch made dissimulation a priority for such people. John Hooper wrote to Bullinger in 1546 of the 'chief supporters of the gospel' who had recently died. He claimed Sir Thomas Wyatt (d.1542) as 'a most zealous defender of yours and Christ's religion,'[237] although his Psalm paraphrases evade easy doctrinal classification.[238] Hooper was also happy to recognise the duke of Suffolk (d.1545), Lord Chancellor Audley (d.1544), Sir Edward Baynton (d.1544), Sir Thomas Poynings (d.1545) and Dr William Butts (d.1545) as 'real favourers of the gospel' who had 'promoted the glory of God to the utmost of their power.'[239] Audley had communicated with Bullinger in 1540 via Gwalther.[240] Hooper himself claimed to have encountered Zwingli and Bullinger's writings 'when I was a courtier' in the late 1530s.[241] MacCulloch proposes that Hooper could have been influenced by the circle around Henry Fitzalan, Lord Maltravers, whose humanist credentials might have predisposed him to Zürich evangelicalism.[242] Brigden observes that the earl of Surrey's contacts could also suggest experimentation beyond Lutheranism.[243]

Alec Ryrie's interpretation of evangelicalism in England between 1539 and 1547 requires attention because it tends to diminish the

---

[235] Ibid., 208.

[236] Ryrie, *Gospel*, 205.

[237] *OL*, 36–37.

[238] Susan Brigden, *Thomas Wyatt: the Heart's Forest* (London: Faber and Faber, 2012), 451–90. See also Cummings, *Literary Culture*, 224–26.

[239] *OL*, 36–37.

[240] MacCulloch, *Cromwell*, 370.

[241] *OL*, 33.

[242] MacCulloch, "Bullinger," 904–5; MacCulloch, *Cromwell*, 370; D. G. Newcombe, "Hooper, John (1495x1500–1555)," *ODNB* (Oxford: OUP, 2004).

[243] Susan Brigden, "Henry Howard, Earl of Surrey, and the 'Conjured League,'" *HJ* 37 (1994): 515.

incidence of Reformed identity. He suggests that 'Reformed dominance was late in coming; that until shortly before the king's death the dominant strain of English evangelicalism was broadly Lutheran in its doctrine and non-confrontational in its politics.'[244] Ryrie advances his interpretation by suggesting that 'moderates' at home differed from those in exile in the following ways: firstly, they were more optimistic about the prospect of national conversion and consequently 'less exacting than the exiles about quite what that true faith might mean, concentrating on a simple willingness to hear the Gospel and on moral renewal.' They hoped 'to minimise and indeed to disguise any doctrinal divisions' to make conversion a less revolutionary step.[245] Secondly, they emphasised justification *sola fide* only, stopping short of its 'more provocative' implications for the Mass.[246] Thirdly, they avoided controversy regarding the Mass; there was 'a firm unwillingness on the part of any of these moderates to be associated with rejection of the Real Presence.'[247] In Ryrie's opinion, they best resembled Lutherans.[248]

Ryrie argues that between 1539 and 1543 the regime appeared sufficiently ambiguous to satisfy moderates 'willing to accept a slow pace of reform, if necessary a glacially slow pace, in the name of good order.' The silence of the Six Articles on justification made this viable.[249] He suggests that in 1543 the restriction of Bible reading to the élites by the Act for the Advancement of True Religion, and the explicit denial of justification *sola fide* in the King's Book, 'piteously exposed' the fragility of conformism. When another crisis began in May 1546 focusing persecution on the question of the Real Presence, the moderate position proved untenable for the majority of its adherents. They were forced to abandon their subtle position—both

---

[244] Ryrie, "Strange Death," 68. Ryrie, *Gospel*, 97–98, 107, 266–170.
[245] Ryrie, *Gospel*, 125–26.
[246] Ibid., 135–36.
[247] Ibid., 138.
[248] Ibid., 145.
[249] Ibid., 254.

theologically and politically—and to choose between Reformed defiance and traditionalist submission. Hence Ryrie sees 'a fundamental shift in evangelicalism's centre of gravity' in 1546.[250] This does not, however, seem adequately to explain a sudden Reformed ascendency under Edward VI.

Reeves has already challenged the idea that the evangelical rhetoric of obedience in this period was the result of the Lutheran political theory of the Two-Kingdoms. He argues that 'early English obedience theory is both Swiss and Lutheran.'[251] Several further reservations can be expressed regarding Ryrie's interpretation. It is not necessarily the case that exiles were more exacting about the doctrinal implications of true faith than evangelicals remaining in England. Guido Latré sees a 'tendency towards compromise in Tyndale' who 'does not insist on all principles of doctrine' but is ready to put them aside if he can thereby secure Scripture in the vernacular. Latré comments more generally on 'the Antwerp readiness to be expedient rather than doctrinal, that both Tyndale and Coverdale seem strongly aware of.'[252] Although evangelicals at home did conform, it does not follow that they were all content to do so. A higher incidence of Reformed opinion may be supposed to have existed than was apparent under hostile circumstances. Whether ten, by Neelak Tjernagel's count, or twenty people, by Ryrie's, were executed as sacramentaries in 1539–47,[253] the threat itself was persecution enough to keep others quiet. MacCulloch writes of the 'curious ecumenism' of these years in which a great plurality of

---

[250] Ibid., 249–56. See also Ryrie, "Strange Death," 89–91; *King's Book*, 152, 158–59.

[251] Ryan Reeves, "'Ye Gods': Political Obedience from Tyndale to Cromwell, c.1528–1540," *ARG* 105, 1 (2014): 254–55.

[252] Guido Latré, "The 1535 Coverdale Bible and its Antwerp Origins," in *The Bible as book: the Reformation*, ed. O. O'Sullivan (New Castle and London: Oak Knoll Press, 2000), 93–94.

[253] N. S. Tjernagel, *Henry VIII and the Lutherans: a study in Anglo-Lutheran relations from 1521 to 1547* (St Louis, MO: Concordia, 1965), 238; Ryrie, *Gospel*, 23.

opinion was possible, albeit with 'murderous lunges against representatives of either religious wing.'[254]

Since exile might be an unrealistic choice, it is probable that only a fraction of those evangelicals seriously discontent with conformity went into exile in the 1540s.[255] Susan Wabuda has highlighted the reality that 'men who wanted to avoid losing their lives or contradicting their faith had little room for manoeuvre. Flight was not always possible.'[256] Whether people decided to leave or to remain is an unreliable guide to the strength and nature of their convictions. While some of those who had participated in the Zürich exchange went into exile, others remained, including Bartholomew Traheron and Nicholas Eliot, demonstrating that some committed Zürichers were prepared to keep a low-profile in the face of the Six Articles' clear rejection of their position.[257] Indeed Zürich theology would strongly dispose someone towards a doctrine of obedience. As Reeves observes, the tendency of evangelicals during the early 1540s 'was to change their tone but not their principles.'[258]

In September 1540 the sacramentary Lascells advised the

---

[254] MacCulloch, *Cranmer*, 275.

[255] This is not to deny subsequent differences between those exiles returning under Edward VI and the 'insular background' of those who had remained in England. See Knappen, *Tudor Puritanism*, 84. There were differences after the Marian Exile too. On religious exile generally, and with particular attention to religious conservatives, see Peter Marshall, "Religious Exiles and the Tudor State," in *Discipline and Diversity*, eds. K. Cooper and J. Gregory, Ecclesiastical History Society (Woodbridge: Boydell Press, 2007), 263–84.

[256] Wabuda, "Equivocation," 228–29; see also Jonathan Wright, "Marian Exiles and the Legitimacy of Flight from Persecution," *JEH* 52, 2 (2001): 220–43. Latimer may have been making for Switzerland when he was caught at Gravesend in July 1539, suggests Hildebrandt, "Protestant Exiles," 12.

[257] MacCulloch, "Bullinger," 909. At least six of the Marian exiles had previously visited Zürich during Henry VIII's reign: Christina Garrett, *The Marian Exiles: a study in the origins of Elizabethan Puritanism* (Cambridge: CUP, 1938), 42.

[258] Ryan Reeves, *English Evangelicals and Tudor Obedience, c.1527–1570* (Leiden & Boston: Brill, 2014), 71, 75.

queen's servant William Smythwyke 'not to be too rash or quick in maintaining the Scriptures, for if we would let them alone and suffer a little time, they [the duke of Norfolk and Bishop Gardiner] would overthrow themselves.'[259] Not only moderates but radicals too were capable of optimistically biding their time.[260] Zwingli himself had emphasised the advantages of not causing 'offence'.[261] In 1542 the seemingly moderate Becon rehearsed Zwingli's argument from Psalm 82 that the civil power is an agent of God's providence.[262] For those taking the risk, remaining in England offered opportunities to share the Gospel there in person. Brinklow observed in 1545 that 'the Gospell was never more sincerely preached in the time of the apostles than it hath been of late in London'—significant acclamation and buoyancy coming from a sacramentary.[263]

Ryrie's judgment that Gough and Mayler 'presumably found the milk-and-water reformism that they were being forced to publish in the 1540s somewhat distasteful' is an understatement.[264] As has been argued in this chapter, there is good reason to suspect that such men were compelled by circumstances 'to conceal more radical views,'[265] and Jennifer Britnell sees no reason to assume that Gough was content.[266] Christopher Bradshaw observes that to dissent openly from the Crown's position 'would have been an option, but polemically it would have been a disaster. Such dissent would

---

[259] *LP*, xvi. #101.

[260] See Ryrie's description of 'moderates' in Racaut and Ryrie, "Between Coercion and Persuasion," 5.

[261] Euler, *Couriers*, 18.

[262] Reeves, *English Evangelicals*, 81–82.

[263] Quoted in Brigden, *London*, 256. This must qualify Reeves' assertion that evangelicals were unable to preach their message: Reeves, *English Evangelicals*, 94.

[264] Ryrie, *Gospel*, 120.

[265] Ibid.

[266] Jennifer Britnell, "John Gough and the *Traité de la Différence des Schismes et des Conciles* of Jean Lemaire de Beiges: translation as propaganda in the Henrician Reformation," *JEH* 46, 1 (1995): 69.

have played right into the hands of Catholic propagandists.'[267] Maria Dowling agrees that mainstream evangelicals feared a fringe 'who might try to bring about a too-rapid reformation and thus jeopardise the whole movement.'[268] Arguably the important difference between conforming and nonconforming evangelicals was not their doctrine but their circumspection. Just as censorship could be ambiguous, writes Cummings, 'so writers were attuned to the possibility of self-censorship and of self-concealment.'[269] Thus, Wyatt's paraphrases freed him to 'keep secrets without telling lies.'[270] As Rupp realised, the stability of Henry's Church in his last decade was secured by a general 'concern for the unity of the realm' by all who knew that obedience to the king was bound up with 'the safety of their own necks.'[271]

Ryrie's attempt to explain the theological polarisation at the end of Henry VIII's reign in terms of the political outflanking of the moderate position is unconvincing. It is hard to understand Euler's affirmation of it, but she does at least venture that the decline of Lutheranism might have begun earlier than Ryrie suggests.[272] Had moderates really been convinced Lutherans, their reaction need only have been to abandon their willingness 'to give the king the benefit of any possible doubt.'[273] They had nothing to gain from adding

---

[267] Christopher Bradshaw, "The Exile Literature of the Early Reformation: 'Obedience to God and the King,'" in *The Education of a Christian Society: Humanism and the Reformation in Britain and the Netherlands*, eds. N. Amos, A. Pettegree, and H. van Nierop (Aldershot: Ashgate, 1999), 112f.

[268] Maria Dowling, "The Gospel and the Court: Reformation under Henry VIII," in *Protestantism and the National Church in Sixteenth Century England*, eds. P. Lake and M. Dowling (London, New York and Sydney: Croom Helm, 1987), 46.

[269] Cummings, *Literary Culture*, 11.

[270] Ibid., 224.

[271] Rupp, *Studies*, 128.

[272] Euler, *Couriers*, 68; Carrie Euler, "Does Faith Translate? Tudor Translations of Martin Luther and the Doctrine of Justification by Faith," *ARG* 101 (2010): 84, 91.

[273] Ryrie, *Gospel*, 67.

further doctrinal anathemas to what Ryrie claims were their largely procedural differences with the king. Indeed, by Ryrie's reasoning, moderates would have had reason enough to lose confidence in the regime much earlier, in 1539, when the Six Articles asserted transubstantiation and five hundred Londoners were arrested in one fortnight during the summer. The regime's essential implacability was certainly evident then and, as Brigden observes, 'those already won to protestantism were only strengthened in their awareness of being part of a persecuted community.'[274] Thus Ryrie's thesis contains difficulties. It seems more likely that Sacramentarianism grew earlier and that, through dissimulation, it remained concealed. After 1543, with both the evangelicals' moderate camouflage and their hope in the king's intentions disintegrating, the restraint of more Reformed opinions was invalidated.

Early Evangelicalism in the Low Countries

During the 1520s and 1530s the English government began to perceive heresy as a foreign infection more than a native threat. A proclamation of 1535 expelling Anabaptists noted apprehensively that 'many strangers, born out of the King's obedience, are arrived and come into this realm.'[275] By the mid-1540s more than one in twenty London residents were foreigners.[276] The immediate point of contact with the continent was the Low Countries; from there most of all people and ideas crossed the Channel, and they travelled both ways. English evangelical exiles highlight the continental dimension to the English Reformation.[277] These exiles were typically quasi-Reformed, even self-professed devotees of Zwingli and Œcolampadius.[278] Many

[274] Susan Brigden, "Popular Disturbance and the Fall of Thomas Cromwell and the Reformers, 1539–1540," *HJ* 24, 2 (1981): 274, 277.
[275] *TRP*, i. #155.
[276] Pettegree, *Foreign Protestant Communities*, 9–22.
[277] Marshall, "Religious Exiles," 283.
[278] Ryrie, *Gospel*, 97–98, 107, 266–70.

of them sought refuge in the Low Countries and were hosted in Antwerp by the Merchant Adventurers. We must not think of men like Tyndale and Coverdale languishing in lonely exile here, but as energetic participants in an industrious network of printers and polemicists producing tracts and translating Bibles into multiple languages.[279] Merchants like Richard Hilles and Thomas Poyntz and customers of the book trade would also have encountered Reformed ideas on their visits.[280]

It is important to understand the proliferation of evangelical ideas in the Low Countries in order to appreciate how Reformed theology could be transmitted so straightforwardly to England from the Alps and upper Germany. Geographical corridors for the dissemination of printed material between the Rhineland and London via the Low Countries are identifiable from the late fifteenth century and the links had existed much earlier. Even at that stage, writes Sorin Ciutacu, there was 'an amazing and staggering network.'[281] These links remained strong in the early sixteenth century, connecting the printers of Strassburg and Basle to England and supported by the Frankfurt book fair every spring and autumn.[282] In October 1526 or 1527 Richard Hall, an ironmonger, wrote to Richard Harman in Antwerp placing an order for 'two books of the New Testament in English.'[283] In 1528 Tunstall reported to Cardinal Wolsey that 'the bringer of these books' to Gough 'this year past was a Dutchman from Antwerp, named Theodoryke, who was for some time

---

[279] Latré, "The 1535 Coverdale Bible," 94.

[280] W. D. J. Cargill Thompson, "The Two Regiments: the continental setting of William Tyndale's political thought," in *Reform and Reformation: England and the Continent c.1500–c.1750*, ed. D. Baker (Oxford: Blackwell, 1979), 33.

[281] Sorin Ciutacu, "Flemish-English Cultural Corridors: William Caxton and his cultural revolution," in L. Hellinga, ed., *The Bookshop of the World: the role of the Low Countries in the book-trade 1473–1941* (t' Goy-Houten: Hes and De Graaf, 2001), 58.

[282] Loades, "Books and the English Reformation," 270; Marcus Loane, *Masters of the English Reformation*, 2nd ed. (Edinburgh: Banner of Truth, 2005), 75.

[283] *LP*, iv/2, 4693.

in London, and has brought many books.'[284] Francis Denham also acquired some of his reforming texts from Antwerp, and Thomas Keyle was no doubt highly exposed to reformism by his connections in the printing trade and in Antwerp and Calais.[285]

Netherlanders were exposed to numerous strains of evangelicalism in the 1520s apart from Lutheranism. Indices of prohibited books included works by Karlstädt, Lambert, Œcolampadius and, from 1529, Zwingli. Many of these were printed in Antwerp—a precarious venture for publishers who were surely working to popular demand[286]—and a significant number were made available in English translation. One Antwerp printer used by Tyndale, Joannes Hillen van Hoochstraten, printed at least thirteen heretical books in English translation.[287] The exiled Simon Fish translated the *Sum of Scripture* from the Dutch while he was in Antwerp.[288] Maerten de Keyser, the first to print Tyndale's English New Testament, was prepared to put his name to this text even though he used false imprints in other reformist publications. Antwerp was a religious melting-pot, Tyndale's refuge, and unquestionably the centre of the English exiles' campaign: of forty-one evangelical books published in exile between 1525 and 1535, thirty-six were printed in Antwerp.[289] Two more were printed in Strassburg, and two of the Antwerp publications claimed to be from Strassburg, highlighting the familiar trade routes through the Rhineland towards the Alps.

The earliest local bookshop inventory extant is from Leuven

---

[284] *LP*, iv/2, 4073.
[285] Brigden, *London*, 116, 125.
[286] Duke, *Low Countries*, 31.
[287] Hellinga, "Bookshop," 24.
[288] Brigden, *London*, 117.
[289] Anthea Hume, "English Protestant Books Printed Abroad, 1525–35: an annotated bibliography," in *The Complete Works of St. Thomas More*, eds. L. Schuster et al. (New Haven & London: YUP, 1973), 8:1063–91; see also John King, "Thomas More, William Tyndale, and the Printing of Religious Propaganda," in *The Oxford Handbook of Tudor Literature, 1485–1603*, eds. M. Pincombe and C. Shrank (Oxford: OUP, 2009), 119.

in 1543. Almost all of its 513 books were printed between 1516 and 1543. Statistical analysis is indicative: approximately thirty-one percent of the books were printed in the German lands, of which forty-four percent were printed in Swiss or upper German towns, that is, nearly fourteen percent of the total inventory.[290] Reformed writings were thus readily available in the Low Countries, regardless of whether they formed the bulk of Dutch printing.

Laurentius Knappert depicted the first decade of the Dutch Reformation as 'the sacramentarian period' because of the blending of Zwinglian eucharistic theology and Erasmian humanism, and because Luther's eucharistic understanding gained few adherents.[291] Few sacramentaries were arrested in the 1520s because they showed no interest in forming large conventicles. As in England they were hard to detect. Moreover, the authorities doubted the efficacy of harsh persecution: on 1 February 1528 the Council of Holland reported that stern measures 'have not been as profitable as one might have expected; but we have found by experience that incarceration has brought to repentance' men who would otherwise have been burnt. This was perhaps overly optimistic, as shown by the persistent heterodoxy of one prisoner named Jan Sartorius.[292]

In February 1521 the papal nuncio reported that spiritual interpretations of the Real Presence following 'Wycliff and Berengar of Tours' were widespread in the Low Countries.[293] The earliest

---

[290] Pierre Delsaerdt, "A Bookshop for a New Age: the inventory of the bookshop of the Louvain bookseller Hieronymus Cloet, 1543," in *The Bookshop of the World: the role of the Low Countries in the book-trade 1473–1941*, ed. L. Hellinga (t' Goy-Houten: Hes and De Graaf, 2001), 86.

[291] Quoted in Duke, *Low Countries*, 6.

[292] Quoted in James Tracy, "Heresy Law and Centralisation under Mary of Hungary: conflict between the Council of Holland and the central government over the enforcement of Charles V's Placards," *ARG* 73 (1982): 287–88.

[293] Quoted in B. J. Spruyt, "Wessel Gansfort and Cornelis Hoen's *Epistola Christiana*: 'the ring as a pledge of my love,'" in *Wessel Gansfort (1419–1489) and Northern Humanism*, eds. F. Akkerman, G. Huisman and A. Vanderjagt (Leiden: Brill, 1993), 136.

incontrovertible case of Dutch Sacramentarianism was recorded in May 1525, within months of the Real Presence first breaking as a matter of public controversy between European reformers.[294] That summer iconoclasm was added to Sacramentarianism in Antwerp and Delft.[295] In 1526 Bucer's then memorialist understanding of the Eucharist was publicised at Antwerp in a free translation of Johannes Bugenhagen's Psalms commentary, and in 1527 a monk blamed Œcolampadius for Flemish Sacramentarianism.[296]

Most Netherlanders were unaware that the various strands of evangelicalism from which they were borrowing were in competition. Confessionalisation had not yet begun and, according to Alastair Duke, it took 'many years' before Dutch evangelicals could differentiate between the theologies of Luther and Zwingli.[297] The prompt translation of the Marburg Articles into Dutch after the colloquy in 1529 would certainly have emphasised points of agreement. Theological allegiance is therefore difficult to define clearly. However, it is interesting that justification *sola fide* was rarely mentioned explicitly.[298] Perhaps solifidian soteriology was poorly understood by the masses or reformers could draw upon a wider base of support if they attacked the Mass, images, and the cult of saints. It may be that relatively relaxed policing by the authorities allowed these more Reformed currents to prevail. Whatever the reason, the doctrine of justification was not the focus, an observation which instantly evokes parallels with the Reformed programme.

Lollardy

The availability and transmission of Reformed ideas from the Low Countries is not the only possible explanation for Sacra-

[294] Duke, *Low Countries*, 19–20.
[295] Ibid., 42.
[296] Ibid., 21–22.
[297] Ibid., 57.
[298] Ibid., 51.

mentarianism in England. Duke thinks it likely that 'crude materialist rejections of the real presence' amongst the lower orders in the Low Countries 'hark back to late medieval oral traditions of dissent.' The arguments martialled by the magisterial reformers in the sacramental controversy were more sophisticated. Popular Sacramentarianism is betrayed by its 'barbarous idiom and a country divinity far removed from the erudite theology of the major reformers.'[299] Some scholars have sought to explain English Sacramentarianism in terms of the native Lollard tradition derived from the teaching of John Wyclif (1328–84) rather than ascribing it to continental Reformed influence.[300] This has proved controversial in certain quarters but the argument needs to be considered.[301] As Duke says of the Low Countries, the influence of late-medieval dissent 'may not have been profound, but it should not be overlooked.'[302] What becomes apparent is that Lollardy cannot sufficiently account for the intellectual substance of English Sacramentarianism in the early Reformation period.

It is clear from prosecutions in Kent (1511), Coventry (1511–12), the West Country (1514) and the Chilterns (1521) that Lollardy was flourishing apart from any rejuvenating impulse from the continent.[303] The heartlands of early English evangelicalism—Geoffrey

---

[299] Ibid., xii, 23.

[300] E.g., A. G. Dickens, *The English Reformation*, 1st ed. (London: B. T. Batsford, 1964), 37, 69, 81; Davis, *Heresy and Reformation*; Margaret Aston, *Lollards and Reformers: Images and Literacy in Late Medieval England* (London: Hambledon Press, 1984); A. G. Dickens, "The Early Expansion of Protestantism in England 1520–1558," *ARG* 78 (1987); Anne Hudson, *The Premature Reformation: Wycliffite Texts and Lollard History* (Oxford: OUP, 1988). The historiographical debate on Lollard influence has resembled a war of attrition.

[301] Haigh suggests that proponents of the view that Lollardy prepared the ground for Reformation are reacting against the revisionist historiography of which he is a part: Christopher Haigh, "Religion," *TRHS* 6th series, vii (1997): 288–89, 293, 295. See more recently on Lollard influence Diarmaid MacCulloch, "Sixteenth-century English Protestantism," 5–6, 14.

[302] Duke, *Low Countries*, 28.

[303] For a complete geographical survey see J. A. F. Thomson, *The Later Lollards 1414–1520* (Oxford: OUP, 1965).

Dickens' 'great crescent'—correlated with some of the areas which experienced renewed persecution of Lollards from the end of the fifteenth century: particularly Suffolk, Essex, London, Kent and the Thames Valley.[304] Margaret Aston has shown how reformers made use of Lollard literature for propaganda purposes, while Anne Hudson cites cases of Lollards recognising the correspondence of Reformation teachings to their own beliefs.[305] Contemporary interrogators themselves often seem to have confused Lollards and evangelicals. This may be because inquisitorial methods had long been calculated to detect Lollardy. Obsolete questioning routines may have failed to penetrate superficial similarities. As Brigden points out, the preaching of Bilney sounded 'for all the world like Lollard invective.'[306] The term 'lollard' had been a generic synonym of 'heretic' for at least a generation and was still used this way by John Bradford in 1548.[307] However, once investigators had been equipped with Fisher's *Assertionis Lutheranae Confutatio* and More's *Responsio ad Lutherum* (both 1523), they ought to have been competent to detect the new breed of heresy.[308] In December 1527 Tunstall's questioning of Bilney began with 'the assertions of Luther,'[309] but the anti-heresy proclamation of March 1529 encompassed 'all manner of heresies and errors, commonly called Lollardies.'[310]

---

[304] Dickens, "Early Expansion," 211.

[305] Aston, *Lollards and Reformers*, 222–24, 231–32; Hudson, *Premature Reformation*, 478–80, 501.

[306] Brigden, *London*, 112. On Bilney see Davis, "The Trials of Thomas Bylney," 775–90.

[307] Hudson, *Premature Reformation*, 446, 498–500; Petrus Artopoeus and John Chrysostome, *The Diuisyon of the Places of the Lawe and of the Gospell, gathered owt of the Hooly Scriptures by Petrum Artopoeum: wher unto is added two orations of prayeng to God made by S. Iohn. Chrisostome*, trans. J. Bradford (London: [S. Mierdman for] Gwalter Lynne, 1548; RSTC 822), A8v.

[308] Richard Rex, *The Theology of John Fisher* (Cambridge: CUP, 1991), 88; Rainer Pineas, *Thomas More and Tudor Polemics* (London & Bloomington, IN: Indiana University Press, 1968), 14–28.

[309] Foxe, *AM* [1563], 3:513.

[310] *TRP*, i. #122.

Lollardy was primarily a phenomenon of the lower orders although it appealed to some significant families and clerics too.[311] Tantalising connections between Lollardy and the 'Christian brethren' remain difficult to prove and, while the revival of Lollardy in high London circles during the early sixteenth century is intriguing, Rupp advises that 'these men on the verge of orthodoxy should not properly be called "Lollards".'[312] The extinction of academic Wycliffism in the universities by the 1430s meant that Lollardy had to survive without intellectual leadership.[313] Although it could perpetuate popular religious attitudes, it was not equipped to generate a sophisticated doctrinal programme. Reformation doctrine appeared first at the academic level via continental interactions and quickly seeped down the social order,[314] where Lollardy readily assisted its popular reception.[315] The direction of doctrinal influence was always from the more educated evangelical to the Lollard.[316] Consequently the intellectual independence of Reformed evangelicalism from Lollardy is well established.[317] Even amongst the exponents of Lollard influence John Davis attributes educated reformism to

[311] Rupp, *Studies*, 2; Hudson, *Premature Reformation*, 467; MacCulloch, "Reform of the Church," 160.

[312] Brigden, *London*, 85, 410; Rupp, *Studies*, 11.

[313] Jeremy Catto, "Theology after Wycliffism," in *The History of the University of Oxford*, eds. J. Catto and R. Evans (Oxford: OUP, 1992), 2:275; Richard Rex, *The Lollards* (Basingstoke: Palgrave, 2002), 132.

[314] See Duke, *Low Countries*, 33; G. Dickens, "Heresy and the Origins of English Protestantism," in *Britain and The Netherlands: Anglo-Dutch Historical Conference 1962*, ed. J. S. Bromley and E. H. Kossmann (Utrecht & Amsterdam: J. B. Walters, 1964), 48–49.

[315] A. G. Dickens, *The English Reformation*, 2nd ed. (London: B. T. Batsford, 1989), 14; Robert Whiting, "Local responses to the Henrician Reformation," in *The Reign of Henry VIII: politics, policy and piety*, ed. D. MacCulloch (Basingstoke: Macmillan, 1995), 223.

[316] Hudson, *Premature Reformation*, 478–79; Margaret Aston, *Faith and Fire: popular and unpopular religion 1350–1600* (London & Rio Grande, OH: Hambledon Press, 1993), 266.

[317] E.g., Thomson, *Later Lollards*, 219; MacCulloch, "England," 173.

humanism and Dickens concedes that 'the Cambridge intellectuals who first took up Lutheran and Zwinglian doctrines owed little to Lollardy.'[318] This may explain why Fisher did not worry himself with Lollardy.[319]

An important contribution to this debate is Patrick Hornbeck's study of doctrinal development within Lollardy. It reveals the extent to which so-called Wycliffites had drifted from their namesake by the sixteenth century, many becoming obsessed with the dramatic and visual aspects of religious practice. There is a risk of being misled by their depositions because they retained much of Wyclif's expression without being either willing or able to articulate his predestinarian soteriology. In particular, their partiality for the Epistle of James and its emphasis on good works was inconsistent with the evangelicals' more Pauline emphases and could hardly have given rise to them.[320] By 1430 many Lollards had also departed from Wyclif's eucharistic theology of 'a real, spiritual, and yet not substantial presence.'[321] A century later they were far from unanimous. There was certainly a higher incidence of crude Sacramentarianism amongst Lollards, yet Hornbeck cautions against a simple shift away from Wyclif's understanding of Real Presence because inquisitors tended to be interested in whether the elements remained after consecration rather than dissecting figurative understandings.[322]

The diversity of Lollard opinion makes it very difficult to quantify their contribution to evangelicalism and almost impossible to link Lollardy to any individual English reformer's doctrine. More evidence is needed to prove Davis's assertion that Lollardy produced

---

[318] Davis, *Heresy*, 65; A. G. Dickens, *Lollards and Protestants in the Diocese of York, 1509–1558* (Oxford: OUP, 1959), 10.

[319] Rex, *Lollards*, 121.

[320] J. Patrick Hornbeck, *What is a Lollard? Dissent and Belief in Late Medieval England* (Oxford: OUP, 2010), 44–67; see also Dickens, "Heresy and the Origins of English Protestantism," 59; Hudson, *Premature Reformation*, 383.

[321] Hornbeck, *Lollard*, 75.

[322] Ibid., 76–103.

a predilection for Swiss theology but Brigden and MacCulloch are right to think that it had this potential.[323] An educated Englishman interacting with continental theology might instinctively have preferred Reformed over Lutheran eucharistic thought because of some pre-existent Lollard disposition. At the same time comparisons can be made between Lollards and more extreme radicals like the Anabaptists.[324]

Of the leading English reformers Tyndale and Frith are most commonly suspected as having had formative Lollard influences. Rex has insisted that Lollard influence in Tyndale's Gloucestershire was 'small, discreet and localised' and he adduces evidence of Tyndale's close connections to thoroughly orthodox gentry.[325] The exposure of the Bristol conventicle probably occurred while Tyndale was away at Oxford where his reading of the Greek New Testament is credited by David Daniell for inspiring his reformist convictions. Tyndale himself denied reliance on the Wycliffite gospels for his 1526 translations.[326] In Frith's case the evidence is

---

[323] Davis, *Heresy*, 65; Brigden, *London*, 276; MacCulloch, "Reform of the Church," 168; Diarmaid MacCulloch, "Putting the English Reformation on the Map," *TRHS* 15 (2005): 80–81. There were further discrepancies over baptism and images which diminish the case for Lollard influence in the 1520s: Hudson, *Premature Reformation*, 302, 307, 469.

[324] See M. T. Pearse, *Between Known Men and Visible Saints: a study in sixteenth-century English dissent* (London & Toronto: Associated University Press, 1994), esp. 17.

[325] Richard Rex, "New Light on Tyndale and Lollardy," *Reformation* 8 (2003): esp. 147, 157, 171; Rex exposes methodological flaws undermining Donald Smeeton, *Lollard Themes in the Reformation Theology of William Tyndale* (Kirksville, MO: SCJ Publishers, 1986). Gloucestershire was in fact typically traditionalist: Caroline Litzenberger, *The English Reformation and the Laity: Gloucestershire, 1540–1580* (Cambridge: CUP, 1997), 28–29. Rex's caution was anticipated by S. L. Greenslade, *The Work of William Tindale* (London & Glasgow: Blackie and Son, 1938), 24–26.

[326] David Daniell, "Tyndale, William (c.1494–1536)," *ODNB* (Oxford: OUP, 2004); William Tyndale, *Doctrinal Treatises and Introductions to Different Portions of the Holy Scriptures*, ed. H. Walter, PS (Cambridge: CUP, 1848), 390.

circumstantial.[327] He protested to More that 'I do not allow this thing because Wickliffe, Œcolampadius, Tyndale, and Zuinglius so say, but because I see them in that place more purely expound the Scripture.'[328] Theodore Bozeman rightly suggests that 'the Wycliffite heritage might have served them more as a broadly congenial native antecedent than as a substantive influence upon their theory of redemption.'[329]

The case for Lollard influence depends to a large extent on reasoning *post hoc ergo propter hoc*, which has its roots in the apologetic search for native antecedents of true religion by evangelicals like John Bale and John Foxe.[330] Although Lollardy can be invoked to explain a choice of Reformed over Lutheran evangelicalism, continental influence might do just as well and with more substantive evidence. England could well have charted a Reformed course without any contribution from Lollardy, just as France, Scotland and the Netherlands embraced Swiss theology apart from any comparable heretical tradition.[331] Lollardy can hardly take credit for the theological programme of the English Reformation.

Humanism

Humanism, like Lollardy, has been offered as a possible explanation for the theological diversity of early English evangelicalism and its deviations from Lutheranism. James McConica for instance

[327] David Daniell, "Frith, John (1503–1533)," *ODNB* (Oxford: OUP, 2004); Thomson, *Later Lollards*, 185–91.

[328] John Frith, *The Work of John Frith*, ed. N. T. Wright, *CLRC*, Vol. 7 (Appleford: Sutton Courtenay Press, 1978), 342; Clebsch, *Earliest Protestants*, 122–23.

[329] Theodore Bozeman, *The Precisianist Strain: Disciplinary Religion and Antinomian Backlash in Puritanism to 1638* (Chapel Hill, NC and London: University of North Carolina Press, 2004), 14; see also Frith, *Works*, 344; Knappen, *Tudor Puritanism*, 9.

[330] E.g., G. J. Mayhew, "The Progress of the Reformation in East Sussex, 1530–1559: the evidence from wills," *Southern History* 5 (1983): 49.

[331] See Rex, *Henry VIII*, 111; Rex, *Lollards*, 120.

claimed Erasmian humanism as the unifying and developing theme of the English Reformation. Lucy Wooding tries to explain English doctrinal formulae on the basis of humanist ideology.[332] This approach has likewise been subject to criticism but it is still necessary to explain why humanism is not a convincing alternative explanation to continental Reformed influence for what we observe in England in this period.[333] This has largely to do with the nature of humanism itself.

Humanists were not committed to any particular theological outlook.[334] As Oscar Kristeller explains, 'Renaissance humanism was not as such a philosophical tendency or system, but rather a cultural and educational programme.'[335] This programme was not fundamentally opposed to medieval scholastic methods like *loci* and *disputationes*, nor is there particular evidence of a struggle between scholasticism and humanism on intellectual grounds.[336] Rather humanists sought to tackle 'scholastic problems, notably the absence of a refined use of classical languages and rhetoric that was rooted in the absence of sound philological training and [. . .] excessively speculative theological argument.'[337] Humanists were

---

[332] McConica, *Humanists*, 12; Lucy Wooding, *Rethinking Catholicism in Reformation England* (Oxford: OUP, 2000), 16–17, 96.

[333] Dickens judged this approach too simplistic. McConica's treatment made him 'more than ever suspicious of blanket-words like "humanist" and "Erasmian"': A. G. Dickens, "Review of 'English Humanists and Reformation Politics under Henry VIII and Edward VI. By James K. McConica,'" *History* 52 (1967): 77–78. Cf. the clear distinction between humanism and theology in Jonathan Arnold, *The Great Humanists: European thought on the eve of the Reformation* (London & New York: I. B. Tauris and Co., 2011), 3–4, 8–9.

[334] Richard Muller, *The Unaccommodated Calvin: Studies in the Foundation of a Theological Tradition* (Oxford: OUP, 2000), 42.

[335] Paul Kristeller, *Renaissance Thought and Its Sources* (New York: Columbia University Press, 1979), 22.

[336] James Overfield, "Scholastic Opposition to Humanism in Pre-Reformation Germany," *Viator* 7 (1976): 398.

[337] Muller, *Unaccommodated Calvin*, 44; see also Overfield, "Scholastic Opposition," 400. On scholasticism see Richard Muller, *After Calvin: Studies in the Development of a Theological Tradition* (Oxford: OUP, 2003), 75–76.

proponents of classical ideals, eloquent forms of expression and, particularly, textual and philological scholarship utilising original sources *ad fontes*. Christian humanism applied these principles to religion by returning to the fount of Scripture and the Church Fathers. As Charles Trinkaus writes, 'humanism, the classical-Christian rhetorical tradition, did not require, nor did it develop a systematic philosophy or a theology.'[338] The pietistic *philosophia Christi* expounded by Erasmus, for example, simply cultivated a suspicion of certain scholastic tendencies and a concern for the apparent decay of Church and society.[339] Humanism was not committed to any particular confessional trajectory but was adapted to serve different confessional goals.[340]

With this in mind, and remembering that Luther himself was misconstrued by many of his contemporaries to be extending the Erasmian programme, it is surprising that humanism has been used to explain the divergence of English reformism from Lutheranism.[341] By the 1520s Oxford was being opened up to the humanist and biblical scholarship that had already been thoroughly inculcated at Cambridge.[342] If humanism and evangelicalism could be linked then this might seem a straightforward explanation for Reformation developments, yet passionate humanists on the eve of the Reformation, like Fisher, More and John Stokesley, could be found amongst the staunchest conservatives a few years later, shocked at the evangelical perversion of humanist techniques. Other humanist scholars placed their skills at the service of the evangelical cause. Preachers of quite different theological colours could employ

---

[338] Charles Trinkaus, *The Scope of Renaissance Humanism* (Ann Arbor: University of Michigan Press, 1983), 243.

[339] See McConica, *Humanists*, 14–15.

[340] Erika Rummel, *The Confessionalisation of Humanism in Reformation Germany* (Oxford: OUP, 2000), 8.

[341] Ibid., 15–18.

[342] Methuen, "Oxford," 76; V. H. H. Green, *Religion at Oxford and Cambridge* (London: SCM Press, 1964), 80–83; Rex, "English Humanists," 23; Rex, "Early Impact," 52.

the same humanist tools in support of the Royal Supremacy for instance.[343] Thus humanism cannot be used to explain the origins of different theological convictions.

A more plausible argument could be made that an evangelical convert espousing humanist learning might have a predilection for the Swiss variety of evangelicalism just as a Lollard might be attracted to Swiss sacramental theology.[344] According to McConica Erasmus' popular *Enchiridion militis Christiani* [*Handbook of the Christian Soldier*] (1501) provided 'a stern and practical guide to pious living in the world.' His was 'a lay religion which exalts the vocation in the world to an unprecedented degree [. . .] it is less the redemptive than the ethical Christ who prevails in the Erasmian gospel.'[345] Humanist biblical criticism and practical piety imbued with evangelical fervour would have found a comfortable niche in the Reformed concern for social transformation by living a renewed life.[346]

Zwingli and Calvin, unlike Luther, were strongly influenced by this ethical strand of humanism.[347] Zwingli's reading of Erasmus in 1515 or 1516 was decisive for his approach to theology; he even offered Erasmus citizenship in Zürich in 1522.[348] He believed that humanist biblical exegesis revealed the necessary measures to transform communities morally, befitting their status as part of Christ's Church.[349] As Bruce Gordon writes, 'the appeal

---

[343] Lucy Wooding, "From Tudor Humanism to Reformation Preaching," in *The Oxford Handbook of the Early Modern Sermon*, eds. P. McCullough, H. Adlington and E. Rhatigan (Oxford: OUP, 2011), 342–43.

[344] See Trueman and Euler, "Reception of Luther," 65. Philip Melanchthon was not a straightforward humanist. Although he was more inclined to humanism than Luther was, he was reluctant to disagree with him publicly.

[345] McConica, *Humanists*, 23, 33.

[346] W. P. Stephens, *Zwingli: an introduction to his thought* (Oxford: OUP, 1992), 70–71.

[347] On Erasmus's involvement with reformers in Zürich and Basle see Christine Christ-von Wedel, *Erasmus of Rotterdam: advocate of a new Christianity* (Toronto & London: University of Toronto Press, 2013), 183ff.

[348] Ibid., 186.

[349] Stephens, *Zwingli*, 14–15; Robert Walton, *Zwingli's Theocracy* (Toronto:

of [Zwingli's] humanist conceptions of doctrine and Church was extensive, and Zwingli used his wide range of personal connections with leading theologians and humanists in his evangelism to the European courts.'[350] Humanist scholars understood religion as a matter of public law over which the emergent state had some jurisdiction. Although Tyndale's *Obedience of a Christian Man* (1528), for instance, drew upon Luther's responses to the tumults of the mid-1520s, the theological model for a theocratic state was rather better expounded in Zürich.[351]

Humanism and Zwinglianism shared some essential traits but Irena Backus has shown that it was Bullinger who first established the link between humanist scholarship and Reformation. In his unpublished *Von warer under falscher leer* [*Of true and false teaching*] (1527) he attributed the revival of patristic studies and the revision of biblical texts to humanist endeavours in ancient languages and emergent literary criticism.[352] Bullinger, following Philip Melanchthon, encouraged the study of *bonae litterae* for 'their value in helping to interpret and understand sacred letters.'[353] Intensive engagement with classical scholarship constituted ideal preparation for biblical exegesis and Bullinger was able to maintain humanist methodology even after the 'theological and ecclesiological parting of the ways

---

University of Toronto Press, 1967), 24, 220–21. See also Alister McGrath, "Humanist Elements in the Early Reformed Doctrine of Justification," *ARG* 73 (1982): 7–10.

[350] Bruce Gordon, "Zurich and the Scottish Reformation: Rudolf Gwalther's *Homilies on Galatians* of 1576," in *Humanism and Reform: the Church in Europe, England, and Scotland, 1400–1643*, ed. J. Kirk (Oxford: Blackwell, 1991), 207.

[351] Rex, "English Humanists," 37.

[352] Irena Backus, "Bullinger and Humanism," in *Heinrich Bullinger: Life—Thought—Influence: International Congress Heinrich Bullinger 2004*, 2 vols. (Zurich: TVZ, 2007), 2:641.

[353] Bullinger, *Studiorum ratio* (1527/28), quoted in Ibid., 649. On Melanchthon, see Charlotte Methuen, *Kepler's Tübingen: stimulus to a theological mathematics* (Aldershot: Ashgate, 1998), 34–35, 96–97.

between Erasmus and the Reformation' in the mid-1520s.[354] Most educated Englishmen were steeped in humanist principles by this time.[355] Evangelical converts with a humanist training would have found the Reformed brand of evangelicalism congenial but humanism was not sufficient in itself to produce a theologically-Reformed evangelical.

Reformed Evangelicalism, 1547–55

There is strong scholarly consensus about the predominantly Reformed nature of the Church under King Edward VI and the evangelicalism of those who suffered under Mary Tudor.[356] Following Luther's death in 1546, the defeat of the Schmalkaldic League at Mühlberg in 1547 threw Germany, and with it Lutheran influence on England, into disarray. Bucer's Strassburg (a part of the Empire) also experienced turmoil. The Reformation's centre shifted decidedly into the Alps where the *Consensus Tigurinus* (1549) established working stability between Zürich and Geneva in spite of the hostility of Basle and Bern.[357] As MacCulloch observes, 'the consolidation of this Reformed identity came just at the time when

---

[354] Peter Opitz, "Bullinger and Paul," in *A Companion to Paul in the Reformation*, ed. R. Holder (Leiden and Boston: Brill, 2009), 244–45.

[355] McConica, *Humanists*; Maria Dowling, *Humanism in the Age of Henry VIII* (London: Croom Helm, 1986); Frederic Seebohm, *The Oxford Reformers: John Colet, Erasmus, and Thomas More*, 3rd ed. (London: Longmans, Green & Co., 1911). See the critique of Seebohm in Daniell, *Tyndale*, 32–37.

[356] Diarmaid MacCulloch, *Tudor Church Militant: Edward VI and the Protestant Reformation* (London: Allen Lane, 1999), 167–74; Ryrie, *Gospel*, 248; Catherine Davies, *A Religion of the Word: the defence of the Reformation in the reign of Edward VI* (Manchester: Manchester University Press, 2002), 18; Philip Benedict, *Christ's Churches Purely Reformed: a social history of Calvinism* (New Haven & London: YUP, 2002), 235; McConica, *Humanists*, 250; Roland Bainton, *The Age of the Reformation* (Princeton: Van Nostrand, 1956), 57.

[357] Lyndal Roper, *Martin Luther: renegade and prophet* (London: Penguin, 2016), 406–11; Euan Cameron, *The European Reformation* (Oxford: OUP, 1991), 346–49; Heal, *Reformation*, 330; Gordon, *Swiss Reformation*, 176, 179.

[. . .] Thomas Cranmer and the English evangelical leadership had also consciously moved out of step with Lutheranism in their eucharistic thought.'[358]

The Edwardian establishment embraced the Reformed identity and welcomed the continental exiles who arrived ready to assist godly Reformation. Among them were the Reformed theologians Bucer and Peter Martyr Vermigli who were given strategic university chairs. Martyr attracted most of the visiting Swiss students to Oxford, recalling the earlier exchange,[359] and with Bernardino Ochino, Jan Łaski, Martin Micron, and Jan Utenhove, he helped to mediate Zürich theology.[360] When Queen Jane was deposed by the Lady Mary in 1553 it was to the Reformed cities that most exiles migrated.[361]

Dramatically unequalled by the Henrician or Elizabethan Reformations, Edward's Reformation was 'a revolutionary act, a dynamic assault on the past, a struggle to the death between Christ and Antichrist.' It was also a recasting of national culture, explains MacCulloch, 'a movement of hope and moral fervour.'[362] The Zürich model, with its strong social dimension, had much to offer the Edwardian programme by way of appropriating biblical narratives and typology. In imitation of the Old Testament kings of Israel, ecclesiastical authority in Zürich was vested in the secular magistrate, aided by a 'prophet,' the *Antistes*. The magistrate was obliged

---

[358] MacCulloch, *Militant*, 169–70.

[359] MacCulloch, "Bullinger," 913; Claire Cross, "Continental Students and the Protestant Reformation in England in the Sixteenth Century," in *Reform and Reformation: England and the Continent c.1500–c.1750*, ed. D. Baker (Oxford: Blackwell, 1979), 35–46.

[360] Ian Hazlett, "Calvin and the British Isles," in *The Calvin Handbook*, ed. H. Selderhuis (Grand Rapids and Cambridge: Eerdmans, 2009), 119; Gottfried Locher, *Zwingli's Thought: New Perspectives* (Leiden: Brill, 1981), 71; Gordon, *Swiss Reformation*, 302.

[361] Garrett, *Marian Exiles*, 8–10. On Jane Grey see Eric Ives, *Lady Jane Grey: a Tudor mystery* (Oxford: Wiley-Blackwell, 2009).

[362] MacCulloch, *Militant*, 9–11, 126.

to lead the people into godly religion.[363] According to Gordon, 'this historical creation proved highly exportable and an attractive advertisement for the Swiss model of reform, especially in England under Edward VI.'[364] The potential for partnership between Reformed religion and the Royal Supremacy was obvious and most warmly enunciated by Edward himself:

> To the honourable and valiant Lords of Zurich, our right entirely beloved friends, [. . .] we [. . .] regard you with especial esteem, and exceedingly value your friendship [. . .] there is also a mutual agreement between us concerning the christian religion and true godliness, which ought to render this friendship of ours, by God's blessing, yet more intimate. We therefore return you our warmest thanks for your singular and favourable disposition towards us, which you shall always find to be reciprocal on our part, whenever an opportunity shall present itself.[365]

Cranmer seemed similarly well-disposed: Hooper reported to Bullinger in 1551 that the archbishop

> could hardly refrain from tears, when he understood your feelings in regard to the king and to the kingdom, and also the perseverance of your church in these most lamentable times. He made most honourable mention both of yourself

---

[363] Stephens, *Zwingli*, 126–30.

[364] Bruce Gordon, "The Changing Face of Protestant History and Identity in the Sixteenth Century," in *Protestant History and Identity in Sixteenth-Century Europe*, ed. B. Gordon, Vol. 1 (Aldershot: Ashgate, 1996), 6.

[365] Edward VI to the Zürich Senate, 20 October 1549, *OL*, 1. Hooper presented a copy of Bullinger's commentary on the book of Kings to Edward on Ascension Day 1550: Alison Dalton, "John Hooper and His Networks: a study of change in Reformation England," DPhil diss. (University of Oxford, 2008), 58. He reported the king's continuing good-will to Bullinger on 27 October 1551, *OL*, 96.

and of your profound erudition. [. . .] I know of a truth that he loves you from his heart.³⁶⁶

The godly examples of David, Solomon, Josiah and Hezekiah, adopted by Henry VIII and celebrated by Reformed apologists, were impressed upon the young sovereign by many. Calvin dedicated his Isaiah lectures to Edward in 1550 citing the model of Hezekiah.³⁶⁷ Dowling's contention that 'Edward was not brought up as a godly young Josias, but after the renaissance model of a Christian prince' is unequal to the evidence.³⁶⁸ In a Court sermon on 5 April 1549, Latimer advised Edward to imitate Josiah who had 'reformed his father's ways who walked in idolatry.'³⁶⁹ The tutors around the king had significant responsibility for his theological precocity, which made him at times more determined than his councillors, as when he refused to tolerate his sister Mary's conservatism.³⁷⁰ John Cheke's unambiguously Reformed nephew Jean Belmaine was Edward's French tutor from 1544. He took the opportunity to encourage the king in his opinions: Edward translated from French the first book of Calvin's *Institutes* as a gift to his royal father.³⁷¹ It is curious therefore

---

³⁶⁶ Hooper to Bullinger, 1 August 1551, *OL*, 93.

³⁶⁷ Hazlett, "Calvin and the British Isles," 120–21. Hazlett advises against underestimating Calvin's influence in England relative to other continental reformers. Meanwhile Pettegree argues for the limited influence of Calvin in England relative to the influence of Zürich: Pettegree, *Foreign Protestant Communities*, 72–73.

³⁶⁸ Dowling, *Humanism*, 214; cf. Murdock, "Josiah," 1048–49; Aston, *Iconoclasts*, 247–50; Eamon Duffy, *The Stripping of the Altars: Traditional Religion in England c.1400–c.1580* (New Haven & London: YUP, 1992), 448.

³⁶⁹ Hugh Latimer, *Sermons of Hugh Latimer*, ed. G. Corrie, PS (Cambridge: CUP, 1844), 175; see also John Hooper, *An answer vnto my lord of Wynthesters booke intytlyd a detection of the deuyls sophistrye wherwith he robith the vnlernyd people of the trew byleef in the moost blessyd sacrament of the aulter* (Zurich: Augustyne Fries, 1547; RSTC 13741), Q2r.

³⁷⁰ Burnet, *Reformation*, ii/1:227; David Loades, *The Reign of King Edward VI* (Bangor: Headstart History, 1994), 17.

³⁷¹ William Jones, "Uses of Foreigners in the Church of Edward VI," *Numen*

that Loach refuses to accept 'any deep or informed interest in Protestant theology' in Edward.[372] By contrast W. K. Jordan recognises that Edward was an 'advanced Protestant [. . .] genuinely and deeply pious' even while emphasising his concern for the Supremacy.[373]

There was undoubtedly relief among Edward's evangelical subjects that previously concealed views could be openly expressed:[374] take Latimer's exhortation above, for example, or the guarded opinions of Cheke in his preface to his Latin translation of Plutarch's *De Superstitione* (1545/46) compared with his later candour before his royal pupil.[375] John King highlights the 'unprecedented degree of religious toleration and freedom of speech, reading, and publication' under Protector Somerset which allowed vast numbers of Reformed books and tracts to be printed.[376] Of course the evangelical clique exercising power still upheld obedience to the Supremacy, as exemplified by the Vestments Controversy. Obedience, Somerset told the Essex rebels in 1549, remained 'the principal lesson of Scripture to subjects.'[377] Yet Edward's government countenanced aggressive reform on a biblical scale. Evangelicals who had trodden the boundaries of Henrician orthodoxy might now count on tacit approval if not outright support.[378]

---

6 (1959): 143; Gordon Kipling, "Belmaine, Jean (fl.1546–1559)," *ODNB* (Oxford: OUP, 2004).

[372] Jennifer Loach, *Edward VI* (New Haven & London: YUP, 1999), 135, 158.

[373] W. K. Jordan, ed., *The Chronicle and Political Papers of Edward VI* (London: George Allen and Unwin, 1966), xxii.

[374] W. K. Jordan, *Edward VI: the Young King* (London: George Allen & Unwin, 1968), 68; Dale Hoak, *The King's Council in the Reign of Edward VI* (Cambridge: CUP, 1976), 180; C. M. Dent, *Protestant Reformers in Elizabethan Oxford* (Oxford: OUP, 1983), 4.

[375] John McDiarmid, "John Cheke's Preface to *De Superstitione*," *JEH* 48, 1 (1997): 118–20.

[376] John King, *English Reformation Literature: The Tudor Origins of the Protestant Tradition* (Princeton: Princeton University Press, 1982), 26, 84–86.

[377] Quoted in MacCulloch, *Militant*, 122.

[378] Foreign threats undoubtedly contributed to official moderation: see Hoak, *King's Council*, 174–77.

The brokering of the *Consensus Tigurinus* by Bullinger and Calvin in 1549 was pivotal for the direction of English sacramental theology.[379] Official pronouncements on the Eucharist were avoided in 1547–48 pending the Swiss decision and Cranmer kept quiet his personal conversion to a spiritual presence.[380] Although he was seen as a disciple of Bucer by the Zürichers, Cranmer had moved beyond Bucer towards Bullinger's position.[381] 'Once the agreement was achieved,' writes MacCulloch, 'tensions relaxed' and the Swiss Reformation became the basic working model of English evangelical aspirations.[382]

Amongst the abolition of chantries and images and the foundations of schools and hospitals which constituted the social revolution of these years, one aspect of reform deserves particular attention for its contribution to a Reformed identity: the Bible was placed at the centre of communal life to a degree unprecedented in England. Although Cromwell had attempted to make the Bible available in every parish through the Injunctions of 1536,[383] in July 1547 the Edwardian regime commanded open access in churches both to the Bible and to Erasmus's *Paraphrases*, suggesting that interpretative engagement with Scripture was crucial to the Christian life. In a further revival of Cromwell's programme there were to be sermons 'every quarter of the year at the least wherein they shall purely and sincerely declare the word of God.'[384] The official homily exhorting Bible reading, with a loaded marginal reference to Psalm 1, concluded:

> Let vs heare, reade, and knowe, these holy rules, iniunccions, and statutes of our christian religion [. . .]. Lette vs with feare,

---

[379] The *Consensus* was published in England in 1552 as an appendix to Jan Łaski and John Calvin, *Breuis et dilucida de sacramentis ecclesiae Christi tractatio* (London: Stephanum Myerdmannum, 1552; RSTC 15259).
[380] MacCulloch, *Cranmer*, 378–79.
[381] Ibid., 380–83, 391–92.
[382] MacCulloch, *Militant*, 170–74.
[383] MacCulloch, *Cranmer*, 166.
[384] *TRP*, i. #287.

and reuerence laie vp (in the cheste of our hartes) these necessarie and fruitfull lessons. Lette vs night and daie muse, and haue meditacion, and contemplacion in theim. Lette vs ruminate, and (as it wer) chewe the cudde [. . .]. Let vs praie to God, (the onely aucthor of these heauenly meditacions) that we maie speake, thynke, beleue, liue, and depart hence, accordyng to the wholesome doctrine, and verities of theim.[385]

This emphasis allowed the reformers to reorganise national culture around the dual authorities of Scripture and Supremacy.[386] While the Supremacy maintained order as it had done under the first Supreme Head, now Scripture was deployed in the quest for a godly society. The people were given a new history and identity, modelled by Zürich and drawing inspiration from the word of God. English writers were concerned, explains Gordon, 'to employ myths and historical memories to construct a literary vision of national identity' as God's elect nation.[387]

Reformed theology was prevalent in England at the highest levels under Edward VI, culminating in a Reformed liturgy in 1552 and the Forty-Two Articles of Religion in 1553. The English leadership clearly valued the relationship with Zürich and drew inspiration from it in these projects. While Reformed convictions did not become dominant in English evangelicalism until Edward's reign there is good reason to believe they had substantial influence and support much earlier in spite of Henry VIII. A minority had access to Swiss ideas in the 1520s and this number undoubtedly grew throughout the 1530s. By the 1540s a relatively large, if cautious, number of Reformed believers can be posited amongst English evangelicals. They emerged in force under Edward.

---

[385] Cranmer, *Homelies*, B4r-v.
[386] Robert Wainwright, "I believe in the English Reformation," *Faith and Worship*, 85, Trinity (2019): 38–53.
[387] Gordon, "Changing Face," 6, 19.

3

Swiss Concepts of Covenant

It is as if Zwingli were our Josiah sent from God, through whom also the idols have been exterminated, the 'Deuteronomy' found, and the covenant which we have with God brought forward again. —Heinrich Bullinger (1527)[1]

For Heinrich Bullinger a new appreciation for the covenantal pattern of relationship with God was a breakthrough of no less importance than Martin Luther's insistence that justification comes by faith alone. Like King Josiah's reformation of Judah in the seventh century b.c., the covenant had once again been rediscovered, this time by Huldrych Zwingli in sixteenth-century Zürich. Zwingli wrote that God 'had determined to recall and renew those teachings in our day by a sort of second revelation.'[2] It was a breakthrough of enormous significance for Reformed theology in the Swiss Confederation and beyond. Among the many Swiss exports to England during the Reformation, which included ideas about worship, political theory, and social policy, the concept of covenant was arguably the most theologically significant. It provided the intellectual basis for Swiss theological influence generally. A careful reading of the

---

[1] Heinrich Bullinger, 14 May 1527, quoted in Lillback, *Binding of God*, 98.
[2] Huldrych Zwingli, *Petition of Certain Preachers of Switzerland to the Most Reverend Lord Hugo, Bishop of Constance* [2 July 1522], *LWHZ*, 1:151.

early Swiss reformers reveals the importance of covenant theology to them, in short because it was closely bound to their core principle of *sola scriptura*. The nature of the Swiss concept of covenant can be established from three representative figures: Zwingli, Bullinger, and John Calvin.[3]

Huldrych Zwingli

Zwingli was never a monk. Whereas Luther entered a cloister in his tortured search for the *acceptatio Dei*, Zwingli remained in the world. While Luther's theological quest was primarily personal, Zwingli's theology emphasised social and political application.[4] In the 1510s his interest in reform was characteristic of emergent Swiss humanism. Alister McGrath writes that, unlike Erasmus, Swiss

---

[3] Johannes Œcolampadius developed a similar formula of a bilateral and conditional covenant in his lectures on Isaiah in 1523–24, probably in Zwingli's wake. The presence of the concept is significant for English evangelical theology considering how often his publications, including his commentary on Isaiah (1525), appear in lists of prohibited books. See John Fines, ed., *A Biographical Register of Early English Protestants and Others Opposed to the Roman Catholic Church, 1525–1558*, Vol. 1 (Abingdon: Sutton Courtenay Press, 1981), unpaginated. Œcolampadius' contribution to early Reformed covenant theology should not be underestimated—the evidence is simply more limited than for Zwingli and Bullinger. See Leonard Trinterud, "The Origins of Puritanism," *CH* 20, 1 (1951): 41; E. G. Rupp, *Patterns of Reformation* (London: Epworth Press, 1969), esp. 26–27; Peter Lillback, *The Binding of God: Calvin's Role in the Development of Covenant Theology* (Grand Rapids, MI: Baker Academic, 2001), 83–87; Peter Opitz, "The Exegetical and Hermeneutical Work of John Oecolampadius, Huldrych Zwingli and John Calvin," in *Hebrew Bible/Old Testament: the history of its interpretation*, ed. M. Sæbo, 3 vols. (Göttingen: Vandenhoeck & Ruprecht, 2008), 2:411–12; Andrew Woolsey, *Unity and Continuity in Covenantal Thought: A Study of the Reformed Tradition to the Westminster Assembly* (Grand Rapids, MI: Reformation Heritage Books, 2012), 210–14.

[4] Heiko Oberman, *Luther: Man between God and the Devil* (New Haven & London: YUP, 1989), 128; Bernhard Lohse, *Martin Luther's Theology: its historical and systematic development*, trans. R. Harrisville (Edinburgh: T&T Clark, 1999), 33–34.

humanists 'were not concerned with the creation of a cosmopolitan republic of letters, but with establishing the literary and cultural identity of the Swiss nation at a time of political uncertainty.'[5] As an army chaplain in the Franco-Italian Wars Zwingli resented the way Swiss mercenaries 'ran upon drawn swords, devoured blades, and incurred all sort of dangers to enrich' foreign powers, and in 1515 he witnessed for himself the disastrous bloodshed of Marignano.[6] After that his public ministry continued in the popular pilgrimage centre of Einsiedeln until he took up the post of *Leutpriester* (people's priest) in Zürich in 1519. That year he narrowly survived an outbreak of the plague, having remained in the city to fulfil his duties.

Zwingli's practical ministry experience and political consciousness helped to shape his pastoral priorities. His preaching focussed primarily, not on the value of works for salvation, but on the immediate problem of idolatry. He lamented the consequences of rapacious Swiss mercenary service, the ceremonies that had displaced true worship, and the venerated images that had usurped the 'true images of God,' that is, the poor. He recognised, too, from personal experience, the idolatry of lust and unchaste behaviour.[7] Zwingli's diagnosis of the human condition revealed present, as well as eschatological, condemnation. By denying their true allegiance to Christ, Swiss troops received the wages of sin and provoked divine retribution. False worship was no less pathogenic. The wounds of Christendom could only be healed by the grace of God.[8]

Recognition of idolatry, false worship, and disloyalty to God led Zwingli to present his theology in terms of broken relationship and

---

[5] Alister McGrath, *The Intellectual Origins of the European Reformation* (Oxford: Basil Blackwell, 1987), 46.

[6] Huldrych Zwingli, *The Fable of the Ox* [1510], *LWHZ*, 1:29.

[7] Robert Walton, *Zwingli's Theocracy* (Toronto: University of Toronto Press, 1967), 32–36; Lee Wandel, *Always among us: images of the poor in Zwingli's Zurich* (Cambridge: CUP, 1990), 59–71; W. P. Stephens, *Zwingli: an introduction to his thought* (Oxford: OUP, 1992), 13–16, 68.

[8] Huldrych Zwingli, *Commentary on True and False Religion* [March 1525], *LWHZ*, 3:49, 132; see Walton, *Zwingli's Theocracy*, 26–28.

accomplished reconciliation to God's lordship. God's sovereignty, or glory and honour, was the consistent conviction colouring all of his thought.[9] Humanity's salvation was proximate to this theocentrism: what God had done in the Gospel of Christ for his covenant people. Salvation was conceived as the restoration of a communal life of true worship under God's law. On 2 July 1522 he explained this aim in a letter to Bishop Hugo of Constance:

> We are aware that our life differs all too widely from the pattern of the Gospel, but is the Gospel on that account to be abolished and done away with? Ought we not rather to devote ourselves vigorously to correcting our faults according to its standard and to subduing our feebleness, since it is the one thing, could we only believe it, from the inspiration of which salvation will come to us, according to the command of Christ when he sent forth his Apostles to preach the Gospel.[10]

The themes of sovereignty and worship, loyalty and disloyalty, law and service, were harmonised in Zwingli's concept of covenant, which he made explicit in the letter:

> Since therefore, as we have said, God, as of old he used to warn Israel time and again by the mouth of his prophets, now deigns in our day to illumine us with his Gospel, in order to renew his covenant which cannot be annulled, we have thought that this opportunity ought by no means to be neglected, nay, that we ought to strive with unremitting effort that as many as possible may share in the glory of this salvation.[11]

[9] W. P. Stephens, "Huldrych Zwingli: the Swiss Reformer," *SJT* 41, 1 (1988): 31. For the chief characteristics of Zwinglianism see Gottfried Locher, *Zwingli's Thought: New Perspectives* (Leiden: Brill, 1981), 342.
[10] Zwingli, *Petition to Hugo, Bishop of Constance, LWHZ*, 1:154.
[11] Ibid.

This was not abstract theology but the basis of a very practical reform agenda. In his letter to the bishop it undergirded a petition to permit clerical marriage. Nevertheless it is apparent that by 1522 Zwingli already perceived the unity of the Old and New Testaments and understood the Christian Gospel as a renewal of God's ancient covenant with Israel.[12] In his answer that summer to the bishop's admonition the Gospel was 'the glad tidings of God's grace' and referred directly to 'the covenant [*commercium*] which God in his grace had entered into with the miserable race of man.'[13]

Zwingli's agenda was clearly indebted both to Erasmus personally and to humanist christocentrism and biblical exegesis, although his evangelicalism soon progressed in a distinctively Reformed direction.[14] The precise intellectual origins of his covenant theology are unclear. If McGrath is correct to see humanism rather than any particular form of scholasticism shaping Zwingli's reform programme then it may simply have arisen out of his own study of Scripture. His affinities with the *via antiqua* at Basle in 1502–6 do not seem to have been influential in this respect. On the other hand, as a student at Vienna in 1498–1502 Zwingli would not only have encountered humanist ideas but also the *via moderna* for which Vienna had been known for a century.[15] Although we cannot point to evidence of a direct link, it seems unlikely that Zwingli would have reproduced many of the key features of late medieval covenant theology if he had not encountered them during his own education. This, rather than the Anabaptist controversy, encouraged and equipped his reading of

---

[12] This is in agreement with Robert Walton who locates the origin of Zwingli's concept in the years 1519–22: Walton, *Zwingli's Theocracy*, 36.

[13] Huldrych Zwingli, *Defence called Archeteles, in which answer is made to an admonition that the Most Reverend Lord Bishop of Constance…sent to the Council of the Great Minster at Zurich called the Chapter* [22–23 August 1522], *LWHZ*, 1:249; *CR*, 88:293.

[14] Berndt Hamm, *The Reformation of Faith in the Context of Late Medieval Theology and Piety*, trans. H. Heron, G. Wiedermann and J. Frymire (Leiden & Boston: Brill, 2004), 13; McGrath, *Intellectual Origins*, 44–52.

[15] McGrath, *Intellectual Origins*, 46, 88–90.

Scripture in covenantal terms.[16] It was not sermons and disputations but a life lived in the service of God that mattered.[17]

The concept of covenant underlay Zwingli's exposition of the articles that he had presented at the First Zürich Disputation on 29 January 1523.[18] The city council wanted to judge competing theological positions against the standard of Scripture and came out in support of evangelical preaching *sola scriptura*. Since its foremost concern was political stability it must have found Zwingli's identification of the contemporary covenant community in terms of King David's lineage appealing. He explained that 'God promises to enter an eternal covenant with us, the sure and faithful heirs of David. Earlier everyone understood this covenant to have been made and

---

[16] Scholars have often concentrated on the relationship between Zwingli's concept and the Anabaptist controversy. Many incorrectly suppose that it was formed in reaction against the Anabaptists, e.g., Gottlob Schrenk, *Gottesreich und Bund im glteren Protestantismus vornehmlich bei Johannes Cocceius* (Gütersloh: Bertelsmann, 1923), 36–37; G. W. Bromiley, *Baptism and the Anglican Reformers* (London: Lutterworth Press, 1953), 38; Robert Letham, "The Foedus Operum: some factors accounting for its development," SCJ 14, 4 (1983): 460; McGiffert, "Grace and Works," 469; J. F. Gerhard Goeters, "Föderaltheologie," in *Theologische Realenzyklopädie*, eds. H. Balz et al. (Berlin & New York: Walter de Gruyter, 1983), 246. Some even claim that Zwingli employed it only in defence of infant baptism, e.g., Jens Møller, "The Beginnings of Puritan Covenant Theology," *JEH* 14 (1963): 47; David Weir, *The Origins of the Federal Theology in Sixteenth-Century Reformation Thought* (Oxford: OUP, 1990), 10; David Steinmetz, *Reformers in the Wings: from Geiler von Kayserberg to Theodore Beza*, 2nd ed. (Oxford: OUP, 2001), 95. In fact Zwingli's concept had emerged by 1522. Similarly Œcolampadius had linked baptism with covenantal initiation in 1523, prior to the Anabaptist controversy of 1525–30: Lillback, *Binding of God*, 83.

[17] Zwingli, *Erläuterungen zur Genesis* [March 1527], *CR*, 100:101.

[18] On the so-called 'First Zürich Disputation' see Huldrych Zwingli, *The Acts of the First Zurich Disputation*, in *Selected Works of Huldreich Zwingli*, ed. S.M. Jackson (Philadelphia: University of Pennsylvania, 1901), 40–117; Heiko Oberman, *Masters of the Reformation: the emergence of a new intellectual climate in Europe*, trans. D. Martin (Cambridge: CUP, 1981), 213–36; Bruce Gordon, *The Swiss Reformation* (Manchester & New York: Manchester University Press, 2002), 57–61.

grounded in the blood of Christ who is an eternal God; hence, the covenant, too, is eternal.'[19] The Davidic covenant had particularly political resonance and, as an expression of Christ's eternal covenant, could be presented as the ongoing basis for a civic community to relate to God. This meant that it had significant political capital quite apart from its later utility in competition with the Anabaptists between 1525 and 1530.

Particular discussion of the eternal covenant appeared under Zwingli's eighteenth article. Here he wrote that '*testamentum, pactum* and *foedus* are often used interchangeably in Scripture. But *testamentum* is used most often. We therefore refer to it here.' He explained that *testamentum* 'means "legacy" [*erbgmächt*], but it is also used to mean "agreement" [*verstand*] or "covenant" [*pundt*], the latter of which one usually makes between two people for the sake of peace.'[20] *Erbgmächt* implies a long-established inheritance. It was a Swiss legal term denoting a conditional variety of last will and testament, distinct from Roman Law, wherein the beneficiary was obliged to demonstrate his fulfilment of the testator's requirements.[21] This interpretation of *testamentum* allowed Zwingli to establish the reciprocal operation of the legacy unilaterally initiated by God. He assigned primacy to this bilateral sense of the term, the opposite of Luther's unilateral definition of *bund/pundt*. Zwingli did not, however, exclude the unilateral sense altogether since

> where there is a testament it can be executed only after the death of him who made it [. . .]. Therefore Luke calls the blood of Christ not only "the blood of the testament" [*das blůt des testamentes*] but rather "testament" [*das testament selbs*, 'the testament itself'] in the following words, "This drink (I thus translate [*tütsch*, German] 'poterion'), is the new

[19] Zwingli, *Exposition of the Articles*, HZW, 1:124.
[20] Zwingli, *Exposition of the Articles*, HZW, 1:106; CR, 89:131.
[21] See Hagen, "From Testament to Covenant in the Early Sixteenth Century," *SCJ* 3, 1 (1972): 16–17.

testament [*testament*] or covenant [*pündtnus*, alliance] in my blood which is poured out for you." These words bring to our attention that the New Testament is confirmed [*gevestet*] by the blood of Christ.²²

The unilateral was thus subordinate to the bilateral meaning. Zwingli undoubtedly assigned priority to a bilateral pact

> which one makes between two people for the sake of peace. In this sense one speaks of the Old or the New Testament, that is: the covenant [*pundt*], agreement [*verstand*] and commitment [*pflicht*] which God has entered in with the patriarchs and which in Christ he entered in with the whole world.²³

The Old and New Testaments were united under the essential category of covenant between two parties, God and humanity.²⁴ 'In Zwingli's eyes,' writes Gordon, 'the people of Zurich were a wayward folk constantly attracted to idols and easily forgot God's demand to serve and worship him in purity. They were the Israelites. As with the ancient people of the covenant, God punished but never abandoned.'²⁵

---

²² Zwingli, *Exposition of the Articles*, 107; *CR*, 89:132. I have modified the English translation to accord with the German in this and the following quotations from the *Exposition*.

²³ Zwingli, *Exposition of the Articles*, 106; *CR*, 89:131; see also Hagen, "Testament to Covenant," 17–20. Woolsey rightly disputes Hagen's claim that Zwingli contrasted the Testaments and recognises the bilateral dimension of Zwingli's discussion of testament: Woolsey, *Unity and Continuity*, 219–20.

²⁴ Zwingli had previously recognised covenantal continuity between the Testaments in his *Supplication to Hugo, bishop of Constance* (2 July 1522), cited in Lillback, *Binding of God*, 82.

²⁵ Bruce Gordon with Luca Baschera and Christian Moser, "Emulating the Past and Creating the Present: Reformation and the Use of Historical and Theological Models in Zurich in the Sixteenth Century," in *Following Zwingli: Applying the Past in Reformation Zurich*, eds. L. Baschera, B. Gordon

Zwingli clearly appreciated the biblical pattern of covenant making. Whenever an 'agreement [*verstand*] was reached in the Old Testament between God and the friends of God, it was customary to strengthen the same through blood and sacrifice.'[26] The same types were repeated in the New Testament:

> For when God made a covenant [*pundt*] and legacy [*erbgemächt*] with the people of Israel and their descendants, that is: a testament [*testament*], death and bloodshed were involved—but of dumb animals only, as stated earlier. But when Christ made his testament [*testament*] with humankind, an alliance [*verpüntnus*] and legacy [*erbgemächt*] which would last unto all eternity, he did not sacrifice by killing animals but by offering himself.[27]

The language of testamental execution and covenantal ratification were interwoven: Christ's death 'executes' the testament; 'strengthens' his legacy; constitutes a covenantal 'seal and sign'; 'confirms' the New Testament; 'affirms' the testament and is 'a seal of that which has been agreed once.'[28]

Zwingli's location of the believer's righteousness in Christ emphasised the centrality of Christ's fulfilment of covenantal obligations on humanity's behalf without undermining the basic reciprocity of the agreement. Zwingli understood believers to be reputed righteous by virtue of their union with Christ. That is, Christ is apprehended as 'our perfection before God'; the believer's justifying righteousness is extrinsic.[29] However in his sermon *On Divine and Human Righteousness* (July 1523) Zwingli could state that, by grace, guaranteed by Christ, the believer 'is made righteous

---

and C. Moser (Farnham: Ashgate, 2014), 6.

[26] Zwingli, *Exposition of the Articles*, 106.

[27] Ibid.; *CR*, 89:131.

[28] Zwingli, *Exposition of the Articles*, 107.

[29] Ibid., 25; see also Zwingli, *True and False Religion*, 118, 148.

through faith.'³⁰ The appearance of imputation and impartation can be reconciled by appreciating the reputation of the believer who both possesses and is possessed by Christ.³¹ Christ was so central to humanity's fulfilment of the covenant in redemption that Zwingli identified the two parties with one another. In his *Commentary on True and False Religion* (March 1525) Christ 'is our propitiation, therefore also our covenant and testament, which God has made with us.'³² The medieval requirement of *fides caritate formata* is overtaken here by a notion of *fides Christo formata* as Christ acts on behalf of the believer to fulfil the conditions of the covenant.

Zwingli's *Subsidiary Essay*, a eucharistic treatise of August 1525 directed against Erasmian conservatives, again treated of the covenant. In it Zwingli explained that Christ's testament was 'an agreement [*conditio*] promised by God' similar to the Abrahamic 'compact [*pactum*] or covenant [*foedus*]' in Genesis 17. The Abrahamic covenant was a relationship 'thought worthy by God in his grace to enter into.' It had clearly specified terms, 'and these terms [*conditiones*] are the real covenant [*foedus*] itself,' thereby emphasising the imposition of reciprocal conditions. All but one of the terms dealt with God's commitment to be the God of Abraham, to bless him and his descendants. The only condition placed upon Abraham was 'you will walk before me most uprightly,' which Zwingli explained to mean worship and faithfulness.³³

---

[30] Huldrych Zwingli, *Divine and Human Righteousness* [July 1523], *HZW*, 2:12.

[31] Ibid., 2:12–13; see also W. P. Stephens, *The Theology of Huldrych Zwingli* (Oxford: OUP, 1986), 159–60; Alister McGrath, "Humanist Elements in the Early Reformed Doctrine of Justification," *ARG* 73 (1982): 10, 18–19.

[32] Zwingli, *True and False Religion*, 72; see Hagen, "Testament to Covenant," 17.

[33] Huldrych Zwingli, *Subsidiary Essay, or Crown of the Work on the Eucharist* [August 1525], *HZW*, 2:223; *CR*, 91:499. It is hard to accept Wayne Baker's view that Zwingli failed to affirm clearly mutual responsibilities and did not hold faith to be a condition. See Baker, *Other Reformed Tradition*, 16; J. Wayne Baker and Charles McCoy, *Fountainhead of Federalism: Heinrich Bullinger*

Zwingli moved seamlessly to discussion of Christ's covenant as the solution to the lasting problem presented by the Abrahamic covenant. He warned that 'the covenant which was struck with Abraham is so strong and valid that unless you keep it you will not be faithful.' That is, if Zwingli's Christian contemporaries could not claim that 'the Lord is your God and you are worshipper of him only [. . .] you have no reason to boast that you are faithful.'[34] Herein Zwingli's understanding of justifying faith in the context of a lifestyle of true worship can be appreciated.

Having depicted humanity as defaulting on its covenantal commitments so as to sunder relationship with God, Zwingli presented Christ as the restitution provided on humanity's behalf by God himself in accordance with his promise of restoration to Adam: 'he gives himself freely to you and casts himself into death for you by which he might reconcile you to himself.' Thus Christ himself discharges mankind's penalty for violating the conditions. The Abrahamic terms of relationship with God were then replaced, because

> when Christ, slain for us, appeased the divine justice and became the only approach to God, God entered into a new covenant with the human race [. . .]. This new covenant or testament, then, is the free remission of sins which God has bountifully granted us through his Son. They, therefore, that trust in God through Christ and lead their own to this trust [. . .] are themselves circumcised, just as Abraham and his seed were circumcised, but with the circumcision of Christ, which is baptism, Colossians 2:11.[35]

---

and the Covenantal Tradition (Louisville, KY: Westminster John Knox Press, 1991), 21.

[34] Zwingli, *Subsidiary Essay*, 224. The problem of unfaithfulness was framed as self-love in Huldrych Zwingli, *An Account of the Faith of Huldreich Zwingli submitted to the German Emperor Charles V, at the Diet of Augsburg. 3 July 1530*, LWHZ, 2:40.

[35] Zwingli, *Subsidiary Essay*, 224.

Here, Zwingli sets out the substantial continuity of the covenant between Abraham and Christ.[36] He also makes the point that God's covenantal promises are fulfilled in Christ.

In 1526 Zwingli responded to concerns that he held 'an unusual doctrine with regard to the pollution of human descent' with his address *On Original Sin*. The covenant model is clarified in the second part of the treatise, which explores the consequences of original sin. The covenant constitutes, in a discussion of Genesis 17, a climactic summary of the argument: 'For between those whose God He is and Himself there is established a friendship; if there is established a friendship, no damnation because of the condition of birth can intervene.'[37] Zwingli equates God's covenantal relationships established with Abraham and with Christians, causing his readers to apprehend his whole discourse on original sin in covenantal terms: Adam's legal guilt; his descendants' propensity to idolatry; the consequences of enmity of God; God's faithful promise of reconciliation by satisfying the demands of his righteousness; and the sacraments attached to the agreement.[38]

It might be objected that the covenant was not discussed explicitly throughout Zwingli's treatise. David Steinmetz, for instance, calls it 'incidental'.[39] Bullinger, however, believed that, through Zwingli, God was setting forth 'in a clear way, as no one has done for a thousand years, the chief point of his religion, as the whole essence and fundamental knowledge of God, namely, the understanding of his one eternal covenant.' He explained that Zwingli was using the covenant as the basis for discussing particular questions: 'in connection with it [i.e., the covenant] are the keys

---

[36] Zwingli's appreciation of the continuity of the Church from the post-lapsarian Adamic covenant, through Abraham, to Christ is discussed by Jaques Courvoisier, *Zwingli: a Reformed Theologian* (London: Epworth, 1964), 50.
[37] Huldrych Zwingli, *Declaration of Huldreich Zwingli regarding Original Sin, addressed to Urbanus Rhegius, 15 August 1526*, LWHZ, 2:20.
[38] Ibid., 2:7–17.
[39] Steinmetz, *Reformers in the Wings*, 95.

to what original sin is, and to what the whole business of baptism amounts to.'[40] Zwingli was primarily concerned to communicate the implications and applications of the covenant, so an absence of direct discussion of the covenant itself need not indicate its absence from his reasoning. On the contrary, writes Gottfried Locher, he 'raises it to the position of a leading thought in the understanding of Scripture'[41] and it became the premise for two important works prepared for the Emperor Charles V and Francis I of France respectively, *Ratio Fidei* (1530) and *Expositio Fidei* (1531).[42]

The covenant was usually made most explicit in Zwingli's discussions of the sacraments. Zwingli published what was perhaps his most significant contribution to the Eucharist controversy in February 1527, the *Friendly Exegesis* addressed to Luther, in which he continued to employ the covenant idea. Zwingli located the ancient covenant-making ritual of cleaving or 'cutting a covenant' in Deuteronomy 6:13 and 10:20, and he quoted Moses: '"You shall worship the Lord, your God, and him only you shall *proskollēthēsē*, that is, cleave to." And Christ repeated that this was to be taken in the sense that the heart was to cleave to no other thing save God alone [Matthew 4:10].'[43] Towards the end of the *Friendly Exegesis* Zwingli gave a definition of the covenant which was resoundingly christocentric: 'For the testament [*testamentum*] or covenant [*foedus*] is that Christ the Son of God is ours, and that through him we have been elected into the number of the children of God. And all this was accomplished [*perfectum*] and ratified [*sancitum*] by his death.'[44]

---

[40] Bullinger, 14 May 1527, quoted in Lillback, *Binding of God*, 98.

[41] Locher, *Zwingli's Thought*, 219.

[42] Zwingli, *Account of the Faith*, e.g. 38–43; Huldrych Zwingli, *A Short and Clear Exposition of the Christian Faith preached by Huldrych Zwingli* [. . .] *thus far not printed by anyone and now for the first time published unto the world* [. . .] *1536* [July 1531], *LWHZ*, 2:245–46, 253, 264–45.

[43] Zwingli, *Friendly Exegesis*, *HZW*, 2:305.

[44] Ibid., 2:362; *CR*, 92:746; see Joel Beeke, *Assurance of Faith: Calvin, English Puritanism, and the Dutch Second Reformation* (New York: Peter Lang, 1991), 28.

Thus the reciprocal agreement governing the relationship between God and humanity had, at its centre, the possession by mankind of Christ in order to meet the price of their reconciliation to familial relationship with God. Thus in March he explained from Genesis 15:18 that Christ was the true means by which our peace and covenant with God was established and confirmed. God becomes our God in Genesis 17:7 not by our own meritorious works but by the terms of the covenant (*ex pacti conditione*) and his gracious mercy.[45]

The relationship between covenant and election was dealt with in the closing section of Zwingli's *Refutation of the Tricks of the Catabaptists* (July 1527). Particularly interesting is Zwingli's assertion of the unity of the covenant throughout salvation history, beginning with the covenant that God conceived for Adam. He implied a pre-temporal conception but, perhaps significantly, not a prelapsarian implementation of the covenant.[46] Zwingli proceeded to consider testamental continuity and discontinuity and maintained the dependence of salvation upon divine election: 'the elect are ever elect, even before they believe.'[47]

Zwingli's concept of covenant focussed his soteriology upon Christ. Not only had Christ ratified the agreement between God and humanity in his own blood, but he had fulfilled the reciprocal obligations required of mankind. Furthermore, the covenant constituted Zwingli's rationale for righteous living in allegiance to Christ. For him, writes Gordon, religion was 'a relationship, a way of living, to which humans could neither add nor take away because it was both gift and command.'[48] As Woolsey observes, the degree to which

---

[45] Zwingli, *Erläuterungen zur Genesis* [March 1527], *CR*, 100:92, 104.

[46] Huldrych Zwingli, "Refutation of the Tricks of the Catabaptists [1527]," in *Selected Works*, ed. Jackson, 219–21.

[47] Ibid., 242. See Lillback, *Binding of God*, 98–106. For Zwingli's treatment of election see Stephens, *Theology of Zwingli*, 99–106. Woolsey's finding of a 'strong implication' of the later idea of a covenant of redemption risks applying anachronistic categories of federal theology: Woolsey, *Unity and Continuity*, 227.

[48] Gordon, "Emulating the Past," 17.

Zwingli emphasised that imperative depended not on shifts in his thought but on the context or controversy he was addressing at any one time.⁴⁹

Heinrich Bullinger

Bullinger began his career in 1522 as a lay teacher in the Cistercian house at Kappel where he refused both monastic vows and attendance at Mass. Between 1523 and 1529 he undertook to reform the monastery by expounding Scripture before eventually leaving for parochial ministry. He first met Zwingli in 1524 and spent time studying at Zürich in 1527. Following Zwingli's death at the battle of Kappel on 11 October 1531, Bullinger assumed religious oversight of Zürich in December. He exerted himself to consolidate the legacy of his divisive predecessor and friend whose martyrdom had traumatised the Zürichers. Like Zwingli he held a high view of the rôle of the magistrate as the shepherd of God's people, maintaining Zwingli's priorities for social order and godly living.⁵⁰

While Zwingli's concept of covenant has hitherto received limited recognition, it is more widely known that Bullinger developed the covenant into an explicit 'constitutive dogmatic principle.'⁵¹

---

⁴⁹ Woolsey, *Unity and Continuity*, 220.

⁵⁰ Gordon, *Swiss Reformation*, 141. On Bullinger's adaptation of Zwingli's approach to polity see Pamela Biel, *Doorkeepers in the House of Righteousness: Heinrich Bullinger and the Zurich Clergy 1535–1575* (Berne: P. Lang, 1991).

⁵¹ Steinmetz, *Reformers in the Wings*, 95; see also Ulrich Gäbler, *Huldrych Zwingli: his life and work*, trans. R. Gritsch (Philadelphia: Fortress Press, 1986), 158; Lillback, *Binding of God*, 311; Philip Benedict, *Christ's Churches Purely Reformed: a social history of Calvinism* (New Haven & London: YUP, 2002), 59; MacCulloch, *Reformation*, 178. Wayne Baker is the leading proponent of this view. His analysis of Bullinger is instructive (see J. Wayne Baker, *Heinrich Bullinger and the Covenant: The Other Reformed Tradition* (Athens, OH: Ohio University Press, 1980); Baker and McCoy, *Fountainhead*) but must be read with caution. He argues that Bullinger's concept of covenant was distinct from those of his contemporaries (see esp. Baker, *Other Reformed Tradition*, appendices A-C). This has been rightly contested by Richard Muller, "Review

Consequently it is important to recognise that Bullinger acknowledged his debt to Zwingli in this area.[52] Bullinger's concept of covenant began to emerge in the early 1520s. A marginal annotation to his *On the use of Scripture* (1523) implied the unity of the Testaments insofar as 'the New Testament is nothing other than the interpretation of the Old.'[53] The concept became explicit in *On Baptism* (late November or early December 1525), where he wrote that God 'made a covenant [*pundt*], testament [*testament*] or will [*gmächt*] with the fathers Adam, Enoch, Noah and especially clearly and explicitly with Abraham and his seed for eternity.' The bilateral nature of the Abrahamic covenant was asserted: humanity gave something 'in return [*herwyderumb*].'[54]

Bullinger's *Letter on the institution and use of the genuine Eucharist* (December 1525) already expressed his mature theology of the covenant which, as Woolsey observes, drew on Zwingli's early polemics against the Anabaptists.[55] Here he wrote that Christ 'explains and makes fresh the covenant of God' which remains unchanged: 'Now therefore when Christ calls this cup a new testament, no one should imagine that God began a new covenant with the human race.'[56] The eternal nature of the covenant convinced Bullinger that

---

of 'Fountainhead of Federalism,'" *Anglican and Episcopal History* 63 (1994): 89–91; Richard Muller, *The Unaccommodated Calvin: Studies in the Foundation of a Theological Tradition* (Oxford: OUP, 2000), 126; Lillback, *Binding of God*, 81–106; Venema, *Bullinger and Predestination*; Woolsey, *Unity and Continuity*, 228–49. Baker competently defends his analysis of Bullinger himself in J. Wayne Baker, "Heinrich Bullinger, the Covenant, and the Reformed Tradition in Retrospect," *SCJ* 29, 2 (1998): 359–76.

[52] Lillback, *Binding of God*, 98, 113; W. P. Stephens, "Bullinger and the Anabaptists with reference to his *Von Dem Unverschamten Frevel* (1531) and to Zwingli's writings on the Anabaptists," *RRR* 3 (2001): 100–101, 106–7; Goeters, "Föderaltheologie," 247.

[53] Quoted in Baker, *Other Reformed Tradition*, 4–5. Baker incorrectly asserts that Bullinger pre-empted Zwingli by two years in unifying the Testaments.

[54] Quoted in Baker, *Other Reformed Tradition*, 4–6.

[55] Baker, *Other Reformed Tradition*, 9; Woolsey, *Unity and Continuity*, 229.

[56] Quoted in Baker, *Other Reformed Tradition*, 9.

the Old Testament contained the whole will of God. In his *Answer to Burchard* (1528) he explained that the Pentateuch included the 'entire testament' of salvation, defining 'testament' (*testament*) in terms of 'a covenant' (*pundt*) and 'an alliance' (*pündtnus*). Again he made the point that mankind is not a passive recipient of a unilateral bequest, for the 'sum total of all Scripture, toward which all Scripture always aims' is none other than that 'this covenant [*pundt*] has been performed continually on both sides.'[57]

Although the important elements of Bullinger's covenant thought had been expressed several times between 1525 and 1533 they were definitively expounded in his account of history *Concerning the one and eternal testament or covenant of God* [*De testamento seu foedere Dei unico et aeterno*] (1534).[58] This was composed during a period of controversy over the relationship between ecclesiastical and civil authorities to which Bullinger had contributed *What the duty of the magistrate is in the church of Christ, who lawfully defends it against the seditions of heretics and the attacks of tyrants* (1534). His advice to magistrates depended on the unity of the Testaments and the enduring validity of Old Testament models.[59] *De testamento* sought to unite the testimonies of the prophets and apostles by employing the covenant hermeneutic.[60]

---

[57] Quoted in Ibid., 12.

[58] Baker, "Retrospect," 360–61. Woolsey acknowledges *De Testamento* as 'a milestone in the history of covenantal thought' but he qualifies the covenant's importance for Bullinger's theology generally. This may be true when compared with the concept's explicit centrality in federal theology; Woolsey cites M. W. Karlberg, "Reformed Interpretations of the Mosaic Covenant," *WTJ* 43 (1980): 11 in calling *De Testamento* 'the first extended exposition of the covenant of grace': Woolsey, *Unity and Continuity*, 230–31. However, while Baker was incorrect in his contrasting of Bullinger and Calvin, his recognition of the foundational importance of the covenant to Bullinger by contemporary standards seems justified. Bullinger's influence on John Hooper is a testament to this.

[59] J. Wayne Baker, "Church, State, and Dissent: the crisis of the Swiss Reformation, 1531–1536," *CH* 57, 2 (1988): 148; see also Opitz, "Bullinger," 250–51, 260–61.

[60] Heinrich Bullinger, *A Brief Exposition of the One and Eternal Testament or*

De testamento begins with an etymological discussion of the different words associated with the concept of covenant. Bullinger presented three possibilities. Firstly, bᵉrît (translated *diathēkē* or *testamentum*) sometimes signifies '*hereditatem quae testamento obvenit*' [the inheritance that results from a will].[61] Secondly, *diathēkē* means '*pactum & conventum & pollicitationem*' [pact, agreement, promise], so *testamentum* in Scripture means '*promissione, nec quauis, sed iureiurando fermata*' [a promise, not of any sort, but confirmed by oath].[62] Thirdly, *diathēkē* means '*pactum*' or '*foedus*.' Bullinger argued that this third meaning best corresponded with bᵉrît.[63] *Foedus* (or *pundt* in the German edition) was therefore to be the subject of the exposition, consistent with Zwingli's definition of *testamentum* as *pundt*. Bullinger explained the ancient Near Eastern ritual of covenant-making to establish peace between hostile parties, noting that 'a pig was "horribly" (*foede*), that is, cruelly, slain' in the ceremony. This was the human custom used by God to enter into fellowship with mankind.[64] Genesis 17:1–14, wrote Bullinger, followed the covenant pattern precisely:

> First, the passage explains who bound themselves together [*couenerint*], namely, God and the descendants of Abraham. Second, the text states the conditions under which they bound themselves together [*conditionibus couenerint*],

---

Covenant of God, 1534, trans. C. S. McCoy and J. W. Baker, in *Fountainhead of Federalism* (Louisville, KY: Westminster John Knox Press, 1991), 117–30.

[61] Heinrich Bullinger, *De Testamento Seu Foedere Dei Unico & Aeterno Heinrychi Bullingeri Brevis Expositio*, Elektronische Bibliothek Schweiz (Zurich: Christopher Froschauer, 1534), A2v; Bullinger, *Brief Exposition*, 101.

[62] Bullinger, *De Testamento*, A3r-v; Bullinger, *Brief Exposition*, 102.

[63] Bullinger, *De Testamento*, A3v; Bullinger, *Brief Exposition*, 103. For Bullinger these meanings were mutually supportive, see Aurelio Garcia, "Bullinger's *De Testamento*: The Amply Biblical Basis of Reformed Origins," in *Heinrich Bullinger: Life—Thought—Influence: International Congress Heinrich Bullinger 2004*, 2 vols. (Zurich: TVZ, 2007), 2:674.

[64] Bullinger, *Brief Exposition*, 102–3.

specifically that God wished to be the God of the descendants of Abraham and that the descendants of Abraham ought to walk uprightly before God [*integre coram Deo debeat ambulare*]. Third, it is explained that the covenant [*foedus*] is made between them forever. And finally, [the entire covenant] is confirmed with a specific ceremony in blood.[65]

Entry into ancient covenants was mutual but 'the chief negotiator who confirms [*foecialis*] the covenant [*pactum*] gives agreement with formalised words and ceremonies.'[66] It was therefore possible for Bullinger to hold that the covenant was reciprocal yet maintain its gracious nature by unilateral initiation: God, 'who holds the primacy in this covenant [*foedere*],' 'joined himself in covenant [*foedere*] with miserable mortals corrupted by sin [. . .] we are saved solely through the goodness and mercy of God.'[67] God's responsibility in the covenant was, consequently, to be himself, 'the all-sufficient God, the God of the faithful and the rewarder of those who fear him.'[68]

The revelation of the divine nature made 'demands from us in return, and what is fitting for us to do [*quid nos facere conueniat*].'[69] 'These,' wrote Bullinger, 'are our duties; these things must be observed by us [. . .]. It is our duty to adhere firmly by faith to the one God [. . .] and to walk in innocence of life for his pleasure.' These

[65] Ibid., 104; Bullinger, *De Testamento*, A5v.

[66] Bullinger, *Brief Exposition*, 103; Bullinger, *De Testamento*, A4r.

[67] Bullinger, *Brief Exposition*, 105, 108; Bullinger, *De Testamento*, A6v, B3v. This distinction offsets criticism of Baker's reading as synergistic by Richard Muller, *Christ and the Decree: Christology and Predestination in Reformed Theology from Calvin to Perkins* (Grand Rapids: Baker, 1986), 41–44. It also undermines Strehle's view that Bullinger's teaching is synergistic: Stephen Strehle, "*Fides aut Foedus*: Wittenberg and Zurich in conflict over the Gospel," *SCJ* 23, 1 (1992): 15–17. On Bullinger's qualified expression of double predestination, see W. P. Stephens, "Predestination or Election in Zwingli and Bullinger," *Heinrich Bullinger: Life—Thought—Influence: International Congress Heinrich Bullinger 2004*, 2 vols. (Zurich: TVZ, 2007), 1:322; Beeke, *Assurance*, 32.

[68] Bullinger, *Brief Exposition*, 109.

[69] Ibid., 108–9; Bullinger, *De Testamento*, B3v.

conditions were later summarised as 'partly faith in God and partly love of the neighbour.' Like Zwingli, Bullinger contrasted godly duties with false worship and idolatry.[70] From the German edition it is clear that Bullinger uses *integer* [uprightly] in a moral sense.[71] The moral law of the Decalogue paraphrased the conditions of the covenant, but these could be traced back to Adam.[72] Both divine and human responsibilities were fulfilled in Christ, making Bullinger's concept of covenant thoroughly christocentric. He himself was 'the seal and living confirmation of the covenant.'[73] God fulfilled his promise by revealing himself in Christ and Christ confirmed the covenant relationship in his blood. Moreover, the apprehension of Christ's righteousness was the means by which faith discharged mankind's responsibilities: 'this same Jesus is the inheritance itself which has been bequeathed to those who trust in the one and eternal covenant of God.' This, too, is the work of God who, as humanity's 'protector, confederate, and saviour,' supplies Christ as liberator.[74]

The consistency of Bullinger's covenant thought is demonstrated in his sermon series the *Decades* (1549–51)[75] by the referral of his readers to *De testamento* (1534) and to *Der alt gloub* [*The old faith*] (1537) 'which treatises I know to be familiar among you.'[76] In short, Bullinger taught that the covenant was initially made with Adam immediately after the Fall, and renewed with Noah, Abraham and Moses. He specified the mutuality, duration, conditions and signs of the covenant. The salvific import in Pauline terms was

---

[70] Bullinger, *Brief Exposition*, 111, 116–17; see also Garcia, "*De Testamento*," 679. Salvation by works was implicitly rejected.

[71] Bullinger, *Brief Exposition*, 104n.

[72] Ibid., 113, 135. Bullinger did not imply a prelapsarian covenant here. See Steinmetz, *Reformers in the Wings*, 95.

[73] Bullinger, *Brief Exposition*, 115.

[74] Ibid., 110, 116.

[75] The covenant concept is traced throughout the *Decades* in Baker, "Retrospect," 364–66.

[76] Heinrich Bullinger, *The Decades of Henry Bullinger*, ed. T. Harding, 5 vols. PS (Cambridge: CUP, 1849–52), iii/8:299.

that humanity 'is justified by grace through faith.'[77] Bullinger held that God's word is reliable on the basis of his irrevocable '*foedus*'.[78] The whole of Scripture was to be received as authoritative, therefore, 'even because we are Christians.' Although certain elements of the Old Testament had been abrogated or surpassed by Christ, others remained binding.[79] The testament was always one, so there was but one means of salvation at all times. This was Bullinger's key point, as Richard Muller emphasises,[80] although he did not refrain from extensive discussion of Testamental continuity and discontinuity.[81]

Scripture was to be interpreted according to the law of love towards God and neighbour.[82] Love was required in the keeping of God's commandments, evidenced by John 14:23–24 and Moses' teaching around Deuteronomy 6:5. The whole heart must be faithful to God alone and, with regard to neighbours, 'fulfil the duties of love and civil humanity.'[83] It is unsurprising, then, that eighteen sermons were devoted to law and an exposition of the Decalogue where 'the conditions of the league [*conditionibus foederis*] were at large written.'[84] Bullinger implied the immutability of the covenant conditions by noting the similarity between the preface to the Decalogue and 'the words of the covenant [*foederis*] which God made with Abraham, and in Abraham with all faithful believers.'[85] The first table 'teacheth us the perfect way to love uprightly and holily in the sight of God. The second is the rule whereby we have to learn our

---

[77] Bullinger, *Decades*, iii/6:169–75, see also v/9:434.
[78] Ibid., i/4:93–94; Heinrich Bullinger, *Sermonum decades quinque, de potissimis Christianae religionis capitibus* (Zurich: Christopher Froschauer, 1557), 14. The PS editor translates *foedus* as both 'league' and 'covenant'.
[79] Bullinger, *Decades*, i/2:58–59.
[80] Richard Muller, *The Unaccommodated Calvin: Studies in the Foundation of a Theological Tradition* (Oxford: OUP, 2000), 126.
[81] Bullinger, *Decades*, iii/8:236ff.
[82] Ibid., i/3:77.
[83] Ibid., i/10:82–83, 190.
[84] Ibid., iii/6:169; Bullinger, *Sermonum decades*, 121.
[85] Bullinger, *Decades*, ii/2:215; Bullinger, *Sermonum decades*, 40.

duty toward our neighbour [. . .] in these two tables are so nearly contained all and every duty looked for at men's hands.'[86] Humanity's obligations to God were explicit: 'if he will be mine, then I again of duty must be his [. . .]. Wherefore in this commandment there is required at our hands, that we do not only acknowledge the true God to be the true God, and so to stay there; but also, that we do take and account him for our God.'[87]

Nevertheless, as in *De testamento*, Christ remained at the centre of the covenant promise with all the Old Testament foreshadowing his appearance.[88] Total reliance upon God was again emphasised. God, wrote Bullinger, 'is the life and righteousness of both the people [Jews and Gentiles]: which righteousness he bestoweth on them by faith: therefore faith doth justify or make them both righteous.' God in Christ is the locus of humanity's righteousness, for 'God alone is righteous,'[89] and in this sense righteousness is bestowed on believers. Christ acted as the means for the fulfilment of the promise:

> God the Father, through the Son, doth pour himself wholly with all good things into the faithful, whom he quickeneth and filleth with all goodness, and last of all doth take them up to himself [. . .]. This doth true faith believe [. . .] that God in Christ doth communicate to the faithful life and godliness.[90]

Undoubtedly Christ's righteousness is the righteousness by which humanity fulfils its part in the covenant.[91] Like Zwingli, Bullinger

---

[86] Bullinger, *Decades*, ii/2:217; see also Philip Melanchthon, *Loci Communes Theologici* [1535], ed. W. Pauck, *LCC*, Vol. 19 (London: SCM, 1969), 53–57.

[87] Bullinger, *Decades*, ii/2:217.

[88] Ibid., iv/1:13–19.

[89] Ibid., iv/1:44–45.

[90] Ibid., i/4:95.

[91] Ibid., iv/2:91. Woolsey is right to emphasise 'unilateral grace' as 'the focal point of the covenant' but his denial that 'Bullinger's was simply a bilateral view' introduces the notion that the bilateral concept implies human merit: Woolsey, *Unity and Continuity*, 235.

located Christ at the centre of his concept of covenant. Christ was integral to Bullinger's explanation of salvation history, social responsibility, and the believer's duty to God.

John Calvin

Calvin spent about twenty-four years of his life interacting with and shaping the Swiss Reformed *milieu*. In 1535–36 he met various reformers in Basle including Bullinger.[92] Then in 1536 at Guillaume Farel's behest he settled in Geneva. Having been expelled in 1538 he matured as a reformer in Martin Bucer's Strassburg and then agreed to return to Geneva in 1542, assured of Zürich's support.[93] In a passage that could as well describe Zwingli, Bruce Gordon writes that 'for Calvin the core of Christianity was the proper worship of God. The decision that he could not live with false religion had been the defining moment of his life.' Indeed, Calvin's departure from France had been 'his deliverance from idolatry.'[94]

Calvin's early intellectual influeneces are difficult to determine. He cannot be linked with any of the French reformist movements in the 1520s but his legal studies in Paris in 1528–30 would have familiarised him with the key debates of the period.[95] The Collège de Montaigu, where he was a student at some stage, was a bastion of the *via moderna* within the university. McGrath writes that Calvin 'could scarcely have avoided such logical and epistemological questions' as were being emphasised by this school, like the rejection of created habits of grace. His theology is continuous with the late medieval voluntarist tradition associated with William of Ockham.[96]

---

[92] Bruce Gordon, *Calvin* (New Haven & London: YUP, 2009), 47–64.
[93] Ibid., 85–102; Bruce Gordon, "Calvin and the Swiss Reformed Churches," in *Calvinism in Europe, 1520–1640*, eds. A. Pettegree, A. Duke and G. Lewis (Cambridge: CUP, 1994), 69.
[94] Gordon, *Calvin*, 195.
[95] Ibid., 17, 20.
[96] McGrath, *Intellectual Origins*, 94–100.

Certainly he would have been *au fait* with conciliarist contract theories and he could hardly have avoided medieval *pactum* theology.[97]

Calvin's concept of covenant has been a focus of scholarly debate. While Perry Miller questioned its existence altogether, others see it as peripheral, or distinct from Zürich theology.[98] Jens Møller differentiated between Calvin's emphasis on grace and obedience and the Puritans' contractual relation of these two 'in the vein of Zürich.'[99] More strongly, Leonard Trinterud argued that Calvin's concept of covenant was incompatible with a reciprocal agreement. Instead, he contends that Calvin's covenant was unilateral and unconditional.[100] Baker agrees that Calvin 'simply amplified the idea of testament,' faith being 'only a hypothetical condition.'[101] Even if exposure to Swiss society did fail to impress upon Calvin's mind the covenantal forms so familiar to Zwingli and Bullinger, there can be no doubt that Calvin's legal training would have led him to consider the question of covenant independently. However, Muller believes that the strong influence of Bullinger's *De testamento* on Calvin's general view of the covenant is undeniable.[102] Peter Lillback has convincingly demonstrated and explored the extensive integration of a mutual, conditional covenant hermeneutic in Calvin's theology.[103]

---

[97] Lillback, *Binding of God*, 36–38.

[98] Miller, *New England Mind*, 366–67; Miller, *Errand*, 62.

[99] Møller, "Beginnings," 64–67.

[100] Trinterud, "Origins," 56; see also Richard Greaves, "The Origins and Early Development of English Covenant Thought," *The Historian* 31, 1 (1968): 32.

[101] Baker, *Other Reformed Tradition*, 193–95. Joel Beeke rejects a dogmatic historiographical tendency to treat a unilateral covenant as exemplary but to disparage bilateral formulations: Beeke, *Assurance*, 44n.

[102] Muller, *Unaccommodated Calvin*, 126. Muller notes that Calvin's *Épitre a tous amateurs de Jésus-Christ* [*Letter to all those who love Jesus Christ*], written as a preface to the New Testament of Olivetan's French Bible (1535), 'presents a survey of salvation-history [. . .] in which Calvin's theology parallels Bullinger's earlier treatise on the covenant,' i.e., *De testamento* (1534): Muller, *Unaccommodated Calvin*, 23. See also Goeters, "Föderaltheologie," 247.

[103] Lillback, *Binding of God*, 126–230. This is affirmed by Cornelis Venema, *Accepted and Renewed in Christ: the 'Twofold Grace of God' and the interpretation*

He concludes that there was substantial agreement with Bullinger and that Calvin's doctrine of predestination was thoroughly reconciled with the covenant.[104]

Woolsey remarks on the heavy use of covenant terminology in Calvin's *Institutes of the Christian Religion*. The final edition in 1559 contained two hundred and sixty-nine references, the most common being *foedus* (seventy-seven times) and its cognates (seventy-four times).[105] The concept's importance is apparent even in the first edition published at Basle in 1536.[106] While he offered no specific etymological discussion, Calvin reasoned that 'since the Lord calls his promises "covenants" [*foedera*] and his sacraments "tokens" of the covenants [*symbola foederum*], a simile can be taken from the covenants [*foederibus*] of men.' He then referred, like Bullinger, to the ancient ratification practice of slaying a pig.[107] Calvin also described sacraments as 'seals' [*sigillum*] of God's 'testament or promise' [*testamentum seu promissio*].[108] It seems that Calvin considered *foedus*, *testamentum*, *pactum* and *promissio* to be synonymous, thereby incorporating discussion of God's promise into his concept of covenant.

---

of Calvin's theology (Gottingen: Vandenhoeck & Ruprecht, 2007), 183–90. See also Woolsey, *Unity and Continuity*, ch. 8–12 for another account of Calvin's concept.

[104] Lillback, *Binding of God*, 306ff; see also Michael McGiffert, "Grace and Works: The Rise and Division of Covenant Divinity in Elizabethan Puritanism," *HTR* 75, 4 (1982): 469. One of Lillback's main concerns, peripheral to this study, is to refute the thesis of discontinuity between Calvin and later federal theologians, e.g., Weir, *Federal Theology*, 9–10, 32. On that debate see Carl Trueman, "Calvin and Reformed Orthodoxy," in *The Calvin Handbook*, ed. H. Selderhuis (Grand Rapids and Cambridge: Eerdmans, 2009), 474–76.

[105] Woolsey, *Unity and Continuity*, 255.

[106] Lillback's study focuses upon the 1559 edition of the *Institutes of the Christian Religion*. There are obvious qualifications to be made in light of the fact that the covenant was not among the *loci* discussed in any of the earlier editions also examined here.

[107] John Calvin, *Institutes of the Christian Religion* [1536], trans. F. L. Battles (Grand Rapids, MI: William Eerdmans, 1986), 88; *CO*, 1:102.

[108] Calvin, *Institutes* [1536], 124; *CO*, 1:142.

Calvin believed that Christ was made incarnate 'to enter a covenant [*foedus*] with us.'[109] The agreement had been initiated by God but it was clearly implied that mankind was also bound, discounting any notion of a unilateral testament. The sense of mutual responsibility began with God's lordship and the problem of sin. Divine service and obedience are 'due him by right,' explained Calvin, 'for his nature's sake alone.'[110] Conversely, 'we call sins "debts" because we owe penalty or payment for them to God.'[111] Humanity's failure and inability to give God his due does not exculpate him from responsibility, for

> we do not cease to owe the very things we cannot supply. Inasmuch as we are God's creatures, we ought to serve his honour and glory, and obey his commandments. And we are not allowed to excuse ourselves by claiming that we lack ability and, like impoverished debtors, cannot pay our debt [. . .] we have not discharged our duty, as was fitting. Yet man is swollen with arrogance and ambition and blinded by self-love.[112]

Mutual responsibility was codified in the Mosaic Law. Calvin evidently did not use God's 'promise' in a unilateral sense because he included conditions: 'For the Lord promises that, if anyone should perfectly and exactly fulfil by his effort whatever is commanded, he will receive the reward of eternal life [Leviticus 18:5].'[113] Again, 'this condition, that we should carry out the law—*upon which the promises depend* and by which alone they are to be performed—will never be fulfilled.'[114] That mutuality continued into the New Testament era

---

[109] Calvin, *Institutes* [1536], 18; *CO*, 1:30.
[110] Calvin, *Institutes* [1536], 15.
[111] Ibid., 81.
[112] Ibid., 16. The problem of self-love is reminiscent of Zwingli's concerns.
[113] Ibid., 17.
[114] Ibid., 33. My emphasis. By 1559 Calvin taught that the Mosaic Law was intended to 'strengthen [the Jews'] expectation' of the fulfilment of the

is demonstrated by the conditionality of Christ's promise.[115] Calvin explained that it 'will be fulfilled for none except those who possess a sure and unvarying persuasion that it has to be fulfilled for them.' This must not be misconstrued as unconditional, for God is obliged to fulfil his promise only for 'those who have faith. When, therefore, faith fails, the promise will not remain in force.'[116]

Although faith was the sole condition for justification, under the third use of the law believers were further 'called to sanctification. The function of the law consists in this: by warning men of their duty, to arouse them to pursue holiness and innocence.'[117] Hamm explains that, for Calvin, 'faith is always love at the same time, and justification is always renewal as well.'[118] Therefore humanity's duty continued after justification under the persisting validity of the moral law which constituted the law of love: 'to worship God with pure faith and piety [. . .] to embrace men with sincere affection.' The law does not constrain the believer by necessity but represents God's will, which true believers desire to obey.[119]

All responsibilities contained in the covenant are fulfilled by Christ. 'In Christ alone,' wrote Calvin, we find 'the good will of God the Father towards us'[120] and, again, 'this is the new covenant that God in Christ has made with us.'[121] For Zwingli and Bullinger, Christ fulfilled the covenant through union with the believer, thereby

---

Abrahamic covenant in Christ: John Calvin, *Institutes of the Christian Religion*, ed. J. T. McNeill, trans. F. L. Battles, *LCC*, 2 vols. (Louisville & London: Westminster John Knox Press, 1960), 348 (II. vii. 1). See the useful discussion of covenant and law in Kendall, *Calvin*, 27.

[115] Conditionality was not restricted to the Mosaic covenant as suggested by Letham, "Foedus Operum," 463.

[116] Calvin, *Institutes* [1536], 34.

[117] Ibid., 177.

[118] Hamm, *Reformation of Faith*, 215.

[119] Calvin, *Institutes* [1536], 215; see also I. J. Hesselink, *Calvin's Concept of the Law* (Allison Park, PA: Pickwick, 1992), 36.

[120] Calvin, *Institutes* [1536], 59–60.

[121] Ibid., 152.

becoming the believer's righteousness. Similarly, wrote Calvin, 'if we partake of Christ, in Him we shall possess all the heavenly treasures and gifts of the Holy Spirit which lead us into life and salvation.'[122] However, Calvin accented the imputation of Christ's righteousness:

> But Christ's righteousness, which alone can bear the sight of God because it alone is perfect, must appear in court on our behalf, and stand surety for us in judgment. Received from God, this righteousness is brought to us and imputed to us, just as if it were ours.[123]

For Calvin, Christ's righteousness was detached and imputed to the believer. It was 'brought to us' and 'put on as our own,' 'just as if it were ours.'[124] Although Zwingli and Bullinger would have said that the believer is 'made righteous,' they did not conceive of Christ's righteousness being transported in any way. For them, the believer's righteousness was not so much Christ's as Christ himself.

Finally, Calvin asserted the continuity of the Old and New Testaments in the context of his sacramental teaching. He claimed that the people of the Old Testament were pointed to Christ.[125] Moreover, the promise or covenant with Abraham was 'the very same thing' promised to Christians.[126] The close relationship of 'covenant' and 'promise' originated in the earliest editions of the *Institutes*. The 1536 edition used the terms synonymously.[127] The 1539 edition spoke with more precision of the covenant (*'foedus'*) including the promise (*'promissionem'*) of eternal life,[128] while the

---

[122] Ibid., 18.
[123] Ibid., 35.
[124] Ibid., 34–35.
[125] Ibid., 93.
[126] Ibid., 102.
[127] Mutual conditionality is what distinguished Calvin's use of 'promise' from Luther's unilateral understanding.
[128] *CO*, 1:817; see also Beeke, *Assurance*, 59; Calvin, *Institutes* [*LCC*], 884 (III. xx. 25), 1334 (IV. xvi. 11), 1347 (IV. xvi. 24).

1541 edition described the promise as being 'comprised [*comprises*] in that Testament [*Testament*].'[129] They were not so much synonymous as inextricably related.[130]

Although Calvin was not expounding the covenant in particular, all the essential elements of the concept, alongside the synonymous idea of promise, were present in the 1536 edition of the *Institutes*. The covenant would not have been a natural framework for a catechetical work but it still underpinned Calvin's teaching. Lillback describes one passage in the *Institutes* on the sacraments of the Church as perhaps 'the most conclusive evidence of Calvin's adherence to a mutual covenant.'[131] It illustrates the early development of Calvin's concept of covenant.[132]

The material originating in 1536 is very limited,[133] but in 1539 Calvin introduced the idea that humanity reciprocates God's promise in the sacraments: '*Ut enim illic se pollicetur Dominus* [. . .] *ita pietatis ac innocentiae professione illi nos mutuo obligamus*' [For as in them the Lord promises ... so do we, in turn, bind ourselves to him],[134] or, in the 1541 edition, '*aussi mutuellement nous nous obligeons à luy de le server*' [we also mutually promise ourselves to him to serve him].[135]

---

[129] John Calvin, *Institutes of the Christian Religion: 1541 French Edition*, trans. E. McKee (Grand Rapids, MI and Cambridge: William Eerdmans, 2009), 387; John Calvin, *Institution de la Religion Chrestienne* [1541], ed. J. Pannier (Paris: Société d'Edition "Les Belles Lettres," 1961), 3:10.

[130] On the consequent necessity of the atonement and Christ's covenant after God's gracious decree to redeem see Paul Helm, *John Calvin's Ideas* (Oxford: OUP, 2004), 333–39.

[131] Lillback, *Binding of God*, 167. On the significance of Calvin's covenant in uniting God's majesty and paternity see Marijn de Kroon, *The Honour of God and Human Salvation: a contribution to an understanding of Calvin's theology according to his Institutes*, trans. L. Bierma and J. Vriend (Edinburgh and New York: T&T Clark, 2001), 42–44.

[132] Calvin, *Institutes* [*LCC*], 1296 (IV. xiv. 19), cf. 685 (III. vi. 1), 1327 (IV. xvi. 4).

[133] Calvin, *Institutes* [1536], 93.

[134] *CO*, 1:952.

[135] Calvin, *Institution* [1541], 3:217; Calvin, *Institutes* [1541], 506.

Again, in the 1539 edition, sacraments are '*professionis notae, quibus palam in Dei nomen iuramus, fidem illi vicissim nostrum obstringentes*' [marks of profession, by which we openly swear allegiance to God, binding ourselves in fealty to him]. Consequently, Calvin argued, '*Scite ergo Chrysostomus ipsa alicubi pactiones nuncupat,* [...] *quibus in vitae puritatem ac sanctimoniam obstringimur*' [In one place therefore Chrysostom has appropriately called them covenants, ... by which we pledge ourselves to purity and holiness of life].[136] This was appropriate, added Calvin in 1559, 'since there is interposed here a mutual agreement [*mutua*] between God and ourselves' in which 'God leagues [*confoederat*] himself with us.'[137] It seems, then, that the concept of mutuality emerged in the 1539 edition.

This development was probably a result of Calvin's reading of other Reformed theologians and his engagement with the Anabaptists. As Woolsey observes, 'Calvin was not introducing a new theological category, but taking up a biblical motif best suited to develop and stress what was already inherent in his thinking.'[138] The 1539 edition made conditionality more explicit than the 1536 edition. Calvin stated: '*hac enim conditione deus noster est, ut in medio nostri habitet*' [he is our God on this condition, that he dwell among us].[139] Of course, God is bound by his nature to fulfil his responsibilities, for '*nihil ad bonorum omnium affluentiam, adeoque salutis certitudinem deesse, modo nobis Dominus sit in deum*' [we lack nothing for an abundance of all good things, and for assurance of salvation, so long as the Lord is our God].[140] Likewise, conditions are explicitly assigned to humanity: for example, in the 1539 edition, it is considered fair for an adult entering into the covenant to learn its conditions

---

[136] *CO*, 1:952. For other examples of Calvin's use of pact, see Calvin, *Institutes* [*LCC*], 1087 (IV. v. 3), 1088 (IV. v. 4), 1136 (IV. vii. 17); *CO*, 2:800–801, 835.
[137] Calvin, *Institutes* [*LCC*], 1296 (IV. xiv. 19); *CO*, ii. 956.
[138] Woolsey, *Unity and Continuity*, 257.
[139] *CO*, 1:807; see also Calvin, *Institutes* [*LCC*], 435 (II. x. 8).
[140] *CO*, 1:806.

beforehand ('*quoniam eum, qui adulta demum aetate in foederis societam recipitur* [...] *eius conditiones antea perdiscere aequuem est*').[141]

All the workings of the covenant were explicitly christocentric in the 1536 edition and this element was emphasised again in 1539.[142] Joel Beeke astutely observes that 'Calvin directs sinners to Christ and to the promise almost as if they were synonymous.'[143] Indeed, Calvin's Christology was 'worked out in the history of the covenant,' writes Cornelis van der Kooi.[144] Christ's death becomes humanity's reconciliation via the covenant. Thus Woolsey highlights the fact that, for Calvin, God's progressive covenantal revelation had always been accomplished through Christ.[145]

This concept of the unity of the Testaments was developed properly by Calvin in the 1539 edition of the *Institutes*.[146] There he wrote that '*patrum omnium foedus adeo substantia et re ipsa nihil a nostro differt, ut unum prorsus atque idem sit*' [the covenant made with all the patriarchs is so much like ours in substance and reality that the two are actually one and the same].[147] Consequently, the Abrahamic covenant applies to the children of Christians today no less than it did to Jewish infants.[148] However, a distinctly new development in that edition was the eternal nature of the covenant. For example,

---

[141] *CO*, 1:985; see also Calvin, *Institutes* [*LCC*], 1151 (IV. viii. 2), 1347 (IV. xvi. 24).

[142] Calvin, *Institutes* [*LCC*], 431 (II. x. 4), 454 (II. xi. 4). Calvin's teaching on righteousness in 1536 was retained in subsequent editions. The believer was 'clothed' with Christ's innocence and 'furnished' with righteousness: Calvin, *Institutes* [*LCC*], 779 (III. xiv. 12), cf. 524 (II. xvi. 16).

[143] Beeke, *Assurance*, 48.

[144] Cornelis van der Kooi, "Christology," trans. G. Sheeres, in *The Calvin Handbook*, ed. H. Selderhuis (Grand Rapids and Cambridge: Eerdmans, 2009), 259.

[145] Quoted in Woolsey, *Unity and Continuity*, 262.

[146] Muller points to this as a continuity between Zwingli and Calvin: Muller, *Unaccommodated Calvin*, 124–25. See further Woolsey, *Unity and Continuity*, 268–75.

[147] *CO*, 1:802; see also Calvin, *Institutes* [*LCC*], 429 (II. x. 2), 434 (II. x. 7).

[148] *CO*, 1:971; see also Calvin, *Institutes* [*LCC*], 1328 (IV. xvi. 5).

Calvin wrote that '*pertinere ab initio mundi ad novum testamentum filios promissionis*' (the children of the promise have belonged to the new testament from the beginning of the world).[149] Not only were the elect included in the covenant at Creation, but it would also endure forever, for it was '*aeternum et nunquam interiturum semel sanctivit*' [once established as eternal and never-perishing].[150] Calvin explained differences in administration of the covenant as its manifestations becoming increasingly radiant during the course of biblical history.[151]

Thus the concept of covenant had emerged in Calvin's theology by 1536 and had developed reciprocal features by 1539. He demonstrated a concern, similar to Zwingli and Bullinger, to place Christ at the centre of his discussion of the covenant. These findings in the *Institutes* are confirmed by studies of Calvin's biblical commentaries and sermons where Richard Muller finds 'numerous bilateral covenant arguments,' notably in his commentary on Genesis 17 and the reciprocal language of his Deuteronomy sermons.[152] Calvin's commentary on Galatians was not published until 1548 but on Galatians 3:15 he remarks that, although 'testament' is the more common meaning for the Greek *diathēkē*, 'it matters little in the present passage whether you translate it contract or testament [. . .]. But here I prefer to take it simply for the covenant God made. For the simile from which the apostle argues [a 'human bargain'] would not apply so strictly to a testament as to a covenant.'[153] Calvin was interested in teaching what Scripture says without further speculation.

---

[149] *CO*, 1:825; see also Calvin, *Institutes* [*LCC*], 459 (II. xi. 10).

[150] *CO*, 1:821; see also Calvin, *Institutes* [*LCC*], 454 (II. xi. 4).

[151] Calvin, *Institutes* [*LCC*], 446; see Peter Opitz, "Scripture," trans. R. Giselbrecht, in *The Calvin Handbook*, ed. H. Selderhuis (Grand Rapids and Cambridge: Eerdmans, 2009), 238–39, 243.

[152] Muller, *Unaccommodated Calvin*, 154–55, 183.

[153] John Calvin, *The Epistle of Paul the Apostle to the Galatians, Ephesians, Philippians and Colossians*, Calvin's Commentaries, Vol. 9. (Edinburgh and London: Oliver and Boyd, 1965), 56–57.

Swiss Concepts of Covenant

There is a marked consistency between the concepts of covenant developed by Zwingli, Bullinger and Calvin. All three agreed that God initiated the covenant unilaterally but that it operated bilaterally between God and humanity. Obligations, which acted as conditions for the fulfilment of salvation, were imposed on each party. While God was obliged to grant salvation to those pleading Christ's atonement, humanity was required to strive for godliness in accordance with divine law. The consequences of defaulting on these conditions amounted to covenantal sanctions.

These ideas, especially those of Zwingli and Bullinger, were developed at an early enough stage to be able to influence English evangelicals under Henry VIII and Edward VI. From 1522 Zwingli used the covenant to structure a christocentric soteriology directed towards true worship according to God's law. He understood Christ's atonement as both the ratification of the covenant and the fulfilment of the righteous demands which the covenant makes upon mankind. A life of godliness and true worship would receive God's promised blessing and salvation. Bullinger was indebted to Zwingli's enunciation of the covenant which he perceived to be the principal idea in theology. From the mid-1520s he refined the concept in its detail and expanded it in its application to the community more generally. He particularly sought to place contemporary Christian obligations to please God and to love neighbour in the context of salvation history. Calvin's concept of covenant developed in the late 1530s in line with the Zürichers, apparently drawing on their ideas. All the main elements of his concept were present by 1539. Thus, the leading theologians of Zürich and Geneva shared a consistent concept of reciprocal covenant. This provides the basis for exploring English reception of the concept.

4

English Concepts of Covenant

And so shall hys ryghteousnesse upon theyr
chylders children: euen unto suche as kepe his couenaunt.
And are mindful of his commaundementes, to fulfyll them.
—*Psalm 103:17–18.*[1]

Among the most theologically sophisticated of the early English evangelicals were those who went into exile abroad. They could access with greater ease the writings of continental reformers, gain from their insights and transmit them home. Many English exiles were carried along by the Reformed currents flowing down the Rhine from the Alps. The formulation of reciprocal concepts of covenant in the writings of William Tyndale, Miles Coverdale, and John Hooper is suggestive of their exposure to Swiss Reformed theology. Wayne Baker hypothesised that these men each developed their concepts 'in connection with their contacts with Zürich' specifically.[2] The fourth figure to be investigated here is John Bradford, an Edwardian evangelical who never experienced exile and received limited exposure to Swiss Reformed theology. It will be suggested below that his unilateral concept of covenant resulted from alternative theological influences that would not have commended reciprocity to him.

---

[1] Miles Coverdale, *The Psalter or Boke of Psalmes Both in Latyn and Englyshe* (London: Ricardus Grafton, 1540; RSTC 2368), fol. lxxxvii.

[2] J. Wayne Baker, "Zwinglianism," in *OER* (New York and Oxford: OUP, 1996), 4:326.

William Tyndale

Tyndale was born in the Forest of Dean and studied at Oxford, travelling to London to be ordained in 1515.[3] The interest he began to take in reform no later than 1516 or 1517 was that of a typical Christian humanist; hence the kind of classical and Erasmian texts he chose for translation in the early 1520s.[4] In 1524, at around the age of thirty, he moved permanently to the continent, living mainly in Antwerp, but not before he had visited Wittenberg. He matriculated at the university there under the pseudonym '*Guillelmus Daltici Ex Anglia* 27 Maij 1524'.[5]

That Tyndale should have visited Wittenberg is unsurprising, and is evidence of his 'Lutheranism' only in the sense of general evangelical conviction. We should not think of him as any more dependent on Luther than his contemporaries in Zürich.[6] He would

---

[3] Andrew Brown, *William Tyndale on priests and preachers: with new light on his early career* (London: Inscriptor Imprints, 1996), 18–26. There is no evidence of value that Tyndale studied at Cambridge. For further discussion of his early life see Brian Buxton, "William Tyndale in Gloucestershire," *TBGAS* 131 (2013): 189–98; Diarmaid MacCulloch, *Thomas Cromwell: A Life* (London: Allen Lane, 2018), 66.

[4] Robert Wainwright, "William Tyndale on Covenant and Justification," *RRR* 13, 3 (2011): 355–56.

[5] Preserved Smith, "Englishmen at Wittenberg in the Sixteenth Century," *EHR* 36 (1921): 422–33; J. F. Mozley, *William Tyndale* (London: SPCK, 1937), 51–53. No substantive details of the alleged visit were recorded by John Foxe, *AM* [1570] (Sheffield: HRI Online Publications, 2011), 8:1265 and *AM* [1583], 8:1100. Arguments against the visit are advanced by David Daniell, *William Tyndale: a biography* (New Haven & London: YUP, 1994), 109, 297–302, 306–9 and E. G. Rupp, *Six Makers of English Religion 1500–1700* (London: Hodder and Stoughton, 1957), 18.

[6] Leonard Trinterud, "A Reappraisal of William Tyndale's Debt to Martin Luther," *CH* 31 (1962): 24–26, 41; Daniell, *Tyndale*, 119–27. Trinterud believes that 'Tyndale's greatest debt was first to Christian humanism and then to the German-Swiss reformers of Zurich and Basle.' Tyndale did not limit himself to Luther's translations but also made use of Zürich scholarship: William Clebsch, *England's Earliest Protestants, 1525–1535* (Westport, CT:

later deny 'confederacy' with Luther even if he had initially been impressed by him.[7] The earliest of his extant writings was printed at Cologne in 1525: the prologue to his English New Testament. Although select material was appropriated from Luther's German New Testament prologue (1522), Tyndale's prologue was twice as long and demonstrated his independence of mind.

In the couple of pages that did follow Luther closely, Tyndale explained 'newe testament' as when a man

> shall dye appoynteth hys goodds to be dealte and distributed after hys dethe amonge them which he nameth to be hys heyres. Even so Christ before hys dethe commaunded and appoynted that suche evangelion[,] gospel[,] er tydyngs shulde be declared through oute all the worlde and there with to geve unto all that beleve all his goodds that is to saye his lyfe.[8]

The understanding of testament is apparently unilateral. There is insufficient detail to be sure whether faith was a conditional prerequisite in Tyndale's view. The apprehension of Christ by faith is affirmed yet emphasis falls on the rehabilitation of humanity which cannot initiate its own salvation because of the bondage of the will. Owing to original sin, humanity is 'full of the naturall poyson where of all synfull deds spryng.'[9] Christ's work is primarily regenerative, effectively involving the impartation of a proleptic righteousness to the believer.[10] When the elect are plucked out of Adam and grafted

---

Greenwood Press, 1964), 142.

[7] William Tyndale, *An Answer to Sir Thomas More's Dialogue*, ed. H. Walter, PS (Cambridge: CUP, 1849), 147.

[8] William Tyndale, *The New Testament* [*Cologne Fragment*, 1525] (Cologne: H. Fuchs?, 1525; RSTC 2823), A3r. The bequeathing of Christ's 'lyfe' may anticipate the apprehension of Christ and his righteousness by the believer enunciated in 1528.

[9] Ibid., A4v-B1r. This emphasis is more akin to Zwingli than to Luther.

[10] Tyndale understood justification as the healing of human infirmity, generally translating *dikaioō* as 'make righteous.' In five of the thirty-one New Testament verses containing the verbal forms of *dikaioō*, Tyndale preferred

into Christ we 'consent to the lawe and love it inwardly in oure hert and desyre to fulfyll it.'[11] Even if Tyndale's 'testament' here appears to be concurrent with Luther's, his ethical emphasis on the fulfilment of the law was undoubtedly different. Since Tyndale did not conceive of justification as a forensic declaration elicited by faith, reciprocity would have been a natural development of his concept.

Tyndale's *Prologue to the Epistle to the Romans* (1526) also demonstrates that he was not slavishly dependent upon Luther.[12] It departed from Luther's own version by specifying thrice that God was not satisfied by outward works 'only'. Whereas Luther wrote that 'faith alone makes a person righteous,'[13] Tyndale claimed that 'nowe is the sprite no nodyr [other] wyse geven then by fayth only,' which allowed him to preserve the subsequent importance of works to the fulfilment of the law. Such fulfilment required that works be done with love from 'the botome of the hert.'[14] Herein lay Tyndale's soteriological interest: the effect of faith in creating desire to fulfil the law. Whereas Luther had weighted his remarks upon the

---

'account' or 'reckon righteous.' This makes for interesting comparison with Zwingli. See also D. Broughton Knox, *The Doctrine of Faith in the Reign of Henry VIII* (London: James Clarke & Co., 1961), 5–8, 19; Carl Trueman, *Luther's Legacy: Salvation and English Reformers, 1525–1556* (Oxford: OUP, 1994), 84–94. Luther himself allowed a breadth of interpretation, primarily, but by no means exclusively, using language of declaration and acquittal: see Bernhard Lohse, *Martin Luther's Theology: its historical and systematic development*, trans. R. Harrisville (Edinburgh: T&T Clark, 1999), 260.

[11] Tyndale, *Cologne Fragment*, B1r; see also Hall, "Lutheranism in England," 110.

[12] Trueman and Euler, "Reception of Luther," 64; Carl Trueman, "Early English Evangelicals: Three Examples," in *Sister Reformations: the Reformation in Germany and in England: symposium on the occasion of the 450th anniversary of the Elizabethan Settlement, September 23rd-26th, 2009*, ed. D. Wendebourg (Tübingen: Mohr Siebeck, 2010), 18.

[13] Martin Luther, *Preface to the Epistle of St. Paul to the Romans* [1522], trans. C. Jacobs, *LW*, Vol. 35 (Philadelphia: Fortress Press, 1960), 368.

[14] William Tyndale, *A compendious introduccion, prologe or preface vnto the pistle off Paul to the Romayns* (Worms: P. Schoeffer, 1526; RSTC 24438), A2v-A3v, A4v.

freedom to work 'without compulsion' brought by faith,[15] Tyndale enthused that faith gives 'strengthe to worke the dedes of the lawe with love even as the lawe requireth.'[16] His emphasis was not on solifidianism so much as true godliness. He did not, however, relate this to his concept of testament.

Tyndale's first treatise, *The Parable of the Wycked Mammon* (May 1528), was inspired by Luther's *Sermon von dem unrechten Mammon* (1522). Although it expounded justification by faith, Tyndale was undoubtedly more interested in Luther's teaching on the works appropriate after justification.[17] The clearest indication of a concept of covenant is located in a marginal note: 'God hath made an everlastynge covenaunt with us yt we shuld no more go astraye after oure good intent.' The adjacent text refers to a testament which is apparently bilateral: owing to humanity's helplessness 'God made a testamente betwene him & us wherin is contayned bothe what he wolde have us do, and what he would have us to [ask] of him. Se therefore yt thou do nothyng to playse god with all but that he commaundeth.'[18] Although this testament was initiated unilaterally by God, it was the first time Tyndale mentioned a relationship carrying reciprocal responsibilities.[19] This was exceptional, however, because Tyndale did not usually make mutuality explicit. Elsewhere in the treatise God is understood to have made a testament in Christ's blood, with all who trust in Christ's blood.[20] Conversely the bishops

---

[15] Luther, *Preface to Romans*, 371; see Trinterud, "Reappraisal," 27–31.

[16] Tyndale, *Romayns*, A5r; see Joan O'Donovan, *Theology of Law and Authority in the English Reformation* (Grand Rapids: Eerdmans, 2004), 59–62.

[17] Michael McGiffert, "William Tyndale's Conception of Covenant," *JEH* 32 (1981): 175n; Carrie Euler, "Does Faith Translate? Tudor Translations of Martin Luther and the Doctrine of Justification by Faith," *ARG* 101 (2010): 85.

[18] William Tyndale, *A treatyse of the iustificacyon by faith only, otherwise called the parable of the Wyked Mammon* [1528] (Southwarke: Iames Nycolson, 1536; RSTC 24455), I8r; see also Trueman, *Luther's Legacy*, 110.

[19] This is 'clearly in the line of Zürich theology,' writes Jens Møller, "The Beginnings of Puritan Covenant Theology," *JEH* 14 (1963): 51.

[20] Tyndale, *Mammon*, H2v, H5r, M6v.

'wolde devyde you from Christ and his holy testament & ioine you to the pope to beleve in his testament and promises.'[21]

Undoubtedly Tyndale regarded God's testament to be at the core of the Gospel message, even if a bilateral concept of covenant was peripheral in his thought in 1528. It is nonetheless possible with hindsight to detect many of the themes that would eventually become a consolidated concept of covenant. God's law 'requireth impossible thynges of us,' so the right response is faith in 'the glad tydyngs & promyses which God hath made and sworne to us in Christ.' This faith should be unwavering, befitting the fact that God 'cannot but fulfyl his promyses.' Not only are his promises necessarily delivered, they also endure perpetually, for 'Goddes worde onely lasteth for ever and that whiche he hathe sworn doth abyde, when al other thinges peryshe.'[22] This promised salvation is elicited specifically by repentance which involves 'consentinge to the law and belevyng the promyses,' or cleaving to God's promises,[23] because 'the consent of the hart unto the law, is unite & peace betwene god & man.'[24] Luther, by contrast, had written in 1520 that the first concern of every Christian should be 'to strengthen faith alone and through faith to grow in the knowledge, not of works, but of Christ Jesus.'[25]

---

[21] Ibid., A5v. The 'testament of the pope' recurs in William Tyndale, *The exposition of the fyrst epistle of Seynt Jhon with a prologge before it* (Antwerp: M. de Keyser, 1531; RSTC 24443), D2v; William Tyndale, *An exposicion vppon the v. vi. vii. chapters of Mathew* (Antwerp?: J. Grapheus?, 1533?; RSTC 24440), L3v.

[22] Tyndale, *Mammon*, A8r-B2v.

[23] Ibid., B6v, E8v, H2r.

[24] Ibid., F3v-4r, cf. I3v. For Tyndale, justification is based specifically upon the apprehension of Christ's righteousness as one's own. Tyndale echoed Luther in writing that 'by good dedes shalt thou be saued, not which thou hast done, but which christ hath done for ye. For christ is thin[e], & al his dedes are thy dedes. Christ is in the[e] & thou in him knyt together inseparable.' However, Tyndale went beyond Luther when he wrote: 'Moreover thy harte is good, right holy & iust. For thy harte is no enemye to the lawe but a frend & a louer. The law & thy hart are agreed & at one, & therfore is God at one with the[e]': Idem.

[25] Martin Luther, *The Freedom of a Christian* [1520], trans. H. Grimm. *LW*,

Although Tyndale did not emphasise it, in practice repentance functions as a condition: 'if we do repent again, we have always mercy laid up for us.' Subsequently the believer turns himself to God's commandments, which Tyndale expounded as duties. He used the term 'law of love' to link love for God with seeking 'the honoure of god in all men, & to drawe (as much as in hym is) all men unto god.'[26]

It was said that Henry VIII praised Tyndale's next book, published five months later, as one 'for me and all kings to read.'[27] *The Obedience of a Christian Man* (October 1528) defended nascent evangelical doctrine from charges of licence by teaching 'what obedience God requyreth of vs vnto father and mother[,] master[,] lorde[,] kinge & all superiours.'[28] Ryan Reeves has shown that Tyndale adopted Zwingli's reading of Psalm 82 to justify the intervention of the civil magistrate in spiritual affairs, providing 'conclusive evidence that he was influenced by Swiss theology.' Since Zwingli had only introduced this interpretation in late 1526 or early 1527, Tyndale must have enjoyed ready access to the latest teachings from Zürich.[29]

The *Obedience* exhibited numerous examples of Tyndale's use of 'testament' as God's promise, good news or last will.[30] He observed that judicial authority extended to the 'turke or sareson' even though they were 'not vnder the everlastinge testamente of God in Christe.' Indeed, only true believers are included under this testament: 'few of vs which are called Christen be and even no mo[re] then to whom God hath sente his promyses and powred his sprite in to their hertes to beleve them and thorow fayth graven lust in their hertes

---

Vol. 31. (Philadelphia: Fortress Press, 1957), 347.

[26] Tyndale, *Mammon*, H3r, see also G2r.

[27] Strype, *Memorials*, i/1:171–72; see Mozley, *William Tyndale*, 142.

[28] William Tyndale, *The Obedience of a Christen Man and how Christen rulers ought to governe* (Antwerp: J. Hoochstraten [Martin de Keyser?], 1528; RSTC 24446), C1v.

[29] Ryan Reeves, "'Ye Gods': Political Obedience from Tyndale to Cromwell, c.1528–1540," *ARG* 105, 1 (2014): 237.

[30] Tyndale, *Obedience*, C2r, I5v, I6v, L4r, L7v-L8v, M5v, O7r, P6v, Q7r, R2v, R7r-v, S8r, T3v, V3r, V5v.

to fulfill the lawe of love.' Infidels, whether Turks or nominal Christians, are instead under the 'testamente of the lawe naturall' which contains 'promyses of worldly thinges.'[31] Later, assailing Bishop Fisher's sermon of 11 February 1526 against Luther, which had recently become available in print, Tyndale insisted that the Gospel included not only the four Evangelists but the 'open preachinge of Christe and the holy testamente and gracious promises that God hath made in Christes bloude to all that repente and beleve.' Christ, the testament and the promises were to be found in all Scripture.[32]

There were some occasions when Tyndale deployed a bilateral concept of covenant, which would have had obvious utility in countering suspicions of antinomianism. It is evident that the testament made demands upon humanity since it was possible to be 'disobedient vnto Gods testamente.' Those who sought to offer satisfaction other than Christ's blood were trying to 'compell God to obeye' another testament.[33] The only means of salvation was that which God had ordained. Hence Tyndale attacked 'hypocrites' who imitate the outward works of the saints, wrongly supposing that 'the saynt for weringe soch a garmente and for soch deades is become so glorious in heven. Yf I doo lyke wise so shall I be also.' Rather than enjoying God's liberality, such people make saints into mediators 'and of their blinde imaginacion make a testamente or bonde betwene the saynt and them[,] the testamente of Christes bloude cleane forgoten.'[34]

In this instance Tyndale used the words 'testamente' and 'bonde' interchangeably for an agreement 'betwene' two parties—the believer and the saint—suggesting that this testament is mutual and at least implying mutuality in Christ's testament. Similarly, the apostles' preaching of Christ had been accompanied by miracles confirming the promises and eternal testament which 'God had

[31] Ibid., G4v-G5r.
[32] Ibid., H4v-H5r.
[33] Ibid., I6v.
[34] Ibid., E5r.

made betwene man & him in Christes bloude.'[35] God, in contrast to inconstant human kings, is reliable because he 'hath also made vs promyses and hath sworne: ye hath made a testamente or a covenaunt and hath bound him selfe and hath sealed his obligacion with Christes bloude and confirmed it with myracles.'[36] Tyndale uses the terms 'testament' and 'covenaunt' here to express God's obligation. Later in the text, humanity's responsibilities are said to have been appointed in Scripture and consist, with regard to God, of believing his testament.[37] Humanity's responsibilities are not, it seems, part of the testament, although the fact that servants in 'covenauntes' with their masters are to obey them as God is perhaps suggestive.[38]

In January 1529 Tyndale was officially denounced by the Imperial authorities. He relocated from Antwerp to Hamburg, suffering shipwreck *en route*,[39] but his translation of the Pentateuch finally appeared in January 1530.[40] The prologues are significant because they represent the turning point in the development of Tyndale's

---

[35] Ibid., P4v.
[36] Ibid., P7v-P8r.
[37] Ibid., T7v.
[38] Ibid., D4r.
[39] Foxe, *AM* [1583], 8:1101. There is no contemporary evidence of Tyndale's being in Hamburg, but the details of Foxe's account are persuasive: after travelling in two ships Tyndale spent Easter (28 March) until December 1529 in Hamburg assisted by Miles Coverdale, residing in the house of Margaret van Emmerson during an outbreak of sweating sickness. Tyndale probably left Antwerp following official searches for him in summer 1528 and his official denunciation in January 1529. Coverdale's presence is also plausible. See Mozley, *William Tyndale*, 150–53; Marcus Loane, *Masters of the English Reformation*, 2nd ed. (Edinburgh: Banner of Truth, 2005), 82–83. Hamburg's Reformation was secured in 1528–29 making it a good sanctuary for Tyndale's work. Foxe is correct about what was an unusual and sudden outbreak of sweating sickness in Hamburg that year. Perhaps a shipwreck explains Tyndale's selection of Jonah for his next translation.
[40] See Dahlia Karpman, "William Tyndale's Response to the Hebraic Tradition," *Studies in the Renaissance* 14 (1967): 115; G. Lloyd Jones, *The Discovery of Hebrew in Tudor England: a third language* (Manchester: Manchester University Press, 1983), 115–23.

concept of covenant, which almost immediately became definitive for the ethical emphases of his soteriology.[41] The bilateral concept of covenant was much stronger here than in his earlier works, beginning in the preface, which mentioned 'the everlastinge testament[,] promises[,] and a[p]poyntemente made betwene god & vs.'[42] In the Genesis text Tyndale variously translated *berit* as 'apoyntement' (Genesis 6:18; 9:13), 'covenaunte' (Genesis 15:18), 'bonde' (Genesis 9:9, 11–12; 17:7, 13, 19, 21; 21:27, 32; 26:28; 31:44), and 'testamente' (Genesis 9:15–17; 17:7, 9–11, 13–14). At the end of Genesis a glossary offered two possible definitions of 'testament'. The unilateral definition came second: a testament was 'goddes promyses.' Priority was given to the bilateral definition: 'an appoyntement made betwene god and man.' Tyndale clearly understood the testament to place obligations on both parties because he invoked Genesis 17 where circumcision

> representeth the promyses of god to Abraham on the one syde and that Abraham and his s[e]ed shuld circumcyse and cut off the lustes of their fleshe on the other syde to walke in the wayes of the lorde: As baptyme which is come in the roume therof now signifieth on the one syde how that all that repent and beleue are washed in Christes bloud: And on the other syde how that the same must quench and droune the lustes of the flesh to folow the steppes of Christ.[43]

The appointment made requirements of both parties: God should fulfil his promises and Abraham should mortify sin and live a godly

---

[41] Arne Dembek locates the turning point in 1533, even later than Clebsch who saw Tyndale's concept as having matured in 1532: Arne Dembek, *William Tyndale (1491–1536): Reformatorische Theologie als kontextuelle Schriftauslegung* (Tübingen: Mohr Siebeck, 2010), 201, 234, 373; Clebsch, *Earliest Protestants*, 180.

[42] William Tyndale, *The Pentateuch* (Antwerp: Johan Hoochstraten, 1530; RSTC 2350), W.T. to the reader. This work is unpaginated.

[43] Ibid., A table expoundinge certeyn wordes.

life. Tyndale appeared to favour the bilateral meaning by his consistent rendering of *berit* as 'covenaunt' in the 1534 revision of the text. Certainly the meaning of 'testament' as God's promise receded in the revision, although Tyndale presumably also intended to translate the same Hebrew word consistently with the same English word.[44]

In the Exodus prologue from the 1530 edition Tyndale explained that God reliably acts for those who 'beleve his promises and herken vnto his commaundmentes and with pacience cleaue vnto him and walke with him: euen so shall he do for vs, yf we receaue the witnesse of Christ with a stronge faith and endure paciently folowinge his steppes.'[45] It seems likely that Tyndale had in mind the condition of Genesis 17:1 to 'walke before me and be vncorrupte.' Indeed, Tyndale suggested the basic continuity of the Old and New Testaments when he wrote that 'the newe testament was euer, euen from the beginning of the world,' since Christ was always promised. Those who default and 'falle from the fayth of the promyses and love of the lawe and ordinaunces of god' are forsaken by God 'for oure dishonouringe of his name and despisinge of oure neghboure.' Then 'god persecuteth us because we abuse his holye testament, and because when we knowe the truth we folowe it not.' Tyndale sought through his Pentateuch prologues to demonstrate the relevance of the covenantal imperatives and sanctions of the Old Testament to the Christian.

It is important to recognise that Tyndale's emphasis on godliness in the Exodus prologue does not undermine the gracious basis of justification. Justification on the basis of meritorious works was disqualified when Tyndale wrote that 'it is not sayde of that testament he that worketh shall lyue: But he that beleveth shall lyue.' Rather, the condition for receiving the promises of Christ is faith alone, 'in which promyses the electe were then iustifyed inwardly

---

[44] William Tyndale, *The Firste Boke of Moses called Genesis newly correctyd and amendyd by W.T* (Antwerp: M. de Keyser, 1534; RSTC 2351).

[45] Tyndale, *Pentateuch*, Exodus Prologue. On claiming God's faithfulness, see McGiffert, "Tyndale," 174.

before God.'⁴⁶ The promises deliver justification by sending the Spirit: 'the sprete entreth the hart [of those who believe] and quyckeneth it, and geueth her lyfe and iustifieth her.' Faith is the means of receiving the Spirit, but justification is graciously based on the Spirit's action on the heart. The Spirit 'also maketh the lawe a lyuely thing in the herte, so that a man bringeth forth good workes of his awne ac[c]ord without compulsion of the lawe, without feare of threateninges or cursinges.'⁴⁷ Rather than law, it is love which 'compelleth me,' and both 'the fayth of the promyses and love of the lawe' are required by God for the individual to be justified. A lack of works indicates their absence and is deserving of 'persecution' by God.⁴⁸

The essential unity of the Old and New Testaments in Tyndale's theology is apparent in the closing passages of *The Practice of Prelates* (late 1530) which concern Henry VIII's 'Great Matter'. The Mosaic Law was divided into three parts: ceremonial, penal, and natural.⁴⁹ The ceremonial laws 'cease assone as christ had offered upp the

---

⁴⁶ Tyndale, *Pentateuch*, Exodus Prologue.

⁴⁷ Ibid.; see Luther, *Freedom of a Christian*, 348–49.

⁴⁸ Tyndale, *Pentateuch*, Exodus Prologue. Tyndale is 'extremely vague' on the atonement (Trueman, *Luther's Legacy*, 88) and although the synthesis here seems justified it is important to remember that Tyndale did not utilise an *ordo salutis* framework (Trueman, *Luther's Legacy*, 87n). In a separate category was justification 'outwardly before the world by kepynge of the lawe and ceremonies' in the sense that works declare the righteousness of the believer in the sight of God. Tyndale was not expounding 'double justification' (wherein justification is partly based on works) since outward justification is only a testimony of the justifying work of the Spirit on the heart and corresponds to what is more commonly known as 'sanctification.' See Trueman, *Luther's Legacy*, 102–4; Dermot Fenlon, *Heresy and Obedience in Tridentine Italy: Cardinal Pole and the Counter Reformation* (Cambridge: CUP, 1972), 53–61. Tyndale's position has therefore been misrepresented by Knox who accuses him of 'overthrowing the whole basis of the Reformation!': Knox, *Doctrine of Faith*, 6, 19–21. Knox's criticism is valid only if the 'basis of the Reformation' is defined as Luther's solifidianism. See Wainwright, "William Tyndale."

⁴⁹ See Philip Melanchthon, *Loci Communes Theologici* [1535], ed. W. Pauck, *LCC*, Vol. 19 (London: SCM, 1969), 53f. Tyndale probably had access to the 1521 edition.

sacrifice of his bodye and bloude for us,' but had functioned in part to signify to the Jews 'the promysse and appoyntement made betwene god and man.'[50] Penal laws bound the Jews only. However, the natural law, the law of faith and love requiring belief, trust and love of God, 'pertayneth unto all nacyons indifferentlye.' This law applied apart from Moses and 'whosoever hath this lawe graven in his harte this same kepeth all lawes.' Tyndale expounded these laws from the Decalogue. He emphasised the efficacy of natural law to propagate true worship of God.[51] This is not legalism, since Tyndale was discussing the life of worshipful obedience of the loving Christian under God's testament rather than the forensic justification of the sinner.[52]

1531 was a prolific year of publication for Tyndale. In May his translation of Jonah appeared, reiterating justification by grace with a reminder that 'the fulfillynge of the law is a fastfayth in christes bloud coupled wt our profession & submyttinge ourselues to lerne to doo better.'[53] A willingness to become godly was essential: 'On

---

[50] William Tyndale, *The Practyse of Prelates, whether the kinges grace maye be separated from hys quene, be cause she was his brothers wyfe* (Antwerp: Joannes Hoochstraten, 1530; RSTC 24465), H8r.

[51] Ibid., I1r.

[52] Clebsch misconstrues Tyndale's increased emphasis on mutuality in 1530 as a radical innovation. Tyndale's first mention of a 'bipartite agreement' was in 1528 and not in *The Practice of Prelates* as Clebsch suggests (Clebsch, *Earliest Protestants*, 161). Trueman's impression of fundamental consistency in Tyndale's writings obscures the increased emphasis on mutuality, and his observations on forensic justification do not reflect Tyndale's own focus on God's promise to 'kepe them that kepe his lawes' after justification: Trueman, *Luther's Legacy*, 106–7, 119; Tyndale, *Practyse of Prelates*, H7r; see also C. S. Lewis, *English Literature in the Sixteenth Century excluding Drama* (Oxford: OUP, 1954), 182f; W. D. J. Cargill Thompson, "The Two Regiments: the continental setting of William Tyndale's political thought," in *Reform and Reformation: England and the Continent c.1500–c.1750*, ed. D. Baker (Oxford: Blackwell, 1979), 26. McGiffert's study concentrating on conditionality and works in Tyndale's theology exonerates him from charges of legalism: see McGiffert, "Tyndale," 167–84.

[53] William Tyndale, *The Prophete Ionas* (Antwerp: M. de Keyser, 1531; RSTC 2788), A4r.

the one syde' God treats with compassion 'his electe which submitte them selues as scolers to lerne to walke in the wayes of his lawes & to kepe them of loue.' 'On the other side' those who do not meet this condition, 'they that hardened their hertes & synned of malice & refused mercie that was offered them & had no power to repent perished at the later ende with all confusion & shame mercilessely.'[54] Within God's sovereign choice there was both blessing and curse, yet the emphasis was on the ability of the believer to act so as to elicit God's compassion. Jonah was the story of 'an obligacion betwene God and thy soule'[55] in which the believer could exercise the will and ability to be godly by faith in God's promise implanted in the heart:

> with Jonas let them that wayte on vanities & seke god here & there & in euery temple saue in their hertes goo & seke thou the testament of god in thyne hert. For in thyne hert is the worde of the law & in thyne hert is the worde of fayth in the promises of mercie in Jesus Christe. So that yf thou confesse with a repentynge herte & knowlege and surely beleue that Jesus is lorde ouer all synne thou art saffe.[56]

Thus faith was a part of Tyndale's concept of true worship according to the testament, giving confidence in the attainment of victory over sin.

In July 1531 Tyndale's *Answer* to Sir Thomas More's barbed *Dialogue concerning heresies* (1529) was published. Tyndale wrote that 'the testament of Christ's blood' is received by Christians and 'in it' they 'walketh and serveth God in the spirit,'[57] suggesting that believers' participation in the testament is not passive. The testament was the forgiveness of sins, built not on works but on faith in Christ's blood. Works deserved no reward, whether their motivation

---

[54] Ibid., A4v-A5r.
[55] Ibid., A6r.
[56] Ibid., C3r.
[57] Tyndale, *Answer*, 108–9.

was 'worldly' or 'heavenly'.[58] Particularly noteworthy with regard to Tyndale's *Answer* is William Clebsch's detection of the influence of *Vom Alten und Neuen Gott* by Joachim Vadian, the reformer of St Gall and a kindred spirit of Zwingli's.[59] This connection increases the likelihood of Tyndale's acquaintance with other Swiss Reformed theological works.[60]

In the autumn of 1531 Tyndale applied his consolidated concept of covenant to the New Testament. He revised his New Testament prologue of 1525 as *A Pathway into the Holy Scripture* with a dozen additions achieving a more nuanced biblical theology of the Christian life. That God fulfils his promises 'for his [Christ's] sake' affirmed justification by grace through faith: 'Christ bringeth the love of God unto us, and not our own holy works.' Nonetheless, at the point of justification 'we receive love unto the law, and power to fulfil it, and grow therein daily.'[61] Tyndale opposed attempts to fulfil the law by 'outward deeds' with the truth that 'love only is the fulfilling of the law.' The believer fulfils the law by having faith, consenting to the righteousness of the law, thereby justifying God its maker, and having the desire to fulfil it. This is the love that fulfils the law: although they cannot 'always' fulfil it in their lives, they genuinely want to.[62] The convert experiences a shift from desire for

---

[58] Ibid., 200, 204.

[59] Clebsch, *Earliest Protestants*, 169–70.

[60] Wayne Baker believes that Tyndale could easily have accessed Zwingli's writings: J. Wayne Baker, *Heinrich Bullinger and the Covenant: The Other Reformed Tradition* (Athens, OH: Ohio University Press, 1980), 208–9; Zwingli's influence is also asserted by Gregory Miller, "Huldrych Zwingli," in *The Reformation Theologians: an introduction to theology in the early modern period*, ed. C. Lindberg (Oxford: Blackwell, 2002), 165. Bullinger's influence is inferred to explain Tyndale's interest in covenant by Patrick Collinson, "William Tyndale and the Course of the English Reformation," *Reformation* 1 (1996): 87. Ralph Werrell's view that Tyndale was completely at odds with continental concepts of covenant is impossible to sustain: Ralph Werrell, *The Theology of William Tyndale* (Cambridge: James Clarke & Co., 2006), 46–47.

[61] Tyndale, *Treatises*, 11.

[62] Ibid., 12–13.

the devil's law to a desire for God's.[63] Although 'we know that good deeds are rewarded, both in this life and the life to come,' they are not rewarded with justification in the sight of God.[64] Instead Tyndale writes of sanctification wherein 'we wax perfecter alway' and perform the true worship of God 'with working according to the doctrine, and not with blind works of our own imagining.'[65]

The covenant hermeneutic which underpinned the *Pathway* was explained in Tyndale's *Exposition of the fyrste epistle of seynt Jhon* published in September 1531. He traced the concept of covenant historically to the ancient world 'when a loue day or a truse was made betwene man and man the couenauntes were rehersid: and upon that they slewe bestes in a memorial and remembraunce of thappoyntement only.'[66] In view of humanity's natural inability to understand Scripture, Tyndale invoked appreciation of the covenant as the necessary tool for comprehension:

> If our hertes wer taught thappoyntment made between god & us in Christes bloud when we wer baptised we had the kay to open the scripture & light to se & perceyve the true meaning of it & the scripture shulde be easy to understonde. And because we be not taght that profession is the cause whi the scripture is so darke & so fare passinge our capacyte.[67]

---

[63] Ibid., 17–19.
[64] Ibid., 20.
[65] Ibid., 23. The *Pathway* is traduced as religion subsumed under morality by Clebsch, *Earliest Protestants*, 168. On the contrary, morality was put to the service of piety, writes McGiffert, "Tyndale," 175. Tyndale was making an impassioned call to a life of worship in truth and love which is different from the ethical imperatives seen by Clebsch, yet more profound than a simple reaffirmation of good works proving inward justification observed by Trueman, *Luther's Legacy*, 102.
[66] Tyndale, *Exposition of the fyrst epistle of Seynt Jhon*, H1r-v.
[67] Ibid., A5v.

The true worship of God is 'to love hym for his mercye,' which love is expressed in good works and personal holiness.[68] Immediately followed 'the conditions of the peace that is made betwene God & us in Christes bloude':

> The lawe is set befor us unto which if we consent and submit oure selves to be scholers therof then are not only al oure forsinnnes forgiven both *p[o]ena* and *culpa* (with our holy fathers licence ever) but also al our infirmities weknes pronite [proneness] redinese and motions unto sinne are pardoned and taken awarth and we translated frome under the damnation of the lawe [. . .]. So that we shal not henceforth as longe as we forsake not our profession be iudged by the rigournese of the lawe But chastised if we do amyse as children that ar under no lawe.[69]

This mutual, conditional covenant was described by Tyndale as an 'indentyd obligation' binding on both parties.[70] It was unilaterally initiated by God for salvation, confirmed by his Spirit, and carried the threat of damnation for the impenitent covenant-breaker:

> For first God which alone hath powere to helpe or hurte hath made apoyntment betwixt hym & us in Christes bloude & hath bounde hym self to g[i]ve us what so ever we [ask] in his name testifiynge therto that ther is no nother name to be savyd by & that he wilbe a father unto us & save us bothe in this life & in the lyfe to come & take us from under the damnation of the lawe & set us under grace and mercie to be scholers only to learne the lawe and that our unperfect dedes

---

[68] Ibid., B8r.
[69] Ibid., B8v, see also C5r, C6v.
[70] Ibid., C5v. *OED*: 'an indenture was a deed between two or more parties with mutual obligations, executed in two or more copies, all having their tops or edges indented or serrated for identification and security.'

shalbe taken in worth ye and thought at a tyme we marre al thoroue oure infirmitie yet if we turne agayne that shabe forgeuen us mercifully so that we shalbe under no damnation: which testament is confirmed with signes and wonders wrought thorowe the holy gost.[71]

Tyndale's literary output during 1531, and his exposition of 1 John pre-eminently so, was the fruit of a consolidation of the concept of covenant which had probably begun in 1529. His writings became more robust in their treatment of the Christian life as compared, for instance, to his Romans Prologue of 1526. The reciprocal covenant was not so much an innovation in Tyndale's theology as the amplification of aspects of his earlier concept of testament. This is suggested by Tyndale's enduring preference for the word 'testament' in 1530–31, albeit redefined as 'appointment'.[72]

The remainder of Tyndale's writings exhibited a soteriology harmonised, but not practically altered, by the consolidated concept of covenant already established by 1531. His *Exposicion vppon the v. vi. vii. chapters of Mathew* (1533)[73] claimed them as 'the keye

---

[71] Tyndale, *Exposition of the fyrst epistle of Seynt Jhon*, C5v; see also John King, "Thomas More, William Tyndale, and the Printing of Religious Propaganda," in *The Oxford Handbook of Tudor Literature, 1485*–1603, eds. M. Pincombe and C. Shrank (Oxford: OUP, 2009), 113.

[72] Clebsch is incorrect to claim that the meaning 'appointment' first appeared in the *Exposition* since Tyndale had given this definition of 'testament' in his Pentateuch glossary twenty-one months earlier. See the otherwise useful analysis in Clebsch, *Earliest Protestants*, 172–73.

[73] Tyndale, like other Reformed theologians, argued that in the Sermon on the Mount Christ was restoring the Old Testament law from the corruption of the Pharisees, a 'spiritual Isaac' re-digging the wells of Abraham. Christ was not introducing new legislation. This opposed both the Roman argument that Christ instituted new 'counsels of perfection' and the Anabaptist rejection of Old Testament commands on the basis of Christ's new law. I am grateful to Dr Sarah Mortimer for discussion of this point. In Tyndale's *Brief Declaration of the Sacraments* he closely aligned salvation through Christ with the keeping of the law: 'they only, w[hich] turne to god to kepe hys Lawes shall haue mercye

and the dore' of Scripture, and his prologue contained 'the whole somme of the couenaunt made betwene God and vs, vppon which we be baptised to kepe it.'[74] Emphasising the conditionality of God's promises, Tyndale wrote that they 'are all made on this condition or covenant on our party, that we henceforth love the law of God, to walk therein, and to do it, and to fashion our lives thereafter.' The promise of justification was not, however, based on law-keeping but, like a king pardoning a murderer, the condition that 'he henceforth keep the law' was imposed, meaning that the law must be kept to remain in God's favour following justification.[75] This meant, for example, that in the case of the petition from the Lord's Prayer, 'if thou wilt entre in to the couenaunt of thy lorde God, and forgeue thy brother: then what so euer thou hast committed agaynst God, if thou repent and [ask] him forgeuenesse, thou art sure that thou art so absoued by these wordes, that none in heauen ner erthe can bynde the.'[76]

The righteousness of the Christian was consequently based upon faith and also upon consent in the heart to the goodness of the law and submission to it.[77] At the point of conversion, or reconciliation, righteousness was entirely alien (it 'cometh of God altogether'), but after atonement and reconciliation 'we be partlye ryghtwesse in oure selves and unrightwese' reflecting our degree of sanctification.[78]

---

for chrysts sake': William Tyndale, *A Briefe Declaration of the Sacraments* (London: Robert Stoughton, 1548; RSTC 24445), C3r.

[74] Tyndale, *Mathew*, title page. McGiffert argues that Tyndale's continued relation of the covenant to the New Testament undermines Clebsch's view that engagement with the Pentateuch was seminal for its 'discovery': McGiffert, "Tyndale," 175n.

[75] William Tyndale, *Expositions and Notes on Sundry Portions of the Holy Scriptures, together with the Practice of Prelates*, ed. H. Walter, PS (Cambridge: CUP, 1849), 6–7 (the corresponding leaf A3r-v is missing in the 1533 edition being used here).

[76] Tyndale, *Mathew*, K3v-4r.

[77] Ibid., C6r.

[78] Ibid., K6r. This seems to be a more nuanced understanding than in the Romans prologue (1526) where righteousness is equivalent to a faith that

Tyndale was nonetheless at pains to separate the discharge of mankind's duty from God's decision to bind himself to the promise of justification. For his part, God was always righteous unless he could be shown to be breaking his own promise to 'them that kepe covenaunt with him.'[79] God had promised to help the believer to keep his part of the covenant, to accept imperfect faith and effort, and to forgive failure.[80]

Why, asked Tyndale, should God bless those who dishonour him? Those who keep the law receive temporal blessing while those who break it are punished.[81] He divided humanity in two: those who 'entre' and 'kepe the covenaunt' who need 'feare no Bugges [bugbears],' and those who 'wilt not come with in the covenaunt' or 'have professed it and [. . .] cast the yoke of the lorde from of thy necke.' Both of the latter were 'bounde by these woordes so fast that none in heaven or in erthe can lowse the.'[82] The covenant thus contained imminent sanctions against transgressors.

The new prologue to Tyndale's revised English New Testament (November 1534) emphasised the concept of covenant as being

---

changes the believer's nature. See Tyndale, *Romayns*, A7r-v. It is also sounds similar to Luther's formulation '*simul iustus et peccator*,' but Tyndale was not teaching extrinsic justification. See Martin Luther, *Lectures on Romans*, ed. H. Oswald, *LW*, Vol. 25 (St Louis, MO: Concordia, 1972), 260.

[79] Tyndale, *Mathew*, C8v-D1r; see Trueman, *Luther's Legacy*, 113–16; Collinson, "Tyndale," 88. Trueman and Collinson distinguish Tyndale's 'covenant' from a legalistic 'contract' making salvation conditional on human works. The term itself seems unproblematic if understood as the Latin *contractio* (a drawing-together), see McGiffert, "Tyndale," 174; Clebsch, *Earliest Protestants*, 189–90. The unmerited, familial nature of the relationship—like the parent who promises a child 'a good thynge for the doynge of some trifle' (Tyndale, *Mathew*, K6r)—can be held together with the image of a king pardoning a murderer: Tyndale, *Expositions*, 7; Tyndale, *Mathew*, A3r-v.

[80] Tyndale, *Mathew*, M7r-v. On the wholly gracious nature of reward, which amounts to sanctification, see Emma Disley, "Degrees of Glory: Protestant Doctrine and the Concept of Rewards Hereafter," *JTS* 42, 1 (1991): 74–75, 100.

[81] Tyndale, *Mathew*, F5r, see also L3r, M5v-M6r.

[82] Ibid., K4r.

what readers needed if they were to understand Scripture. It began boldly: 'Here thou hast (most dear reader) the new testament or covenant made with us of God in Christ's blood.' The 'general covenant' referred to God's binding himself to the promise of mercy in Christ for those who keep his laws. Within this general covenant were subsidiary covenants (or promises) which Tyndale noted in the margins (he cited Matthew 5:7; 6:14; 7:7). Whenever there was a 'promise' lacking mention of a 'covenant,' 'there must thou understand a covenant. For all the promises of the mercy and grace that Christ hath purchased for us, are made upon the condition that we keep the law.'[83] Again, 'on that condition that we love and work, is mercy given us.'[84] Faith yielded salvation 'according to the covenants and appointment made between God and us.' Both faith and active repentance were needed to 'begin a Christian man.' Repentance involved fighting against 'our corrupt nature perpetually' to keep God's law.[85]

In this ongoing battle God chastened the believer until 'he be at utter defiance with his flesh.' Antinomianism was excluded by the conditionality of covenant membership which was maintained by good deeds: 'Let us walk in the fear of God, and have our eyes open unto both parts of God's covenants [faith and law], certified that none shall be partaker of the mercy, save he that will fight against the flesh, to keep the law.'[86] Those who refuse God's offer of covenant mercy and 'will not come under the covenant' become more degenerate through the withdrawal of grace. Unbelievers were liable because the 'general covenant' applied to all humanity, whereas in 1528 the 'testament' was a promise to believers only. Meanwhile, those who have a faith 'built on the sand of their own imaginations, and not on

---

[83] William Tyndale, *The New Testament* [1534], ed. D. Daniell (New Haven & London: YUP, 1995), 4–5.

[84] Ibid., 274. Trueman thinks that this means that 'a justified man can finally fall away,' but Tyndale was not discussing the doctrine of perseverance here: Trueman, *Luther's Legacy*, 87n.

[85] Tyndale, *New Testament* [1534], 4–5.

[86] Ibid., 7.

the rock of God's word according to his covenants'—seen by a lack of love for God's law—will face judgment with a sense of desperation.[87]

Finally, in 1535, in his exposition of William Tracy's ardently evangelical will, Tyndale made it clear that a person must discharge a covenantal requirement in order to benefit from God's promise. He wrote that 'God neuer made promes but apon an appoyntment or couenaunt vnder which who so euer wyll not come can be no partaker of the promes.' God's promise was always conditional on a proper response and, having responded, 'damnable is yt alto to leaue the couenaunt made yn Chrystes bloude.'[88]

Tyndale's concept of covenant gradually evolved from being one strand of his theology in 1525 into his central understanding of God's testament by 1530. It seems highly likely that Swiss Reformed theology was a significant contributor to his concept of covenant.[89] Tyndale's early ethical emphases were harmonised within the covenant framework which co-ordinated the justifying work of the Spirit with the responsibilities of the believer in the pursuit of godliness. One of his principal aims in the 1530s was to equip Christians with the covenant framework that they would need to understand Scripture.

Miles Coverdale

When the Luther controversy broke in England in the early 1520s Coverdale was an Augustinian friar in Cambridge under the

---

[87] Tyndale, *New Testament* [1534], 5–6.

[88] See John Frith and William Tyndale, *The Testament of Master Wylliam Tracie Esquier, expounded both by William Tindall and Ihon Frith* (Antwerp: H. Peetersen van Middelburch?, 1535; RSTC 24167), A6r, A8r; see also McGiffert, "Tyndale," 179–80.

[89] See Clebsch, *Earliest Protestants*, 199; Trueman, *Luther's Legacy*, 117–18. Tyndale's own Bible study could have sufficed for the development of his concept, claims Theodore Bozeman, *The Precisianist Strain: Disciplinary Religion and Antinomian Backlash in Puritanism to 1638* (Chapel Hill, NC and London: University of North Carolina Press, 2004), 23.

reformist prior Robert Barnes, whom we have already met in connection with Richard Bayfield. This Yorkshireman became, in the words of John Bale, 'one of the first to make a pure profession of Christ.'[90] In 1525–27 he was studying Scripture and working to strengthen connections amongst religious dissidents, and he was indebted to the patronage of Thomas Cromwell.[91] By Lent 1528 Foxe recounts that he had abandoned regular orders when he toured Essex preaching in favour of a commemorative understanding of the Eucharist and against the veneration of images.[92]

Later that year Coverdale began his first exile to the continent to escape Bishop Tunstall's wave of persecution,[93] and he must have completed the first of his translations of continental theology about this time. He chose a Zürich text: Bullinger's *Christen state of matrimonye*.[94] Bullinger defined wedlock as a 'couenaunt' which he explained in terms of God's covenant with his people and wrote that this covenant required 'the good consent of them both,' man and woman.[95] From this Coverdale might have begun to appreciate Bullinger's idea of mutuality in the biblical concept of covenant.

Coverdale's travels allowed him to be in Hamburg to help Tyndale prepare his Pentateuch in 1529.[96] He was a colleague, therefore,

---

[90] Quoted in J. F. Mozley, *Coverdale and His Bibles* (London: Lutterworth, 1953), 3.

[91] Miles Coverdale, *Remains of Myles Coverdale, Bishop of Exeter*, ed. G. Pearson, PS (Cambridge: CUP, 1846), 490–91; MacCulloch, *Cromwell*, 69.

[92] Foxe, *AM* [1570], 8:1228–29.

[93] Mozley, *William Tyndale*, 121.

[94] The translation was recorded in a list of prohibited books: *TRP*, i. #122.

[95] Heinrich Bullinger, *The Christen State of Matrimonye*, trans. M. Coverdale (Antwerp: M. Crom, 1541; RSTC 4045), unpaginated leaf between 3v and 4r. This reprint from 1541 is the earliest extant copy of Coverdale's translation.

[96] See John Vowell, ed., *The Antient History and Description of the City of Exeter* [. . .] *with a catalogue of all the bishops to the year of our Lord 1578* (Exeter: Andrews and Trewman, 1765), 279; Mozley, *Coverdale*, 4–5; Esther Hildebrandt, "A Study of the English Protestant Exiles in Northern Switzerland and Strasbourg 1539–47, and Their Role in the English Reformation," PhD diss. (University of Durham, 1982), 56. Coverdale's command of Hebrew and

at the very time when Tyndale's concept of testament was consolidated into a bilateral, conditional form. He returned with, or followed, Tyndale to Antwerp, where he worked as a printer's assistant for Martin de Keyser, Tyndale's publisher.⁹⁷ Coverdale was certainly in Antwerp when John Rogers arrived in 1534, for he and Rogers were described by George Joye in February 1535 as Tyndale's 'two discipl[es] that gaped so longe for their masters morsel,' that is, the revised New Testament.⁹⁸ Coverdale must have been very familiar with Tyndale's mature concept of covenant, even assisting Tyndale with the translations which would eventually be incorporated into Matthew's Bible (1537).⁹⁹

In October 1535, five months after Tyndale's arrest, Coverdale published his own English Bible, supplementing the texts of Tyndale and Joye with his own translations. He relied heavily upon the Zürich Bible and Luther's recently published German Bible.¹⁰⁰ The

---

Greek was very limited but he would have been a valuable English proofreader. There is no reason to identify Coverdale as Tyndale's earliest assistant in the production of the New Testament in 1525–26, that is, the 'faythfull companyon which now hath taken another vyage apon him to preach Christ where (I suppose) he was never yet preached': Tyndale, *Mammon*, A2r. Coverdale was in London with Barnes in February 1526 when Tyndale's New Testament appeared there. Otherwise he was in Cambridge.

⁹⁷ J. P. Gelbert, *Magister Johann Bader's Leben und Schriften, Nicolaus Thomae und seine briefe* (Neustadt: A. P. Gottschict-Witter, 1868), 275.

⁹⁸ George Joye, *An Apolgye made by George Ioye to satisfye (if it maye be) W. Tindale to pourge & defende himself ageinst many sclaunderouse lyes fayned vpon him* (London: J. Byddell, 1535; RSTC 14820), C6v; see also John Foxe, *AM* [1576], 11:1439.

⁹⁹ Foxe, *AM* [1576], 8:1074; Miles Coverdale and William Tyndale, *The Byble* [. . .] *truly and purely translated into Englysh by Thomas Matthew*, ed. John Rogers (Antwerp: Matthew Crom for Richard Grafton and Edward Whitchurch, 1537; RSTC 2066).

¹⁰⁰ Miles Coverdale, *Biblia the Bible* [. . .] *faithfully and truly translated out of Douche and Latyn in to Englishe* (Cologne?: E. Cervicornus and J. Soter?, 1535; RSTC 2063). Scholars have successively favoured Zürich, Cologne and Marburg as the likely place of publication, but now Antwerp is established as such: Guido Latré, "The 1535 Coverdale Bible and its Antwerp Origins," in

opening argument of the prologue deployed the Zwinglian interpretation of Psalm 82 to support the Royal Supremacy.[101] In the prologue Coverdale emphasised the divine law of the Pentateuch, mentioned that God comforts 'with his promes' in Genesis, and explained how the New Testament was related to those promises: 'the New Testament or Gospell, is a manyfest and cleare testymony of Christ how God perfourmeth his ooth and promes made in the olde Testament, how the New is declared and included in the Olde, and the Olde fulfylled and verifyed in the New.'[102] For Coverdale, the divine promises harmonised the Testaments, but he did not attempt to delineate mutuality or conditionality in the prologue. In his translation of Genesis 15 and 17 he consistently translated *berit* as 'covenant,' following Tyndale's revisions of 1534. In 1537 Coverdale's prologue to *A goodly treatise of faith, hope, and charitie* emphasised the necessity of good works to 'true fayth' and being 'made righteous': 'By thys workynge or endeuoure to please God' there comes hope of eternal life, 'not of dewtye [. . .] but only of Gods bounteous goodnesse and mercye.'[103] Coverdale's insistence on godly living in order to enjoy God's promise was consistent with Tyndale's emphases but the concept of covenant was not made explicit.

Why did Coverdale appear relatively indifferent to Reformed

The Bible as book: the Reformation, ed. O. O'Sullivan (New Castle and London: Oak Knoll Press, 2000), 89–102. See also G. Paisey and G. Bartrum, "Hans Holbein and Miles Coverdale: a new Woodcut," *Print Quarterly* 26 (2009): esp. 244–46. On the influence of Zwingli and Zürich on Coverdale see Miller, "Zwingli," 165; Bruce Gordon, *The Swiss Reformation* (Manchester & New York: Manchester University Press, 2002), 299–300.

[101] Reeves, "Ye Gods," 250.

[102] Miles Coverdale, *Biblia the Byble [. . .] faithfully translated in to Englyshe* (Southwark?: J. Nycolson, 1535; RSTC 2063.3), +5v-+6r. Clebsch observes that Coverdale 'adopted Tyndale's covenant theology' in the preface: Clebsch, *Earliest Protestants*, 193.

[103] Miles Coverdale, *A goodly treatise of faith, hope, and charite necessary for all Christen men to know and to exercyse themselues therein translated into Englyshe* (Southwark: James Nicolson, 1537; RSTC 24219.5), A1v.

theology in the late 1530s despite his collaboration with Tyndale?[104] Significant evidence of his concept of covenant only emerges in the early 1540s. The explanation is probably political: as we have seen, official negotiations with the German Lutherans presented the most promising prospect for evangelical progress in England between 1534 and 1539. Coverdale must have recognised that the cause of reform was advancing at Cromwell's instigation; it was with Cromwell's support that he had been able to publish his English Bible.[105] Thus he returned to England late that year and translated several Lutheran texts in 1537 and 1538,[106] no doubt mindful of renewed talks with the Saxons from the summer of 1537 and the inclusion of Robert Barnes on the discussion committee in 1538.[107] In 1538 Coverdale was in Paris occupied with Cromwell's commission to revise Matthew's Bible. He seemed eager to express the loyalty of those working on the revision to the Crown, reporting to Cromwell on 30 October 1538: 'all we, that be here of the king's nation, are even of one heart and humble mind toward God and

---

[104] Leonard Trinterud, "The Origins of Puritanism," *CH* 20, 1 (1951): 44. It is arguable that Trinterud's examination of English Bibles before 1550 demonstrates neither indifference to mutuality nor preference for a unilateral promise, but rather the interchangeable meaning of 'testament'. In Taverner's Bible (1539) 'testament' was defined as 'the olde testament (that is to saye the couvenaunt [. . .]. The newe testament consysteth [. . .] in the sprite, which is gyven thorow fayth, and which doth write his lawes in our hertes.' The marginal note to Genesis 17 reads: 'Testament is in scripture taken for the moste parte for a couvenant bargayne or leage': Richard Taverner, *The Most Sacred Bible* [. . .] *translated into English* (London: John Byddell, for Thomas Barthlet, 1539; RSTC 2066), 'definitions' and 5r. The covenant teaching in Matthew's Bible might have influenced many readers (Møller, "Beginnings," 54) and Clebsch points out that the majority of Tyndale's Bibles printed from 1535–52 included the prologues and notes of 1534 which contained covenant teaching: Clebsch, *Earliest Protestants*, 188–89.

[105] MacCulloch, *Cromwell*, 363.

[106] RSTC 16999; 18878; 16979.7; 17000. Coverdale included no prologues to reveal his evaluations of these texts.

[107] Rory McEntegart, *Henry VIII, the League of Schmalkalden and the English Reformation* (Woodbridge: Royal Historical Society, 2002), 78, 92–93, 108.

our sovereign.' He was also prepared to censor his personal views on unspecified 'dark places of the text,' writing on 13 December: 'As for any private opinion or contentious words, as I will utterly avoid all such [. . .] if it be your lordship's good pleasure that I shall so do.'[108] In February and March 1539 he was in Newbury exhorting people still favouring the pope 'to increase in due obedience towards the king's highness.'[109]

The Great Bible was printed in April 1539, a month before Lutheran negotiations finally collapsed. In the Genesis text 'testament,' 'covenant' and 'bond' were used interchangeably to translate *berît*, in spite of Tyndale's and Coverdale's consistent preference for 'covenant' in 1534 and 1535 respectively.[110] In the late 1530s Coverdale exemplified the kind of cunning conformity to official Reformation discussed in chapter two. His earlier propensity to Swiss theology could easily have been a hindrance and plenteous evidence of his concept of covenant from the early 1540s seems to suggest that he had been hiding his views.

In response to the Act of Six Articles (28 June 1539) Coverdale returned into exile and made directly for Strassburg with his new wife, arriving there in the autumn of 1540. For three years, writes Esther Hildebrandt, he was 'a student of the Reformation, somewhat in the style which Hooper was to adopt.'[111] The Coverdales were made welcome by another newly-wed couple, John Calvin and Idelette de Bure.[112] Perhaps they discussed the concept of covenant developed by Calvin in the first edition of his *Institutes* in

---

[108] Coverdale, *Remains*, 492–98; see MacCulloch, *Cromwell*, 492.

[109] Coverdale, *Remains*, 498–502.

[110] *The Byble in Englyshe* [The Great Bible] (Paris: Francis Regnaut; London: Rychard Grafton and Edward Whitchurch, 1539; RSTC 2068); see Trinterud, "Origins," 44.

[111] Hildebrandt, "Protestant Exiles," 57–58. It was during this period that Coverdale took his doctorate from Tübingen University. The choice of Strassburg seems significant because Coverdale's sister and brother-in-law first went to Wittenberg, and Coverdale could have done the same: Mozley, *Coverdale*, 8.

[112] Coverdale, *Remains*, 526.

1536. Certainly, Coverdale utilised the concept in his subsequent publications.

Before the end of 1540 Coverdale published at Marburg his *Fruitfull lessons, vpon the passion, buriall, resurrection, ascension, and of the sending of the holy Ghost*. It was modelled on Zwingli's treatise *A brief commemoration of the death of Christ out of the four Evangelists*, but was so expanded as to be substantially original.[113] Coverdale must have begun it before, or very soon after, his flight abroad. Its primary concern is to teach sanctification and godly living after the example of Christ,[114] and some notable points are made: love fulfils all the law and must be expressed through the keeping of God's precepts;[115] grace will be withdrawn from those who do not work;[116] the commandments are kept by means of God's strength in us;[117] salvation depends upon faith and submission to Christ's yoke.[118]

The covenant principle of interpretation is not everywhere explicit but when it comes to the surface it does so forcefully. Coverdale prayed, with reference to the eternal and mutual covenant, 'O Lord Iesu Christ, drawe thou our hearts vnto thee, ioyne them together in vnseparable loue, that they may feruently burne: that wee

---

[113] Hildebrandt, "Protestant Exiles," 57–58. Coverdale must have had access to a manuscript copy before Leo Jud published Zwingli's text in 1544. See Gottfried Locher, *Zwingli's Thought: New Perspectives* (Leiden: Brill, 1981), 366. *Fruitfull Lessons* is dated 1540–47 in Miles Coverdale, *Writings and Translations of Myles Coverdale, Bishop of Exeter*, ed. G. Pearson, PS (Cambridge: CUP, 1844). The earliest extant copy dates from 1593.

[114] Miles Coverdale, *Fruitfull Lessons, vpon the Passion, Buriall, Resurrection, Ascension, and of the sending of the Holy Ghost gathered out of the foure euangelists: with a plaine exposition of the same* (London: Thomas Scarlet, 1593; RSTC 5891), ¶1r-¶2v. According to Bozeman, 'this work assesses the human condition largely in terms of personal and social "wickedness and iniquity" and gives far more play to the self's moral reconstruction and empowerment than to pardon and comfort': Bozeman, *Precisianist Strain*, 19n.

[115] Coverdale, *Fruitfull Lessons*, C2v.
[116] Ibid., D3v, F1r.
[117] Ibid., D4r.
[118] Ibid., G3r-v.

may abide in thee, & thou in vs, & that the euerlasting couenant betweene vs may stand sure for euer.'[119] The passionate love which defines the relationship is inescapable, and Coverdale located it within a familial context in which Christians enjoy fellowship with the Trinity. Christ's incarnation and atonement made this relationship possible:

> Christ also calleth those that bee his, not seruants, but friends and brethren: he will be our God, and wee his people: our father, we his children: and his couenant which he hath made with vs, shall bee euerlasting, for it is sealed and confirmed with the bloud of his onely begotten sonne. Now haue wee fellowshippe and companie with God the father, the sonne, and the holy Ghost.[120]

Perseverance in covenant relationship depended upon God's sanctification of believers to conform them to his pleasure. Another prayer a couple of paragraphs later asked for faith and love to

> lead a godly and heauenly lyfe vpon earth. Set vp the spirituall kingdome of Christ Iesu in our hearts, that in vs thy name may be sanctified and thy will performed: that wee may become thy virtuous children, and neuer displease thee our gracious father[,] that we continuing stil in thy mercifull couenant, doe neuer fall away from the companie and fellowship of thee and thy soune.[121]

The godly activities of the believer are properly attributed to God, but the covenant makes it possible to talk of believers doing the work of the Father. In preaching, for instance, the apostles were said

---

[119] Ibid., T4v.
[120] Ibid., Z2r-v.
[121] Ibid., Z3r.

to absolve from sin 'for the gracious father of his aboundant loue and kindnesse (and by reason of the couenant that he hath made with vs) doeth oft ascribe vnto vs many things, which can properly belong vnto none, saue onely to himselfe.'[122] Yet 'note this condition wel,' wrote Coverdale in the margin: we will be forgiven only if we believe on Christ to the point of hating sin and actively desiring heavenly things.[123] Grace is promised to us 'so farre as we abide in his couenants.'[124]

On 7 December 1540 Coverdale 'mourned sore' to read a treatise written against his late superior's protestation of faith at the stake.[125] Barnes had been burnt at Smithfield on 28 July. Coverdale's 'theologically gritty'[126] *Confutacion of that treatise, which one Iohn Standish made agaynst the protestacion of D. Barnes* (1541) reveals his personal convictions at the time and, according to the colophon, it was printed at Zürich. Much of it was concerned with defending evangelical doctrine against charges of antinomianism: 'we are bound to do good workes to the which though god ioyne his louing promes (as he doth comonly thorow out the scripture) yet calleth he not them the satisfaction to him for sinnes.' Even though works which God requires of humanity cannot make satisfaction for sin, God adds 'a louinge promes to the fulfillers therof.'[127] It is noteworthy that Coverdale saw the predicament of sinners in terms of the covenant: those 'that haue broken their couenaunt with god.' Restoration was possible, 'though we haue fallen from the profession of

---

[122] Ibid., Hh1r.

[123] Ibid.

[124] Ibid., Oo3r.

[125] John Standish, *A Lytle Treatyse [. . .] against the Protestacion of Roberti Barnes at the tyme of his death* (London: Robert Redman, 1540; RSTC 23209).

[126] David Daniell, "Coverdale, Miles (1488–1569)," *ODNB* (Oxford: OUP, 2004).

[127] Miles Coverdale, *A confutacion of that treatise, which one Iohn Standish made agaynst the Protestacion of D. Barnes in the yeare. M.D.Xl. wherin, the Holy Scriptures (peruerted and wrested in his sayd treatise) are restored to their owne true vnderstonding agayne* (Zurich: C. Froschauer, 1541; RSTC 5888), E4r, L8r-v.

our faith,' through repentance.[128] Then the believer cheerfully tries to obey:

> to them that loue god are his commaundementes not greuous (not thorow anye possibilite of man) but partly because Christ hath taken awaie the curse of the lawe and deliuered them from the he[a]uy burthens of their soules and partly because they deli[g]te in gods commaundementes and esteme his word sweter then hony as Dauid did. For loue maketh all thinges light.[129]

Coverdale approved of Barnes' teaching men to do good works and his threatening damnation to those who do not do them. Coverdale believed that God had commanded that good works be done in order that believers might be justified outwardly before men.[130] Then he came to the point and explained the covenantal principle undergirding his argument:

> Now to do good dedes, to bring forth good frutes, to walke in a new life, to shew gods wonderfull workes, to lead an honest conuersacion in the world, what is it els, but to shew and set forth our profession, the life that we haue promised and taken us to at the font stone, euen the holy couenaunt and appoyntment that we haue made with the eternall god?[131]

The baptismal covenant was clearly bilateral because the Christian entered into it with God. For Coverdale the obligations imposed under this appointment were inescapable:

---

[128] Ibid., F7v.
[129] Ibid., G8r.
[130] Ibid., H8v.
[131] Ibid., H9r.

> Is not oure profession the promes and couenaunt that we haue made with god to seke his glory and oure neghbours profet euen to loue him with all oure herte with all our soules and with all oure strength and oure neghbour as oure selues In the which two pointes hangeth all the lawe and the Prophetes? Are not we bound then (by gods commaundement) to set forth the glory of god oure neghbours profit and loue to them both?[132]

Coverdale seems to overemphasise mutuality in these examples when he writes that humanity makes the covenant with God rather than *vice versa*. However, in the context of Coverdale's discussion of Genesis 18:16–33, where God reveals his intention to destroy Sodom, Coverdale claimed that God was willing to reveal this to Abraham 'because Abraham was vnder his couenaunt and did faithfully cleue to his promes and because he knew that Abraham wolde commaunde his children and housholde to kepe the waie of the lorde.'[133] Abraham's covenant faithfulness through trust and obedience to the covenant and promise belonging to God is clear.

Coverdale selected Bullinger's *Der alt gloub*, or *Antiquissima Fides et vera Religio* (1537) for the first of his translations at Strassburg, probably having received the book directly from the author.[134] He published this chronological overview of the Bible in 1541 as *The olde faith*,[135] which was particularly significant because it was the first English translation of a continental covenant text.[136] Scripture,

---

[132] Ibid., I2v.

[133] Ibid., L6r.

[134] Coverdale's publications of Bullinger's *Christen state of matrimonye* in 1541 and 1543 (RSTC 4045 and 4046) were editions of his earlier translation, probably completed in 1528.

[135] Coverdale almost certainly produced his *Confutation of Standish* before working on this translation, but Coverdale had probably considered Bullinger's work before 1541 and so Bullinger's influence is not impossible in the *Confutation*.

[136] Michael McGiffert, "Grace and Works: The Rise and Division of

Coverdale wrote in his prologue, imputes the cause of justification to faith, 'not without other vertues folowynge but without any other worke or dede iustfyenge.'[137] False believers fail to 'lyue thereafter' and 'practise not the lawe of godly loue' consistent with 'the effectuous the workynge and lyuynge fayth that Abraham and Rahab had.'[138] Importantly,

> where as by theyr profession ooth & allegiaunce (which they owe to theyr mooste hye soueraygne the kynge of heauen) they shulde in a vertuous conuersacion maynteyne all godlynesse are become euen enemies suppressours and ouerthrowers therof.[139]

The believer is clearly bound to godly living by an oath, indicating that the divine-human relationship carries reciprocal responsibilities.

Coverdale's concept of covenant was undoubtedly augmented by Bullinger's discussion, which began with Eden where 'it was equall that man [. . .] shulde shew thankfulnesse and obedience unto God [. . .]. Yee God him selfe [. . .] requyreth the same of him and that by the meanes of the commaundement.'[140] The Fall prompted God's 'devyce' of salvation through Christ and this, determined from eternity, was available from the time of Adam.[141] Love and obedience were demanded of Adam, signified by a sacrament, and this command was revealed to be a covenant with Adam when it was renewed with Noah:

Covenant Divinity in Elizabethan Puritanism," *HTR* 75, 4 (1982): 472–73; Baker, *Other Reformed Tradition*, 209.

[137] Heinrich Bullinger, *The Olde Fayth, an euydent probation out of the Holy Scripture, that the Christen Fayth (which is the right true, old & undoubted faith, hath endured sens the beginnyng of the worlde)*, trans. M. Coverdale (Antwerp?: Thomas Vautroullier, 1541; RSTC 4070.5), *4r.

[138] Ibid., *5v.
[139] Ibid., *6r.
[140] Ibid., A3v-4r.
[141] Ibid., A5r.

> Noe also was he, with whome God first renued the covenant made with Adam. For it is but one covenaunt onely even the foresayde promesse & ende made by God unto Adam. Howe beit the same covenaunte was afterwarde at certayne tymes renewed by reason of certayne occasions.

Coverdale would have understood from Bullinger that the covenant had operated consistently throughout salvation history because 'what soever pertayneth to [God's] couenaunt' with Adam would 'surely and constantly' be made good for Noah. Similarly, the laws given to Noah were part of the law written on human hearts concerning the love of God and neighbour.[142] The same covenant applied to Abraham: 'all thys now is but one promes one sauyoure and one faith. Abraham also beleued in Jesus Christ and was saued by fauth.'[143] Although 'God then made a couenaunt with Abraham when he ordeyned the circumcision[,] it serveth more to the confirmacion of oure holy christen faith then to the mayntenaunce of the Jewish ceremonyes.'[144]

Coverdale would also have noted that Bullinger used the terms 'testament' and 'covenant' synonymously.[145] The covenant extended into the New Testament era when true religion consisted of true faith and innocent life and, although outward virtue could not justify, 'the children of God are bounde to kepe them selves from the workes of darckenesse and to applye them to lyve in righteousnes and in the light.'[146]

In exile Coverdale was free to compose and translate Reformed theological works using the concept of covenant. The Cromwellian project of the 1530s was over. He had known of Bullinger's work for at least thirteen years when in 1541 he sent his *Confutation of Standish*

---

[142] Ibid., B8r-v.
[143] Ibid., C1v.
[144] Ibid., C2v-C3r.
[145] Ibid., C7v.
[146] Ibid., F8v-G1r, see also E8r, F7r.

to be printed at Zürich and published *The olde fayth*. Perhaps these projects triggered their correspondence in September 1541 which could plausibly have included theological consultation.[147] On 27 July 1542 Coverdale recalled how Bullinger had received his letters kindly and with a favourable interpretation. He expressed his 'pain' at being unable to join Richard Hilles and Henry Butler on their visit to Zürich in the summer of 1542, for he was 'very anxious to enjoy your society, and to behold your church.' He was nonetheless grateful for the benefit of Bullinger's ministry and friendship at a distance.[148]

From September 1543 Coverdale concentrated on his rôle as assistant pastor and headmaster at Bergzabern, where he finally learnt Hebrew. There he opposed the 'ravings of the Anabaptists' who, being generally 'tolerated,' caused 'great misfortune to the people.'[149] He chose to keep a low profile and his direct influence on fellow exiles was diminished,[150] but he was visited by Bucer and corresponded with other reformers.[151] Hilles reported that Coverdale's translation of *Der alt gloub* had caused Bullinger's book to be 'much

---

[147] Much is yet unknown about Coverdale's network and correspondence, according to Hildebrandt, "Protestant Exiles," 154.

[148] I suggest that Coverdale's letter, dated 27 July, should be assigned to 1542, contrary to the opinion of the Parker Society editor who suggests the range of years 1543 to 1548: Coverdale, *Remains*, 502–3. Coverdale's initial letter in September 1541 could have been sent with Hilles' letter to Bullinger from Strassburg on 25 September 1541. In a second letter, dated 23 November 1541, Hilles seems to assume that Bullinger at least knew of Coverdale. Bullinger certainly sent greetings to Coverdale in his replies to Hilles, who had visited Zürich by the time of his letter to Bullinger dated 18 December 1542. See *OL*, 221, 223, 229; David Loades, "Hilles, Richard (c.1514–1587)," *ODNB* (Oxford: OUP, 2004). On 15 April 1545 Hilles thought that Coverdale was 'somewhat known' to Bullinger 'both by my commendation, and also by his own letters sent to you some time since.' Perhaps Coverdale had not corresponded with Bullinger since 1542, but Hilles appears to have forgotten that he himself had written of Coverdale to Bullinger only six months earlier: *OL*, 247.

[149] Coverdale, *Remains*, 521; Daniell, "Coverdale, Miles."

[150] Hildebrandt, "Protestant Exiles," 154–55, 160.

[151] Coverdale, *Remains*, 510.

commended' by English evangelicals,[152] which is evidence of the circulation of its ideas.[153]

In October 1545 Coverdale translated from German *The defence of a certayne poore Christen man* by 'a right excellent and noble prince,' adding a *Short Recapitulation unto the Reader* which summarised its intention

> to put the (moste Christen reder) in remembrance of some paerte of thy dewty: and to render thanckes unto the lorde for the great strength and power he gaue unto this Christen prynce to confesse his lord & god before all men hym shalle the lorde confesse agayne before the father of heven.[154]

Coverdale reassured the persecuted Christian of God's covenanted justice:

> For evyn as owre lorde and god doeth all ways and at all tymes preserue kepe and defende the poore persecuted & afflicte in al extremities: so doeth he caste downe and never rayse up agayne all soche that so obstinatly and wilfully resistyth his eternall testament and worde.[155]

God's reliability and humanity's duty, as well as the sanctions imposed on covenant-breakers, were thus appended to a treatise which had not itself employed the concept.

On 8 July 1546 Coverdale's books were condemned in England and in September a dozen were burnt.[156] However, Edward VI's

---

[152] *OL*, 245.

[153] MacCulloch, "Bullinger," 911.

[154] Miles Coverdale, *The defence of a certayne poore Christen man who els shuld-haue bene condemned by the popes lawe* (Antwerp: S. Mierdman, 1545; RSTC 5889), E7r-8r.

[155] Ibid.

[156] *LP*, xxi/1, #1233; Daniell, "Coverdale, Miles."

accession in January 1547 prompted reprints of several of them in London, including his Bullinger translations.[157] He was summoned home in 1548 and served first as almoner to Katherine Parr before becoming a royal chaplain. He was consecrated bishop of Exeter in August 1551. These rôles reduced his literary output: in 1549 he contributed considerably to the English translation of Erasmus' *Paraphrases*; in 1550 a new edition of his 1535 Bible translation was published by Froschauer in Zürich, and he translated the *Precious Pearl* by the Zürich pastor Otto Werdmüller.

As one would expect of a Zürich text, this latter work contained the themes of mutuality and conditionality. The careful burdens of a governor or father fell upon God while 'our partes and duty is no more, but to trust and beleue in hym, and to serue in that vocacyon & condycyon of lyfe wherevnto we are called & appointed of god, faithfully.'[158] Readers were invited to 'consider & wey, as it were in a true balance the righteousnes, which god requireth of vs on the one syde, & again the whole trade of our life, on the other syde.'[159] Since we have not conformed to God's law, Christ treats the believer as a scholar and disciple and 'makyth condicions wyth him most necessary for euery Christen man, whyche are expressyd in the. xvi. chapter of Mathew,' that is, the requirement to take up our cross and follow him. The word of God becomes 'the rule, whereby we should be orderyd'[160] and God requires that our awareness of sin and judgment grow so that we repent 'and so daylye amende and waxe better.'[161] Godliness was never required for justification but, being inseparable from faithfulness, was imperative afterwards.

---

[157] RSTC 2756, 4048, 4048.5, 4071, 20423.

[158] Otto Werdmüller, *A spyrytuall and moost precyouse pearle teachyng all men to loue and imbrace the crosse* [. . .] *sett forth by the Moste Honorable Lorde, the Duke Hys Grace of Somerset*, trans. M. Coverdale (London: S. Mierdman for Gwalter Lynne, 1550; RSTC 25255), K3v.

[159] Ibid., B3v.

[160] Ibid., D1v.

[161] Ibid., E3r.

Although he had encountered the concept of covenant during his early work with Tyndale, Coverdale utilised it in his own way. During the late 1530s, the priority of Bible translation, combined with political pragmatism, led to an absence of Reformed theology in Coverdale's publications. However, his second exile permitted theological engagement and expression, initially with Bullinger. Coverdale, unlike Tyndale, tended to expound a theology of good works grounded in the legal and familial categories of the covenant, rather than explaining the concept of covenant itself. Evidence from his declining literary output during the late 1540s and 1550s indicates continued engagement with Zürich theology, as well as the growing influence of Calvin.[162]

Coverdale's third, Marian exile is beyond the bounds of this study, but it reaffirmed his Swiss Reformed links. In February 1555 he went first to Denmark,[163] soon continued to Bergzabern, before moving in 1557 to Aarau and in 1558 to Geneva.[164] This was a period of radicalisation for Coverdale who, back in England from 1559, was among the more recalcitrant nonconformists.[165] The question of whether his concept of covenant changed considerably as a result of these experiences deserves investigation.

John Hooper

Of wealthy parentage, Hooper took a degree from Oxford in 1519 and entered the Cistercian house at Cleeve in Somerset

---

[162] Calvin's influence on Coverdale may have begun from as early as 1540 but seems to have increased in the mid-1540s.

[163] Coverdale refused preferment in Denmark. This may have been because the Danish king required exiles to conform to Lutheranism, which would be further evidence of Coverdale's Reformed convictions. See Christina Garrett, *The Marian Exiles: a study in the origins of Elizabethan Puritanism* (Cambridge: CUP, 1938), 132–34; Andrew Pettegree, *Marian Protestantism: Six Studies* (Aldershot: Ashgate, 1996), 58–59.

[164] Garrett, *Marian Exiles*, 52.

[165] Hildebrandt, "Protestant Exiles," 61–63; A. G. Dickens, *The English Reformation*, 1st ed. (London: B. T. Batsford, 1964), 131.

that was dissolved in 1536.[166] Afterwards he became steward to the conservative courtier Sir Thomas Arundell in whose service he nevertheless encountered 'certain writings of master Huldruch Zwinglius' and Bullinger's Pauline commentaries. He later described to Bullinger how 'I thought it well worth my while, night and day, with earnest study, and an almost superstitious diligence, to devote my entire attention to your writings.'[167] His conversion must have occurred by mid-1539 since Arundell arranged for Bishop Gardiner to conduct a 'long conference with M. Hooper 4. or 5. dayes together'[168] within five months of the enactment of the Six Articles.

Hooper felt sufficiently threatened to hasten to Paris but soon returned into the service of Arundell's evangelical nephew, Sir John St Loe, in Somerset.[169] There he remained until 1543 or 1544 when

> he was agayne molested and laid for: whereby he was compelled (vnder the pretence of being Captayne of a ship going to Ireland) to take the Seas, and so escaped he (although not

---

[166] D. G. Newcombe, *John Hooper: Tudor Bishop and Martyr* (Oxford: Davenant Press, 2009), 9–13; Alison Dalton, "John Hooper and His Networks: a study of change in Reformation England," DPhil diss. (University of Oxford, 2008), 15–17; Robert Dunning, "The last days of Cleeve Abbey," in *The Church in Pre-Reformation Society*, eds. C. Barron and C. Harper-Bill (Woodbridge: Boydell Press, 1985), 59. Franke disputes the traditional identification of Hooper with the 'John Hoper' admitted to the degree of Bachelor of Arts in 1519. He argues that Hooper was not born until 1510/15 and supplicated for the degree in 1542: John Franke, "The Religious Thought of John Hooper," DPhil diss. (University of Oxford, 1996), 10–22. Rex speculates whether Hooper might have been a friar rather than a monk: Richard Rex, "Friars in the English Reformation," in *The Beginnings of English Protestantism*, eds. P. Marshall and A. Ryrie (Cambridge: CUP, 2002), 47.

[167] Hooper to Bullinger, Strassburg, 27 January [1546], *OL*, 33–34. On the greater influence of Zwingli and Bullinger relative to Calvin see W. M. S. West, "John Hooper and the Origins of Puritanism [1]," *BQ* 15, 8 (1954): 346, 363; Locher, *Zwingli's Thought*, 365n; Newcombe, *Hooper*, 40. On Hooper's deteriorating relationship with Bucer in 1547–49 see Newcombe, *Hooper*, 33–34.

[168] Foxe, *AM* [1583], 11:1526.

[169] Ibid., 11:1527.

without extreme perill of drowning) through Fraunce, to the higher partes of Germany.[170]

He matriculated at Basle University for the academic year 1545–46 and applied himself to the study of Hebrew, but by January he was recuperating from illness in Strassburg.[171] He wrote to Bullinger on 27 January of his intention, 'in about a month's time,' to visit his father, who was hostile to reform, to obtain his inheritance 'wherewith I may be able to subsist upon my slender means among you at Zürich.' Ready to immerse himself in Zürich theology, he explained that 'by reason of my love and respect towards you, I had often proposed to visit you, though I have always been prevented hitherto' by ill-health and parental opposition.[172] This trip home occasioned two brief imprisonments in Exeter before he returned to Basle and the house of Simon Grynaeus.[173] In February 1547, shortly after the accession of Edward VI in England, Hooper married Anna de Tscerlas and in March they moved to Zürich.[174]

For two years Hooper studied under Bullinger at Zürich.[175] Three treatises date from this seminal period of his life and all exhibit a concept of covenant. In April 1547 he obtained Stephen Gardiner's book on the Eucharist and in September published a refutation, *An answer vnto my lord of wynthesters booke*, before the official doctrine of the Eucharist in England had begun to change. Hooper began by comparing Gardiner to the Jews in Romans 9–11 where Paul discusses 'there departure and reiection ffrom the promesse of god.'[176] Thus, on the second page of his prologue, Hooper introduced

---

[170] Ibid.
[171] Hildebrandt, "Protestant Exiles," 75, 146; Foxe, *AM* [1583], 11:1527; *OL*, 251–52; see also Dalton, "Hooper's Networks," 36–37.
[172] *OL*, 34–35.
[173] Ibid., 41; Hooper, *Wynthester*, G2v-3r; Newcombe, *Hooper*, 25–26.
[174] Hildebrandt, "Protestant Exiles," 75–76; *OL*, 42.
[175] *OL*, 635; West, "Hooper [1]," 352–53; Dalton, "Hooper's Networks," 38.
[176] Hooper, *Wynthester*, A2v.

the possibility of abandoning the divine promise. He proceeded to expound the imperative to learn doctrine and godliness from God's law. The Mosaic Law, he wrote, 'was not yeuen to be wroten in perschement or paper but in the hart of man not to bable and prate of it, but to lyue as it byddyth. not to bare it in the bosom but to shew it unto the worold in godly conuersacyon and uertues lief.' Obedience to this same authority in Scripture was demanded of the Christian.[177]

In the course of this discussion of his sacramental theology Hooper affirmed the unity of the Testaments by connecting God's people from Adam to the apostles: 'As well was the promes of eternall lief made unto them as unto us, as well they belyuid to be sauyd by Christ as we. They were of Christes church as well as we.'[178] Christ was 'the Mediatour betwene god and man from the beginning.'[179] Israelites and Christians are together God's people by virtue of receiving the same promise which establishes 'the unyon peace and concord betwen god and us [. . .] the loue and peax that is betwen god and us.'[180] The relationship is unilaterally initiated by God but continues bilaterally. Like Zwingli, Bullinger, and Calvin, Hooper's explanation of the sacraments as sealing an agreement revealed his mutual conception of this relationship which was contractual and covenantal:

> As the seale annxyd unto the wryting is a stablyshment an makyng [good] of all thinges conteynid and specified within the wryting this is usid in all bargayns, exchanges, purcheses an contractes. When the mater intreydyd betwene too partes is fully concludyd upon, it is confirmyd with obligacions sealyd entrechangeble that for euer those sealys may be awytnis of souch couenantes as hath ben agreyd upon betwen the booth parthes.[181]

[177] Ibid., B3r.
[178] Ibid., D4v.
[179] Ibid., R4v.
[180] Ibid., E2r.
[181] Ibid., F2v.

No man, Hooper supposed, would pledge a debtor's obligation prior to agreeing a contract with his creditor. Likewise, a contract is needed between humanity and God. The first step is revelation from, and repentance of enmity towards, God:

> There must ffyrst be had acommunicacion betwen god, an[d] the man to know how he [the man] can mak ony contract of frendshippe with his ennymie, the lyuing god[.] He confessith his default and desirith mercy, usith no purgacion, nor translation of his sinne.

Rather, humanity pleads Christ's atonement for sin:

> But onlie besechithe mercy, and lay[e]th Christ to gayge [to accept the challenge] and saith for asmouch as thow hast yeuen thy only sone for the sinne of the worold mercyfull lord, hast thow not likewice yeuen all thing unto sinners that repent with hym. Then likewice lord for[g]eue me, and be my god, booth in fayth and also in thy sacramentes.[182]

Humanity must also make a promise of godliness:

> and as trewlie shall I serue the[e] during my lief as thes[e] wordes passe my mo[u]the, I renownce the deuil, the worold an sinne upon this fayth and promesse mad[e] to god we be markyd in godes mark. An[d] none other wice. For the church euer teachyth amendement of life before he promese grace.[183]

The establishment of the contract thus involved repentance, faith in Christ and a promise by the believer to God. The Church could not confidently promise that God would be gracious unless

---

[182] Hooper, *Wynthester*, F2v.
[183] Ibid., F3r.

all of these were evident. Reception of God's promise of grace was conditional upon that determination to amendment of life which accompanied genuine repentance in Christ. Godliness, achieved by grace,[184] was vital to perseverance in God's promise or testament:

> let them cast the testament into the fier, for they know to there damnacion that will not folow there knolege. To be achristiane it is not so light as men make it, of all the craftes in the worold it is the hardyst, not to pratle and prate of it. But to practyse it in lief. For it is a sciens practyue and not speculatyue. Consisti[ng] in Actione & non in lingua.[185]

Christian obligation occasioned Hooper's repetition of his earlier point about the authority of Scripture in that 'God hath bound his church and all men that be of the churche to be obedient unto the word of god.'[186] In the Decalogue specifically 'is euery mannes office and dewty describid, what is to be donne whether it be to wardes god or man.' Consequently Hooper, in line with Zürich soteriology, attacked solifidian reductionism: 'But faith is aryght persuacion and willing consent unto the [w]hole word of god. For he that sayth, Credes in deum patrem, filium, & spiritum sanctum, the same god saith, Ambula coram me & esto integer, What auaylith the bragg of fayth, where as is no uerteues lief.'[187] This invocation of Genesis 17:1 to 'walk before me and be blameless' implies that Hooper was cognisant of the requirements of the Abrahamic covenant. The heavenly bliss enjoyed by the patriarchs 'appertainith not to souche as know only the faythe of them,' warned Hooper, 'but unto souche as obey the commaundement of god as they dyd.'[188] Moreover, unscriptural practice, or making an

[184] Ibid., X4r.
[185] Ibid., F3r-v.
[186] Ibid., F4r.
[187] Ibid., G4r.
[188] Ibid., M3v.

English Concepts of Covenant

alternative, idolatrous covenant, was equivalent to treason against a prince and had comparable consequences:

> the kyng of equite is bound to kyll the body of thes treatur and god can do nolesse of his iustice then kyll booth body and soulle of this ydolater if he repent not. And as noman is permittid to by or sell or to mak ony other contractes in ony Realme for his commodite except in the doyng therof he obserue the law of the land, nomore can noman use to bargayne or contract with god for his commodite in t[h]e churche of Christes, except he obserue the lawes prescribid by god.[189]

It was this concern for scriptural godliness that prompted Hooper's calls throughout the treatise for pure practice informed by expository preaching.[190]

Hooper's second treatise was entitled *A declaration of Christe and of his office* (December 1547). Trueman calls it 'an English expression of Zurich theology' and compares Hooper's concept of covenant here with Bullinger's and Tyndale's.[191] The treatise was addressed to Protector Somerset and concerned the priest-king rôle of Christ, a motif favoured by the Edwardian regime. A covenant hermeneutic was not pressed on the reader, but the concept undoubtedly informed Hooper's discourse. The only explicit reference to God's 'pact' specifies its conditionality and sanctions:

> souche as be sanctified by Christe must lyue an honest and holy lief or else his sanctification auaylith not, as god for soke the chylder of Israel for sinne so wil he do us, they were electyd to be his people with this condition si audiendo

---

[189] Ibid., S2v.
[190] E.g. Ibid., Q4v-R1r, T1r.
[191] Trueman, *Luther's Legacy*, 208, 214; see also Felicity Heal, *Reformation in Britain and Ireland* (Oxford: OUP, 2003), 332.

audieris uocem uocem meam, & custodieris pactum meum Exo. 19. Eritis mihi in peculium de cunctis populis [if, when hearing, you (sing.) hear my voice and keep my pact, you (pl.) will be my own/for myself out of all the peoples]. He that fauoryd not the Israelites but toke cruell uengence upon them because they walkid not in there uocation will do and dooth dayly the same unto us, Rom. 11.[192]

Election as God's people carries the condition of heeding God's word and keeping his pact on pain of punishment for defaulting. Later, Hooper described the reciprocal responsibilities of the relationship unilaterally imposed by God. This included the prospect of reward for obedience:

> as god hath bound hymselfe by his promes to be our god and helper for Christ, so hathe he bound man by his commaundement to be his seruant and in his worde to folow Christ and in Christ god for the commaundementes sake untill souche tyme as thend wherfore man was made be optaynid, whiche is eternall foelicite and man restoryd and made like unto the ymayge of god.[193]

There were other implicit suggestions of the concept. For example, Hooper approved of those who fast to improve their prayerfulness: they 'doothe well and as they be bound to do.'[194]

Owing to Christ's sacrificial office, Hooper concluded that justification is by faith, but this is conditional. Faith in the divine promise to justify on the basis of Christ's meritorious sacrifice obliges God to remit sin and have favour on believers 'whiche he is

---

[192] John Hooper, *A Declaration of Christe and of His Offyce* (Zurich: Augustyne Fries, 1547; RSTC 13745), K1r.
[193] Ibid., L4r.
[194] Ibid., D1r.

bound to do for his promesse sak[e].'¹⁹⁵ However, while 'sole fayth and only exclude the merites of other uertews and optaynith soly remission of sinne for Christes sake,' it 'exclude not other uertews to be present at the conuersion of euery sinner.' These virtues or 'workes that go before iustificacion, nether those that folow iustification deserue remission of synne'¹⁹⁶ but still 'it be necessary and requysyt that in the iustification of a synner contricion to be present and that necessaryly cherite and uertews lieffe moost folow.'¹⁹⁷ Without a virtuous life God's grace is received 'inuayne'.¹⁹⁸ David Newcombe describes Hooper's doctrine as *'conditionally* unconditional,'¹⁹⁹ which helps to describe the way in which he situated obligation within a context of grace.

Christ not only justifies but also sanctifies his people.²⁰⁰ By sanctification Hooper 'means none other but a trew knolege of God in Christ' which brings awareness of how 'wear clensid by Christ' of the uncleanness caused by Adam's sin. On the basis of this expiation God 'doothe not only remitt the sinnes wrowght willyngly agaynst the word of God, but also the imperfection and naturall concupiscens whiche remaynythe in euery man as long as the nature of man is mortall.'²⁰¹ Indeed, Christ insists upon his Father's obligations: 'thow must most holy father sanctifie them, and accept them as sanctified.'²⁰² Thus God forgives the imperfection of believers, both making them holy and counting them as holy, which is a

---

¹⁹⁵ Ibid., F2r.
¹⁹⁶ Ibid., G1r-v.
¹⁹⁷ Ibid., F2v.
¹⁹⁸ Ibid., G5r.
¹⁹⁹ Newcombe, *Hooper*, 65.
²⁰⁰ Hooper does not seem to have understood sanctification as a process since he wrote that 'affter we be sanctified' it is our office to proclaim Christ's power: Hooper, *Christe and His Offyce*, I8r-v.
²⁰¹ Ibid., I3r. Like Zwingli, Hooper understood original sin as a disease. See Hooper, *Christe and His Offyce*, L5v.
²⁰² Hooper, *Christe and His Offyce*, I4r. Hooper appears to teach the impartation as well as imputation of righteousness.

plainly Reformed view. They are restored to be 'apt for thy kingdom,' enabling them to be godly: we 'must lyue an honest and holy lief or else his sanctification auaylith not.'[203] Like justification, sanctification is efficacious only to the godly and so it is conditional. Hooper's soteriology is covenantal in all but name.

The preface to Hooper's third Zürich treatise, *A declaration of the ten holy commaundementes of allmygthye God*,[204] was dated November 1549, although it was actually published in 1548. It began with a bold statement of the mutual, conditional covenant:

> for asmouche as there can be no contract peace aliaunce or confederacye betwene too persones or more except fyrst the persones that will contract agre within them selfes vpon souche thinges as shal be contractyd as thow right well knowyst: also seyng these ten commaundementes ar nothing else but the Tables or wrytinges that contayne the conditions of the peace betwene God and man Gen. 19. and declarithe at large how and to what the persones namyd in the wrytinges ar bounde unto the other [. . .]. It is necessary to know how God and man was made at one that souche conditions could be agreyed upon and confirmyd [. . .]. The contentes wherof byndithe God to ayede and succur kepe and preserue warrant and defend man from all yle boothe of body and solle and at the last to yeue him eternall blysse and euerlasting felicite [. . .]. Man bounde of the other part to obey serue and kepe Godes commaundementes to loue him honor him and fere him aboue all thinges.[205]

---

[203] Ibid., K1r.

[204] Hooper's doctrine of predestination in this treatise, expressed in a similar style to Bullinger's doctrine, led to conflict with followers of Calvin. See Trueman, *Luther's Legacy*, 215ff; Stephen Strehle, "*Fides aut Foedus*: Wittenberg and Zurich in conflict over the Gospel," *SCJ* 23, 1 (1992): 13–14.

[205] John Hooper, *A Declaration of the Ten Holy Commaundementes of Allmygthye God* (Zurich: Augustin Fries, 1548; RSTC 13746), A2r-v; see Trinterud,

Hooper commented on how surprising it was, in light of sin, 'now we se bound in le[a]ge to gather as very frendes' God and mankind in 'aliaunce and confederacye.' Mercy was the only explanation: God's 'testament' confirmed by the death of the testator, Christ.[206] This operated 'within certaine limetes and bondes: the whiche if men neglect or passe ouer they exclude them selfes from the promes in Christ.'[207] Such boundaries were transgressed by those

> whiche will not h[ea]re nether receaue the promes of the gospelle: or else after he hathe receauid it by accustomid doing of ile he fall ether in a contempt of the gospell will not studie to liue there after or else hat[eth] the gospell because it condemnithe his vngodly liefe.[208]

The promise of salvation was demonstrated by the Ninevites who received Jonah's warning 'and toke God for there God and God toke them to be his people.' The Ninevites 'likewyce promisyd obedience vnto his holy Lawes and commaundementes,' and Hooper prayed that God would give us grace to do the same 'that thowghe we be infirme and weacke to all vertewes we exclude not oure selfes by contempt or negligence from the grace promisid to all men.'[209]

The observance of the law, as a covenantal condition for continuing in grace, was integral to Hooper's soteriology. Newcombe is wrong therefore to suggest that Hooper's 'book on the commandments and adoption of Bullinger's covenant theology' can be separated from his wider concern for salvation.[210] Morris West rightly understands Hooper's view that if people fail to believe in Christ and act accordingly 'they would be judged according to their acts,

---

"Origins," 43.
[206] *Ten Holy Commaundementes*, A3r-v.
[207] Ibid., A5r.
[208] Ibid., A8r.
[209] Ibid., B2r-v.
[210] Newcombe, *Hooper*, 42–43; see Hooper, *Ten Holy Commaundementes*, 36.

or rather by their failure to believe and walk in the right paths.'²¹¹ Hooper acknowledged this difficulty of explaining how 'the workes of the law cannot deserue remission of synne nor sa[ve] man and yet God requyrythe our diligens and obedi[e]nce vnto the Lawe.'²¹² By themselves, human works were like Israel's 'le[a]ge and confederatie' with Egypt which excluded God and 'auaylid nothing.' Believers were not to trust more in 'confederacie with men: th[a]n in God.'²¹³ On the other hand, mercy was assured to all those who entered 'aliaunce' with God, but 'if they think to haue God for there God let them obserue his aliaunce.' Just as 'Godes mercy is commune for all men whiche is the fyrst part of the condicion expressyd in the le[a] ge so alike is the obedience towardes the law requiryd of all men.'²¹⁴

These three treatises encapsulated the essential theological position held by Hooper for the rest of his life.²¹⁵ West is justified, in spite of Jens Møller's criticisms, in seeing Hooper's reciprocal concept of covenant as the controlling idea in his theology.²¹⁶ Newcombe argues that West's conclusions rely too much upon Hooper's exposition of the Decalogue, and it is true that J. H. Primus and John Franke also depended too much for evidence on *A declaration of the ten holy commaundementes*.²¹⁷ However, the influence of the covenant idea upon Hooper's sacramental, Christological and soteriological thought can be detected in all his Zürich treatises. The pastoral nature of Hooper's writing may not have lent itself to a systematic exposition of the covenant, but his Zürich mentors had already laid that foundation.²¹⁸

---

²¹¹ West, "Hooper [1]," 358.
²¹² Hooper, *Ten Holy Commaundementes*, 19.
²¹³ Ibid., 42.
²¹⁴ Ibid., 211–12, see also 209.
²¹⁵ Newcombe, *Hooper*, 43.
²¹⁶ West, "Hooper [1]," 356–59; Møller, "Beginnings," 56.
²¹⁷ Newcombe, *Hooper*, 42, 42n; J. H. Primus, "The Role of the Covenant Doctrine in the Puritanism of John Hooper," *Dutch Review of Church History* 48, 2 (1968): 184–87; Franke, "Religious Thought," 113–23.
²¹⁸ Andries Raath and Shaun de Freitas, "From Heinrich Bullinger to

On 16 May 1549 Hooper returned to London where he was promptly engaged in controversy by readers of his treatise on the Decalogue.[219] He was undeterred by Cranmer's cold reception, which he blamed on the influence of Bucer, and was determined to disseminate Zürich teachings in public lectures twice daily.[220] Those who favoured him called him 'a true friend of the liberties of the church and commonwealth of Zürich, and their defender from every calumny,'[221] and even 'the future Zwingli of England.'[222] His influence and popularity grew throughout the year and by 27 December he could report that Cranmer 'is now very friendly towards myself.'[223] He lectured in London and at Court in early 1550, and his efforts bore fruit on 5 February when Cranmer ordered him to deliver the Lenten addresses at Court, for which he selected the book of Jonah 'which will enable me freely to touch upon the duties of individuals.'[224] His avowed aims when he came to preach were to show the unity of evangelical doctrine with that of the prophets and apostles, in contrast to Rome, and to 'declare whych way the synfull worlde may be reconcyled vnto God.'[225] Duty and salvation were closely related.

Hooper used his seven Jonah sermons to present a Zürich-inspired reform programme to the king and privy councillors. These sermons undoubtedly encapsulate his core beliefs.[226] As was typical

---

Puritanism: John Hooper's Theology and the Office of Magistracy," *SJT* 56, 2 (2003): 221–22.

[219] Dalton, "Hooper's Networks," 103–7.

[220] *OL*, 64–65; Dalton, "Hooper's Networks," 53–54.

[221] John Stumphius to Bullinger, May 1549, *OL*, 462.

[222] Martin Micron to Conrad Pellican, quoted in W. M. S. West, "John Hooper and the Origins of Puritanism [2]," *BQ* 16, 1 (1955): 24. About this time Hooper disputed with Anabaptists as Zwingli had done.

[223] *OL*, 71.

[224] Ibid., 75.

[225] John Hooper, *An ouersight, and deliberacion vpon the holy prophete Ionas: made, and vttered before the Kynges Maiestie, and his Moost Honorable Councell, by Ihon Hoper in Lent last past. Comprehended in seuen sermons* (London: Ihon Daye and Wylliam Seres, 1550; RSTC 13763), 5r.

[226] West, "Hooper [2]," 26–27.

of Hooper, the technical terminology of covenant does not appear in the transcript, but the concept is present. The obligation which humanity is required to discharge is a recurrent theme which makes the divine-human relationship conditional on humanity's obedience to divine law. Hooper reasoned in the prologue (written for publication in September 1550) that just as a human prince expects adherence to his 'statutes, lawes, and testament,' so God stipulates precise obedience:

> Shulde not the same glory, maiesty, and honour be geuen vnto the lawes and testament of Christ, that is sealed wyth hys precious bloude? The worde of God wherwyth he gouerneth and ruleth his church, is a septer of yron. Psal. ii. and not a rod of wylowe to be bowed wyth euerye mans finger, either a rede to be broken at mans wyll.[227]

Christ's 'lawes and testament' function together, emphasising the legislative significance of Christ's death and suggesting that Hooper utilised 'testament' in the same mutual sense as Tyndale. The impetus for Hooper's call for 'a perfecte and Apostolicall reformacion' sprang not from the New Testament but the Old, 'seynge I see in the writynges of the Prophets, God to require the obseruacion of his lawe onely.'[228] Thus the two Testaments were held together and the Mosaic Law had enduring relevance.

The first sermon began with the premise that children of God must 'know perfectly the nature and condicion of hys fathers wyl' in order to fulfil their duties contained in Scripture.[229] Hooper attacked those who diminished the offence of disobedience to God, illustrating the consequences of Jonah's disobedience to his duty and vocation.[230] 'We se our duetye,' said Hooper in his second sermon,

[227] Hooper, *Ionas*, +3v.
[228] Ibid., +5v–+6r.
[229] Ibid., 1r–v.
[230] Ibid., 16v–17r.

'that as GOD freelye geueth healpe, so we muste trayuell, and do the beste we canne wyth prayer, not onelye to receyue, and obtayne the free helpe of God, but also to kepe it.'[231] Doing our best, dependent nonetheless upon the grace of God, is required, and there should be expectation of success in the fulfilment of duty.

In his third sermon Hooper included godliness within the true Christian profession, saying that 'the people shoulde heare the word of God, geue faithe vnto it, and folow it,'[232] and in the fourth he warned that 'Gods promyse appertayneth' to 'he that wyl study the amendement of lyf' but not to the 'impenitent and neuer myndynge synner to amende.' 'The former promyses were not so sweete,' remarked Hooper, mindful of God's judgment, 'but these threatnynges be as bytter.'[233] Godly living was not required merely as a declaration of faith in the eyes of the world.[234] Like Jonah we must 'liue obedyentlye vnto the commaundement of god [. . .] and not vse healthe and quyetnes as an occasyon to syn, libertie, & filthines of lyfe.'[235] His fifth sermon began by placing obedience second only to right judgment of Scripture in the pleasures of God, subjecting godliness to the standards of God rather than the world.[236]

Jonah's example teaches us 'to be diligente, we see all our doinges, actes, and obedience to be according, and as the worde of God biddeth.'[237] Meanwhile the repentance of the Ninevites, preached Hooper in the sixth sermon, shows 'that to afflicte the bodye wyth fastynge, to praye, and to chaunge the olde wycked lyfe is verye expediente to wynne hys [God's] fauoure.' The king's hope of divine mercy in spite of divine wrath reminds us of 'the fyghte & battayle that is always betwene the spyrite, and the flesh aboute

---

[231] Ibid., 26r.
[232] Ibid., 45v.
[233] Ibid., 69v-70r.
[234] Ibid., 73v.
[235] Ibid., 96r.
[236] Ibid., 99v-100r; see Newcombe, *Hooper*, 130–31.
[237] Hooper, *Ionas*, 111r.

Goddes promises.'[238] In other words, in the seventh sermon, 'al the threatnings of god be condicionally, that is to say: to fal vpon vs if we repent not of our [evil] de[e]ds.'[239] The Ninevites having repented, God 'coulde do none other then saue them,'[240] indicating that he is bound by the terms of his promise. The condition remains at the Last Judgment when good works will be counted since 'God sleepeth not but seeth all oure actes, aud noteth oure dooynges.'[241] Finally Hooper urged, 'let vs therfore beleue and amende, or els we must peryshe.'[242] Both faith and godliness were necessary for salvation.

The Vestment Controversy that engulfed Hooper's appointment as bishop of Gloucester from April 1550 until his consecration on 8 March 1551 demonstrated the rigidity of his devotion to the practices of Zürich against the counsels of Bucer, Vermigli, Calvin, and even of Bullinger himself. Jan Łaski, the overseer of the London Stranger Church, was Hooper's only faithful supporter of note.[243] Hooper lost official support and then caused further embitterment by the illicit publication of his *Godly confession and protestacion of the christian fayth* in December 1550, which is of interest here for its plain statement of the place of works in Hooper's soteriology.[244] Not

---

[238] Ibid., 161v-162r.
[239] Ibid., 164r.
[240] Ibid., 165v.
[241] Ibid., 180r.
[242] Ibid., 183v.
[243] See West, "Hooper [2]," 30–42, esp. 41n; John Opie, "The Anglicising of John Hooper," *ARG* 59, 2 (1968): 171; Andrew Pettegree, *Foreign Protestant Communities in Sixteenth-Century London* (Oxford: OUP, 1986), 30–45; Dalton, "Hooper's Networks," 59–72, 107–16. Bullinger's letter to Utenhoven, dated 8 November 1551, conjectured that the experience might help Hooper to trust less in himself and more in God: George Gorham, ed., *Gleanings of a few scattered ears, during the period of the Reformation in England* (London: Bell and Daldy, 1857), 276.
[244] John Hooper, *A Godly Confession and Protestacion of the Christian Fayth, made and set furth by Ihon Hooper, wherin is declared what a Christian manne is bound to beleue of God, hys kyng, his neibour, and hymselfe* (London: John Daye, 1550; RSTC 13757). *A Brief and Clear Confession*, also appearing about this

only is belief in the promises of God achieved entirely by grace apart from works, but all the believer's works and obedience towards God throughout their lives depend upon mercy and grace, for Christ's sake, to be of value before God.[245] Hooper never considered his calls for amendment of life to depart from dependence upon grace and it was with this intention that he summarised humanity's obligation thus: 'Vnto god they owe both bodye and soule, to laude and prayse him according to gods boke. To cal vpon him in the daies of their trouble, and vpon none els, to conforme both their doctrin & their lyues, to promote and set forth the glory of God.'[246]

Like Coverdale, Hooper's episcopal exertions distracted him from further publication,[247] but his activities spoke of his Zürich commitment, particularly his establishment of a version of the Zürich prophesyings in his diocese.[248] In his fifty Visitation Articles (1551) he stressed the necessity of good works following justification and that they were required of 'every Christian man.'[249] Morris West notes that this emphasis was typical of Hooper and plausibly suggests derivation from his concept of covenant, both here and in the ordering of public penance.[250] Hooper recovered his

---

time, was not Hooper's work, according to D. S. Ross, "Hooper's Alleged Authorship of *A Brief and Clear Confession of the Christian Faith*," *CH* 39, 1 (1970): 18–29.

[245] Hooper, *Godly Confession*, C1r-v. Works were never to be held in higher estimation than the merits of Christ: John Hooper, *A funerall oratyon made the xiiij. day of Ianuary* [. . .] *vpon the texte wrytyne in the Reuelatyone of Sayncte Iohne. ca. 14* (London: S. Mierdman for Edwarde Whitechurch, 1549 [1550]; RSTC 13753), B2v-3r.

[246] Hooper, *Godly Confession*, H1v-2r.

[247] The dedicatory epistle to his unpublished *De vera ratione inveniendae et fugiendae falsae doctrinae* (December 1554) is recorded in Strype, *Memorials*, iii/1:283–84; iii/2:267–73.

[248] W. M. S. West, "John Hooper and the Origins of Puritanism [3]," *BQ* 16, 2 (1955): 68–69.

[249] John Hooper, *Later Writings of Bishop Hooper*, ed. C. Nevinson, PS (Cambridge: CUP, 1852), 121–22.

[250] West, "Hooper [3]," 72, 79.

popularity within the Edwardian establishment, shown by Cranmer's letter to Bullinger on 20 March 1552 describing Hooper as being 'in such great esteem among us [. . .] and is at this time living in my house upon the most intimate terms, during the sitting of parliament.'[251]

The king's death was the harbinger of Hooper's imprisonment and eventual martyrdom outside his cathedral on 9 February 1555. He was the first English bishop to suffer death at the stake,[252] and his commitment to Zürich theology won from his persecutors the appellation of 'greatest hereticke in all England.'[253] Hooper's concept of covenant, honed in Zürich, caused him to emphasise humanity's obligation to keep divine law. Although human works by themselves were worthless for salvation, the conditions of the divine league included, not only God's gracious promise of mercy, but the requirement that believers strive for godliness in dependence upon Christ.

John Bradford

When Bradford visited the continent during the 1540s he went to assist military operations in France rather than to escape religious persecution. His affections eventually did become evangelical but Philip Johnston is right to suggest that Bradford's prologues to works of continental theology 'do not bear the hallmark of a great mind brought to bear upon them.'[254] Indeed, considering Bradford's contribution to the Edwardian Reformation, his engagement with continental theology was surprisingly limited outside of Bucer's teaching at Cambridge. The hypothesis that Swiss Reformed theology was the source of the reciprocal concept of covenant in England is sustained

---

[251] *OL*, 23–24.
[252] Newcombe, *Hooper*, 229.
[253] Foxe, *AM* [1583], 11:1535.
[254] P. F. Johnston, "The Life of John Bradford, the Manchester Martyr, c.1510–1555," BLitt diss. (University of Oxford, 1963), 109.

by the fact that Bradford, whose concept lacked significant mutual or conditional elements, was hardly touched by Swiss influence. His ethical emphases stopped short of reciprocal obligation.

Between 1544 and 1547 Bradford ably served Sir John Harington, vice-treasurer of the English forces at Boulogne, as an auditor and confidential clerk. Foxe justly described Bradford as living 'as a child of this world';[255] in other words, as Gordon Rupp puts it, he was 'fiddling the accounts.'[256] With Harington's assistance he left Boulogne to read law at the Inner Temple in April 1547 and about this time became an evangelical.[257] After his conversion, Foxe says that 'Bradford did forsake his worldly affaires, and forwardnes in worldlye wealthe'[258] under the guidance of Hugh Latimer, who was not afraid to threaten unscrupulous accountants with the choice of 'either restitution, or else endless damnation.'[259]

Bradford's extreme anxiety about his complicity in a fraud committed by Harington against the Crown gives an insight into his thoughts about what God demands of the believer. He sought the advice of a Manchester trader, John Traves, 'an old and intelligent friend whose religion,' according to Christopher Haigh, 'was

---

[255] Foxe, *AM* [1563], 5:1241.

[256] E. G. Rupp, "John Bradford, Martyr. ob. 1 July, 1555," *The London Quarterly and Holborn Review*, 6th series, 32 (1963): 50.

[257] Foxe's account could imply that Bradford's conversion occurred before leaving Harington's service, but Johnston observes that 'there is certainly no hint that he became acquainted with Continental Reformed Theology [whilst abroad], and to adduce such in the face of non-existent evidence would be ingenious but inappropriate': Johnston, "Bradford," 19.

[258] Foxe, *AM* [1563], 5:1241.

[259] Hugh Latimer, *Sermons of Hugh Latimer*, ed. G. Corrie, PS (Cambridge: CUP, 1844), 262; see John Bradford and Thomas Sampson, *Two Notable Sermons. Made by that worthy martyr of Christ Maister Iohn Bradford, the one of repentance, and the other of the Lordes Supper neuer before imprinted* (London: Iohn Awdely and Iohn Wyght, 1574; RSTC 3500.5), A4v. Bradford was exposed to Reformed theology implicit in Latimer's sermons, writes Celia Hughes, "Two Sixteenth-Century Northern Protestants: John Bradford and William Turner," *Bulletin of the John Rylands Library* 66, 1 (1983): 106.

following a similar course' to Bradford's own.[260] In February 1548 Traves counselled Bradford on his fears of dying without making amends:

> God hath given you a desire to pay it, but not a power. Is God so cruel, trow ye, that he will exact of you to do that that is impossible for you to do? Are ye able to pay it? Then pay it. Are ye not able? Have a continual desire, which is to be begged of God, to pay; and in the name of God work so long as ye live, as God shall lead you toward the payment of it. And, if ye die before the satisfaction, yet I think ye shall go without peril; for I believe the sin is forgiven already for Christ's sake. There remaineth then by the doctor's mind but restitution; and I believe that you have *animum restituendi* [a spirit of restitution]; and [he that] earnestly laboureth and followeth upon God's preparation toward the restitution, the same hath made a good restitution, if he die before a full restitution.[261]

Traves's advice is fairly consistent with the late-medieval 'theology of piety,' placing minimal human effort in tension with the sufficiency of Christ's atonement. In order for Bradford to benefit from Christ's satisfaction, he must exercise a genuine desire to make satisfaction.[262] Although he has, in reality, contributed nothing to his salvation by his 'labour,' his 'labour' is accepted by God. Bradford's reply in early March went beyond Traves in demonstrating a stronger conviction of humanity's total inability to act in his own power:

---

[260] Christopher Haigh, *Reformation and Resistance in Tudor Lancashire* (Cambridge: CUP, 1975), 170.

[261] Traves to Bradford, February 1548, John Bradford, *The Writings of John Bradford, M. A., Martyr, 1555. Containing Letters, Treatises, Remains*, ed. A. Townsend, PS. 2 vols. (Cambridge: CUP, 1853), 2:3.

[262] Bradford seems to have shared this view: Johnston, "Bradford," 27.

> You know the cross, the fatherly cross, the loving Lord hath laid upon me; but I am little or nothing moved therewith; I work therein (yet not I, but God's Spirit), not of a repentant faithful mind, but, I cannot tell how, of a slothful, blind, [w]retchless intent.[263]

Bradford interpreted 'tribulations' as 'the cognizances of God's election, the letter *Thau*, the instruments which work *suspiria aeternae vitae* [the sighs of eternal life], and therefore to be embraced.'[264] The elect are provoked to work, or, more precisely, the Holy Spirit in them works.[265] When Bradford's restitution was completed a couple of years later, he assigned the credit to God: 'God wrought the restitution of the great thing [. . .] the which benefit should bind me to all obedience.'[266]

On 22 March 1548 Bradford wrote again to Traves, lamenting his own obstinacy in responding to God. He used a series of mixed metaphors related to God's call that demonstrate his interconnected reading of the Old Testament: 'I hide me with Adam in the garden, I play not only Samuel running to Eli, but I play Jonas running to the sea, and there I sleep upon the hatches, tumbling into Jezebel's bed.'[267] He saw himself as being too feeble even to answer God's summons, so he attributed salvation entirely to God, recognising that 'it cometh not of man, it cometh not of works, to repent, to

---

[263] To Traves, early March 1548, Bradford, *Writings*, 2:5.

[264] Ibid. The Hebrew letter 'thau' supposedly represented the 'mark' of election in an allusion to Ezekiel 9:4.

[265] As Trueman observes, 'in situations where [Bradford] is dealing with a troubled conscience, he almost always points towards Christ as the sole means of assurance. It is only when faced with complacency that he goads individuals into action by stressing the moral imperatives of Christianity': Trueman, *Luther's Legacy*, 274.

[266] To Traves, about February 1550, Bradford, *Writings*, 2:33.

[267] To Traves, 20 March 1548, Ibid., 2:13. Bradford had similarly cited Jezebel (Revelation 3:20–22) in his previous letter, highlighting his feelings of hypocrisy: Bradford, *Writings*, 2:5.

believe, to fear, and to love. Work thou therefore in me, for Jesus Christ's sake, which am thy creature and most unthankful hypocritical servant.'[268]

Bradford severely doubted his own ability to become a minister of God's word. While in London he undertook what he hoped to be the first of many translations of theological texts in order to avoid being an 'unprofitable and idle member.'[269] He chose to begin with *The division of the places of the lawe and of the Gospell* by Petrus Artopoeus, a Lutheran theologian in Szczecin.[270] In his prologue Bradford urged the theological use of the law and the sweetness of the Gospel of Christ before proceeding to condemn antinomian 'carnall gospellers.' God's 'testament' was mentioned only as the promise of salvation which the gospellers say the papists will never 'loke upon.'[271] The sole significance ascribed to godliness was to 'proue whether ye be in fayth [. . .] for fayth is not, where the feare of God is not.'[272] There was no indication of mutual or conditional concepts in this work.

In the same volume Bradford published two orations by John Chrysostom on prayer. His preface emphasised the numerous 'duetyes' which constitute a right response to the Gospel,[273] mindful of the fact that God's wrath, both in the Old Testament and today, is ignited by 'wanton receyuyng' of his word, by which he meant 'ingratitude and unthankfulness.' Together with repentance the Gospel 'cryeth for amendment of liuyng [. . .] God regardeth more obedience than sacrifice [. . .] if we wyll obey hym, we shall eate the

---

[268] To Traves, 22 March 1548, Bradford, *Writings*, 2:13–14.

[269] To Traves, late May/early June 1548, Ibid., 2:21.

[270] Petrus Artopoeus and John Chrysostome, *The Diuisyon of the Places of the Lawe and of the Gospell, gathered owt of the Hooly Scriptures by Petrum Artopoeum: wher unto is added two orations of prayeng to God made by S. Iohn. Chrisostome*, trans. J. Bradford (London: [S. Mierdman for] Gwalter Lynne, 1548; RSTC 822).

[271] Ibid., A6r.

[272] Ibid., A8r.

[273] Ibid., N5v.

good thynges of the lande.' Obedience, particularly in prayer, was the God-given means to 'exercyse' the faith that was needed to 'reteygne and kepe styll the grace of God gyuen unto us.'[274] Bradford still held faith to be the sole basis on which the Christian is justified before God, yet he considered obedience to be important to the enjoyment of the continuing blessing of God's grace. Although this has vestiges of a mutual covenant concept, Bradford did not develop his theology in that direction.

In the summer of 1548 Bradford went up to Cambridge to read divinity; having taken his M.A. in October 1549, he became a fellow of Pembroke Hall.[275] His theological indebtedness to Bucer, the Regius Professor of Divinity, whose lectures he attended, was 'truly decisive.'[276] Bradford was also conversant with the works of numerous patristic and medieval theologians as well as those of Erasmus, Ridley, Melanchthon, and Œcolampadius.[277] When, in the context of a discussion about transubstantiation at his examination in 1555, Bradford referred to those who had influenced him, it was in the negative: 'my faith is not builded on Luther, Zwingli, or Œcolampadius, in this point and indeed, to tell you truly, I never read any of their works in this matter [of the Eucharist].' He was, nonetheless, prepared to vouch that 'as for their persons, whatsoever their sayings were, yet do I think assuredly that they were and are God's children and saints with him.'[278] It may be significant for

---

[274] Ibid., N6r-7r.

[275] See Haigh, *Lancashire*, 166–67.

[276] Trueman, *Luther's Legacy*, 251n. For general comparisons see Johnston, "Bradford," 49–52, 109–19. Johnston concludes that Bradford's primary theological debt was to Bucer. Bradford did translate some passages of Bucer but it is otherwise hard to establish a 'clear demonstrable relationship between Bucer's writings and those of Bradford,' writes Basil Hall, "Martin Bucer in England," in *Martin Bucer: reforming church and community*, ed. D. Wright (Cambridge: CUP, 1994), 157n.

[277] Johnston, "Bradford," 59–60; Haigh, *Lancashire*, 171; Bradford, *Writings*, 2:55n.

[278] Bradford, *Writings*, 1:525.

Bradford's concept of covenant that he claimed that he had engaged with the sacramental theology of neither Zwingli, Œcolampadius, nor, indeed, Luther.[279]

Bradford's personal piety at Cambridge was remarkable for its depth of emotion and discipline.[280] He understood profoundly that he must one day give 'account even for every hair-breadth' of his sin.[281] His meditations (collected for publication in 1562) may profitably be considered here for their explicit reference to the concept of covenant. His *Meditation on the Ten Commandments* drew ethical principles from the Decalogue in line with Reformed theology. He considered how God

> vouchsafed [. . .] gratiously to enrich me concerning fortune, frends, liuinge, name [. . . and that I] should be called into the number of thy people, enroledde in thy boke, & now in thy couenaunt, so that thou with all that euer thou hast arte mine.

Bradford clearly places the covenant relationship after election. This relationship involves the possession of God with all his benefits through the 'couenaunt of peace vnfallible and euerlasting,' which is spoken of in the same breath as the relationships enjoyed

---

[279] In Bradford's treatise on the Mass the names of Calvin, Viret, Bullinger, and Hooper are printed in the margin where his text reads 'dyuerse haue wrytten of it ynough,' but this is more likely to be an editorial insertion than an indication of Bradford's own influences. See John Bradford, *The Hurte of Hering Masse* (London: Wyllyam Copland for Wyllyam Martyne, 1561; RSTC 3494), A2v.

[280] Bradford and Sampson, *Two Notable Sermons*, A5v; Strype, *Memorials*, iii/1:363. Marcus Loane remarks on 'an intolerance and an intensity in his nature which were just as vivid as his gentleness or his piety. This strand [. . .] was the result in part of his firm grasp of the Reformed Theology, and in part of his clear knowledge of God's grace in his own experience': Marcus Loane, *Pioneers of the Reformation in England* (London: The Church Book Room Press, 1964), 159.

[281] To Traves, late May/early June 1548, Bradford, *Writings*, 2:20.

by Abraham and the Israelites.²⁸² Bradford reflected that in Christ's blood 'shedde vpon the crosse, ye hast made a couenaunt with me, whiche thou wilt neuer forget.' God had promised 'that thou art and wilt be my lord and my god, that is, thou wilt forgeue me my sinnes and be wholy mine.'²⁸³ For Bradford, God guides us in all that we do:

> most iustely and reasonably thou requirest that as thou arte my lord god: so I should be thy seruaunt and one of thy people: As thou haste giuen thyself wholy vnto me, to be mine with all thy power wisedome &c (For he that geueth himself geueth all he hath) so shuld I be wholy thine, and geue ouer myself vnto thee to be guided with thy wisedome, defended with thy power, holpen, releiued, and comforted by thy mercy.²⁸⁴

This passage concerns the covenant relationship once salvation has been granted. God's covenant 'iustely and reasonably' elicits an appropriate response, but with no suggestion of human obligation, for Bradford had a stronger sense than Tyndale, Coverdale or Hooper of God working through believers. Humanity should submit itself to God, not only because those who do not fear the Lord will perish, but also that blessing may be poured out, 'that thou mightest reueale thy sonne to me, and thy mercye might be vpon me from generacion to generacion.'²⁸⁵ Humanity's part in the relationship does not attain the reciprocal character of a mutual covenant.

---

²⁸² John Bradford, *Godlie Meditations vpon the Lordes Prayer, the Beleefe, and Ten Commaundementes* [. . .] *a Defence of the Doctrine of Gods Eternall Election and Predestination* (London: Rouland Hall, 1562; RSTC 3484), F1r-v.

²⁸³ Ibid., E8v. Greaves, on the assumption that Calvin's concept of covenant was unilateral, claims that Bradford's concept was a reflection of Calvin's concept: Richard Greaves, "The Origins and Early Development of English Covenant Thought," *The Historian* 31, 1 (1968): 25, 28.

²⁸⁴ Bradford, *Godlie Meditations* [. . .] *Defence of Election*, F1v-2r.

²⁸⁵ Ibid., F2v; compare Genesis 17:7.

Bradford considered reasons 'to put my trust in thee, to loue, feare, and obey thee.' These reasons were 'not only in respect of the hurt which els will ensew, but also in respect of the commoditie that herby cometh vnto me.'[286] Although this 'commoditie' is received by relating properly to God, the alternative 'hurt' is being the poorer, having rejected God's benefits, rather than a punishment for disobedience. Bradford acknowledged that

> in times paste horribly I haue broken this thy lawe, in trusting in thy creatures, calling vpon them, louing, fearing, and obeying many thinges besydes thee, and rather then thee [. . .] by reason wherof I am worthy of eternall damnation.

This led him to reiterate the assurance of Christ's atonement on account of which God graciously grants salvation to those who believe.[287] There is a sense in which faith operates as a condition when Bradford recognises that God could fairly object 'that I doe not beleue, and therfore notwithstandinge thy trueth & promise, in that I beleue it not, thou maiest most iustly after thy Iustice, dampne me.' However, this being so, Bradford's advice is that the faithless

---

[286] Ibid., F3r.

[287] Ibid., G1r-v. Bradford, similar to Tyndale, based justification on the apprehension of Christ's righteousness: he was made incarnate so that we 'by hym myghte be made thy chyldren, children of grace, communicatinge with him rightuousnes, holines, & immortality by the working of the spirit, as he communicated wyth vs fleshe and bloude [. . .] by the working of the same holy spirit': Bradford, *Godlie Meditations* [. . .] *Defence of Election*, E7v-8r. Hence the importance of mystical union in Bradford's concept of covenant, 'that I mighte dwel in thee and thou in me': Idem., F3r. This informed his understanding of imputation as well as the law-Gospel dialectic in a *Comparison between the old man and the new* in John Bradford, *Godly Meditations vppon the Ten Commaundementes, the Articles of the Fayth, and the Lords Prayer* [. . .] *a Comparison Betweene the Old Man and the New: the Lawe and the Gosple* (London: William Seres, 1567; RSTC 3493.5), 92–96. However, Bradford did not teach 'double justification' as has been suggested by Hughes, "Two Northern Protestants," 115–17; see also Trueman, *Luther's Legacy*, 282–83.

should cast themselves on God's mercy, rather than urging them to work at their faith.[288]

The other explicit references to the covenant also concerned divine promises. In *A confession of sinnes, and a praier for the mitigation of goddes wrath and punishment for the same*, Bradford prayed, with regard to salvation: 'indue vs wyth thy holie spirit according to thy couenant and mercy.' Bradford unequivocally stated that it is God who acts in us, and that it is divine action which accomplishes all that is required of God's children:

> write thy law in our hartes & so to worke in vs, that we maye now begyn and goe forwardes in beleuing, liuing, fearing, obeyng, praying, hoping & seruinge thee as thou doest requyre most fatherly and most iustly of vs, acceptinge vs as perfecte throughe Christ and by imputation.[289]

Although the Christian should follow a godly pattern of life, Bradford's point is that God works this in his people, accepting them by virtue of the imputed, alien righteousness of Christ.

In *A prayer for the remission of sinnes*, Bradford implored God to remember his 'promise & euerlasting couenant' of Isaiah 54:9. God's oath that he will never again be angry as in the time of Noah is called the 'bond of my peace' which 'shal not faile thee.' Again, Bradford emphasised the divine action working in the Christian by means of the covenant written on his heart:

> that I maye loue thee with all my harte for euer: that I may loue thy people for thy sake: that I may be holy in thi sight through Christ: that I may always not only striue against sinne, but also ouercome the same daily more and more, as thy children doe, aboue all thinges desiringe the sanctification of

[288] Bradford, *Godlie Meditations* [. . .] *Defence of Election*, F3r-v.
[289] Ibid., N2v.

thy name, the comming of thy kingdome, the doyng of thy will here on earth as it is in heauen.[290]

Similarly, in *The Flesh and the Spirit*, Bradford explained that 'so much as we are regenerate and endued with God's Spirit, we do strive and fight against all the powers of our souls and bodies.'[291] The practical outworking of Bradford's position, writes Johnston, is that 'godly living is of paramount importance to the elect.'[292] However, godliness is characterised as a response to having been chosen by God rather than a responsibility of being elect.

In the fly-leaves of his copy of Tyndale's New Testament Bradford wrote that although the Spirit-empowered works of the Christian are yet imperfect, through faith imperfection is not 'imputed or laid to their charge for the covenant's sake.' Therefore the regenerate man 'never can nor will sin against God,' and is 'free to do good and nothing else.' This righteousness in God's sight, insofar as believers 'walk in his laws,' gives 'certainty of salvation.' Bradford's focus was on God's covenanted means of accepting believers 'finally and perpetually,' rather than on ethical instruction.[293]

Bucer encouraged Bradford to become a preacher and on 10 August 1550 Ridley ordained him deacon with licence to preach.[294] Before Bucer died in February 1551, Bradford urged him to remember Christ's promises and 'to consider who he was, what he taught, and what steadfastness, faith, and devotion, he had always exercised,'

---

[290] Ibid., N6r-v.
[291] Bradford, *Writings*, 1:301–2.
[292] Johnston, "Bradford," 145.
[293] Bradford, *Writings*, 1:250–51. On the reception history of Bradford's copy see Michael Graham and Gretchen Minton, "The Word as as an Artifact of Remembrance," *Reformation* 18, 1 (2013): 68f.
[294] Foxe, *AM* [1563], 5:1242. Bradford's objection at his ordination, unspecified by Foxe, was almost certainly against the invocation of the saints rather than against vestments, since Ridley would never have conceded the latter in the midst of Hooper's Vestments Controversy. Bradford was probably ordained priest eventually: Johnston, "Bradford," 217.

and the satisfaction made by God alone. Bradford's confidence for salvation was based on faith, but a faith characterised by discipline. Bucer seems to have felt that Bradford's advice was too introspective since, according to Nicholas Carr's report, Bucer was concentrating wholly 'upon Christ crucified, that God dwelt in his heart, and [. . .] nothing but heaven and a speedy departure from this body.'[295]

In December 1551 Bradford became a royal chaplain, one of six élite, itinerant preachers.[296] Ridley likened him to Latimer and John Knox in his sharp rebuke of social ills.[297] According to Haigh, Lancashire evangelicalism came to include 'a pronounced Puritan strain' in response to Bradford's preaching.[298] Throughout 1552 Bradford toured Lancashire and Cheshire, and that summer he preached his *Sermon of Repentance* (published in July 1553).[299] In it the concept of covenant was used explicitly only in reference to complacent law-breakers: Bradford asked, 'tell me nowe good brother why do you so lightely consyder Gods cursse, that for your sinnes past you are so careles as though you had made a couenaunt with death and damnation as the wicked dyd in Esayes time?'[300] The reference is to Isaiah 28:15–18 where the covenant with death and hell requires nothing of sinners. In Bradford's sermon, as in Isaiah, humanity initiates an anti-covenant which is neither reciprocal nor conditional.

Johnston observes of this sermon that 'in Bradford's redemptive scheme, it is difficult to see anything but the doctrine of substitutionary atonement.'[301] The exclusion of human merit from

---

[295] Nicholas Carr to John Cheke, Bradford, *Writings*, 2:xxiii–xxiv.

[296] W. K. Jordan, ed., *The Chronicle and Political Papers of Edward VI* (London: George Allen and Unwin, 1966), 101.

[297] Nicholas Ridley, *The Works of Nicholas Ridley*, ed. H. Christmas, PS (Cambridge: CUP, 1843), 59.

[298] Haigh, *Lancashire*, 175.

[299] For general discussion see Johnston, "Bradford," 164–80.

[300] John Bradford, *A Sermon of Repentaunce* (London: S. Mierdman for Iohn Wight, 1553; RSTC 3496), D5r.

[301] Johnston, "Bradford," 173.

justification is a pervasive concern.[302] To understand the value of works we must appreciate that in Bradford's theology 'repentance and its resultant, godly living, are synonymous.'[303] Bradford asserted that 'pennaunce is the thynges whereto all the scripture calleth vs.' He defined penance as 'a hartye sorow for our sinnes, a good hope or truste of pardone thorough Christe, whiche is not withoute an earneste purpose to amende, or a new lyfe.' Repentance, faith and the intention of godliness 'must be continuallye in vs, and not for a lent season, as we haue thoughte[.] This must increase dayly more and more in vs, without this we cannot be saued.' It is God who provides these three 'partes' of penance unto salvation.[304]

For Bradford the distinction between law and Gospel was that

> these promyses of the gospell doe not hange on the condicion of oure worthynesse as the promyses of the law do: but they depende and hange on Godsses [sic.] trueth, so that they cannot, but be perfourmed to al them which lay holde on them by faith, I had almost sayd which cast them not away by vnbelefe.[305]

Bradford assumes belief when he asserts the unconditionality of the Gospel promise. Recipients must not 'wyth Sathan say, GOD is false.' If they declare God to be a liar, 'GOD is faythful, and cannot denye himselfe: as thou shalt feele by hys plages in hell, for so dishonoringe God to thinke that he is not true.'[306] Assurance stems from the reliability of God's word and can only be forfeited by incredulity.

The truly faithful believer is always one who attempts to be godly, since the faithful have the Spirit 'to worke in you, with you, & by you here in this lyfe, sanctificacion.' The faithful are exhorted not

---

[302] E.g., Bradford, *Repentaunce*, B7r-C2r, H2r.
[303] Johnston, "Bradford," 164.
[304] Bradford, *Repentaunce*, C5r, 6v.
[305] Ibid., F1v-2r.
[306] Ibid., F4r.

to 'moleste the good spyryt of God by rebellinge agaynste it, when it prouoketh and calleth you to go on forewardes, that he which is holy, myght yet be more holy, he whyche is righteous myghte be more righteous.'[307] Bradford's understanding of God's call to holiness was integrated into the reception of God's benefits by faith. He was particularly concerned to show that the godly works required of humanity were done through the internal action of the Spirit, and his teaching was constructed to be as consistent as possible with his understanding of grace from first to last.

In November 1552 Ridley identified Bradford as a potential bishop,[308] and Bradford was invited to preach before the king in Lent 1553.[309] Shortly after Edward's death in July 1553 Bradford published his translation of Melanchthon's *A treatyse of prayer*, using the preface to blame God's wrath on the impiety of the English people.[310] However, Bradford did not depict this retribution as a covenantal sanction.

On 16 August 1553 Bradford was imprisoned in the Tower, whence he contributed to the public divisions over the resumption of the Latin rite a treatise on *The Hurt of Hearing Mass*, warning 'week gospellers' not to conform under worldly pressure.[311] Bradford

---

[307] Ibid., H5v-6r.

[308] Ridley to John Gate and William Cecil, 18 November 1552, Ridley, *Works*, 337.

[309] Bradford and Sampson, *Two Notable Sermons*, A3v-4r. On the assumption that Bradford was ordained, it seems reasonable to speculate that he, like Hooper, might have been made a bishop following his Court sermons had not Edward VI died. For John Knox's account of Bradford's preaching at Court, see Bradford, *Writings*, 1:111.

[310] Philip Melanchthon, *A Godlye Treatyse of Prayer*, trans. J. Bradford (London: S. Mierdman for Iohn Wight, 1553; RSTC 17791), A3r, A4v.

[311] Bradford, *Hurte of Hering Masse*, E4v. Bradford was by far the most prolific of the prison writers, producing some 128 items: Megan Wheeler, "Protestants, Prisoners and the Marian Persecution," DPhil diss. (University of Oxford, 2006), 75, 102. His enduring respect for the national Church under Mary is seen as indicative of a Swiss ecclesiology by Hughes, "Two Northern Protestants," 115.

built his argument on God's law in the Decalogue: 'out of the furste table I haue shewed that euery commaundemendemente [*sic*.] theirin is broken by hearinge & seynge Masse [. . .] so could I shew out of the second table that it is a breach of all and euerye commaundementes there.'³¹² His first point reiterated, yet again, the propriety of godliness:

> [when God] hath tolde vs what he is vnto vs: euen oure lorde and oure god, wyth all that euer he is and hathe [. . .] then of equitee he requireth that we shulde be content wyth hym and geue oure selues to hym to be hys wyth all that euer we haue [. . .]. [God] demaundeth the soule, wyll, vnderstan[d]ynge, and harte, that is our fayth feare, loue, thankefulnes, inuocasion, & inwarde adoracion, or worshippynge to be gyuen to hym onelye, and for hys sake as he shall appoynte [. . .]. He generallye requereth for the outwarde seruyce of hym, that we shulde followe his worde in seruinge of hym.³¹³

God has given himself to humanity, and humanity must act as God's possession. Of equity mankind must worship God alone and serve God according to his express instruction, but again, Bradford did not relate this to the covenant.

Bradford was transferred to the King's Bench Prison in the spring of 1554. In the summer he entered into controversy with sectarian 'free-willers' who sought, in this dispute, to preserve human free will in salvation.³¹⁴ Trueman claims that election was axiomatic to Bradford's soteriology.³¹⁵ Although a predestinarian emphasis

---

³¹² Bradford, *Hurte of Hering Masse*, C5v.
³¹³ Ibid., B7r-v.
³¹⁴ Thomas Freeman, "Dissenters from a Dissenting Church: the Challenge of the Freewillers, 1550–1558," in *The Beginnings of English Protestantism*, eds. P. Marshall and A. Ryrie (Cambridge: CUP, 2002), 134–35.
³¹⁵ Trueman, *Luther's Legacy*, 256; see also Johnston, "Bradford," 135–36.

need not preclude a bilateral concept of covenant it seems to have done so in Bradford's case. Thomas Freeman writes that 'Bradford and his associates felt obliged to defend predestination at almost any cost: assurance of immutable election was a paramount concern of their followers.'[316] The most obvious source of his doctrine of election is Bucer, although Calvin's predestinarianism had begun to circulate in England.[317] Bradford had probably attended Bucer's lectures on St Paul's Epistle to the Ephesians in 1550–51 and he shared Bucer's emphasis on divine revelation over human reason.[318]

Writing to the free-willers, Bradford contended that God's will to save the elect was 'determined, and therefore immutable.'[319] From a human perspective, God 'doth seem in some things to alter his will, before not determined, but dependant on man's behaviour,' yet God's will is not altered 'in respect of himself.' Thus, Jonah declared to the Ninevites that 'God's sentence pronounced was not determined but hanged upon condition [. . .] as by the alteration of it we perceive.'[320] Meanwhile, 'the sentence of God for those which he hath given to Christ' is seen to be determined both by Christ's prayer in John 17:20–26 and by the fact that they 'refuse [redemption] not finally.' It is possible to distinguish between what is determined and what is undetermined 'by the word and of the end.'[321]

---

[316] Freeman, "Dissenters," 135; see also J. W. Martin, "English Protestant Separatism at its Beginnings: Henry Hart and the Free-Will Men," *SCJ* 7, 2 (1976): 69.

[317] Ian Hazlett, "Calvin and the British Isles," in *The Calvin Handbook*, ed. H. Selderhuis (Grand Rapids and Cambridge: Eerdmans, 2009), 120–21.

[318] Trueman, *Luther's Legacy*, 251n; see also Heal, *Reformation*, 331. Bucer's lectures would also account for Bradford's emphasis on discipline. Bucer said that the knowledge of election 'actively kindles in us a zeal for purity' and 'an amazing longing and desire to cleave to the benefits of God': Martin Bucer, *Lectures on Ephesians* (1550–51), in *Commonplaces of Martin Bucer*, ed. D. F. Wright (Abingdon: Sutton Courtenay Press, 1972), 109–11.

[319] To a free-willer, 1554, Bradford, *Writings*, 2:129.

[320] Ibid., 2:130.

[321] Ibid.; To Cole and Sheterden, Ibid., 2:133.

Similar to Luther's argument in *De Servo Arbitrio*,[322] Bradford rejected a synergistic interpretation of salvation that implied the insufficiency of Christ's atonement to elicit grace:

> if you will say that salvation dependeth partly on ourselves, and not simply, wholly and altogether on God's mercy and truth in Christ and his merits, you deny salvation to come of grace, contrary to the prophets and apostles; for grace to us is not but in respect of grace to Christ.[323]

Bradford suspected that the free-willers were 'adversaries to grace by maintaining free-will' and he assumed that they must lack assurance 'because you are never certain of your power how much and free it is.'[324] The denial of human cooperation was fundamental to Bradford's defence of salvation by grace.[325] The development of a reciprocal concept of covenant would have militated against his line of argument.

Nevertheless, the unconditional nature of Bradford's concept of covenant did not permit antinomianism. He insisted that, as 'God's providence bindeth not our hands, so it hindereth not in us any good thing, but rather provoketh us thereunto mightily.'[326] Christians 'pray, watch and fast, and do good deeds, and yet still hang on God's eternal and immutable decree and grace in Christ.' These activities do not 'infirm their faith' regarding their election; instead they are recognised as 'God's instruments to their salvation' on the

---

[322] Martin Luther, *De Servo Arbitrio* [1525], trans. P. Watson, *LCC*, Vol. 17 (Philadelphia: Westminster Press, 1969), 178.

[323] To a free-willer, Bradford, *Writings*, 2:130.

[324] Ibid.

[325] D. A. Penny, *Freewill or Predestination: the battle over saving grace in mid-Tudor England* (Woodbridge: Royal Historical Society, 1990), 116. Bradford's determination to exclude human cooperation might fruitfully be compared with later Puritan attitudes. On the free-willer view that God's promise was contingent on mankind's actively putting himself under the covenant, see Martin, "English Protestant Separatism," 65, 71–72.

[326] Bradford, Writings, 2:130–31.

understanding that God 'can and will make his counsel to stand for ever, as we see he doth with the elect infants without these things.'[327]

Bradford's *Defence of the doctrine of gods eternall election and predestination* was written in late 1554. In the dedication, written on 11 October 1554, he claimed that faith in divine election was 'the whole sum' of what God 'requireth of us,'[328] yet faith not only undermined human 'power, ableness, and choice,' but also

> enforceth men to love and carefully travail for their brethren [. . .]. It provoketh to piety, and is the greatest enemy to ungodliness that can be, by teaching us of what dignity we be [. . .]. It maketh man wholly and continually to give over himself to be careful, not for himself, but for his brethren and those things which make to God's glory.[329]

Bradford argued that godliness was

> grounded in predestination in Christ. For who liveth 'godly,' but he that believeth? and who believeth but such as are 'ordained to eternal life?' Who liveth 'justly,' but such as love their neighbours? and whence springeth this love, but of God's election 'before the beginning of the world, that we might be blameless by love?' Who liveth 'soberly' but such as be holy? and who are they but only those that be endued with the Spirit of sanctification? Which is the 'seal' of our election, which by election do believe.[330]

Godliness was an assurance, rather than a requirement, of election, but they were closely linked in the treatise.[331] Bradford pointed

---

[327] Ibid., 2:131; see Trueman, *Luther's Legacy*, 224.
[328] Bradford, *Writings*, 1:307.
[329] Ibid., 1:308.
[330] Ibid., 1:309.
[331] Bradford, *Godlie Meditations* [. . .] *Defence of Election*, O6r.

out that Christ had attributed 'to election the cause of finall perseuerance.'³³² God 'cannot condemne the penitent and beleuer, for that were against his promise,' wrote Bradford, and believers were exhorted to claim the promise: 'Let us therefore labour, studie, crye and praye for repentance and faith, and then cannot we be damned.'³³³

In the second part of Bradford's treatise on election he discussed the relationship between election and the covenant. He reported the opinion of a free-willer that election

> putteth away (saith he) the covenaunt of god p[ar]tely on gods parte, but wholly on mans p[ar]te. On gods parte (saieth he) bicause christ is denyed to be a generall savior [...] he writeth that election putteth away the covenaunt on mans behalf wholy for it taketh away (saieth he) the power and holynes, w[hi]ch god hath before given from hym.³³⁴

Bradford did not hesitate to deny that Christ was a 'generall savior' because that would, he believed, lead either to universalism or to a denial of divine sovereignty. To the accusation that election confounds human 'power and holynes,' Bradford responded that Paul 'taketh from man the thought which is the best part of any good workes[.] As for the consent and deede elsewhere he taketh it from man and gevethe it to god.'³³⁵

Bradford progressed to attack the free-willer's view that 'as god called in adam all men so all men came in Adam: unto him whereuppon he made the covenaunt.' Bradford objected that Adam had not responded to God's call in Genesis 3, 'much lesse all in hym.'³³⁶ Bradford also criticised the free-willer for making humanity's response

---

³³² Ibid., O8v.

³³³ Ibid., P1v.

³³⁴ Bodleian Library, Oxford: MS. Bodl. 53, fol. 59r. Only part one of the treatise was published in 1562.

³³⁵ Ibid. fol. 59v.

³³⁶ Ibid.

to God into the basis of the covenant: 'Agayn gode[s] covenaunt whose grounde is his mercy and truthe: he maketh now our coming so greatly dothe he Impugne the mercie and goodnes of god.' In Bradford's view, the free-willer had failed to discern 'betweene the fre promes and covenaunt, for els he would not call the fre promes a covenaunt but on gode[s] behalf onlye: ffor what is required here on mans behalf if he have respect to infants and children which can not beleve[?]'[337] For Bradford, the word 'covenant' implied responsibility and ought to be applied only to God's unilateral action in salvation. Although God had made covenants with both David and Jeroboam in 1 Kings 11:34–39, Bradford claimed that the free-willer 'confoundethe the covenaunts as appearethe by his testimonies: and examples. the covenaunt to David and Jeroboam were not a like as a child can tell that readeth the booke of the kinge.'[338] David and Jeroboam were both required to keep God's law but, as Bradford suggests, the Davidic covenant was distinguished by the fact that it was ultimately unconditional.

Bradford's prison disputes strongly suggest that his concept of covenant was subordinated to and controlled by his emphasis on unconditional election, seemingly encouraging the development of a unilateral version of the concept. In this respect Bradford's predestinarian theology, although similar to Calvin's, had different theological consequences. In January 1555 Bradford was transferred from the King's Bench to the Compter Prison. There he composed farewells to those he had known and preached to.[339] In his *Exhortation to the brethren throughout the realm of England*, he reminded them that they had 'made a covenant with God to forsake yourselves in this world and Satan also.'[340] It was the first time that Bradford had

---

[337] Ibid.

[338] Ibid. Greaves cites this passage to show that Bradford took more care than Calvin to distinguish between the free promise and covenant of grace: Greaves, "Origins," 28.

[339] See Wheeler, "Protestants, Prisoners," 90.

[340] Bradford, *Writings*, 1:415. On the importance of suffering in Bradford's

written of humanity making a covenant with God, but he did not develop the idea. Bradford himself forsook this world for the next at the stake on 30 June 1555.

This analysis of the writings of four English reformers has revealed their engagement with, and strongly pastoral approach to, the concept of covenant. Although logical theological exposition tended to give way to the achievement of their didactic ends, Tyndale, Coverdale and Hooper developed their understandings of covenant in a direction comparable with the Swiss reformers explored in chapter three. While they had been directly exposed to continental theology during their periods in exile, Bradford imbibed other influences and his concept of covenant did not come to resemble the Swiss formulation.

Tyndale was undoubtedly reading Swiss Reformed theology by the late 1520s. His development of a reciprocal concept of covenant in 1529–31 was probably precipitated by his own work on the Pentateuch, although his reading of Swiss texts would have strongly encouraged this extension of his earlier ethical emphases. He co-ordinated faith and love within the covenant framework so that it was incumbent upon the believer to fulfil the law in the context of the gracious indwelling of the Spirit. While Tyndale's gradual accentuation of ethical emphases is striking, in Coverdale's case there is a concentration of evidence of his covenant thought in the early 1540s. It is probable that Coverdale's concept initially arose through Tyndale's influence, but his direct links with Zürich theology are clearer than Tyndale's. Coverdale made available in English Bullinger's *Der alt gloub*, thereby disseminating covenant ideas among English-speakers. Coverdale applied the legal and familial nature of mutual obligation in his writings with an emphasis on sanctification. He maintained his interest in Swiss ideas throughout Edward VI's reign, but by that time Hooper was the most renowned

---

theology and its link to godliness and reward, see Johnston, "Bradford," 161–62.

exponent of Zürich theology in England. Hooper's concept of covenant had been fully developed in Zürich between 1547 and 1549. It was the basic principle expounded, explicitly and implicitly, in his writings. The covenant guaranteed God's salvation to believers on the condition that they met the requirements of faith and godliness. Tyndale, Coverdale and Hooper all exhibited a reciprocal concept of covenant consistent with that of Zwingli, Bullinger, and Calvin.

Bradford's continental influences were largely indirect, although the most significant was Bucer's teaching at Cambridge. Bradford aspired to high moral standards for his personal relationship with God and he developed strong ethical impulses in his theology. However, his concept of covenant cannot account for this. For Bradford, following Bucer, God's eternal decree made it impossible to attribute anything to humanity in salvation that could be construed as a condition. Owing to the particular circumstances of the free-will controversy in 1554, he applied 'covenant' to God's unilateral commitment only, since he could not risk assigning any salvific efficacy to human action, even if it were within the context of God's sovereign grace.

The similarity between the Swiss reformers and Tyndale, Coverale, and Hooper in their reciprocal concept of covenant points to the reception of Swiss theology into English Reformed identity. Bradford's unilateral concept of covenant, under Bucer's influence, appears to confirm the link between the development of a reciprocal covenant and Swiss influence. The next two chapters will add further definition to these influences through an examination of the covenant idea in relation to sacramental theology.

5

Swiss Sacramental Theology

Whoever honours idols, before and after holds them in his heart as god, that is, as father or helper. For this reason they are idols. For who honours the stone ape in the fish market or the golden hen in the small tower? Who burns candles before them? No one. For what reason? For the reason that man perceives divine help in no ape or hen.
—*Huldrych Zwingli (1525)*[1]

The Fourth Lateran Council (1215) declared transubstantiation of the bread and the wine into the body and blood of Christ in the course of the Mass to be *de fide*.[2] Communicants received divine grace through the corporal reception of Christ. The efficacy of the sacrifice of the Mass made it the elaborate centrepiece of the sacramental cycle which would be shaken by Martin Luther's rejection, not only of transubstantiation, but of five medieval sacraments in his treatise *The Babylonian Captivity of the Church* (1520). In Luther's opinion baptism and the Eucharist alone contained divine

---

[1] Huldrych Zwingli, *Answer to Valentin Compar* (1525), translated in Lee Wandel, "The Body of Christ at Marburg, 1529," in *Image and Imagination of the Religious Self in Late Medieval and Early Modern Europe*, eds. R. Falkenburg, W. Melion and T. Richardson (Turnhout: Brepols, 2007), 204–5.

[2] Gary Macy, "The Dogma of Transubstantiation in the Middle Ages," *JEH* 45, 1 (1994): 23, 40.

promises confirmed by a sign. He wrote that 'in every promise of God two things are presented to us, the word and the sign, so that we are to understand the word to be the testament, but the sign to be the sacrament.'³ It was the Eucharist rather than baptism that generated fierce debate between magisterial reformers when the *Abendmahlsstreit* (Supper controversy) erupted in 1525 between the Swiss and upper German reformers and the Lutherans. The Eucharist was the only subject on which agreement could not be reached when Philip of Hesse arranged for Luther and Zwingli to meet at Marburg in 1529.⁴

Luther insisted that Christ's 'real flesh and real blood are present in no other way and to no less a degree than the others [the Catholics] assert them to be under their accidents.'⁵ His explanation of the Eucharist as 'Christ's testament' united his sacramental theology to his definition of a testament, compact, or covenant as a unilateral and unconditional last will and testament.⁶ His understanding of the Real Presence was inextricable from his conception of Christ's testament. Similarly Martin Bucer concentrated his sacramental theology upon the 'divine promises' and united the sacraments to an understanding of testament akin to Luther's.⁷

---

³ Luther, *Babylonian Captivity*, *LW*, 36:44. On signs, see Euan Cameron, *The European Reformation* (Oxford: OUP, 1991), 157.

⁴ *Marburg Colloquy and Articles*, *LW*, 38:85–89.

⁵ Luther, *Babylonian Captivity*, 29. The term 'consubstantiation' does not accurately describe Luther's position because he rejected the Aristotelian language of 'substance' and 'accident'.

⁶ Ibid., 38; see Hagen, "From Testament to Covenant in the Early Sixteenth Century," *SCJ* 3, 1 (1972): 10; Bernhard Lohse, *Martin Luther's Theology: its historical and systematic development*, trans. R. Harrisville (Edinburgh: T&T Clark, 1999), 175.

⁷ See Ian Hazlett, "Eucharistic Communion: Impulses and Directions in Martin Bucer's Thought," in *Martin Bucer: reforming church and community*, ed. D. Wright (Cambridge: CUP, 1994), 75; W. P. Stephens, *Zwingli: an introduction to his thought* (Oxford: OUP, 1992), 79; Stephens, *Bucer*, 216–19; Gordon Jeanes, *Signs of God's Promise: Thomas Cranmer's sacramental theology and the Book of Common Prayer* (London: T&T Clark, 2008), 144. For Bucer's account

Zwingli, Bullinger, and Calvin developed equally vibrant sacramental theologies which were similarly integrated into their concepts of covenant. Unlike Luther, their high regard for the Eucharist did not depend upon the belief that Christ was physically present in the elements.[8] Although their concepts of covenant all conformed to the reciprocal pattern, they offered different interpretations of Christ's spiritual presence in the sacraments and of the relationship between the sacraments and their spiritual signification. While all of them agreed that the Holy Spirit conferred grace, they differed on the utility of the sacraments as instruments, means, mediators or vehicles of grace. Many of the developments in Swiss sacramental thought from the 1520s until the 1550s arose from attempts at concord amongst evangelicals. The brokering of the *Consensus Tigurinus* (1549), when comparable agreement with the Lutherans had proved elusive, was partly due to the shared covenantal basis of distinct sacramental understandings between Zürich and Geneva.

Huldrych Zwingli

The abolition of the Mass by the city council of Zürich in April 1525 was a seminal moment in the implementation of Zwingli's vision for a new Christian society. Zwingli located the sacraments within his concept of covenant, arguing that they existed primarily for the covenant community, the Church, rather than for the individual.[9] Zwingli's sacramental theology was predicated upon

---

of the development of his sacramental theology towards Luther's position in the early 1530s see Martin Bucer, *Account of the Concord entered into in 1536 at Wittenberg* (1536), in *Commonplaces of Martin Bucer*, ed. D. F. Wright (Abingdon: Sutton Courtenay Press, 1972), 357–58.

[8] There is much confusion in Basil Hall's claim that 'a covenant theology is always inimical to a sacramental theology': Hall, "Lutheranism in England," 110. Hall refers to a bilateral covenant, thereby restrictively associating 'sacramental theology' with Luther's concept of unilateral testament.

[9] Jaques Courvoisier, *Zwingli: a Reformed Theologian* (London: Epworth, 1964), 64.

his Christology. His primary concern was to uphold the unique efficacy of Christ's Passion for salvation. A positive statement of the sacraments for Zwingli was one that maintained Christ's exclusive sufficiency for the people of God. As Bruce Gordon explains, 'the Son of God's work of reconciliation on the cross was complete and in no need of repetition, and from grateful people he required obedience.'[10]

In his exposition of the eighteenth of his Sixty-Seven Articles (1523) Zwingli contrasted Christ's sacrifice with the sacrifice of the Mass. His christocentric conception of the covenant is evident in his ascription of the Roman profanation of the Eucharist to ignorance of the covenant, which he already understood to be bilateral and conditional. He complained: 'that which is a testament, legacy or covenant and memorial, they have called a sacrament or offering.'[11] Zwingli's contention was that the legacy of peace (or the peace agreement) which the sacrament signified could not be a sacrifice or offering to God. Even the Roman definition of sacrament as 'a sign of a holy thing' was inconsistent with the assertion of Christ's corporal presence in the elements, for what did Christ's corporal body and blood signify? Zwingli would agree to the definition of *sacramentum* as 'a sure sign or seal'[12] but not as the oblatory means of grace inferred by Catholic theologians. Like Luther, he considered a sacrament to be a particular kind of sign 'on which God has spoken an express word and made a promise in his word,'[13] but he proceeded in the same article to place God's promise in a bilateral, covenantal context,[14] noting 'the likeness of the words of Moses (by which he affirmed

---

[10] Bruce Gordon with Luca Baschera and Christian Moser, "Emulating the Past and Creating the Present: Reformation and the Use of Historical and Theological Models in Zurich in the Sixteenth Century," in *Following Zwingli: Applying the Past in Reformation Zurich*, eds. L. Baschera, B. Gordon and C. Moser (Farnham: Ashgate, 2014), 5.

[11] Zwingli, *Exposition of the Articles*, *HZW*, 1:98.

[12] Ibid., 1:99.

[13] Ibid., 1:100.

[14] Ibid., 1:106–7.

the testament), to the words of Christ, concerning his blood.'[15] Thus an understanding of sacraments as confirmations of God's covenant was already emerging in Zwingli's theology in 1523.

Zwingli's sacramental theology was intended to uphold salvation *solo Christo* in the face of perceived threats during the Eucharist controversy. In November 1524 he expounded the 'figurative language of Christ' in John 6:63—'It is the Spirit who gives life; the flesh profits nothing'—to prove that 'salvation can come in no other way than through Christ, and therefore not through the sacramental eating of bread and wine.'[16] The importance of the sacraments had to be found elsewhere than as vehicles of grace.[17] Zwingli believed that he had identified a category error in the evaluation of the sacraments by his Catholic and Lutheran opponents.

In *Of Baptism, Rebaptism and Infant Baptism* (May 1525) Zwingli affirmed that 'only Jesus Christ and no external thing can take away the sins of us Christians and make us holy.' Since Christ has superseded any other means of atonement, including the Mass, 'we are not to hope in them or look to them for justification.' Faith in Christ alone is sufficient, but the Old Testament sacraments were 'transformed' 'as a concession to our frailty: "for a bruised reed shall he not break."'[18] That is, sacraments do not effect salvation or have 'power to take away sin and to make us holy,' but they do make allowance for humanity in the weakness of sin. Zwingli's intention was to 'let the sacraments be real sacraments' pointing to, rather than displacing, that which they signify.[19] He held the significatory function of the sacraments in high estimation:

---

[15] Ibid., 1:106.

[16] Huldrych Zwingli, *Letter to Matthew Alber concerning the Lord's Supper* [November 1524], *HZW*, 2:135–37.

[17] For comparable criticism by Œcolampadius see Jaroslav Pelikan, *Reformation of Church and Dogma (1300–1700)*, The Christian Tradition, Vol. 4 (Chicago and London: University of Chicago Press, 1984), 188–89.

[18] Zwingli, "Baptism," in *Zwingli and Bullinger*, ed. Bromiley, 130–32.

[19] Ibid., 131.

the word "sacrament" [*sacramentum*] means a pledge of allegiance [*pflichtszeichen*]. If a man sews on a white cross, he proclaims that he is a Confederate [. . .]. Similarly the man who receives the mark of baptism is the one who is resolved to hear what God says to him, to learn the divine precepts and to live his life in accordance with them. And the man who in the remembrance or Supper gives thanks to God in the congregation testifies to the fact that from the very heart he rejoices in the death of Christ and thanks him for it. [. . .] So baptism is a sacrament that pledges [*verpflicht*] us to Jesus Christ. The memorial reminds us that Christ suffered death for us. They are signs and pledges [*zeichen und verpflichtungen*] of the holy things. You find the true meaning of these things in the requirement [*pflichtung*] of circumcision and the thanksgiving of the Easter Lamb.[20]

The sacraments are proclamations and testimonies of obedience, resolution, commitment, determination, membership of the Church, gratitude and jubilation. Like a soldier's uniform or the ring of a faithful spouse, they are rich and emotive signs and badges of the reality signified.[21] Zwingli's sacramental theology was not 'merely' memorialist; rather, the sacraments recalled the meaning of the divine covenant and the atonement themselves.

What, then, for Zwingli was the connection between signifier and signified? In the *Subsidiary Essay* (August 1525) Zwingli taught that the 'testament, covenant or agreement [*testamentum, foedus aut pactum*]' was won by Christ's blood, the 'blood of the testament.'

---

[20] Ibid.; *CR*, 91:218. I have modified the English translation to accord with the German. Zwingli used *bundszeichen* (God's pledge) and *pflichtzeichen* (man's pledge) interchangeably: Andrew Woolsey, *Unity and Continuity in Covenantal Thought: A Study of the Reformed Tradition to the Westminster Assembly* (Grand Rapids, MI: Reformation Heritage Books, 2012), 221.

[21] Zwingli, *True and False Religion*, *LWHZ*, 3:180–81; W. P. Stephens, *The Theology of Huldrych Zwingli* (Oxford: OUP, 1986), 190.

Christ's blood was not itself the testament but 'that through which the testament [*testamentum*] of free remission was made and confirmed.' The Eucharist was 'the symbol or figure of the blood of the testament [*testamenti*],'[22] two removes from the testament itself. The connection was tropological:[23]

> The figure, therefore, receives the name of the thing typified [. . .]. The sacrament, therefore, of the covenant and testament [*foederis et testamenti sacramentum*], if you use "sacrament" for the external sign of the chief covenant or oath [*principali foederis aut iurisiurandi*], is baptism; the symbol of the passion of Christ, through which this covenant [*foedus*] and testament [*testamentum*] was perfected [is the Eucharist or commemoration].[24]

In other words, God has established terms 'and these terms are the real covenant itself. But there are added to covenants signs, which though also called by the name of covenants yet are not covenants.'[25]

To summarise how Zwingli understood the specific signification of the sacraments: in 1523 he saw them as signifying God's covenantal promise; by May 1525 his emphasis had shifted towards understanding them as humanity's pledge rather than God's,[26] but the latter idea had been revived again by August.[27] Both were valid significations in Zwingli's theology: sacraments were a 'sign of duty' and a sign of 'effected grace.'[28] Gerrish suggests that Zwingli's use of

---

[22] Zwingli, *Subsidiary Essay*, *HZW*, 2:225; *CR*, 91:501.

[23] For Zwingli on the tropological sense of scripture, referring to figurative meaning, see Zwingli, *Friendly Exegesis*, *HZW*, 2:352, 355; Zwingli, *Original Sin*, *LWHZ*, 2:20–21; Zwingli, *Account of the Faith*, *LWHZ*, 2:52.

[24] Zwingli, *Subsidiary Essay*, 225; *CR*, 91:501.

[25] Zwingli, *Subsidiary Essay*, 223.

[26] Stephens, *Theology of Zwingli*, 181, 192.

[27] Zwingli, *Subsidiary Essay*, 223–24.

[28] Zwingli, quoted in Gottfried Locher, *Zwingli's Thought: New Perspectives* (Leiden: Brill, 1981), 215–16.

the word 'pledge' (*sicherung*) recedes by 1530.²⁹ In fact, this simply represents the reversion of its use specifically for divine assurances, as in the *Exposition of the Articles* (1523) and the *Commentary on True and False Religion* (March 1525).³⁰ Mankind's pledge was recast as 'certifying' grace and an 'oath of allegiance.'³¹

On the utility of the sacraments as means of grace, Zwingli maintained that God's Spirit worked directly on the heart and could not be tied to the sacraments. In 1525 he acknowledged 'a mistake which once deceived me [. . .] that signs are given for the confirmation of an existing faith [. . .]. But this is not so.' While miraculous signs (*'wunderzeichen'*) can confirm faith, 'seals [*zeichnenden*] and pledges [*pflichtenden zeichen*], like circumcision under the old covenant,' cannot.³² Similarly,

> baptism in the New Testament is a covenant sign [*pflichtzeichen*]. It does not justify the one who is baptised, nor does it confirm his faith, for it is not possible for an external thing to confirm faith. For faith does not proceed from external things. It proceeds only from God who draws us. Therefore it cannot be grounded in any external thing. The same applies to the Lord's Supper as well.³³

In 1526 Zwingli wrote that God had not 'so bound His grace and spirit and election [. . .] that he refused to draw unto Himself any but those that were signed with this sign.'³⁴ 'Blessedness and

---

²⁹ B. A. Gerrish, *The Old Protestantism and the New: essays on the Reformation heritage* (Edinburgh: T&T Clark, 1982), 120; see Zwingli, *Account of the Faith*, 39.

³⁰ Zwingli, *Exposition of the Articles*, 112; Zwingli, *True and False Religion*, 100, 123–24; Zwingli, *Exposition of the Faith*, LWHZ, 2:253; cf. B. A. Gerrish, *Continuing the Reformation: essays on modern religious thought* (Chicago and London: University of Chicago Press, 1993), 64.

³¹ Zwingli, *Account of the Faith*, 47; Zwingli, *Exposition of the Faith*, 259.

³² Zwingli, "Baptism," 138–39; *CR*, 91:227–28.

³³ Ibid.

³⁴ Zwingli, *Original Sin*, 12.

grace are from election,' he explained, 'not from the participation in signs or sacraments.'³⁵ The sacraments could neither effect salvation nor mediate grace:

> Signs, therefore, are nothing but externals, by which nothing is effected in the conscience but faith is the only thing through which we are blessed [. . .] they are by no means themselves spiritual, nor do they perfect anything spiritual in us, but they are the badges, as it were, of those who are of the spirit.³⁶

Grace is mediated by the Spirit through faith, and Zwingli took this to its logical conclusion: the sacraments themselves perfect nothing.

The fact that Zwingli could agree with Luther on the fifteenth article produced at the Marburg Colloquy demonstrates how closely Zwingli's theology allowed him to associate the work of the Spirit with the sacraments. Article 15 stated that God had ordained the Eucharist 'in order that weak consciences may thereby be excited to faith by the Holy Spirit.'³⁷ This might have been indicative of a development in Zwingli's thought. In *Ratio Fidei* (1530) he admitted the possibility that the Spirit might occasionally act in relation to the external sign. However, this admission was appended to his insistence that the Spirit dispenses grace directly to the soul:

> a channel or vehicle is not necessary to the Spirit, for He Himself is the virtue and energy whereby all things are borne; neither do we read in the Holy Scriptures that visible things, as are the sacraments, carry certainly with them the Spirit, but if visible things have ever been borne with the

---

[35] Ibid., 20.
[36] Ibid., 29.
[37] *Marburg Colloquy and Articles*, 88.

Spirit, it has been the Spirit, not the visible things that have done the bearing.[38]

Sacraments 'are so far from conferring grace that they do not even convey or dispense it.'[39] Nevertheless, Zwingli did not consider the sacraments to be devalued by their inability to mediate grace. They

> should be religiously cherished, that is, highly valued and treated with honour. For though they are unable to bestow grace, they nevertheless associate visibly with the Church us who have been received into it invisibly; and this should be regarded with the highest veneration, since with their administration the words of the divine promise are declared and pronounced.[40]

To suggest as Gerrish does that in Zwingli's view 'the sacraments merely testify in public that grace has been received in private' does not do justice to Zwingli's understanding.[41]

The possibility of a relationship between signs and the work of the Spirit, anticipated in the Marburg Articles and *Ratio Fidei*, became clearer in *Expositio Fidei* (1531), wherein Zwingli 'seems to allow that things happen together at two levels.'[42] Zwingli continued to define the spiritual eating of Christ as 'trust in spirit and heart upon the mercy and goodness of God.' Sacramental eating, 'if we wish to speak accurately, is to eat the body of Christ in heart and spirit with the accompaniment of the sacrament.'[43] Therefore truly 'sacramental' eating cannot occur without faith.[44] Zwingli also

---

[38] Zwingli, *Account of the Faith*, 46.
[39] Ibid.
[40] Ibid., 48.
[41] Gerrish, *Old Protestantism*, 119.
[42] Stephens, *Theology of Zwingli*, 189.
[43] Zwingli, *Exposition of the Faith*, 252.
[44] Ibid., 254.

maintained his view that 'none but the Holy Spirit giveth faith [. . .] and no external thing giveth it. Yet the sacraments do work faith, but historical faith [*fidem faciant sacramenta, sed historicam*]: that is, call to mind that a certain thing once took place, the memory of which is thus refreshed.'[45] Hence the sacraments give historical faith (*fides*) to believers and unbelievers alike that Christ indeed suffered, 'but that he suffered for us, it signifies to the pious believer only. For no one knows that Christ suffered for us, save those whom the Spirit within has taught to recognise the mystery of divine goodness.' Therefore saving faith or trust (*fiducia*) is not mediated by the sacraments: 'nothing gives confidence [*fiduciam*] in God except the Spirit.'[46] Zwingli's opinion that the sacraments could not confirm faith had not fundamentally altered since 1525; it had become more nuanced.

Zwingli enumerated seven virtues of the sacraments, all consistent with his theology. The only apparent anomaly is the sixth virtue: sacraments 'bring increase and support to faith [*fidei*].'[47] Zwingli does not mean that faith itself is confirmed or strengthened, but that 'all the senses, are as it were, reclaimed and redeemed from fleshly desires, and drawn into obedience to faith.'[48] The 'contemplation of faith' is aided indirectly by the sacraments because they are 'a sort of bridles by which the senses, when on the point of dashing away to their own desires, are checked and brought back to the service of heart and of faith.'[49] Thus Zwingli consistently rejected the idea that the sacraments were vehicles of grace.

Having seen how Zwingli understood sacraments to work in general we can give specific consideration to Zwingli's view of baptism and the Eucharist. In *Of Baptism* Zwingli presented baptism as

---

[45] Ibid.; *CR*, 93:151–52.

[46] Zwingli, *Exposition of the Faith*, 255; *CR*, 93:152.

[47] Zwingli, *Exposition of the Faith*, 258. There is no distinction between *fides* and *fiducia* here.

[48] Ibid.

[49] Ibid., 259.

'a covenant sign'[50] and 'an initiatory sign or pledge' by humanity to God.[51] The signification included: (1) pledging individuals to God, (2) pledging ourselves to God, (3) testifying that pledge to others, and (4) imposing obligation. Firstly, baptism marked out sheep for the true shepherd,[52] 'dedicating,'[53] 'introducing' or 'pledging'[54] individuals to Christ's salvation. Secondly, in baptism 'we bind ourselves to God.'[55] In this sense 'it is like the cowl which is cut out for initiates into an order,'[56] signifying their intention to learn the rule, or their commitment to mortify sin 'like the soldier at his enlistment.'[57] Thus it begins a 'process of development'[58] in sanctification. Thirdly, baptism is 'given and received for the sake of fellow-believers.'[59] It is a public testimony of the pledge to our neighbour,[60] an 'outward sign that we are incorporated and engrafted into the Lord Jesus Christ.'[61] In other words it is a mark of communion with Christ's body, the Church.[62] Fourthly, baptism conferred obligations in that 'it requires us to amend our lives, to turn to Christ and to believe in him.'[63] Zwingli maintained throughout that faith results from divine election, so baptism itself neither justifies nor confirms faith,

---

[50] Zwingli, "Baptism," 138, 141; see also Zwingli, *True and False Religion*, 121.

[51] Zwingli, "Baptism," 141, 145–51, 156.

[52] Ibid., 145.

[53] Ibid., 146.

[54] Ibid., 151.

[55] Ibid., 148.

[56] Ibid., 141.

[57] Ibid., 147.

[58] Ibid., 146.

[59] Ibid., 136.

[60] Ibid., 148; see also Zwingli, *True and False Religion*, 184.

[61] Zwingli, "Baptism," 156.

[62] Zwingli drew no particular distinction between visible and invisible churches, nor did he seek to distinguish between the elect and the reprobate, although he knew that the Church in this world was a mixed body: Gordon, "Emulating the Past," 7.

[63] Zwingli, "Baptism," 169.

nor is there necessarily any correlation between water-baptism and saving faith.[64]

Like the Anabaptists Zwingli considered baptism to be a symbol of belonging to God, but he anathematised their innovation of believers' baptism.[65] As early as May 1525 Zwingli launched a consistent defence of infant baptism on the basis of continuity with circumcision and the inclusion of the offspring of believing parents in the covenant community.[66] Both depended upon the unity of the Testaments, with Christian children having no less right to the sacrament of initiation than Jewish children. As we have seen, over the summer of 1525 he accentuated the significance of sacraments as God's covenant pledge rather than humanity's. This made baptism more readily applicable to infants. In August he wrote that 'baptism is just as much the symbol of the Christian people that has received from God the covenant that his son should be ours, as circumcision was once the symbol that the Lord should be their God and they should be his people.'[67] His *Reply to Balthasar Hubmaier* in November illustrated the point by tabulating the covenants with Abraham and with Christians side by side. Circumcision (*bschnydung*) and baptism of younger children and adults (*touf junger kinden und alter*) were both the covenant pledge (*pundtszeichen*) of what God had done in respectively promising and sending the Saviour.[68] In *On Original Sin* (1526) he asserted that Christian infants are to be

---

[64] Ibid., 135, 138. See W. P. Stephens, "Bullinger and the Anabaptists with reference to his *Von Dem Unverschamten Frevel* (1531) and to Zwingli's writings on the Anabaptists," *RRR* 3 (2001): 98–99.

[65] Ulrich Gäbler, *Huldrych Zwingli: his life and work*, trans. R. Gritsch (Philadelphia: Fortress Press, 1986), 128–29.

[66] Stephens, *Theology of Zwingli*, 203. Euler incorrectly asserts that Zwingli failed to offer positive theological arguments for infant baptism: Carrie Euler, *Couriers of the Gospel: England and Zürich 1531–1558* (Zurich: TVZ, 2006), 25–26.

[67] Zwingli, *Subsidiary Essay*, 224.

[68] Huldrych Zwingli, *Antwort über Balthaser Hubmaiers Taufbüchlein* [November 1525], *CR*, 91:368.

given the 'token' because 'our children are included in the covenant just as much as they were, for we are sons of the promise.'[69]

The difference between baptism and the Eucharist in Zwingli's mind is clearly seen in his *Refutation of the Tricks of the Catabaptists* (1527) where 'boys are not competent' to prove themselves in the Eucharist 'while they are for baptism and circumcision.' He restated his argument that 'we are under the same covenant with them and are renewed by the same Spirit, and by it are circumcised.' In both cases the pledge was God's who marks out his people: 'our circumcision is baptism.'[70] He concluded, as in all his polemical works against the Anabaptists, that 'since there is one immutable God and one testament only, we who trust in Christ are under the same testament, consequently God is as much our God as he was Abraham's, and we are as much his people as was Israel.'[71] The same reasoning applies in each case as to how the sign of covenant initiation functions.

Turning, then, to Zwingli's eucharistic theology, it is hard to gauge the importance of the Dutch theologian Cornelisz Hoen to his thought. Their views were not identical, but Zwingli did claim that Hoen's letter had helped him to identify *est* as the 'trope' he already suspected in the words *hoc est corpus meum*.[72] The rendering *hoc significat corpus meum* first appeared in his *Letter to Matthew Alber* on 16 November 1524.[73] The symbolic understanding seems implicit, however, in his earlier descriptions in 1523 of the Eucharist as a covenantal 'seal' or memorial of Christ's sacrifice: 'the term "memorial" has its name from the custom we have, namely, that whenever we eat and drink the body and blood of Christ—which are a testament

---

[69] Zwingli, *Original Sin*, 21, see also 30. See also Zwingli, *Account of the Faith*, 42–46; Stephens, *Theology of Zwingli*, 206–11, 215.

[70] Zwingli, "Refutation" in *Selected Works*, ed. Jackson, 249–50. See also Zwingli, *Erläuterungen zur Genesis* [March 1527], *CR*, 100:105.

[71] Ibid., 100:235.

[72] B. J. Spruyt, *Cornelius Henrici Hoen (Honius) and his Epistle on the Eucharist (1525)* (Leiden and Boston: Brill, 2006), 205–8. On their use of the ring metaphor, see idem., 91.

[73] Zwingli, *Letter to Alber*, 138.

of Christ—we do so in remembrance of that which has been transacted only once.'[74] The body and blood are really eaten, but only by faith, signified by the elements which 'make more concrete to the simple of heart the essential nature of the testament.' Believers are 'strengthened in their faith through the visible act,' and the faith which recognises the signification strengthens the soul, rejoicing in salvation.[75] As Gottfried Locher helpfully explains, the memorial 'displays the soul's power of actualisation and awareness' in that 'the past is brought into our present time, becoming contemporary with us and effective in us' (rather than the believer being transported back to Calvary); the Holy Spirit 'renders present' the death of Christ.[76] Additionally, the Eucharist proclaims or testifies to Christ's salvation.[77] This public aspect was enlarged in *A Proposal Concerning Images and the Mass* (May 1524), in which the Eucharist signified 'an inward and outward union of Christian people' in which we 'testify to all men that we are one body and brotherhood.'[78] Gerrish has suggested the label 'symbolic memorialism' for Zwingli's sacramental theology. This is convenient provided that the rich meaning of 'memorialism' is appreciated in its full scope.[79]

---

[74] Zwingli, *Exposition of the Articles*, 103–4, 107, 111; see Stephens, *Theology of Zwingli*, 218–21.

[75] Zwingli, *Exposition of the Articles*, 115.

[76] Locher, *Zwingli's Thought*, 59, 222–23. Zwingli coined the term *Wiedergedächtnis* to describe this recollection of Christ's Passion: see W. M. S. West, "John Hooper and the Origins of Puritanism [1]," *BQ* 15, 8 (1954): 360. Christ's Passion is made present to the faithful. See also Clifford Dugmore, *The Mass and the English Reformers* (London: Macmillan, 1958), 10.

[77] Zwingli, *Exposition of the Articles*, 114–16.

[78] Quoted in Stephens, *Theology of Zwingli*, 225.

[79] Gerrish, *Old Protestantism*, 128. Gerrish does not clarify the positive implications of Zwingli's position. In 1523 Zwingli's term 'memorial' was a polemical reaction to late-medieval teaching and in 1531 the believer is said to recognise God's grace in the memorial: Zwingli, *Exposition of the Articles*, 111; Zwingli, *Exposition of the Faith*, 255. For Gerrish's classifications of Reformed sacramental theology as symbolic memorialism, parallelism, and instrumentalism see B. A. Gerrish, *Grace and Gratitude: the eucharistic theology of John Calvin*

In the *Letter to Alber*, besides spiritual eating and the figurative words of consecration,[80] Zwingli expounded the communal, confessional purpose of the Eucharist. This sacrament does 'nothing but make it plain to your brother that you are a member of Christ, and one of these who trust in Christ.' The intention is to testify that you reject idolatry and faithfully believe, to unite with other Christians in 'this oath of allegiance as it were (whence it is called a sacrament),' and to 'bind' yourself to the Christian life under sanction of excommunication.[81] The themes of mutuality and conditionality are evident here within a communal context. In 1527 the communion of believers was called 'the people of the blood of Christ,' which Zwingli understood as the blood of the testament, hence he identified the Church by the covenant.[82] The Eucharist was so important that unworthy participation was 'treason' against the Church communion:

> It would be a small matter to put a morsel into one's mouth or to taste a cup with the edge of one's lips, but it is not a small thing to have done this in the church of Christ. Those who do this give evidence of themselves that they are of that body and people who have faith in Christ, the Son of God, and who give thanks for the death he underwent for us. He who sho[w]s the password to the enemy is adjudged worthy of the punishment of Mettius.[83] And whoever sits down at this banquet (which is not just a password but a public profession and sacrament), and straightway does the same

---

(Edinburgh: T&T Clark, 1993), 167.

[80] Stephens, *Theology of Zwingli*, 228–29.

[81] Zwingli, *Letter to Alber*, 141–42.

[82] Zwingli's ecclesiology was based on the visible parish but it was not a major feature of his theology. Positive ecclesiological ideas did not occupy much space in contemporary reforming literature: Peter Blickle, *Communal Reformation: the quest for salvation in sixteenth-century Germany*, trans. T. Dunlap (London and New Jersey: Humanities Press International, 1992), 126.

[83] Mettius Fufetius was a traitor who was torn in two by being chained to chariots moving in opposite directions.

by sacrifices to idols, is that one not guilty of treason? Does this person not only betray the body and blood of Christ, to which he falsely pretends to give thanks for his redemption, but also that congregation which is distinguished by the name of the body and blood of Christ because of the public profession?[84]

The nature of the Real Presence was Zwingli's primary interest in his *Subsidiary Essay* (1525). Christ's blood was necessary to establish the testament, and Christians drink 'a symbol of the blood of the testament.'[85] As with circumcision and baptism, the Paschal lamb symbolising the Passover corresponds with the Eucharist, one commemoration substituted for another. As the Jews ate the lamb as a figure, so Christians eat Christ figuratively in the Eucharist.[86] Zwingli then discussed sensible faith: the physical eating of Christ's bodily flesh makes faith a 'silly notion' and 'blind recklessness.'[87] Zwingli further rejected a spiritual feeding on flesh as paradoxical. Instead, the eating of bread signifies faith in Christ because 'that is salutary and like bread unto humans.'[88] Sensible faith upholds salvation *solo Christo* by trusting the 'new covenant or testament' granted through Christ, which Zwingli expounded at length.[89]

In *The Lord's Supper* (February 1526) Zwingli introduced the argument of Christ's bodily session at the right hand of the Father,[90] yet in his *Answer to Strauss's Book* (January 1527) he could write that Christ is present to the believer because 'the faithful have the body and blood of Christ present in the mind.' Conversely, 'in contemplation, faith, hope, and love' the believer is present with Christ

---

[84] Zwingli, *Friendly Exegesis*, 295–97.
[85] Zwingli, *Subsidiary Essay*, 200.
[86] Ibid., 210.
[87] Ibid., 214–20.
[88] Ibid., 219–20.
[89] Ibid., 223–25.
[90] Stephens, *Theology of Zwingli*, 237; see also Locher, *Zwingli's Thought*, 177.

in heaven.[91] Bodily, Christ was 'truly absent,' wrote Zwingli in his *Friendly Exegesis*, but by alloiosis we may speak of Christ's flesh as 'true meat' (John 6:55) because '"flesh" is used to mean the divine nature.'[92] Lee Wandel explains that the substantial bread could, 'following Zwingli's sense of human psychology, be connected in the mind to the body of Christ, and that connection was not simply 'spiritual' or even, in the modern language, psychological, but visceral.'[93] This reasoning was summarised in *Ratio Fidei*.[94] In *Expositio Fidei* Zwingli argued that the spiritual eating of Christ could be independent of the sacraments altogether.[95]

Zwingli's sacramental theology was clearly formed around the concept of the covenant sign. It was his guiding conviction that the sacraments are signs of Christ's historic ratification of the covenant. He was careful to separate signs from spiritual realities, but in 1529–31 he showed a willingness to allow a supporting rôle to the sacraments in augmenting faith.

Heinrich Bullinger

Bullinger's sacramental theology was not strictly Zwinglian but he often defended a Zwinglian position in his capacity as Zwingli's successor at Zürich. Like Zwingli, Bullinger emphasised the covenantal significance of the sacraments, but he was more comfortable with the idea that the spiritual reality was received in conjunction

[91] Quoted in Stephens, *Theology of Zwingli*, 243.
[92] Zwingli, *Friendly Exegesis*, 322, 327. Alloiosis is a rhetorical device whereby words describing one object are used of another so that the meaning of a proposition is not literally but figuratively true. The one is named, the other understood. See Richard Cross, "Alloiosis in the Christology of Zwingli," *JTS* 47, 1 (1996): 113–19.
[93] Wandel, "Body of Christ," 206. Wandel offers valuable insights into the importance of different conceptions of body and matter in the Eucharist controversy.
[94] Zwingli, *Account of the Faith*, 49.
[95] Zwingli, *Exposition of the Faith*, 252.

with the sign. He nevertheless maintained that the sign could not confer grace. Gerrish has labelled his view 'symbolic parallelism'.[96]

Zwingli and Bullinger discussed the Eucharist on their first acquaintance on 12 September 1524. Bullinger recorded in his diary that 'I in good faith expounded to him my views, which I drew from the writings of the Waldensians and the books of Augustine.'[97] In a letter to Christoph Stiltz on 27 February 1526, Bullinger echoed Zwingli's understanding of the connection between signifier and signified. Linking covenant and sacrament, Bullinger maintained that

> the testament is the blessing or forgiveness of sins, Christ is the mediator of the testament, the dead body and blood of Christ are truly the revealing and sealing of the testament, the bread and wine are symbols of the confirmed testament, which remind [us] of redemption and union.[98]

Thus sacraments were signs of Christ's confirmation of God's testament. Their purpose was to commemorate Christ's revelation and accomplishment of redemption from sin and his union with

---

[96] Gerrish, *Old Protestantism*, 124, 128.

[97] Quoted in Paul Rorem, *Calvin and Bullinger on the Lord's Supper*, Alcuin Club (Nottingham: Grove Books, 1989), 14. Rorem provides the most thorough account of Bullinger's position available in English. He suggests that Bullinger may have been influenced by Wessel Gansfort (1419–89). On Gansfort, see B. J. Spruyt, "Wessel Gansfort and Cornelis Hoen's *Epistola Christiana*: 'the ring as a pledge of my love,'" in *Wessel Gansfort (1419–1489) and Northern Humanism*, eds. F. Akkerman, G. Huisman and A. Vanderjagt (Leiden: Brill, 1993), 134. The argument for 'Bullingerism' is overstated by George Ella, *Henry Bullinger: shepherd of the churches* (Eggleston, Durham: Go Publications, 2007), 97–102.

[98] Quoted in Rorem, *Supper*, 13. Rorem supposes the influence of Luther's *Babylonian Captivity* here, which Bullinger had read in 1520/21. However, the approximation with Zwingli and the conditional understanding of *erbgmächt* in Switzerland make it unlikely that Bullinger drew indiscriminately upon Luther.

believers. This is indistinguishable from Zwingli's view. Bullinger concurred with Zwingli's insistence that the Holy Spirit was neither reliant upon the sacraments nor utilised them as vehicles of grace.[99] In *De origine erroris, in negocio eucharistiae, ac missae* [*The origin of the error, in the matter of the Eucharist, and of the Mass*] (1528) Bullinger attacked the Roman understanding of the Mass as a sacrifice,[100] just as Zwingli had done in 1523. Bullinger repeatedly affirmed the sacraments as God's proclamation and confirmation of the present work of the Spirit on the heart.[101]

After Zwingli's death in 1531 it is likely that Bullinger initially felt compelled to uphold Zwingli's sacramental theology publicly. The Zürichers' confidence in the Reformation had to be restored. Moreover, the theologians of Bern strongly opposed deviation from Zwingli's teachings.[102] Bullinger's comments on the sacraments in *De Testamento* (1534) pertained principally to the concept of covenant. He generally followed Zwingli's commemorative line that sacraments were 'symbols of the covenant [*foederis*] and of divine grace already confirmed through Christ.' The contemplation of the visible led to thoughts of the invisible. Bullinger concentrated on the covenantal significance of the sacraments, avoiding questions of sacramental power and efficacy. Circumcision had been administered to those to whom God had already offered grace and covenantal relationship, binding them to himself.[103] It was the consecration of

---

[99] Rorem, *Supper*, 16.

[100] Ibid., 13.

[101] Ibid., 15. Rorem believes that Bullinger held this view from the early 1520s.

[102] Amy Nelson Burnett, "Heinrich Bullinger and the Problem of Eucharistic Concord," in *Heinrich Bullinger: Life—Thought—Influence: International Congress Heinrich Bullinger 2004*, 2 vols. (Zurich: TVZ, 2007), 1:239. See also J. N. Bakhuizen van den Brink, "Ratramn's eucharistic doctrine and its influence in sixteenth-century England," in *Studies in Church History*, ed. G. Cuming, Vol. 2 (London: Thomas Nelson, 1965), 64.

[103] Bullinger, *Brief Exposition*, 132; Heinrich Bullinger, *De Testamento Seu Foedere Dei Unico & Aeterno Heinrychi Bullingeri Brevis Expositio*, Elektronische

that covenant with blood, 'testifying' (*obtestantes*, Bullinger's preferred term) to the penalty which would apply to those who 'entered into covenants [*foedera*]' with God but 'did not stand firm by the pacts [*pactis*].'[104] 'Despising' the sign was serious because it showed contempt for the covenant that it signified, but Bullinger reassured parents that infants who died without the sign of baptism were 'saved by the grace and mercy of God.'[105] While the Old Testament sacraments had prefigured Christ's confirmation of the covenant, the New Testament sacraments signified 'completion of the most perfect justification.' Meanwhile there was continuity in that 'the entire covenant [*foedus*] was contained in the sacrament of the covenant [*sacramento foederis*, that is, circumcision]; in the same manner, the entire essence of the renewed covenant [*foederis*] is contained in our sacraments.'[106] Baptism and the Eucharist testified to the same covenant with the same conditions.

In 1536 Bullinger helped to compose the First Helvetic Confession at Basle, where he first encountered Calvin. The framing of the articles was influenced by Bucer, who hoped to unite the Swiss and Lutheran reformers, and the articles won Luther's approval.[107] While Zwingli had admitted a correspondence between spiritual realities and their signification in the sacraments, the Confession claimed that the sacraments consisted of *'signis simul et rebus'* (both signs and essential things).[108] Zwingli, had he lived to comment, could have affirmed the statement that '*in rebus ipsis totus fructus*

Bibliothek Schweiz (Zurich: Christopher Froschauer, 1534), F3v.

[104] Bullinger, *Brief Exposition*, 130; Bullinger, *De Testamento*, F1v-2r.

[105] Bullinger, *Brief Exposition*, 131.

[106] Ibid., 132.

[107] Alan Cochrane, ed., *Reformed Confessions of the Sixteenth Century* (London: SCM, 1966), 97–98.

[108] "*Confessio Helvetica Prior* (1536)," in *The Creeds of Christendom*, ed. P. Schaff, Vol. 3 (Grand Rapids, MI: Baker, 1977), 223. Gerrish translates *simul* as 'at the same time,' but there is no equivalent in the German version: '*in Zeichen und wesentlichen Dingen*' (in signs and essential things). See Gerrish, *Old Protestantism*, 123.

sacramentorum est' (the entire fruit of the sacraments lies in the thing itself).[109] However, he probably would not have agreed that, in the Eucharist, Christ may '*suis vere ad hoc offerat*' (truly offer to his people) his body and blood.[110] By contrast, Bullinger's agreement testifies to his belief that sign and reality occur in parallel,[111] and indicates that the idea of the sacraments 'offering' communion with Christ was not incompatible with his position.

Luther's scathing description in 1544 of Zwingli as 'an enemy of the holy sacrament and a full-blown heathen'[112] prompted Bullinger's *Warhaffte Bekanntnus* [*True Confession*] (February 1545), a strident defence of Zwinglianism denouncing Luther's own understanding of the Real Presence as heretical.[113] Here Bullinger asserted that remembrance of Christ's sacrifice was the 'real chief part and purpose' of the Eucharist.[114] Such sacramental remembrance could not occur correctly in the absence of true faith; faith gave the sacrament value. Thus Zwingli's complex memorialism was reiterated: 'the one who has truly eaten the flesh of Christ and has drunk his blood is the one who believes in Christ, true God and human crucified for us. Thus believing is eating and eating believing.'[115] Like Zwingli, Bullinger restricted the means of grace to faith, leaving the sacraments to point to this means and to exercise the faith which receives grace: 'the Lord of the church keeps his

[109] "*Confessio Helvetica Prior*," 223.
[110] Ibid., 225.
[111] Gerrish, *Old Protestantism*, 123.
[112] Martin Luther, *Brief Confession Concerning the Holy Sacrament* [1544], trans. H. Lehmann, *LW*, Vol. 38 (Philadelphia: Fortress Press, 1971), 289–90.
[113] This and the next paragraph rely upon Rorem, *Supper*, 18–26; see also Burnett, "Eucharistic Concord," 240. Calvin urged restraint on Bullinger in a letter dated 25 November 1544: George Gorham, ed., *Gleanings of a few scattered ears, during the period of the Reformation in England* (London: Bell and Daldy, 1857), 27–29. On 3 December 1544 Bullinger invited Melanchthon to Zürich, but Melanchthon's failure to respond ended Bullinger's interest in conciliation: Gordon, "Calvin and the Swiss Reformed Churches," 71.
[114] Quoted in Gerrish, *Old Protestantism*, 123.
[115] Quoted in Rorem, *Supper*, 19–20.

suffering and our redemption in fresh remembrance in the church so that he might refer to and point out his grace and great gifts, which are received in faith, faith which he exercises through these external acts.'[116]

Bullinger wrote to Melanchthon on 1 April 1546, soon after Luther's death: 'the gifts of life are conferred and exhibited by God himself alone; nevertheless they are received by us by faith, are announced by the Word, and are sealed by the Sacraments.'[117] If Bullinger had rallied to the public defence of Zwinglianism, his privately-circulated opinions in *Absoluta de Christi Domini et Catholicae eius Ecclesiae Sacramentis tractatio* [*Complete Treatise on the Sacraments of our Lord Christ and His Catholic Church*] (1546) also suggest his agreement with Zwingli in denying that the sacraments give grace, despite his own view of the analogy between signs and the spiritual reception of grace. The sacraments, argued Bullinger, almost certainly against Melanchthon's *Confessio Augustana Variata* (1540),[118] 'do not exhibit [*non exhibere*] that which they signify.' That is, 'they do not give grace, neither have grace included in them.'[119] Sacraments could not confer grace because they did not contain it.[120]

The sixth and seventh sermons of Bullinger's *Fifth Decade* (1551) practically reproduced the text of the *Absoluta*, and therefore represent Bullinger's thought at a time prior to the *Consensus Tigurinus* (1549). Bullinger repeatedly denied that the sacraments confer grace or justify participants.[121] If grace is defined as God's favour, he

---

[116] Quoted in Ibid.; see also Pelikan, *Reformation of Church*, 204.

[117] Gorham, ed., *Gleanings*, 37.

[118] *Confessio Augustana Variata*, Article 10: '*De coena Domini docent quod cum pane et vino vere exhibeantur corpus et sanguis Christi vescentibus in Coena Domini.*' Philip Melanchthon, *Opera quae supersunt omnia*, eds. H. Bindseil, *CR*, Vol. 26 (Brunswick: Schwetchke et Filium, 1858), 357.

[119] Quoted in Rorem, *Supper*, 21–26. I have amended the English translation.

[120] See Ibid.

[121] Heinrich Bullinger, *The Decades of Henry Bullinger*, ed. T. Harding, 5 vols. PS (Cambridge: CUP, 1849–52), v/7:302–4.

asked, 'doth not the very gross absurdity of the thing plainly prove, that grace is not contained in the signs?' The elect 'enjoy the things before they be partakers of the signs.'[122] Like Zwingli, Bullinger argued that 'the sign and the thing signified do retain their natures distinguished in the sacraments.'[123] If forced to choose, he wrote, 'I had rather confess them to be void than full,' but in his opinion they were 'effectual' and 'full' without being instruments of grace.[124] As Bullinger had written to Melanchthon, Abraham's circumcision was 'not, indeed, vain and useless, although he was justified.'[125]

Bullinger defined a sacrament in covenantal terms as 'a mark or token whereby a thing is understood, as slaughter by blood';[126] 'through partaking of the sacraments, we are bound to God and to all the saints, as it were by obligation; and that God himself also, by the testimony of the sacraments, hath, as it were by an oath, bound himself to us.'[127] Thus Bullinger understood sacramental 'testimony' in the context of an oath and mutual obligation, integrating his sacramental theology into his concept of covenant.[128] Obligation was created between God and believers, as well as amongst individuals within the Church, yet it was the covenant that bound and the sacraments that 'visibly gathered.'[129] Bullinger, like Zwingli, drew a comparison with soldiers' oaths of allegiance: 'we are bound by them, as by an oath, to the true worship of one God.'[130] Bullinger also quoted Zwingli's metaphor of a ring given as an assurance of fidelity by an absent husband to his wife, even though Bullinger's own version of this image usually expressed a present 'promise, or covenant' being

[122] Ibid., v/7:309, 311.
[123] Ibid., v/6:274.
[124] Ibid., v/7:314.
[125] Gorham, ed., *Gleanings*, 37.
[126] Bullinger, *Decades*, v/6:227, 240.
[127] Ibid., v/6:235.
[128] Ibid., v/6:235, 245, 280; v/6:237; v/7:294. Mutuality is particularly explicit in v/7:318–19.
[129] Ibid., v/7:333–34.
[130] Ibid., v/6:235; v/6:237; v/7:333.

made ('passing') between a bride and bridegroom,[131] reflecting his willingness to construe the sign and the spiritual reality in parallel.

In the sacraments, wrote Bullinger, God visibly represents his kingdom 'to renew it afresh, and by lively representation to maintain the remembrance of the same among us.'[132] The theme is Zwinglian but the accent is Bullinger's. He explained that, to appreciate the sacraments,

> we have to mark the analogy, which is a certain aptness, proportion [. . .] without this analogy, the reason of a sacrament cannot be fully and perfectly understood: but this analogy [. . .] offereth to the beholder, without any labour at all, the very αναγωγη [*anagōgē*], that is to say, the hidden and secret meaning of the sacrament.[133]

The characteristic emphasis of Bullinger is that the sacraments offer to the participant a symbol of the promised grace conferred by God. Bullinger praised God's wisdom in employing covenantal signs to testify to his faithfulness:

> as in making leagues, or in confirming promises in earnest and weighty matters, men use signs or tokens of truth to win credit to their words and promises; even so the Lord, doing after the manner of men, hath added signs of his faithfulness and truth in his everlasting covenant and promises of life.[134]

Bullinger related God's sacraments to ancient covenant-making rituals wherein the parties passed between the two parts of a torn carcass in order to symbolise covenantal sanctions.[135] The 'sacraments'

---

[131] Ibid., v/6. 237–38; v/7:324–25; see Spruyt, *Hoen*, 87–91.
[132] Bullinger, *Decades*, v/6:242.
[133] Ibid., v/6:244.
[134] Ibid., v/6:245.
[135] Ibid.; see also Philip Melanchthon, *Loci Communes Theologici* [1535], ed.

of the Old Testament covenant could be compared with their New Testament counterparts.¹³⁶

Bullinger rejected the physical presence of Christ in the sacraments on the basis of the absence of a covenant: God does not 'tie himself to the signs [. . .]. For in no place has Christ promised to be present corporally [. . .] but mystically and sacramentally.'¹³⁷ Christ was seated at the Father's right hand. Bullinger refuted the existence of another covenant ostensibly appointing grace in the sacraments.¹³⁸ He used the image of a wax seal to explain how Christ might be present symbolically in the sacraments:

> Wax, before it be sealed, is common and usual wax; but when, by the king's will and commandment, that which is engraven in the king's seal is printed in the wax, and is set to evidences and letters patent, by and by it is so esteemed, that whoso shall deface the sealed evidences is attached as guilty of treason.¹³⁹

Unbelievers cannot benefit from sacramental testimony because they do not appreciate the signification. Believers 'corporally and sensibly [. . .] receive the signs, but,' in parallel, 'spiritually they possess, comprehend, renew, and exercise the things signified.'¹⁴⁰ The signs are 'superfluous or vain' except for those 'who receive them by faith.'¹⁴¹

Circumcision was equivalent to baptism which, as in Zwingli's later writing, was administered on the basis of covenantal election rather than present faith. God commanded paedobaptism as a

---

W. Pauck, *LCC*, Vol. 19 (London: SCM, 1969), 134.

¹³⁶ Bullinger, *Decades*, v/6:287–90; v/7:298–301.
¹³⁷ Ibid., v/6:253.
¹³⁸ Ibid., v/7:311.
¹³⁹ Ibid., v/6:270; see also John Calvin, *Institutes of the Christian Religion* [1536], trans. F. L. Battles (Grand Rapids, MI: William Eerdmans, 1986), 87.
¹⁴⁰ Bullinger, *Decades*, v/6:279.
¹⁴¹ Ibid., v/7:340.

sign of his commitment.¹⁴² Jewish boys were circumcised 'and were in league with God.' Christian infants were likewise to be sealed and, 'when they come to age and commit wickedness [. . .] they are received again by faithful repentance.'¹⁴³ The relationship between signifier and signified was clear: 'they therefore which before by grace invisibly are received of God into the society of God, those selfsame are visibly now by baptism admitted into the selfsame household of God.'¹⁴⁴

Bullinger entered the discussions with Calvin that preceded the *Consensus Tigurinus* (May 1549) defending his long-held view that the sacraments did not confer grace. On 26 May 1548 he stated that 'Christ communicates himself totally to us in his Spirit, by faith, insofar as this is necessary for our salvation'; the sacraments 'testified' to the word and it was thereby 'inculcated'.¹⁴⁵ This view of the sacraments as testifying to, or symbolically offering, God's covenant promise represented Bullinger's parallel understanding of the relationship between sign and reality. Consequently, he resisted Calvin's understanding of the sacraments as conferring the grace which they signify:

> It is God who saves and receives us in grace. But this you [Calvin] ascribe to an instrument through which it is worked, some implement or flow-sluice or canal, the very sacraments, through which grace is infused into us [. . .]. But we do not believe this [. . .]. God alone works our salvation [. . .]. God, and no created thing, confers and indeed confers through the Spirit and faith [. . .]. The sacraments neither offer nor confer, nor are they instruments of offering and conferring, but they signify, testify, and seal.¹⁴⁶

[142] Ibid., v/7:313.
[143] Ibid., v/7:323.
[144] Ibid., v/7:329, see also 344.
[145] Quoted in Rorem, *Supper*, 29.
[146] Quoted in Ibid., 34.

In the *Consensus Tigurinus* Calvin acquiesced to Bullinger's terms in order to achieve unity between Zürich and Geneva.[147] The conferral of grace was established before the sacraments were introduced: Article 5 stated that, for Christ to be 'exhibited' or given to us, he 'must be made one with us, and we must be ingrafted into his body.'[148] In Article 6 the sacraments were said to 'testify' to an existing 'spiritual communion' which 'all who believe' have with Christ 'by his Spirit.'[149] Bullinger's understanding had clearly prevailed over Calvin's.

These articles are revealing of Bullinger's differences with Zwingli as well as Calvin. Article 7 on the purpose of the sacraments described them in covenantal terms as 'contracts,' 'marks and badges of Christian profession and fellowship or fraternity,' and 'incitements to gratitude and exercises of faith and a godly life.'[150] Perhaps this placated the Zwinglian clergy of Zürich.[151] The sacraments' 'principal' purpose was 'that God may, by means of them, testify, represent, and seal his grace to us.' This meant, firstly, that the sacraments made 'a deeper impression on the senses, by bringing the object in a manner directly before them, while they bring the death of Christ and all his benefits to our remembrance, that faith may be the better exercised.'[152] This was as much Bullinger's view as Zwingli's. Secondly, however, the principal purpose indicated 'that what the mouth of God had announced is, as it were, confirmed and ratified by seals.'[153] This reflected Bullinger's emphasis on the analogous relationship between sign and reality. Hence, in Article 8, in

---

[147] Bruce Gordon, *Calvin* (New Haven & London: YUP, 2009), 179; see also Burnett, "Eucharistic Concord," 234; Ella, *Bullinger*, 13–14.

[148] "Mutual Consent as to the Sacraments [*Consensus Tigurinus* (1549)]," in *John Calvin: Tracts and Letters*, ed. H. Beveridge, Vol. 2 (Edinburgh: Banner of Truth, 2009), 213. Article 5 was inserted in July 1549.

[149] Ibid., 214.

[150] Ibid.

[151] Rorem, *Supper*, 42.

[152] "*Consensus Tigurinus*," 214.

[153] Ibid.

view of the sacraments' true testimony, God 'truly performs inwardly by his Spirit that which the sacraments figure to our eyes and other senses; in other words, we obtain possession of Christ.'[154] The sacramental signification and spiritual reality were, in Bullinger's view, both present occurrences in parallel with one another. This is much more characteristic of Bullinger's position than Zwingli's.

Article 9 also represented Bullinger's view as opposed to Zwingli's. Although sign and reality may be distinguished from one another, they cannot be 'disjoined': 'though we distinguish, as we ought, between the signs and the things signified, yet we do not disjoin the reality from the signs, but acknowledge that all who in faith embrace the promises there offered receive Christ spiritually.'[155] Nevertheless, in Article 10 Bullinger qualified Calvin's view that the sacraments confer grace: it is not the sacraments, but the promise annexed to the sacraments, 'whose office it is to lead us to Christ by the direct way of faith—faith which makes us partakers of Christ.'[156] Bullinger's view was that the sacraments offer, or represent, the divine promises which themselves confer grace.

Although the sacraments were described in Article 13 as 'instruments by which God acts efficaciously when he pleases,' this was qualified so as to exclude Calvin's interpretation. According to Article 12, when God 'uses the instrumentality of the sacraments, he neither infuses his own virtue into them nor derogates in any respect from the effectual working of his Spirit, but, in adaptation to our weakness, uses them as helps.'[157] Thus, in Article 14, 'the whole effect resides in his Spirit' and, in Article 15, 'the Spirit alone is properly the seal' because 'all these attributes of the sacraments sink down to a lower place, so that not even the smallest portion of our salvation is transferred to creatures or elements.'[158] This definition

---

[154] Ibid., 214–15; see Rorem, *Supper*, 42–43.
[155] "*Consensus Tigurinus*," 215.
[156] Ibid.
[157] Ibid., 216.
[158] Ibid., 216–17.

of instrumentality, reflecting Bullinger's doctrine, disqualified any sense that the sacraments conferred grace. While Bullinger and Calvin could agree, in Article 17, that the sacraments did not confer grace 'on all' participants irrespective of faith, Bullinger could not accept any statement on how they might confer grace to the elect.[159] Article 19 stated explicitly that without the use of the sacraments 'believers receive the reality which is there figured.' They already have communion with Christ by faith. Nevertheless, Bullinger and Calvin, like Zwingli, believed that 'inasmuch as faith is confirmed and increased by the sacraments, the gifts of God are confirmed in us, and thus Christ in a manner grows in us and we in him.'[160] However, Article 20 stated that this 'advantage' was not temporally restricted 'as if the visible sign, at the moment when it is brought forward, brought the grace of God along with it.'[161] The *Consensus* contained only sacramental doctrine with which Bullinger was comfortable.

The eighth and ninth sermons of the *Fifth Decade* (1551) tackled practical issues regarding the sacraments and were doctrinally consistent with those sermons first drafted for the *Absoluta*.[162] Bullinger encouraged parents not to delay baptism of their child because Moses disapproved of delaying circumcision. Christians were to be mindful of God's words in Genesis 17:14 that the uncircumcised boy 'shall be cut off from his people, because he hath broken my covenant.'[163] However, the infant who dies before baptism is 'received into the covenant by the grace of God' regardless.[164] All children of Christians are already 'joint partners in the league' by

---

[159] Ibid., 217; see Rorem, *Supper*, 44–45.
[160] "*Consensus Tigurinus*," 218.
[161] Ibid.; see Rorem, *Supper*, 44.
[162] Rorem, *Supper*, 52.
[163] Bullinger, *Decades*, v/8:366.
[164] Ibid., v/8:372; see also Heinrich Bullinger, *A Brief Exposition of the One and Eternal Testament or Covenant of God, 1534*, trans. C. S. McCoy and J. W. Baker, in *Fountainhead of Federalism* (Louisville, KY: Westminster John Knox Press, 1991), 131.

virtue of God's promises, 'fastened [to Christ] with the spiritual knot of the covenant.'¹⁶⁵

The ninth sermon placed eucharistic communion in the context of the covenant. Bullinger noted that the Eucharist was called the 'breaking of bread' by St Luke, and observed that 'in times past firm leagues were performed by breaking of bread.'¹⁶⁶ He explained that 'the church is joined and united unto Christ in the holy supper by a most strait league: and to conclude, the members themselves are therewith joined very fast together.' This mutual 'agreement' was also described as a 'testament.'¹⁶⁷ As in most of Zwingli's writings, God was the initiator.¹⁶⁸ Bullinger described eucharistic communion, both with Christ and with other believers, as 'a league or confederacy. We are knit invisibly with Christ and all his members by unity of faith and participation of one Spirit.'¹⁶⁹ Bullinger finished with a warning against Satan's schemes to corrupt 'the token of a covenant never to be broken.'¹⁷⁰ In effect, Satan's attack on the sacrament of the covenant was an attack on the Christian league.

Bullinger's sacramental theology was similar to Zwingli's in its covenantal context and denial that the sacraments mediated grace. Its distinctive emphasis was on the analogy between sign and reality, allowing that the sacraments offered, by way of testimony, God's promise of grace.

John Calvin

Calvin drew a strong link between covenant and sacrament, closely identifying the spiritual reality with the external sign.¹⁷¹ He

---

¹⁶⁵ Bullinger, *Decades*, v/8:377, see also 383, 387–89.
¹⁶⁶ Ibid., v/9:402.
¹⁶⁷ Ibid., v/9:402–3.
¹⁶⁸ Ibid., v/9:469.
¹⁶⁹ Ibid., v/9:467.
¹⁷⁰ Ibid., v/9:477–78.
¹⁷¹ Lillback, *Binding of God*, 242–63.

believed that the sacraments were vehicles employed by the Spirit to confer the grace that they signified. Consequently Calvin came closer than either Zwingli or Bullinger to Luther's understanding of the sacraments. In 1540 he signed Melanchthon's *Confessio Augustana Variata* and was assigned to a Lutheran delegation at the Worms Colloquy with the Strassburg reformer Johannes Sturm.[172] However, like Zwingli and Bullinger, Calvin denied the physical presence of Christ in the elements and by 1545 Luther had come to group him among the Sacramentaries.[173]

Although Calvin moved towards the sacramental positions of Wittenberg and Strassburg in the late 1530s, the first edition of his *Institutes* (1536) drew on Zwinglian themes. Calvin defined a sacrament as 'an outward sign by which the Lord represents and attests to us his good will toward us to sustain the weakness of our faith'; in other words, 'a testimony of God's grace,'[174] or 'ceremonies by which the Lord wills to exercise and confirm the faith of his people.'[175] Like Zwingli, Calvin emphasised God's provision 'for the ignorance of our mind and for the weakness of our flesh.' Human faith 'is slight and feeble unless propped on all sides and sustained by every means,' hence the sacraments 'confirm and seal the promise itself,' like seals confirming government documents.[176]

Although Calvin drew on Luther's 'testament' concept from the *Babylonian Captivity*, he did not associate it with a unilateral and unconditional promise.[177] On the contrary, Calvin identified 'promise' and 'covenant' in such a way as to define the 'token' or sacrament in relation to ancient covenant rituals. He asked what distinguished a ritual slaughter of a pig from any other killing except its signification

---

[172] Gordon, *Calvin*, 99–100.

[173] Ibid., 170.

[174] Calvin, *Institutes* [1536], 87.

[175] Ibid., 93.

[176] Ibid., 87, 92; see also Melanchthon, *Loci Communes*, 133; Gordon, "Calvin and the Swiss Reformed Churches," 66.

[177] Calvin, *Institutes* [1536], 116.

of ratifying 'the laws of covenants.' Again, the ratification is to make humanity more certain of God's fidelity: the sacraments 'lead us by the hand as tutors lead children.'[178] Conversely, exclusion from the token signifies exclusion from the promise.[179] Nevertheless, Calvin's sacramental theology clearly differed from Zwingli's. He attacked Zwingli's views that 'faith cannot be made better'[180] and that the sacraments signify God's act of receiving the believer, although he accepted that baptism serves 'our confession before men.'[181] Calvin argued that God had established the sacraments 'to nourish, exercise, and increase' faith and that they 'offer us mercy and grace.'[182] Furthermore, while Calvin placed 'no power in creatures,' he believed that the sacraments were 'means and instruments' of grace: God 'nourishes faith spiritually through the sacraments.'[183]

Calvin was careful, nonetheless, to exclude any misperception that sacraments could 'justify and confer grace [...] apart from faith' or 'bring [...] those things given us by divine bounty.'[184] He warned that they ought not to become objects of faith themselves. Instead, faith 'ought to rise up to him, the author of the sacraments.'[185] While, according to Calvin, the Zürichers recognised only the blessing of the Spirit, he identified three blessings:

> For first, the Lord teaches and instructs us by his Word. Secondly, he confirms it by the sacraments. Finally, he illumines our minds by the light of his Holy Spirit and opens

---

[178] Ibid., 88, see also 92.

[179] Ibid., 89–90.

[180] Ibid., 88. Calvin does not appear to have been aware of Zwingli's more nuanced position in 1529–31.

[181] Calvin, *Institutes* [1536], 90–91, 94; see Alexandre Ganoczy, *The Young Calvin*, trans. D. Foxgrover and W. Provo (Edinburgh: T&T Clark, 1987), 151–153.

[182] Calvin, *Institutes* [1536], 88.

[183] Ibid., 90.

[184] Ibid., 91–92.

[185] Ibid., 90.

our hearts for the Word and sacraments to enter in, which would otherwise only strike our ears and appear before our eyes, but not at all affect us within.[186]

The 'ancient sacraments [i.e., circumcision and Temple sacrifice] looked to the same purpose to which ours now tend: to direct and almost lead men by the hand to Christ.'[187] Sacraments show the essential unity of the Testaments: circumcision and baptism indicate cleansing from sin; sacrifice and the Eucharist indicate God's satisfaction. All point to the work of Christ.[188] Baptism, then, performed two functions for Calvin: to 'serve' and strengthen our faith before God and our confession before men. Baptism achieves the former by testifying to our cleansing, our mortification and our union with Christ. The believer is offered certainty of these things. Calvin can say that 'Christ's purity has been offered us in it' and 'in baptism we are covered and protected by Christ's blood.'[189] Baptismal vows therefore include a 'plea for pardon' (justification) and a 'petition for help' (sanctification), so that humanity's obligations are met by grace.[190] It is, like Zwingli's baptism, 'an initiation into faith.'[191] Confession before men was briefly explained from 1 Corinthians 1:13 where

> in being baptised in Christ's name, they had devoted themselves [*devovisse*] to him, sworn allegiance [*iurasse*] to his name, and pledged their fealty [*fidem obstrinxisse*] to him before men. As a result, they could no longer confess any other but Christ alone, unless they chose to renounce the confession they had made in baptism.[192]

---

[186] Ibid., 88–89.
[187] Ibid., 93.
[188] Ibid., 93–94.
[189] Ibid., 94–98.
[190] Lillback, *Binding of God*, 247.
[191] Calvin, *Institutes* [1536], 120.
[192] Ibid., 98; *CO*, 1:114.

The reciprocal obligation towards Christ is evident here, and it sounds remarkably like Zwingli's view. Baptism, explained Calvin, is to be received 'from the hand of God' and 'we should see and ponder spiritual things in the physical.' He denied that grace is 'bound and enclosed in the sacrament' and even seems to contradict his earlier general discussion by further denying that baptism 'is an organ and instrument to confer [grace] upon us.' Here it is only a token of grace from which 'we obtain only as much as we receive in faith.'[193] Although God's promise in baptism remains 'fixed and firm and trustworthy,' a child benefits only when he grows old enough to have faith in it. Faith is so emphasised by Calvin that he even ascribes to it the salvation of an elect infant who dies.[194] By contrast, a lack of faith is 'evidence of our being accused before God,'[195] later clarified as being rendered 'chargeable before God.'[196] The sacraments thus express the sanctions of the covenant.

The Eucharist confirms that Christ's body and blood are given to us, and Calvin suggested three reasons, the first of which is to strengthen faith. Believers recognise their union with Christ and his union with them in the sacrament. Calvin's understanding of Presence is that these benefits are 'so perfectly promised in this sacrament, that we must certainly consider him truly shown to us, just as if Christ himself present were set before our gaze and touched by our hands.' Believers are to perceive an analogy between the physical elements and the spiritual significance of sealing and confirming God's promise.[197] Importantly, the elements are not body and blood but 'the

---

[193] Calvin, *Institutes* [1536], 99; see David Steinmetz, *Calvin in Context* (Oxford and New York: OUP, 1995), 164–65.

[194] Calvin, *Institutes* [1536], 100–102. Calvin's position attempts to reconcile Zwingli's emphasis on initiation with Luther's dual emphasis on promise and faith: see Lohse, *Luther's Theology*, 300.

[195] Calvin, *Institutes* [1536], 99.

[196] John Calvin, *Institutes of the Christian Religion*, ed. J. T. McNeill, trans. F. L. Battles, *LCC*, 2 vols. (Louisville & London: Westminster John Knox Press, 1960), 1315 (IV. xv. 15).

[197] Calvin, *Institutes* [1536], 102–3.

testament in body and blood.'[198] Secondly, the Eucharist strengthens believers' witness, 'publicly and all with a single voice to confess openly before men that for us the whole assurance of life and salvation rests upon the Lord's death, that we may glorify him by our confession, and by our example exhort others to give glory to him.' Thus it is an exercise in remembrance and proclamation.[199] Thirdly, the Eucharist exhorts believers to unity in Christ and is a 'pledge' of mutual love.[200] Calvin wrote that 'as often as we partake of the symbol of the Lord's body, as a token given and received, we reciprocally bind ourselves to all the duties of love.'[201] The mutual commitment undertaken by believers is therefore akin to that between God and believers.

The following year, in 1537, Bucer and Wolfgang Capito subscribed to Calvin's *Confession of Faith concerning the Eucharist* in an attempt to deflect suspicion that Strassburg was conceding too much to the Lutherans. With brevity Calvin stated that participation in Christ occurred through the Spirit 'but in such a manner that he really feeds us with the substance of the body and blood of the Lord to everlasting life.' This participation was offered 'under the symbols of bread and wine.'[202] Christ's symbolic yet 'substantial' presence in the elements was thus asserted.

The ancient origin of the sacraments as covenantal seals was expanded in the 1539 edition of the *Institutes* where Abraham's circumcision was described as 'the seal of the covenant by faith in which he had already been justified.' The believer was to look beyond the physical elements to 'contemplation of those lofty mysteries [*sublima mysteria*] which lie hidden in the sacraments'[203]—'we are lifted up to heaven with our eyes and minds, to seek Christ there in the glory of

---

[198] Ibid., 107.
[199] Ibid., 109.
[200] Ibid., 109–10.
[201] Ibid., 112.
[202] John Calvin, "Confession of Faith Concerning the Eucharist (1537)," in *Calvin: Theological Treatises*, ed. J. Reid, Vol. 22 (London: SCM, 1954), 168.
[203] Calvin, *Institutes* [*LCC*], 1280 (IV. xiv. 5); *CO*, 1:941.

his Kingdom.'²⁰⁴ The sacraments were instituted by God to 'establish and increase faith,' but Calvin clarified that they do not contain 'some secret force' in themselves. Rather, they benefit faith when the Spirit works through them:

> Therefore, I make such a division between Spirit and sacraments that the power to act rests with the former, and the ministry alone is left to the latter—a ministry empty and trifling [*inane ac frivolum*], apart from the action of the Spirit, but charged with great effect when the Spirit works within and manifests his power.²⁰⁵

By assigning credit to God's preparation of the heart to receive the sign, Calvin argues that he avoids doing an injustice to the Spirit who 'transmits those outward words and sacraments from our ears to our soul.'²⁰⁶ Calvin resisted both divorcing sign from mystery, alluding to Hoen and Zwingli, and immoderately exalting signs, alluding to Luther. However, his scepticism towards the Zwinglian position was not hostile: he recognised that there was no unanimity amongst Christians and refrained from the vitriol of which he was capable. His understanding was couched in the phrase 'it seems to me.' The difference, he wrote, is that for Hoen and Zwingli 'eating is faith; for me it seems rather to follow from faith.'²⁰⁷ 'Eating is the result and effect of faith,' by which Calvin meant an infusion of Christ's life into believers.²⁰⁸ Calvin perhaps overestimated his distance from Zwingli's position, which allowed that both faith and the soul are 'strengthened'. However, Calvin conceived of eating as occurring 'under the symbols' of the elements (*'sub panis symbolo'*),²⁰⁹ assigning

---

²⁰⁴ Calvin, *Institutes* [*LCC*], 1381 (IV. xvii. 18); *CO*, 1:1009.
²⁰⁵ Calvin, *Institutes* [*LCC*], 1284 (IV. xiv. 9); *CO*, 1:944.
²⁰⁶ Calvin, *Institutes* [*LCC*], 1285 (IV. xiv. 10); *CO*, 1:945.
²⁰⁷ Calvin, *Institutes* [*LCC*], 1365 (IV. xvii. 5); *CO*, 1:999.
²⁰⁸ Calvin, *Institutes* [*LCC*], 1365 (IV. xvii. 5).
²⁰⁹ Ibid., 1381 (IV. xvii. 18); *CO*, 1:1009.

the Eucharist an instrumentality uniformly rejected in Zürich. In terms of the covenant, Christ unites his body with believers in the sacrament, and that unity is exhibited (*'exhibetur'*) in the bread.[210] In 1559 Calvin described the bread as Christ's body 'because it is the covenant in his body.'[211]

On the believer's part, the sacraments represent vows of perfect obedience, 'marks of profession, by which we openly swear allegiance to God, binding ourselves in fealty to him.' Calvin drew attention to the 'covenantal' significance.[212] This binding of God and humanity is the basic significance of the sacraments for Calvin.[213] The believer cannot invalidate the sacrament through violation of the reciprocal covenant itself, for 'the symbol of the covenant remained ever firm and inviolable by virtue of the Lord's institution.' The 'sole condition of repentance' allowed covenant-breakers' restoration 'into the covenant.'[214]

The 1539 edition of the *Institutes* saw the addition of Calvin's chapter on paedobaptism (IV. xvi) written in light of the Anabaptist controversy. Arguing, like Zwingli and Bullinger, for an essential continuity of the covenant of circumcision, Calvin wrote that *'per baptismum Deo initiamur, ut eius populo adscibamur, et ipsi mutuo in eius nomen iuremus'* (through baptism we are initiated by God, we are reckoned his people, and in turn we swear fealty to him). For the Jews, circumcision had been their first entry into the church (*'primus illis erat in ecclesiam ingressus'*).[215] Entry into a covenant community is clearly intended and infants of both Testaments enter into a common covenant by hereditary right (*'haereditario iure'*).[216] Rejection of

---

[210] *CO*, 1:1014.

[211] Calvin, *Institutes* [*LCC*], 1384 (IV. xvii. 20).

[212] Ibid., 1296 (IV. xiv. 19); see Ronald Wallace, *Calvin's Doctrine of Word and Sacrament* (Edinburgh: Oliver & Boyd, 1953), 141.

[213] Peter Lillback, *The Binding of God: Calvin's Role in the Development of Covenant Theology* (Grand Rapids, MI: Baker Academic, 2001), 246.

[214] Calvin, *Institutes* [*LCC*], 1317 (IV. xv. 17).

[215] *CO*, 1:970; see also Calvin, *Institutes* [*LCC*], 1327–1329 (IV. xvi. 4–6).

[216] *CO*, 1:985; see also Calvin, *Institutes* [*LCC*], 1347 (IV. xvi. 24). Calvin

infant baptism is therefore a 'violation of the will of God.' It is not 'superfluous' for

> God's sign, communicated to a child as by an impressed seal, confirms the promise given to the pious parent, and declares it to be ratified that the Lord will be God not only to him but to his seed; and that he wills to manifest his goodness and grace not only to him but to his descendants even to the thousandth generation [Exodus 20:6].[217]

Calvin argued that infants, even from the womb, can be saved by God due to his prerogative of regeneration; this in spite of their lack of understanding and inability to 'swear to the provisions of the covenant.' Adults, by contrast, who wish to enter the 'fellowship of the covenant' must 'learn its conditions' before receiving the sign.[218] Participation in the Eucharist was reserved for adults because only they were capable of self-examination and remembrance.[219] Both infant offspring and adult proselytes are Abraham's descendants. The Jewish people still have a claim on Christ to 'discharge the pledge made once for all by his Father [. . .] for the salvation of the Jewish nation.' However, natural covenant-members could be 'forsaken' if they became complacent and disobedient in their reciprocal obligations.[220]

Calvin's *Short Treatise on the Lord's Supper* (1541) was written at the high ebb of his hopes for *rapprochement* between the Lutherans and the Swiss.[221] Calvin explained that believers' 'heavenly inheritance'

---

clearly explained his covenantal understanding of paedobaptism to John Knox on 8 November 1559: Gorham, ed., *Gleanings*, 418.

[217] Calvin, *Institutes* [*LCC*], 1331–1332 (IV. xvi. 8–9), see also 1336–38 (IV. xvi. 14–15).

[218] Ibid., 1340–1347 (IV. xvi. 17–24), quotations at 1347.

[219] Ibid., 1353 (IV. xvi. 30).

[220] Ibid., 1336–1337 (IV. xvi. 14–15); see Lillback, *Binding of God*, 252, 255–56.

[221] John Calvin, "Short Treatise on the Lord's Supper (1541)," in *Calvin:*

is not only to be grasped in the future but that God 'has already in a measure installed us in its possession.' Believers are already 'translated' into life and, to be sustained in it, they feed on the 'spiritual bread' of the Word, the 'instrument by which Jesus Christ, with all his benefits, is dispensed to us.' Calvin argued that what pertains to the Word also belongs to the Eucharist. Weak human faith fails to receive Christ from teaching and preaching alone, so God attaches signs to the Word 'to sign and seal in our consciences the promises contained in his gospel concerning our being made partakers of his body and blood.' The signs also promote praise and sanctification.[222] The Eucharist, then, is a testimony or mirror of contemplation of the benefits of Christ. Believers cannot enjoy his benefits until they receive him, and he is 'given' in the Eucharist. Therefore 'the manner and substance of the sacraments is the Lord Jesus Christ, and the efficacy of them are the gifts and blessings which we have by means of him.' The Eucharist is 'frivolous and useless' without 'the true communication of Jesus Christ [...] offered us in the Supper.'[223] Believers are to look beyond the symbol to that signified, for God certainly performs it and 'we must then receive in the Supper the body and blood and Jesus Christ.' The sacraments further 'impel us to do our duty' in gratitude, public confession and holy living.[224] Thus they are signs which are instrumental in communicating Christ to believers.

The 1543 edition of the *Institutes* was consistent with Calvin's teaching in the *Short Treatise*. Sacraments were defined not only as signs to sustain weak faith, as in earlier editions, but signs in which 'we in turn attest our piety toward him [God] before men [*apud homines testamur*].' That signified now included reciprocal or 'mutual attestation of our piety.'[225] In the Eucharist God 'in some measure renews, or rather continues, the covenant which he once and for all

---

Theological Treatises, *LCC*, Vol. 22 (London: SCM, 1954), 164–66.
[222] Ibid., 143–44.
[223] Ibid., 145–46.
[224] Ibid., 148–49.
[225] Calvin, *Institutes* [*LCC*], 1277 (IV. xiv. 1); *CO*, 1:938–39.

ratified with his blood (as far as it pertains to the strengthening of our faith).'[226]

Concerning the instrumentality of sacraments, Calvin stated that God 'imparts spiritual things under visible ones.'[227] Likening sacraments to preaching, he argued that St Paul gloried in the ministry of the Spirit (2 Corinthians 3:6) 'as if the power of the Holy Spirit were joined by an indissoluble bond to his preaching.' Divinely ordained instruments really express the power of the Spirit, 'nevertheless, this distinction is to be kept: we should remember what man can do of himself, and what is reserved to God.'[228] Calvin endeavoured to strike this balance. One sentence in the 1536 edition had read:

> we are said to receive, obtain, and acquire what we believe given to us by God, whether we first recognise it, or become more certain of it as previously recognised.[229]

By 1543 the same sentence had been significantly altered to:

> we are said to receive, obtain, and acquire what, according as our faith is aware, is shown forth to us by the Lord [*nobis a Domino exhibetur*], whether when he first testifies to it, or when he confirms more fully and more surely what has been attested.[230]

Calvin's modifications serve to exaggerate the rôle of faith in apprehending the significance of the sacrament and to stress the primacy of God in testifying and confirming that significance over humanity's recognition of it. Sacramental instrumentality and efficacy depended upon divine activity. The same distinction governed his separation of

[226] Calvin, *Institutes* [*LCC*], 1361 (IV. xvii. 1).
[227] Ibid., 1278 (IV. xiv. 3); *CO*, 1:940.
[228] Calvin, *Institutes* [*LCC*], 1286–87 (IV. xiv. 11); *CO*, 1:945–46.
[229] Calvin, *Institutes* [1536], 99.
[230] Calvin, *Institutes* [*LCC*], 1315 (IV. xv. 15); *CO*, 1:965.

baptism from the grace of regeneration: children of Christians are adopted by God before birth 'when he promises that he will be our God and the God of our descendants after us [Genesis 17:7].'[231] The natural lineage of the covenant promise is thus maintained after Christ.

Calvin's sacramental theology was essentially complete by 1539 and fully integrated with his concept of covenant. While the covenant was sometimes obscured by his concerns in the Eucharist controversy, the definition of sacraments as covenant seals was the consistent basis of Calvin's sacramental theology.

The concept of covenant was central to the sacramental theologies of Zwingli, Bullinger, and Calvin, but they each came to different conclusions about the relationship between grace and the sacraments. Zwingli's prioritisation of the uniqueness of Christ's historic work led him to deny altogether that sacraments could confer grace. He regarded sacraments as tangible memorials of divine faithfulness and human allegiance. Only in 1529–31 did he concede that the sacraments could support faith indirectly. To a great extent Bullinger defended and shared the Zwinglian position, but he amplified Zwingli's connection between sign and reality, emphasising the analogous rôle of the sacraments in testifying to, or offering, the promise of grace without conferring grace themselves. Calvin's position was characterised by the idea that the sacraments conferred the grace that they signified. This stemmed from his close identification of covenant and sacrament. For Calvin, sacraments had no intrinsic worth except as seals of the covenant in Christ's body, but as such they conveyed Christ himself.

The concepts of covenant belonging to Zwingli, Bullinger, and Calvin are distinguishable, not on the basis of any variation between their concepts, but according to the distinct sacramental theology that each of them developed from their concept. In the next chapter these distinctions will undergird an investigation of the sources of reciprocal covenant themes in the English context.

[231] Ibid., 1321 (IV. xv. 20).

6

English Sacramental Theology

Hast thou auctority to absolue me or geue me penaunce[?]
Nay, thou maist kepe shepe. Christ saied mas[s] upon the
Mount of Calvary and that is suffisient for my soule.
—*Archibald of Faversham (1543)*[1]

Controversy in England over the sacraments exhibited the same 'theological mediocrity' that Alister McGrath observes in the English Reformation generally.[2] When read *à propos* of continental contributions the English discourse seems more preoccupied with pastoral application. Diarmaid MacCulloch has commented upon 'the English lack of capacity for abstract theological invention.'[3] Where more sophisticated sacramental doctrine is found in England continental influence may be suspected.[4] The reception of the Swiss concept of covenant by English evangelicals had

---

[1] Parker Library, Cambridge: CCCC MS. 128, 64.
[2] Alister McGrath, *Iustitia Dei: a history of the Christian Doctrine of Justification*, 3rd ed. (Cambridge: CUP, 2005), 258.
[3] MacCulloch, "England," 169.
[4] See Patrick Collinson, "The Fog in the Channel Clears: The Rediscovery of the Continental Dimension to the British Reformations," in *The Reception of Continental Reformation in Britain*, ed. P. Ha and P. Collinson, *PBA*, Vol. 164 (Oxford: OUP, 2010), xxx.

significant implications for their sacramental theology. This means that sacramental theology can be used to suggest particular continental sources of English concepts of covenant.

William Tyndale

A passing reference to the sacrament of baptism in Tyndale's *Prologue to Romans* (1526) states that it 'signifieth the mortifyinge of sinnes and the newe life of grace.'[5] Although the Holy Spirit 'laboureth and enforceth to kill the remnaunte of sinne and luste which remayne in the flesshe after oure iustifinge,' Tyndale opined that 'we are not so fre from sinne thorowe fayth that we shuld henceforth goo vppe and doune ydle carlesse and sure of oure selves as though there were nowe no more sinne in vs.'[6] He does not say much here but he does link the sign with sanctification: in order to 'fulfill oure bapti[s]m' we must 'tame oure bodies and to compell the members to obeye the sprite and not the appetites.' This was equivalent to living in light of regeneration through Christ's death and resurrection rather than living in order to fulfil any kind of baptismal vow.[7]

Tyndale began to engage more particularly with the sacraments in *The Obedience of a Christian Man* (1528). There he defined a sacrament as 'an holy signe and representeth allwaye some promise of God.'[8] It functioned as 'an outwarde signe that maye be sene to signifie[,] to represente and to put a man in remembraunce of some spirituall promyse which can not be sene but by fayth only.'[9] His exemplar was the rainbow of Genesis 9 to 'represent and signifie

---

[5] William Tyndale, *A compendious introduccion, prologe or preface vnto the pistle off Paul to the Romayns* (Worms: P. Schoeffer, 1526; RSTC 24438), B4r.
[6] Ibid.
[7] Ibid.
[8] William Tyndale, *The Obedience of a Christen Man and how Christen rulers ought to governe* (Antwerp: J. Hoochstraten [Martin de Keyser?], 1528; RSTC 24446), M1r.
[9] Ibid., M7r.

vnto all men an o[a]the that God sware to Noe and to all men after him.'[10] The definition of the promise in terms of God's oath makes clear that the sacramental 'remembraunce of the promyses' had only God's commitments in view.[11]

Following Luther, Tyndale claimed that only baptism and 'the Sacrament of the Body and Blood of Christ' were properly called sacraments. Marriage, ordination, anointing, penance, and confirmation had 'no promise coupled therwith,' and the final two were signified in baptism anyway.[12] A short paragraph emphasising the necessity of faith 'when thou seist the sacrament or eatest his body or drinkest his bloude' implied the bodily presence of Christ in a manner consistent with Luther's understanding of Christ's presence in the elements.[13] The promise signified was the forgiveness of sins. Tyndale asserted that communicants were 'saved and justified' by seeing the sacrament, eating the bread, or drinking the wine 'yf [. . .] thou have this promyse fast in thine herte (that his body was slayne and his bloud shed for thy synnes) and belevest it.' Participation was efficacious only to the believer. A marginal note clarified that 'the promyse which the sacrament preacheth iustifieth only,'[14] thereby excluding the Roman idea of eucharistic sacrifice in which, Tyndale claimed, they 'make us believe that the work itself, without the promise, saveth us; which doctrine they learned of Aristotle.'[15]

Tyndale's two paragraphs on baptism in the *Obedience* began by insisting that God's promise be taught to the people in English. Paedobaptism was assumed, and the priest 'appon this faith [of the

[10] Ibid., M1r.
[11] Ibid., O1r.
[12] Ibid., M3r.
[13] Ibid., M1r-v; see Martin Luther, *The Sacrament of the Body and Blood of Christ—against the Fanatics* [1526], trans. A. Steinhauser, *LW*, Vol. 36 (Philadelphia: Fortress Press, 1959), 335, 343; Martin Luther, *That These Words of Christ, "This Is My Body," etc., Still Stand Firm against the Fanatics* [1527], ed. R. Fischer, *LW*, Vol. 37 (Philadelphia: Fortress Press, 1976), 64.
[14] Tyndale, *Obedience*, M1v.
[15] Ibid., O3r.

congregation] baptiseth the childe.'[16] As with the Eucharist the ceremony itself was said to avail nothing 'but thorow the worde it purifieth and clenseth vs.'[17] This is at least consistent with Luther's language if not with regard to the value of the ceremony.[18] Tyndale defined the 'worde' as God's promise. He established a close connection between the preaching of the word and the administration of the sacraments reminiscent of Luther's position in 1526.[19] He compared baptism to preaching in that both 'represent' the divine promise in Christ and thereby have salvific value, but only to those who believe the word. Baptism

> preacheth vnto vs that we are clensed with Christes bloudeshedinge which was an offeringe and a satisfaction for the sinne of all that repente and beleve consentinge and submittinge them selves vnto the will of God. The plunginge in to the water signifieth that we dye and are buryed with Christ as concerninge the olde lyfe of synne which is Adam. And the pullinge out agayne signifieth that we rise agayne with christe in a new lyfe full of the holy goost which shall teach vs and gyde vs and worke the will of God in vs.[20]

Evidently it is Christ's atonement, rather than baptism, that is of real efficacy for believers, but the sacrament, like preaching, presents an opportunity to believe God's promise. In his discussion of penance Tyndale added that 'repentaunce and all the good deades which accompanie repentaunce to sley the lustes of the flesh are signified by bapti[s]m.'[21] The sign of baptism reminds believers that

---

[16] Ibid., M1v.
[17] Ibid., M2r.
[18] See Bernhard Lohse, *Martin Luther's Theology: its historical and systematic development*, trans. R. Harrisville (Edinburgh: T&T Clark, 1999), 299.
[19] See Luther, *Sacrament of the Body and Blood*, 349.
[20] Tyndale, *Obedience*, M2r.
[21] Ibid., M7r.

their inclusion in Christ's atonement assumes that they will battle for holiness. Although this could be interpreted as the believer's mutual responsibility, Tyndale did not link baptism to a bilateral understanding of testament.

Tyndale rejected the idea that the Holy Spirit was received through ceremonies, arguing instead that the Spirit was 'received through preaching of the faith.'[22] Tyndale concluded that, since the sacraments also preach God's word, they

> therfore iustifie and minister the sprite to them that beleve as Paul thorow preachinge the Gospell was a minister of righteousnes and of the sprite vnto all that beleved his preaching [. . .]. Christes sacramentes preach the fayth of Christ as his apostles did and therby iustifie.[23]

Tyndale's primary interest in 1528 seems to have been to oppose late-medieval beliefs about the efficacy of the ceremonies themselves. At this stage his sacramental theology seems to have been closer to Luther's than to Zwingli's but Tyndale was already beginning to exhibit traits more characteristic of Zürich theology.

A mutual concept of covenant became central to Tyndale's theology between 1528 and 1530. In his earlier works the sacraments had not even been related to his peripheral notion of covenant, but in his Pentateuch prologues (1530) they were integrated. The prologues were further conspicuous for their omission of the physical presence of Christ in the sacraments, firmly distancing Tyndale from Luther. In the glossary to Genesis Tyndale defined a sacrament as 'a signe representinge soch an appoyn[t]ment and promeses;' that is, a sign representing the bilateral appointment 'betwene god and man and goddes promyses.'[24] In the Old Testament the rainbow was a sign

[22] Ibid., O2r.
[23] Ibid., O8v.
[24] William Tyndale, *The Pentateuch* (Antwerp: Johan Hoochstraten, 1530; RSTC 2350), A table expoundinge certeyne wordes. This text is unpaginated.

of God's promise of preservation to Noah, which was apparently unilateral. Meanwhile circumcision signified both God's promise to Abraham and, 'on the other side,' Abraham's obligation to 'circumcyse and cut off the lustes of their fleshe [. . .] to walke in the wayes of the lorde.' Baptism had now 'come in the roume' of circumcision and so 'signifieth on the one syde how that all that repent and beleue are washed in Christes bloud: And on the other syde how that the same must quench and droune the lustes of the flesh to folow the steppes of Christ.'[25] For Tyndale, like Zwingli, baptism had come to signify a reciprocal obligation of godliness following the model of circumcision.

In the Leviticus prologue Tyndale argued that sacrifices and ceremonies helped the Jew to serve God according to the 'appoyntement made betwene him and God.' The Jewish ceremonies had spoken to them 'after their awne capacyte' in the era 'before Christ [. . .] in the infancye and childhod of the worlde,' but now,

> as the shadowe vanisheth awaye at the comynge of the light, euen so doo the ceremonyes and sacrifices at the comynge of Christ, and are henceforth no moare necessarye then a token left in remembraunce of a bargayne is necessary when the bargayne is fulfilled.[26]

The New Testament sacraments, by contrast, perform a different function from those of the Levitical cult. Once we have come to know Christ, ceremonies continue to be useful as

> figures, that is to saye allegoryes, similitudes or examples to open Christ and the secrettes off God hyd in Christ euen vnto the quycke, and to declare them more lyuely and sensebly with them than with all the wordes of the worlde. For

---
[25] Ibid.
[26] Ibid., Leviticus prologue.

similitudes haue more vertue and power with them than bare wordes, and lead a mans wittes further in to the pithe and marye [marrow] and spirituall vnderstondinge of the thinge, than all the wordes that can be imagined.[27]

This pedagogical function of the sacraments is not identical to Zwingli's notion of accommodation to humanity's weakness, since Tyndale wrote here of the 'vertue and power' of the signs. He believed that the sacraments were designed to aid remembrance of the bargain with God, like 'a ringe of a rush aboute one of their fingers.'[28] Tyndale's use of the ring metaphor is too brief to be identified with either Zwingli's or Bullinger's use of it, but the ring was equivalent to an oath confirming a bargain: 'it is not ynough to make a bargayne with wordes onlye, but we must put thereto an o[a]th and geue ernest to confirme the faithe off the person with whom it is made.'[29] Tyndale was certainly more confident than Zwingli in his repeated statement that the sacraments were 'a token and remembraunce to sturre vppe their faythes wyth all,' suggesting that they strengthen faith in God's promises so that believers can hold God to his commitments.[30]

A more clearly Zwinglian comparison can be drawn from Tyndale's use of the military metaphor for baptism. It was 'oure comen ba[d]gge and sure ernest and perpetuall memoriall that we pertayne vnto Christ and are separated from all that are not christes' (that is, those who are not pledged to God), just as circumcision signified that the Jews 'were all so[l]diars off God to warre his warre and separatinge them from all other nacyons disobedient vnto God.'[31] Baptism was not only the sign of initiation into God's people. It further signified that we should walk in godliness, echoing the Genesis glossary. The emphasis here is on baptism as divine action rather than

[27] Ibid.
[28] Ibid.
[29] Ibid.
[30] Ibid.
[31] Ibid.

human,³² although in the Numbers prologue it is stated explicitly that Christians 'hast vowed in thy baptyme [. . .] that thou shuldest wayte on his will and commaundmentes and puryfye thy membres acordynge to the same doctryne that hath purifyed thyne harte.' The sacrament signifies reciprocal obligations; humanity enjoys God's help and 'the comforte of the rewarde to come,' which is based on God's goodness rather than human merit.³³

Tyndale expounded a concept of sacramental instrumentality in the Leviticus prologue as he had done in the *Obedience*, referring, for instance, to 'the nature power and frute or effecte of bapti[s]m.' The Jewish ceremonies 'saued them and iustified them and stode them in the same steade as oure sacramentes doo vs: not by the power of the sacrifice or deade it selfe, but by the vertue of the faith in the promysse whiche the sacrifice or ceremonye preached and wherof it was a token or sygne.' Again, 'the sacramentes clense vs and absolue vs of oure synnes as the preastes doo, in preachinge of repentaunce and faith.'³⁴ Tyndale held that 'if bapti[s]m preach me the wasshing in christes bloude, so doth the holy gost accompany it,'³⁵ thereby connecting the work of the Spirit with the faithful reception of the sacraments.

Tyndale also linked Jewish ceremonies with Christian preaching and sacraments in *The Practice of Prelates* (1530). Here his emphasis was on their signification rather than instrumentality. Ceremonies were

> signes that put men in remembraunce other of the benefites of god done all readye as the esterlambe: ether signes of the promysse and appoyntement made betwene god and man as circumcysion: or signes that testifye unto the people that the wrath of god is peaced and their synnes forgeuen as all

---

³² See Zwingli, *Subsidiary Essay, HZW*, 2:224.
³³ Tyndale, *Pentateuch*, Numbers prologue.
³⁴ Ibid., Leviticus prologue.
³⁵ Ibid.

maner sacrifyces: which all cease assone as christ had offered upp the sacrifyce of his bodye and bloude for vs. And in steade of them come the open preachinge of christ and oure signes which we call sacramentes.[36]

There were, then, several possible significations: memorials of God's blessings, signs of the covenant, and confirmations of the atonement. This wealth of meaning was held together in Tyndale's sacramental theology as different aspects were emphasised for polemical ends.

The human obligation contained in the sacrament of baptism and mentioned in the Numbers prologue was clearly identified in Tyndale's prologue to Jonah (1531). In Jonah 2:9 the prophet declares that he will 'paye that I haue vowed that sauinge cometh of the lorde.' Tyndale commented: 'to beleue that god only is the sauer [saviour] is the thynge that all the Jewes vowed in theyr circumcision as we in oure bapti[s]m. Which vowe Jonas now tawght with experience promiseth to paye.'[37] The baptised Christian is, therefore, under obligation to recognise God as the only saviour, which is the condition of faith. Trusting in the sacraments without consciousness of this signification is a form of idolatry.[38] To another error—that baptism does not cleanse from subsequent sin—Tyndale answered that the ongoing application of that sign to infants renews its signification for the whole community:

> though when we synne of frailtie after oure bapty[s]m we receaue the sygne no moare yet we be renewed agayne thorow

---

[36] William Tyndale, *The Practyse of Prelates, whether the kinges grace maye be separated from hys quene, be cause she was his brothers wyfe* (Antwerp: Joannes Hoochstraten, 1530; RSTC 24465), H8r-v. The influence of Swiss Reformed theology is noted by Carl Trueman, *Luther's Legacy: Salvation and English Reformers, 1525–1556* (Oxford: OUP, 1994), 106n.

[37] William Tyndale, *The Prophete Ionas* (Antwerp: M. de Keyser, 1531; RSTC 2788), B4v, see also C3v.

[38] Ibid., B5r.

repentaunce and faith in Christes bloude whych twayne the sygne of bapty[s]m ever contynued amonge vs in baptisynge oure younge childern doeth euer kepe in mynde and call vs backe agayne vn to oure profession if we be gonne astraye & promiseth vs forgeuenesse.[39]

In Tyndale's view, therefore, paedobaptism involves not only the individual but the whole community.

Tyndale's *Answer* to Sir Thomas More (1531) tackled numerous questions relating to 'sacraments, ceremonies, or signs (three words with one signification).'[40] Tyndale's focus was to dispute More's traditional doctrine. Tyndale argued that the sacraments, like the word of God, are to be believed, not to be the object of belief.[41] He argued that 'the priest toucheth not Christ's natural body with his hands,' but affirmed that

> he that repenteth toward the law of God, and at the sight of the sacrament, or of the breaking, feeling, eating, chamming [chewing], or drinking, calleth to remembrance the death of Christ, his body-breaking and blood-shedding for our sins, and all his passion; the same eateth our Saviour's body and drinketh his blood through faith only, and receiveth forgiveness of all his sins thereby.[42]

Here Tyndale's understanding of participation comes close to Zwingli's position, with its emphasis on memorialisation and 'faith in the doctrine.'[43] Thus,

---

[39] Ibid., C4r-v.
[40] William Tyndale, *An Answer to Sir Thomas More's Dialogue*, ed. H. Walter, PS (Cambridge: CUP, 1849), 74.
[41] Ibid., 180.
[42] Ibid., 162–163.
[43] Ibid., 172; see Trueman, *Luther's Legacy*, 106n.

the shewing, breaking, and eating of the host, the shewing and drinking of the cup of Christ's blood, and the words, and the consecration, help us not a pin, nor are God's service; save only in that they stir up our repenting faith, to call to mind the death and passion of Christ for our sins.[44]

Sacraments were no more than aids to the weak, possessing no intrinsic value. All sacraments signify that we should 'keep the faith purely and the law of love undefiled,'[45] which is consistent with a signification of a reciprocal relationship between God and mankind. Baptism makes demands in signifying 'that I must repent of evil, and believe to be saved therefrom by the blood of Christ.'[46]

A similar point was made in the strongly covenantal *Exposition of the fyrste epistle of Seynt Jhon* (1531) where baptism is described as the 'sacrament of repentance.' Tyndale noted significations of commitments pertaining both to God and to humanity:

> For the plunging in to the water as it betokenith on the one parte that christ hathe washed oure soules with his bloude euen so on the other part it signifieth that we haue p[ro]mised to quench & sley the lustes of the fleashe with prayer fasting & holy meditacion after the doctrine of Christ.[47]

Tyndale explained that the Jews 'could beleue no wordes thoughe an aungell had spoken without a token [. . .]. And likewise what so euer they were bidde to doo they must haue had a token of remembraunce thoughe it had bene but a ringe of a rushe.'[48] Tyndale repeated the 'ring of rush' image from his prologue to Leviticus, but of greater

---

[44] Tyndale, *Answer*, 177.
[45] Ibid., 30.
[46] Ibid., 171.
[47] William Tyndale, *The exposition of the fyrst epistle of Seynt Jhon with a prologge before it* (Antwerp: M. de Keyser, 1531; RSTC 24443), C2r, see also G5r.
[48] Ibid., H1v.

interest is the use of the sign to confirm what the Jews had been told to do. 'Euen so,' Christian sacraments are 'oure memorialles and signes of remembraunce only,' recalling us to our profession.[49] In the case of the Eucharist,

> to kepe this testament euer in mynde [. . .] he left vs with the sacrament or signe of his body and bloude to strengthe oure faithe and to certify oure conscience that oure synnes were forgiuen assone as we repentyd and had reconcyled oure selues unto oure brethern: & to arme oure soules thorou the contynuall remembraunce of Christes deeth unto the despising of the worlde mortifyeng of the fleashe and quenching of the lustes and thurst of worldly thinges.[50]

Tyndale allowed a positive function of the Eucharist in strengthening assurance of forgiveness that was consistent with Zwingli's contemporary view. Alongside assurance was the call to arms against sin which must accompany repentance and faith. The Eucharist signified mutuality in the redemptive bargain:

> the sacrament was ministred for the confirmation of the faith of the gospell & of the testament made betwen God and vs of forgiueness of synnes in Christes bloude for oure repentaunce and faith: as ye se howe after all bargens there is a signe therof made.[51]

Thus, both sacraments included some signification on humanity's part, either of initiation into Christ's body, or continuing faithfulness and love as a member of Christ's body.[52]

---

[49] Ibid., H1v-2r.
[50] Ibid., H3r.
[51] Ibid., H4v.
[52] Ibid., H3v; see William Clebsch, *England's Earliest Protestants, 1525–1535* (Westport, CT: Greenwood Press, 1964), 172–73.

The *Exposicion vppon the v. vi. vii. chapters of Mathew* (1533) made mention of sacraments in a broader sense. Good works 'are as it were verye sacramentes and visibile and sensibile signes, tokens, yernest, obligacions, wittnesses, test[i]monies,' in the sense that they provide confirmation of God's faithfulness to his promise.[53] Of course works, like sacraments, do not avail justification. 'God onlye iustifieth vs as cause efficient or workeman,' wrote Tyndale, clearly in line with Zürich emphases. He affirmed that 'God promiseth to iustifie whosoeuer is baptised to beleue in Christ, and to kepe the law of God,'[54] yet, as Zwingli had emphasised, 'the wasshynge' simply testifies to God's commitment. It helps those whose faith is weak,

> as the popes lettres doo certifie the beleuers of the popes pardones. Now the letters helpe not or hindre, but that the pardon were as good without them as with them, saue onlye to stablishe weake soules that coulde not beleue excepte they reade the letters, loked on the seale and saw the printe of saynt Peters keyes.[55]

For Tyndale, the value of the sacraments was to confirm the reliability of God's promise to those who doubted.

Tyndale's single most important work of sacramental theology was *A briefe declaration of the sacraments* written sometime after 1533.[56] He began by observing that the Hebrews instituted

---

[53] William Tyndale, *An exposicion vppon the v. vi. vii. chapters of Mathew* (Antwerp?: J. Grapheus?, 1533?; RSTC 24440), K6v.

[54] Ibid.

[55] Ibid., K7r.

[56] William Tyndale, *A Briefe Declaration of the Sacraments* (London: Robert Stoughton, 1548; RSTC 24445). This is the earliest extant edition. See Clebsch, *Earliest Protestants*, 185. *The Souper of the Lorde* (1533) is now attributed to George Joye rather than Tyndale: W. D. J. Cargill Thompson, "Who wrote 'The Supper of the Lord'?" *HTR* 53 (1960), 77–91; William Clebsch, "More evidence that George Joye wrote the Souper of the Lorde," *HTR* 55 (1962), 63–66.

signs as memorials 'yf any notable thyng chaunced among them.' 'Lykewyse in all the couenauntes,' he explained, 'they not onely promysed one to another & sweare theron. But also set vp signes & tokens therof and gaue the places names to kepe the thynge in mynde.'[57] The sacraments reminded the Hebrews to hold God to his promises, 'byndyng him with his owne wor[d]es and brynging fourth the oblygation and seale thereof in all tymes of necesite and temptation.'[58]

The Hebrews were also reminded of their obligations to God. The sacrament of circumcision 'bounde' the whole community to God 'to truste in hym and to kepe hys lawes.' This included females without the sign in their own bodies. Physical circumcision was of no intrinsic worth except to aid those who are 'truly circumcysed in the hart & soul before god' to fulfil their profession. Those who bore the physical sign but were not 'truly circumcysed' were all the more liable to condemnation, for God was 'not bounde to them but hadde good ryght therby to punyshe them.'[59]

Whether or not a Hebrew infant had been circumcised, it had become part of God's covenant 'assone as it lyuing in the mothers wombe.' The Abrahamic covenant had stipulated that a boy must die if he had not been circumcised by the eighth day (Genesis 17:12–14), but this was due to his parents' contempt of the signified covenant rather than the necessity of the sign for salvation.[60] As for Zwingli, circumcision provided the basis for Tyndale's understanding of paedobaptism. The covenant in Christ's blood applies to all believers and their 'sede assone as it hath life in the mothers wombeyer [womb ever before] the sygne be put on.' It is God's covenant rather than the sacrament which saves, yet baptism is 'comanded to be put on at due time to styr vp faith of the couenaunt that saueth vs.'[61]

[57] Tyndale, *Sacraments*, A2r.
[58] Ibid., A3v.
[59] Ibid., A4r-v.
[60] Ibid., A4v-5r.
[61] Ibid., A5r.

The covenantal nature of the Christian sacraments was repeatedly expressed by Tyndale. Signs had been instituted

> in all [God's] promyses and couenauntes not for hys necessitye, but for oures, that suche thynges shulde be a wytnesse and testymony betwene hym and vs to confyrme the fayth of his promys, that we shuld not wauer or doubt in them, when we loke on the seales of hys oblygac[i]ons, wher with he hath bound hym selfe, and to kepe the promyses and couenauntes beter in mynde, and to make them the more depe synke into our harts, & to be more earnestlye regarded, and that we shulde [ask] what such thyngs mente, and why god commaunded them to be obserued that ignoraunce shulde not excuse, yf we knowe not what we ought to do and beleue.[62]

Numerous points are raised here. The sacraments were 'not a seruice to god, but a seruice to man, to put him in minde of the couenant & to styrre vp fayth and loue w[hich] are goddes spyrytual sacrifyce in mans hart.'[63] This might suggest that faith, which Tyndale saw as a human obligation towards God, is God's work in the heart, thereby placing mutuality in a clearly gracious context. However, it should probably be interpreted as Tyndale's reiteration of the spiritual sacrifice required by God from humanity. The sacraments were instituted 'for our infyrmities sake,'[64] in the sense that humanity's faith in God's promise is weak. Although words might be doubted in retrospect, 'a manne is more sure of that he heareth seythe, feleth, smelleth and tasteth, then that he heareth only.'[65] By way of example, Tyndale, like Bullinger, compared the Eucharist with an engagement ring: 'If a yonge man breake a rynge betwene him & a mayde doth not

[62] Ibid., C1v.
[63] Ibid., A7r.
[64] Ibid., A5v.
[65] Ibid., B7v-8r.

the facte testyfye and make a presumpcyon to all men, that hys hart meant as hys wordes spake.'⁶⁶ Furthermore, the sacraments are testimonies: Christ used the elements of bread and wine to signify 'the couenaunt of hys bodye and bloud.'⁶⁷ The Eucharist is a memorial of God's 'euerlastyng testament and mercyfull Promysse' that Christ's blood 'was shedde for vs, for the remyssyon of our Synnes.'⁶⁸

Alongside this commemoration of God's action is the indication of how humans ought to believe and act. This is particularly clear in baptism, an initiation into Christ's Church, 'wherby we be bound to beleue in Chryst & in the father thorow hym for the remissyon of sinnes & to kepe the law of Chryst to loue e[a]ch other as he loued vs.' Tyndale succinctly summarised its reciprocal, conditional nature, including its sanction: 'by baptysme we be bound to god & god to vs, and the bond and seale of the couenaunt is wryten in our fleshe by whych seale or wryting God chalengeth fayth and loue vnder paine of iust dampnacyon.'⁶⁹ The sign is sufficiently important, and imposes such obligation, that the baptised apostate or unbeliever is under 'greatter dampnacyon [. . .] by the reason of the sygne and ba[d]ge and of there owne consent, graunt and promysse' which gives God 'more ryght to callynge of them the kepyng of hys law.'⁷⁰ As with circumcision, 'they baptysed in the flesh & not in the hart hath no part in [Christ's] bloud.'⁷¹ We must in practice 'beleue and cleaue fast to the profession of our baptysme.'⁷²

The Eucharist, Tyndale explained, takes the place of the Passover as baptism replaces circumcision.⁷³ It is used to rehearse the 'couenaunt and testament.'⁷⁴ As well as proclaiming the atonement

---

⁶⁶ Ibid., B8v.
⁶⁷ Ibid., B4v.
⁶⁸ Ibid., B3v.
⁶⁹ Ibid., A5v.
⁷⁰ Ibid., B5r.
⁷¹ Ibid., A6r.
⁷² Ibid., B3r.
⁷³ Ibid., A8v.
⁷⁴ Ibid., C5v.

the Eucharist marks the culmination of repentance and therefore, claimed Tyndale, it pronounces absolution. The penitent participant has asked God's forgiveness, satisfied his neighbours and submitted himself to the discipline of the congregation.[75] Compared to the terms of the Mosaic covenant Christians are 'partakers of a more easy & kynde testamente, vnder w[hich] yf you synne thorowe fragylyte[,] you shalbe warned louingli & receyued to merci yf you wyl turne agayne and amende.'[76] The participant makes a resolution to godliness, offers thanksgiving and renews his obligations:

> Howe muche he is bounden for Chrystes sake to loue hys neyghbour, to helpe hys neade, and to beare hys infyrmitye, and to forgeue hym if he haue offended and desyre forgeuenes, promysyng to amende, where vnto Chryste byndeth all that wyll be partakers of hys Bloude.[77]

Hence Tyndale's paraphrase of Christ's words of institution emphasises their significance for the mutual covenant:

> Take bread and wyne and reherse the couenaunt and testament ouer them[.] How that my body was broken and mi bloud shed for them & the[n] geue[n] [to] them the people to eate and drynke, to be a sygne an earneste and the seal of the testament, and cry vppon them withowt sesing to beleue in me only for remyssyon of sinnes, & not to dispraue how weak so euer they be, only yf they hange on me & desyre powre to kepe the lawe after my doctryne and ensample of my lyfe and do morne & be sory by cause they can not do that good thynge whych they wold.[78]

---

[75] Ibid., B4r-v.
[76] Ibid., C4r-v.
[77] Ibid., B5v.
[78] Ibid., C5v-6r.

The beneficiaries of atonement, those for whom 'the body was geuen to death & the bloud shed,' were limited to those who continue in faith and obedience to the law, who, in comparison to the numbers who 'loue not the law,' are 'very fewe [. . .] euen that lytle Flocke that gaue them selues whollye to followe Chryst.'[79] Unworthy reception for Tyndale meant participation without 'forsakyng the olde luste of his flesh' or 'porposynge to folowe chryst,' an action which counts the 'bloude of the testamente [. . .] as an vnholye thing.'[80] It demonstrates blasphemous contempt for the significance of the sacrament.

Alongside this particularly covenantal conception of the sacraments Tyndale repeatedly implied that they were not instruments of grace, emphasising that only cognisance of their signification was beneficial. Without understanding the sacraments 'be clene vnprofitable.' They are 'bokys of storyes only and that ther is none other vertu in them then to [testify] the couenauntes and promysses made in chrysts bloud.'[81] It is quite possible to be saved without sacraments, by preaching only, yet the daily rehearsal of the covenant in the Eucharist is a powerful *aide-mémoire*.[82] The sacrament properly understood from John 6 is but 'a confyrmacion to weake conscyences,' yet it is 'in no wyse to be dyspysed how beyt many haue lyued by fayth in the wyldernes which in 20. 30. or 40. yers haue not receyued the sacrament.'[83] In view of this Zürich-style sacramental theology it is no surprise to find the later Tyndale rejecting the Lutheran understanding of Christ's presence in the Eucharist as tantamount to transubstantiation.[84]

[79] Ibid., C2v-3r.
[80] Ibid., C6r.
[81] Ibid., B5r.
[82] Ibid., B6r-v.
[83] Ibid., D1r-v.
[84] Ibid., C7v-8r, see also E6v-7r. Tyndale's dismissal of corporal presence militated against his own plea to John Frith not to 'meddle' with a divisive issue amongst evangelicals: Tyndale, *Treatises*, liii-liv. This might explain why the *Briefe Declaration* was not immediately printed.

Although Tyndale had shared much of Luther's sacramental theology in the 1520s, his views developed in 1529–30 towards the Zürich position as his covenantal ideas assumed centre-stage. His understanding progressed in the 1530s so that, while he could conceivably have been comfortable with Bullinger's later doctrine, he may have found the contemporary Zürich position restrictive. He affirmed Zwingli's views on the sacrament as a memorial together with a complex sense of the sacraments as having a power for the believer which excelled acts of historical remembrance. This suggests the residual effect of late-medieval or Lutheran influences earlier in Tyndale's life in spite of his theoretical exclusion of sacramental instrumentality.

Miles Coverdale

The earliest indication of Coverdale's Reformed sacramental theology dates from early 1528, from the recantation of Thomas Topley, a friar who had read *Wyclif's Wicket*. Initially Topley was troubled by the book 'which did make the Sacrament of Christes body, in forme of bread, but a remembraunce of Christes Passion.' On hearing Coverdale preach, however, Topley's 'mynde was sore withdrawen from that blessed Sacrament, in so much that I tooke it then but for the remembraunce of Christes body.'[85] This deposition suggests that Coverdale had abandoned the physical presence of Christ in the Eucharist to adopt a commemorative view.

Direct evidence of Coverdale's sacramental theology is scarce before the 1540s. In view of his rejection of the physical presence of Christ and his translation of Bullinger's *Christen state of matrimonye* around 1528, Coverdale was arguably more theologically Reformed than Tyndale when they collaborated in 1529.[86] None of Coverdale's

---

[85] John Foxe, *AM* [1570] (Sheffield: HRI Online Publications, 2011), 8:1228; see also Anne Hudson, *The Premature Reformation: Wycliffite Texts and Lollard History* (Oxford: OUP, 1988), 481.

[86] I have suggested that Tyndale's concept of covenant influenced Coverdale's.

continental translations executed in the 1530s were concerned with sacramental theology, although *The original and sprynge of all sectes and orders by whome, wha[n] or w[h]ere they beganne* (1537) might be suggestive. This catalogue included some sects which 'are not farre from Christ nor his fayth yet the moost parte (specyally of them that be brought in by the B. of Rome) are no lesse contrary vnto Christ, then were the false prophetes in tymes past.'[87] Neither the Lutherans nor the Reformed were included as 'sects,' but Coverdale quietly approved Hussite utraquism for its dissent from Rome and he praised the Waldensians: 'They haue no image at all, they knele not afore them nor pray to them. They say the sacrament ought not be worshipped, but Christ at the ryghthand of hys father, & God in sprete & truth.'[88] A passing reference was made to baptism in Coverdale's prologue to *A goodly treatise of faith, hope, and charitie* (1537), stating that 'it is not ynough to be baptysed' and to know the articles of faith which 'a Christian is bounde to beleue & to know' if these are not practised in godly living.[89] These clues from the 1530s are limited but they are consistent with a broadly Reformed view.

Coverdale's residence in Strassburg overlapped from 1540 to 1542 with that of Calvin, who at that time was still hoping for reconciliation with the Lutherans on the Eucharist. However, in

---

It is equally possible that Coverdale's sacramental theology and awareness of Bullinger's work made an impression on Tyndale. Euler suggests that Coverdale actually exaggerated the extent of Bullinger's covenant concept in his doctrine of marriage by translating not only *bundt* but also *vereinigung* (union) and *verkumnuß* (coming together) as 'covenant': Carrie Euler, *Couriers of the Gospel: England and Zürich 1531–1558* (Zurich: TVZ, 2006), 145.

[87] Miles Coverdale, *The original and sprynge of all sectes and orders by whome, wha[n] or w[h]ere they beganne. Translated out of Hye Dutch in Englysh* (Southwarke: James Nicolson for Jhon Gough, 1537; RSTC 18849), +2r.

[88] Ibid., 47v-48r.

[89] Miles Coverdale, *A goodly treatise of faith, hope, and charite necessary for all Christen men to know and to exercyse themselues therein translated into Englyshe* (Southwark: James Nicolson, 1537; RSTC 24219.5), A1v.

1540–41 Coverdale's writings exhibited a greater affinity with the sacramental theology of Zürich. Commenting on Acts 2:37–41 in his *Fruitfull lessons, vpon the passion, buriall, resurrection, ascension, and of the sending of the holy Ghost* (1540), Coverdale gave directions on 'how faithfull beleeuers vse themselues in the outward Sacraments.' The prior 'inspiration of the holy Ghost in theyr hearts' was emphasised first of all, something which seems not to be a part of Tyndale's presentation. This direct work of the Spirit was the means of hearing 'the eternall word preached, giuing credite vnto it, & gladly receiuing it.'[90] Coverdale evidently recognised that the sacraments could therefore seem superfluous since 'without the presence of Gods spirite vnprofitable is the worde preached, vnprofitable are the Sacraments ministred.'[91] Nonetheless, like Zwingli, he stressed that believers 'doo not afterward despise the outward Sacraments, which GOD hath instituted for the welfare of his Church: but vse the same with all obedience, good will and reuerence.' The sacraments were for mankind's benefit and would be embraced gladly by true believers. Indeed, only those with true faith could profit from them; others would be hurt by their use.[92]

Believers know that baptism is an external washing which has no expiatory value, yet they respect the wisdom of Christ's institution of 'outward tokens' which are, firstly, wrote Coverdale, 'to couple and knit together the members of his holy Church, in obedience and loue one towards another, whereby they knowing one another among themselues, might by such exteriour things, stirre and prouoke one another to loue and godlynesse.'[93] The congregation is the locus of blessing; grace is not received in the sacraments. As well as signs of

---

[90] Miles Coverdale, *Fruitfull Lessons, vpon the Passion, Buriall, Resurrection, Ascension, and of the sending of the Holy Ghost gathered out of the foure euangelists: with a plaine exposition of the same* (London: Thomas Scarlet, 1593; RSTC 5891), Oo3r.
[91] Ibid., Qq3r.
[92] Ibid., Oo3r.
[93] Ibid., Oo3v.

love amongst the brethren and spurs to love and godliness, sacraments are, secondly, 'euidences of the promise & grace of God, which they after a visible and palpable manner, do set forth declare, and represent vnto vs.'[94] Thus the sacraments have a practical function among believers by virtue of what they signify about God. Following Zwingli, Coverdale claimed that they are used most devoutly and reverently by those who are already 'certified and assured of the gracious fauour of God.'[95]

Coverdale expounded four things which proceed from faith in Christ from Acts 2:42: apostolic doctrine, fellowship amongst believers, the breaking of bread, and prayer. The third of these was 'the token of the new and everlasting covenant, which Christ upon the cross confirmed with his body and blood.'[96] Bread and wine were ideal symbols due to their traditional significance:

> And euen from the beginning of the world, it hath alw[a]yes beene the vse among men, that with breade and wine, they haue made and confirmed great friendshippe and league: And euen so Christ with the distributing of the bread among his disciples, would establish an euerlasting friendship with them.[97]

The covenantal friendship and league established by Christ was signified in the Eucharist, 'a joyful and glorious memorial of Christ's death,' marked with thanksgiving.[98] Coverdale listed the various purposes of such 'tokens':

---

[94] Ibid.
[95] Ibid.
[96] Miles Coverdale, *Writings and Translations of Myles Coverdale, Bishop of Exeter*, ed. G. Pearson, PS (Cambridge: CUP, 1844), 418. The corresponding page is missing from the 1593 edition.
[97] Coverdale, *Fruitfull Lessons*, Qq2v.
[98] Coverdale, *Writings*, 418.

to signifie and represent vnto vs high and greate things, to gather together and vnite the Church, that beeing dispearsed euerie where ouer the face of the whole earth, might gather together into one communion and fellowshippe in Christ, and bee made partakers of his promises, and inioye those comfortable blessings which hee hath promised from the beginning, namely, such as bee faithfull and true beleeuers, and that the exteriour and outwarde sense, might from all corporall thinges bee withdrawen to that which is spirituall.[99]

In commemorating the covenant the Church is united in its enjoyment of participation in Christ and his promised benefits. Among those things signified are the 'renewal' of the divine promise and the fellowship of the Church. The outward senses are presented with these significations and are consequently freed from worldly preoccupations for contemplation of the spiritual. Coverdale wrote that Christ had instituted the Eucharist

> that over and besides faith, which inwardly liveth in the heart, the outward senses also might have somewhat to stir and draw them unto that, which faith inwardly considereth and looketh upon.[100]

Here Coverdale's exposition resembles Zwingli's teaching in *Expositio Fidei* about sacraments reclaiming the senses from worldly desires. Coverdale's treatise was based on one by Zwingli so it is unsurprising to find it largely in agreement with Zürich theology. At the end of the section the covenantal significance of the Eucharist was reiterated by Coverdale, drawing on the parallels with Old Testament ceremonies:

---

[99] Coverdale, *Fruitfull Lessons*, Qq1v.
[100] Coverdale, *Writings*, 418.

> To the intent then that this excellent and worthie propitiation and sacrifice should not [be] out of theyr eyes and heartes, he added visible signes, not bare signes, but seales of his couenant (as was the Circumcision and Passah [Passover]) and common tokens of loue and friendshippe amongst men, euen bread and wine, which haue no bloud, to declare that all bloud for sinne is onely in Iesus Christ, Christs minde was also, in one bodie to couple and knit together in one bodie the whole multitude of his Church.[101]

Coverdale is perfectly consistent with Zwingli in denying that sacraments are 'bare signes' and in affirming their function in displaying amity between the brethren.

Coverdale's *Confutacion of that treatise, which one Iohn Standish made agaynst the protestacion of D. Barnes* (1541) made occasional reference to the sacraments. Since Barnes had held to the physical presence of Christ in the Eucharist, Coverdale was obviously reluctant to discuss the subject at length, brushing Barnes' understanding aside with the general exoneration that Barnes 'wold haue the sacrament rightly vsed and acording to holy scripture.'[102] In a discussion of 1 Corinthians 11 Coverdale outlined the proper preparation for the Eucharist, beginning with detailed self-examination against the standards of God's commandments,

> and by occasion therof haue hartely [ac]knowleged and confessed oure synnes[,] beynge sory and penitent for them[,] beleuynge stedfastly in the promises of god[,] receaued the absolucion of his worde[,] entred in to true repentaunce and ernest amendment of oure liuinge[,] beinge reconciled and

---

[101] Coverdale, *Fruitfull Lessons*, Qq2r-v.
[102] Miles Coverdale, *A confutacion of that treatise, which one Iohn Standish made agaynst the Protestacion of D. Barnes in the yeare. M.D.XI. wherin, the Holy Scriptures (peruerted and wrested in his sayd treatise) are restored to their owne true vnderstonding agayne* (Zurich: C. Froschauer, 1541; RSTC 5888), K5r.

at one with all men purposinge without fayle so to contynue till oure lyfes ende[.] Then to come and suppe with the lorde.[103]

The supper at the Lord's Table assumed that the participant had already completed the process of repentance and received absolution of sin from God's word. The meal should be shared only by the faithful, who were committed to God, to godliness, and to one another.

If the Eucharist spoke of the commitment and godly resolve of communicants, baptism had been the call to realise it. Baptism was given, not to describe a present state, but 'to the intent that we shulde now [walk] in a new life.' It is the ordination, choice and call of God in baptism, yet on humanity's part baptism is 'our profession[,] the life that we haue promised and taken us to at the font stone[,] euen the holy couenaunt and appoyntment that we haue made with the eternall god.'[104] Baptism is an initiation into that life to which God calls his people and that his people themselves enter into. This was not a profession of faith but a profession of the life of the covenant. Coverdale, Barnes, and Standish were, at least, united in their 'abhorrence' of 'the Anabaptistes heresie concerning the bapti[s]me of infauntes.'[105]

Coverdale's understanding of the sacraments at this time was influenced by Bullinger with whom he corresponded and whose account of salvation history he translated as *The olde fayth* (1541). As the first continental covenant text translated into English it is important to appreciate how Bullinger's argument would have reinforced Coverdale's figurative understanding of sacraments as memorials, aids for the weak, and symbols of Church unity. Bullinger explained that both the covenant of circumcision and the Passover were figures of salvation by faith in Christ to come. Circumcision

---

[103] Ibid., D8r.
[104] Ibid., H9r.
[105] Ibid., C6r.

'serueth more to the confirmacion of oure holy christen faith then to the mayntenaunce of the Jewish ceremonyes.'[106] Likewise, the Hebrews in Egypt were saved 'for the bloudes sake of the blessed sede that was promised,' 'oure Easter lambe & passeouer,' rather than the 'bloud of beastes.' Their deliverance was 'a figure of the true redempcion [. . .] thorow Jesus Christe.'[107]

According to Bullinger, God gave signs to 'set the cause of Jesus Christ clearly afore the eyes of the people,' as with the 'lambe of the Passeover' or the 'serpent in the wildernesse.' Those who saw it 'had a token of health' in the sign, but the believer 'was not made whole by the outward thynge whiche he sawe.' Plainly 'the outward beholdynge of the brazen serpent saued not them that were poisoned.'[108] Abraham had become 'gods frende and iustified or made righteous' many years before he was outwardly circumcised.[109] Faith was the essential component in both cases. Bullinger described the rites of the Jews as

> sacramentes and tokens of heauenly inuisible good thynges and were not the heauenly riches themselues. Wherfore they nether serued nor pleased God that used and did soche seruyce without fayth and lyftinge up of the mynde. But they that put their trust in God cleuynge onely unto hym & lifting up their hertes higher and remayned not in the visible thynge[,] those pleased God.[110]

Bullinger's emphasis on engagement with the heart and mind rather than contemplation of the visible suggests that the heavenly

---

[106] Heinrich Bullinger, *The Olde Fayth, an euydent probation out of the Holy Scripture, that the Christen Fayth (which is the right true, old & undoubted faith, hath endured sens the beginnyng of the worlde)*, trans. M. Coverdale (Antwerp?: Thomas Vautroullier, 1541; RSTC 4070.5), C3r.
[107] Ibid., C5r, see also G3r.
[108] Ibid., D1r.
[109] Ibid., C2v.
[110] Ibid., D1v-2r.

riches are 'not in the visible thynge.' The 'outwarde visyble and corporall thynge' could not serve God who is a spirit. Rather, his people 'shulde lift up their myndes aboue the same [the sacrament] to the spirituall thynges[,] pondrynge the mercy of God.' According to Bullinger, 'faithfull consideracion (whiche is the true beleue)' pleases God and, since it was helped by the Jewish sacraments, their performance pleased God too, 'not for the letters sake but by reason of the sprete.'[111] The idea that tokens are aids in humanity's weakness is also articulated in Bullinger's text. Weak mankind is more capable of understanding 'spirituall heauenly thynges [. . .] whan they are shewed unto it by corporall visible thynges.' Since Christ's himself has now been revealed, the outward sacraments of the Mosaic Law are obsolete.[112] These ideas were applied to the New Testament sacraments near the end of Bullinger's book:

> With suche sacramentes thorow outward visible fourmes (for our infirmities sake) pleased it the lord to shew & set before our eyes his hevenly & invisible grace: not that we shuld continue still hanginge in the visible thing but that we shulde lyft up our myndes & with a true beleue to holde fast[,] to prynte sure in oure myndes[,] to worshippe[,] and to enioye the thinges that faith sheweth us by the outward sacraments. With these outward sacraments also hath it pleased him to open[,] declare and shewe unto us his grace and louynge kyndnesse.[113]

The sacraments point the mind to Christ, signifying that God has given himself wholly to his people. Faith, not the sacraments, is God's instrument of grace: 'For the outward enioyeng of the sacramentes of it selfe alone doth not reconcile us with God: but yf

---

[111] Ibid., D2v.
[112] Ibid., D4r.
[113] Ibid., G5r.

they be used with fayth than (as S. Peter saieth. Act. xv.) thorow faith doth God purifye the hertes.'[114] If the sacraments occasion the contemplation of God, their purpose is twofold: they are a 'remembraunce' of God's blessings and they gather together believers 'to marke us in hys churche and people & to put us in remembraunce of oure dewty[,] how we are one body together and ought to applye our selues to all righteousnsse.'[115]

Coverdale's work on Bullinger's text would have reinforced the Zwinglian themes in his sacramental theology, but his acceptance of Zürich theology was not, or rather, did not remain, exclusive. At the end of 1542 Coverdale briefly visited his brother-in-law John MacAlpine who had become a chaplain to King Christian III of Denmark and a professor of theology at Copenhagen. Coverdale was sufficiently interested in Denmark's Lutheran Reformation to produce in 1544 *The Order that the Church and Congregation of Christ in Denmark, and in many places, countries and cities of Germany, doth use*.[116] However, the order concentrated upon the practical administration of the sacraments rather than sacramental theology, so when Coverdale commended it as 'not varying from the moste wholsome doctrine' he seems to be trying to present the Lutheran practices as agreeing with his own position.[117]

The manner of feeding on Christ was construed realistically in *The Order*. It stated that 'we at his supper in the Sacrament, shoulde

[114] Ibid.

[115] Ibid.

[116] Miles Coverdale, "The Order that the Churche and Congregacion of Christe in Denmarke [...] doth vse," in John Calvin, *A Faythfull and Moost Godlye Treatyse Concernyng the Most Sacred Sacrament of the Blessed Body and Bloude of Our Sauioure Chryst*, ed. M. Coverdale (London: John Day for William Seres?, 1548; RSTC 4411), E3r-F8v. The first edition of *The Order* was burnt at Paul's Cross in 1546. See Esther Hildebrandt, "A Study of the English Protestant Exiles in Northern Switzerland and Strasbourg 1539–47, and Their Role in the English Reformation," PhD diss. (University of Durham, 1982), 58; David Daniell, "Coverdale, Miles (1488–1569)," *ODNB* (Oxford: OUP, 2004).

[117] Coverdale, "Denmarke," E3v.

eate his very body and drynke his very bloude,'[118] which are in 'the Sacramente in fourme of breade [. . .] also in the fourme of wyne.' They 'nouryshed and fedde our soules' with 'spiritual and heauenly foode.'[119] This Lutheran, corporal language was balanced with a description of the Eucharist as 'a sacramente of continuall thankfulnesse, of daylye remembraunce and of charitable vnyte,'[120] which would be easier to reconcile with Coverdale's Reformed views. The petition at baptism also fitted with it being a sign of God's promise, the sign of baptism following regeneration itself: 'graunt to this childe the gyfte of fayth, wherin thou wylt seale and assure his hert in the holy gost, according to the promes of thy sonne, that the inward regeneracion of the spirite may be truely represented by the outwarde baptysme.'[121] Thus Coverdale's presentation of the Danish Order highlights the emergence of common evangelical practices rather than Coverdale's attraction to Lutheran sacramental theology. Later, in 1555, he would decline preferment by the Danish king.

Coverdale's interest in Lutheran Denmark may be explained by his engagement with Calvin's work, particularly Calvin's *Short Treatise on the Lord's Supper* (1541) which was intended as a formulation that Luther might approve. Calvin's eirenic account of the Eucharist controversy might have persuaded Coverdale to reconsider his position:

> When Luther began to teach, he regarded the matter of the Supper in such a way, that, with respect to the corporal presence of Christ, he appeared ready to leave it as the world generally conceived it. For while condemning transubstantiation,

---

[118] Ibid., E6v.

[119] Ibid., E8v-F1r; see Cranmer's similar exhortation in the second Book of Common Prayer: *The Two Liturgies, A.D. 1549, and A.D. 1552: with other documents set forth by authority in the reign of King Edward VI*, ed. J. Ketley, PS (Cambridge: CUP, 1844), 275.

[120] Coverdale, "Denmarke," F1r.

[121] Ibid., F2r.

he said that the bread was the body of Christ, insofar as it was united with him. [. . .] On the other hand, there arose Zwingli and Œcolampadius, who [. . .] thought it wrong to dissimulate; since this view implied an execrable idolatry, in that Jesus Christ was adored as if enclosed under the bread. Now because it was very difficult to remove this opinion, rooted so long in the hearts of men, they applied all their mind to decry it [. . .]. While they were absorbed with this point, they forgot to define what is the presence of Christ in the Supper in which one ought to believe, and what communication of his body and blood one there received.[122]

How early Coverdale read this treatise is unknown. He still hoped to visit Zürich in mid-1542, and according to J. F. Mozley, he was shocked by Luther's violent attack on the eucharistic theology of Zwingli and Œcolampadius in 1544.[123] However, his work on the Danish Order is, perhaps, indicative of a growing conviction that the Zwinglian position needed to be recast in a less polemical form. He wrote affectionately to Calvin in March 1548, enclosing his own translations (presumably into Latin) of the new English Order of Holy Communion, which appeared to advance an instrumental understanding of the Eucharist: Christ 'doth vouchesaufe in a Sacrament and misterye, to geue us his sayd body and bloud spiritually, to fede and drynke upon.'[124] Coverdale's adoption of Calvin's position was confirmed in 1548 by his publication of Thomas Broke's translation of the *Short Treatise*.[125]

---

[122] John Calvin, "Short Treatise on the Lord's Supper (1541)," in *Calvin: Theological Treatises*, ed. J. Reid, Vol. 22 (London: SCM, 1954), 164–65.

[123] J. F. Mozley, *Coverdale and His Bibles* (London: Lutterworth, 1953), 10.

[124] Miles Coverdale, *Remains of Myles Coverdale, Bishop of Exeter*, ed. G. Pearson, PS (Cambridge: CUP, 1846), 525; *The Order of the Communion* (London: Richard Grafton, 1548; RSTC 16458.3), A4r.

[125] John Calvin, *A faythfull and moost godlye treatyse concernyng the Most Sacred Sacrament of the Blessed Body and Bloude of our Sauioure Chryst*, trans. T. Broke, ed. M. Coverdale (London: John Day for William Seres?, 1548; RSTC 4411).

Coverdale retained Broke's preface to *A faythfull and moost godlye treatyse concernyng the most sacred Sacrament of the blessed body and bloude of our sauioure Chryst* (1548), adding only a short commendation. Broke attacked the 'natural, essencial, and real presence' of Christ advanced by traditionalists and Lutherans.[126] Christ did not mean 'that he had chaunged the nature of bread into the nature of fleshe.'[127] Rather, the elements represent 'the misterie of the participation you haue in me by fayth.' The Eucharist was a commemoration and sign of 'communion' with Christ.[128] It was also a confirmation of grace, although Broke would not go so far as to 'deny it to be possible for any man to tarye in Christe or to haue Christe taryinge in hym vnlesse he receyue these visible sacramentes or signes.' Broke clarified:

> No doubte (christian reader) the belefe & truste in Christe, is the mea[n]e wherby Christ taryeth in vs and we in hym. But thys beliefe and trust are established and confirmed by the vse of these visi[b]le signes. As thys beliefe and truste therfore, are necessarye to the abydynge in Chryst: so is the vse of these holye Sacramentes also, for that it is the establyshment and confirmyng of the sayd beleue and trust. To all them therfore to whom this beleue and trust are necessarie: are these sacred Sacramentes also necessary.[129]

Clearly Coverdale had endorsed the symbolic instrumentalist understanding of the sacraments propounded by Calvin.[130] Its

[126] Ibid., A4v.
[127] Ibid., A4r.
[128] Ibid., A5r.
[129] Ibid., B1r-v.
[130] E.g., Ibid., B6r; see Gerrish, *Grace and Gratitude*, 167. I suggest that Celia Hughes is mistaken as to the general direction of Coverdale's development. He was not moving away from Luther but towards him, inasmuch as he was moving from the Zürich position towards Calvin's. See Hughes, "Coverdale," 103–5.

relation to the concept of covenant in Calvin's theology, although hardly discussed in this particular treatise, would have been consistent with Coverdale's earlier views, which he would have found no cause to abandon. His handful of later writings did not deal with the sacraments.

John Hooper

John Foxe did not specify the subject upon which Bishop Gardiner sought to instruct Hooper during their 'conference of learning' in 1539. He did imply that Richard Smith's dislike of Hooper at that time concerned the pronouncements of the Six Articles which enforced, among other things, belief in transubstantiation and communion in one kind.[131] Hooper was reading voraciously books by Zwingli and Bullinger so there is ample ground to suppose that he had rejected the physical presence of Christ in the Eucharist by 1539, especially when his first publication, in 1547, was a reaction to Gardiner's *A Detection of the Devil's Sophistrie, wherwith he robbeth the unlearned people, of the true byleef, in the most blessed Sacrament of the aulter* (1546).[132]

The Zürichers' formulation of the concept of covenant was the basis for Hooper's view of the sacraments.[133] His refutation of Gardiner, *An Answer vnto my lord of wynthesters booke*, was published at Zürich in September 1547.[134] It constituted his most extensive exposition of sacramental theology. The signature Zwinglian argument

[131] Foxe, *AM* [1583], 11:1526; Alison Dalton, "John Hooper and His Networks: a study of change in Reformation England," DPhil diss. (University of Oxford, 2008), 14.

[132] Stephen Gardiner, *A Detection of the Deuils Sophistrie wherwith he robbeth the vnlearned people, of the true byleef, in the Most Blessed Sacrament of the Aulter* (London: Ihon Herforde, 1546; RSTC 11591.3).

[133] Trueman notes that the 'idea of a bilateral arrangement between God and man is also central to Hooper's sacramental theology, indicating the Reformed roots of his theology': Trueman, *Luther's Legacy*, 213n.

[134] Hooper, *Wynthester*.

against Christ's physical presence in the Eucharist, that Christ's human body was at God's right hand and therefore could not be in the elements, was made enthusiastically by Hooper. He mocked the notion that Christ would repeatedly descend 'at the commanudement of euery pryst when he speakyth these wordes *Hoc est corpus meum.*' Christ would return corporally only at the end of the world, so Hooper enjoined his readers to 'belyue Chrystes body to be really and corporally in the sacrament when tho[u] seist him there with thy corporall yeies and not before.'[135] Like Zwingli, Hooper held that baptism and the Eucharist 'in effect be one' with circumcision and the Passover, representing Christ's promise unto Christ's Church; a correct understanding of one ensures a correct understanding of both.[136] Hooper used the word '*foederis*' (covenant) of circumcision, in the same way that Noah's rainbow was 'a signe of the couenant betwen god and him.'[137] The sacraments provide opportunities for the 'exercyse'—rather than strengthening—of faith and, departing from Zwingli's view, for 'godly conuersacion' with Christ, but Hooper clarified that this was 'not bodely, yet in spryt.' The physical consumption of Christ is excluded by the fact that we eat him spiritually in the same way as Old Testament believers did prior to his Incarnation.[138]

These opportunities to exercise faith stemmed from the institution of sacraments as 'externall signes' which 'sett before oure yeis the benefitz of gods mercy dew unto oure faith in Christ.' In this respect they are comparable to 'seals and confirmacions of godes promises where he warrantyd and assuryd his churche openlye that he would be her god, and she to be his spouse for euer.'[139] Their reference to the divine-human relationship is clear, including the condition of faith. The covenantal language of sealing and confirming was explained by Hooper in terms of the sealing of 'bargayns, exchanges, purcheses

---

[135] Ibid., B4v, see also K3v-4r.
[136] Ibid., D4v, see also O1v, Q1r.
[137] Ibid., O3r, see also P1v.
[138] Ibid., E1r.
[139] Ibid., D4v-E1r.

an[d] contractes.' 'These wrtingz and seales makith not the bargaine,' wrote Hooper. Rather, the seal is 'awytnis of souch couenantes as hath ben agreyd upon betwen the booth parthes [parties].'[140]

Hooper's analogy between sacraments and seals did not imply that the sacraments were 'a bare signe and token of [Christ's] death only.' There was a great difference between the royal arms depicted in stained glass and a prince's seal on a charter containing 'the princes right and title that he hathe unto his Realme.'[141] Following Bullinger, Hooper wrote that the prince's seal would be esteemed as much as the charter which it confirmed, 'thowghe the mater of the seale be nothing but wax.' Owing to its function, the seal commands respect; contempt of the seal is tantamount to treason against the prince himself.[142] Hooper also followed Zwingli and Bullinger in his formulation of the analogy of the sun and sunlight:

> as the sone in heauen dooth extend downe his beames, and ligthyn the hearthe. So dooth Christes body, by fayth in sprit, expulse all darknis and sinne out of the hart mouith not bodely, but is euery where, where faythe is spiritually, an at one tyme.[143]

Just as sunbeams are present though the sun is absent, so Christ is spiritually present while being physically absent in heaven.[144]

---

[140] Ibid., F2v; see also D. G. Newcombe, *John Hooper: Tudor Bishop and Martyr* (Oxford: Davenant Press, 2009), 77.

[141] Hooper, *Wynthester*, O3v.

[142] Ibid.; see Heinrich Bullinger, *The Decades of Henry Bullinger*, ed. T. Harding, 5 vols. PS (Cambridge: CUP, 1849–52), v/6:270.

[143] Hooper, *Wynthester*, O4r; see Zwingli, *Account of the Faith*, *LWHZ*, 2:50.

[144] Morris West explains that Calvin and Bucer (to whom Luther may be added) used the same analogy to argue for the believer's participation in Christ's substance on the basis that the sun transmitted its substance in its beams: West, "Hooper [1]," 362; see Calvin, *Institutes* [*LCC*], 1373 (IV. xvii. 12). Bucer's analogy is quoted and discussed in Thomas Cranmer, *Writings and Disputations [...] relative to the Sacrament of the Lord's Supper*, ed. J. Cox, PS (Cambridge: CUP, 1844), 90–91.

According to Hooper, the sacraments are 'tokens' 'because of godes promis and contract made with his churche.'[145] The nature, use and office of a sacrament is 'to shew unto us [o]uttwardly, that the merites of Christ is made oures for the promes sake, which god hath made unto those that belyue.' These sacraments outwardly apply by faith the grace, mercy and benefits of God to the faithful recipient. However, these are not conveyed by the sacraments as if the believer 'were not before assuryd of the same graces and benefites representid by the sacramentes.'[146] The signifier is not the same as that signified: 'as circumsicion was an under signe and cutting away of the fore ffleshe[,] thalliance sign[i]fied by the signe, was the knot and chayne where with all, god and Abraam was co[u]plid to gather as ffrendes thone to be as master, thother as seruaunt.'[147] Clearly that which was signified was the bilateral covenant between God and humanity. The rainbow of Genesis 9 was the 'arke of his allyaunce betwen hym, of the one party, man, and best of the other party.'[148]

The sacraments testify to existing benefits, declaring 'unto the church of Christ' that the faithful recipients truly are 'the people that god hath chosen.' The benefits of Christ's death belong to the believer now. Using Zwingli's favoured metaphor, they are 'a ba[d]gge and open signe of godes ffauour unto us.' The recipients, for their part, 'by this liuery declare our selfes to lyue and dy in his fayth agaynst the deuyll the worold and sinne.'[149] The reciprocal signification was further elucidated by Hooper's insistence that outward participation was of no value apart from an existing relationship with God. The sacrament 'makyth not the unyon peace and concord betwen god and us but it ratifith[,] stablisshyth and confirmyth, the loue and peax that is betwen god and us before.'[150]

---

[145] Hooper, *Wynthester*, P3r.
[146] Ibid., E1v.
[147] Ibid., R2r, see also R3v-4r.
[148] Ibid., P3v.
[149] Ibid., E1v.
[150] Ibid., E2r.

Hooper was keen that the sacraments should be used more often and more reverently, and that participants should be properly instructed: 'he that ys ygnorant of the causes can neuer iudge aright of theffect.' They are 'signes and remembrances' of God's will for his people and, for Hooper, the effect ought to be the study of God's word in Scripture.[151] He speculated that not one in a thousand Christians 'knowith what a sacrament is, more then an Asse. And to souch the sacramentes be not profetable, but damnable.'[152] Only Christians with understanding should be allowed to participate. An inward faith and an outward profession were first of all required 'to acertayne the church, that he is godes ffrende, and reconsilid in Christ.' It would be 'praeposterous,' wrote Hooper, for the sacrament to be administered before this were ascertained, 'lik as if the Kynges maiestis officers, shuld [g]eue his lyuery, unto him that the Kyng neuer ment, to take into his seruise. So to we[a]re, his liuere without profeit.'[153] To partake of the sacraments was to be declared 'the membres of one church. Wear unit[ed] and knyt to gather, made one by one sprit of trewyth.'[154] Conversely, the Church was differentiated from everyone else in declaring itself 'to be deuidid ffrom all other nacions that use not the same sacramentes,' which suggests the exclusivity of the covenant people. This distinction was not, however, to obscure the testimony of God's will in his sacraments.[155]

In baptism 'we ar consecratyd, dedicatid and offeryd unto god, and godes name inuocatid upon us.' It is a mark assuring us of forgiveness received spiritually by faith, which Hooper assumed here would occur before the ceremony, although it was not faith but 'the promesse made unto thy father and his posterite' in Genesis 17 which constituted the basis for baptism.[156] Baptism declared to the

---

[151] Ibid., F3v-4r, see also N2r.
[152] Ibid., G4v.
[153] Ibid., H1r.
[154] Ibid., I1r.
[155] Ibid., P4r-v.
[156] Ibid., E2r-v.

whole Church the 'secret' dwelling of Christ in the heart and stood as a 'record of this loue, amyte, peax, an concord, that is betwen god and hym by Christ.' Thus, it also marked the 'acceptacion of this crystenid person into the comune wealth of his sauid people.'[157]

This signification of entry into the Church was considered so necessary by Hooper that only those people 'thus callid openly into the uisible church and congregacion (except death preuent the act)' were 'appertayning unto god.'[158] His insistence on baptism did not betray a doctrine of baptismal regeneration; it was a measure against those who held the sacrament in contempt as 'not of god.' No faithful Christian should omit to be baptised by a Church-appointed minister, and parents who failed to bring their children for baptism were censured.[159] However, Hooper condemned emergency baptism by midwives because this implied the necessity of the external sacrament for salvation, 'as thowgh his holy sprit could not be caryd by fayth into the penitent and sorowfull consciens except it ryd allwayes in a cheroot [chariot] and externall sacrament.'[160] Hooper, like Bullinger and Calvin, did not deny that the sacrament could be an occasion of grace but, like Bullinger, he was determined to preserve the independence of the Spirit's activity. He was insisting on the necessity of spiritual baptism being proclaimed whenever possible.

Perhaps because Hooper's criticism of midwives appeared to muddle his defence of paedobaptism, he proceeded to reaffirm paedobaptism's covenantal basis. The sacraments must be applied to all those to whom the promise *'Ero deus tuus & seminis tui post te'* (I shall be your God & [the God] of your offspring after you) pertained, including infants of believers. Hooper agreed that baptism signified the salvation of the elect but denied that all the elect received the sign. The elect without the sign certainly included unbaptised infants of believers ('of whois saluacion we may not dout'), while

[157] Ibid., E2v.
[158] Ibid., E2v, cf. P3v-4r.
[159] Ibid., E2v, E3v.
[160] Ibid., E2v-3r.

the infants of infidels could not be excluded with confidence since their destination was unknown.¹⁶¹ Hooper's treatment of election as a mystery is reminiscent of Bullinger's.¹⁶²

The delay between God's promise in Genesis 12 and the institution of circumcision in Genesis 17 indicated to Hooper that the sacraments were not the giving but the confirmation of God's promise to mankind. Abraham received the sacrament already assured of God, so he did not seek God in the sign. The precedence of faith over sacrament meant that the parents of a 'specheles infant' were 'bo[u]nd to [g]eue accompt of his fayt[h], before he be Christenid,' and Hooper claimed confidently that 'Abraam belyuid. Thinfant belyuith, Cornelius belyuid.'¹⁶³ Presumably this was deduced from the promise of Genesis 17.

Christ's words of institution at the Last Supper precluded, for Hooper, any change in the elements at the Eucharist.¹⁶⁴ One of his arguments was that a physical presence would falsify Christ's words, 'for he bid them do it in t[h]e Remembraunce of hym.' The memorial itself could not be the object of remembrance. 'As many men use to remem[b]re aweyghty mater, by alitle ring upon there finger,' the ring had to point to something else: 'If Christes moost honorable body were present corporally in the sacrament it were no nede remembraunce at all, for the thing present, presentith it selfe without thealpe of memory.'¹⁶⁵ However, Hooper positively taught that Christians are 'pertakers of the spirituall graces and communion of Christes body and blud representyd by the breade.' Although 'that gloriouse body of Christe, be in heauen, that this holy and moost honorable sacrament representyth, yet when with

---

¹⁶¹ Ibid., E3r.
¹⁶² See J. Wayne Baker, *Heinrich Bullinger and the Covenant: The Other Reformed Tradition* (Athens, OH: Ohio University Press, 1980), 210.
¹⁶³ Hooper, *Wynthester*, F1r.
¹⁶⁴ On Hooper's confutation of transubstantiation, see Newcombe, *Hooper*, 82–83.
¹⁶⁵ Hooper, *Wynthester*, H1v.

trew penitence we receaue the externall sacrament, faith receauithe theffect of that precious body representyd by the sacrament.'¹⁶⁶ Here Hooper is unusually imprecise regarding whether or not the sacrament is an instrument of grace, so this passage could concur with both Bullinger's and Calvin's views.¹⁶⁷ A similar lack of clarity around the connection between the sacrament and the Spirit's work is evident in Hooper's explanation that

> when the minister delyuerith unto me the thing that is in his poure to delyuer to say the bread and wynne rehersing the wordes of Christes institucion, the holy goost deliuerithe unto my fayth which is mountyd and ascendid into heauen the precious body and bludd of my sauiour Iesus Christ spiritually, and not corporally, so dooth the merites of this precious body in heauen fede my poure wrechid soule upon therthe, and no contradiction or impossibilite for Christes body so to do.¹⁶⁸

The ascent of faith into heaven to feed on Christ is reminiscent of Calvin's description of participation in the 1539 edition of the *Institutes*, but Calvin's view is clearer in Hooper's statement that the mind is not only reassured 'by deuine operacion of godes sprit that his sinnes be for gyuen, but also by thobiect representyd unto thexternall senses.'¹⁶⁹

Eucharistic participation was designed not only to confirm our own union with God but 'to shew the le[a]ge of amyte unto the

---

¹⁶⁶ Ibid., H3v.

¹⁶⁷ This kind of distinction, supporting comparisons with Bullinger and Calvin rather than Zwingli, is lost in Newcombe's generalisation that Hooper's sacramental theology was 'entirely Zwinglian': Newcombe, *Hooper*, 79. Dalton rightly recognises that there was some distinction between Zwingli and Bullinger but implies that it concerned corporal presence rather than the reception of grace: Dalton, "Hooper's Networks," 86n.

¹⁶⁸ Hooper, *Wynthester*, O4r.

¹⁶⁹ Ibid., N4v.

church' and to understand better the meaning of 'communion.' It was a pledge of allegiance to Christ:

> for as all the trew subiectes, sworn to the Kyng by there fayth and alegaynce, ar prest, and redy, where so euer the se the Kynges Baner spleyde, resort ther unto and say, what so euer the Kyng hath to do, or with whom so euer he hath Ennymite with all, I will associat my selfe, to be of this part, tyde what be tyde may, happe well, or woo. Vnto this prince I unit my liefe, and death, the cause. He is my lord, the making good and reason of the cause. I am his sworn subiect fayth yeuen, and mi consciens bound. Therefore to manifest myne obedience and loue, by this baner I procleame liefe and death agaynst his contraries.[170]

Another metaphor Hooper used was the surrendering of the keys of a city to a prince as a sign of obedience.[171] Each individual does this in the Eucharist, which was 'institutyd by Christ, to confirme and manifest oure societie and communion in his body and blud untill he cumme to iudgment.'[172] The effect of reception depended on having a community of fellow believers, so Hooper prohibited 'priuat masse or receauing of the sacrament by one man.' The sick person must receive it in the company of 'souch other as shalbe present at the declaracion of his fayth.'[173] At least three people, including the minister, were required. The prime significance of the Eucharist as being for the congregation is reinforced by Hooper's remark that someone who cannot participate in the congregation (perhaps due to ill-health) is 'nothing the warse Christiane man.'[174]

Hooper's presentation of his sacramental theology in the

[170] Ibid., I1v.
[171] Ibid., P2r-v.
[172] Ibid., M1r.
[173] Ibid., L2v.
[174] Ibid., L3r.

Answer to Gardiner was so thorough that his subsequent writings on the subject could only reiterate what had been stated. The covenantal themes tended to be overshadowed by the pastoral priorities of later works, but having established their place in Hooper's theology, it is not difficult to detect their ongoing influence.

At the end of the *Answer* Hooper defended the Sacramentarianism of Tyndale and Frith and, acknowledging that Luther and Bucer upheld a corporal presence, concluded that faith 'commithe not into the so[u]lle of man because he is lernid.'[175] In Hooper's next work, *A declaration of Christe and of his office* (1547), he referred again to Luther 'who preachyd the gospell of iustificacion noman better yet in the cause of the sacrament he [erreth] concerning the corporall precens of Christes naturall body that there is no man can [err] more.'[176] Apparently Hooper equated the seriousness of Luther's error with that of transubstantiation.

Hooper sought to correct error by reiterating in the *Declaration* a number of his established covenantal ideas about sacraments as 'signes tokens and testimonijs of the promesse.'[177] The mode of reception of Christ in the Eucharist was compared with the Hebrew sacrament of the serpent in the desert (Numbers 21:8–9):

> Not to eat his body, transformid into the form of bred, or in the bred with the bread: under the bread, behind the bred or before the bread, corporally, or bodely substancially, or realli, inuisible, or ani souch wayes as mani men to the great iniurijs of Christes body dooth teach, but as the children of Israel only by fayth eat the body spiritually not yet born, so by faythe dooth the Christianes eat hym now being ascendyd into heauen.[178]

---

[175] Ibid., X3r-v.
[176] John Hooper, *A Declaration of Christe and of His Offyce* (Zurich: Augustyne Fries, 1547; RSTC 13745), C5v.
[177] Ibid., I8v.
[178] Ibid., F8v.

Hooper perceived those who believed in the corporal presence of Christ, both Catholic and Lutheran, to be denying the integrity of the natural, physical body of Christ in heaven. They claimed that the 'trewe body' was in the elements 'and yet lackith all the qualites and quantites of a body.'[179] At the Last Supper Christ had not instituted a corporal presence but 'a memory of the body slayne resuscitatyd, ascendid into heuen and from thense to cum unto iudgment.' By means of spiritually eating and drinking 'that sacrament the promis of god [is] sealyd and confirmid in us.'[180]

Later in the treatise Hooper attacked the doctrine of baptismal regeneration, warning that attribution of the forgiveness of sin to the sign was offensive. Baptism was the mark and declaration of entry into the Church, 'so that externall baptisme was but an inauguracion or externall consecracion of these that first belyuyd and were clensid of there sinne.' Baptism itself causes no additional change in a person.[181] However, 'souch as be baptisyd must remembre, that penenc[e] and fayth presedyd this external signe and in Christ the purgacion was inwardely optaynyd before the externall signe was yeuen.' They are encouraged to reflect on the spiritual benefits of their repentance and faith, 'at the contemplacion of the which faith God purchith [purges] tha soule.'[182] The Spirit appears to work alongside the sacrament here.

Although baptism does not change the state of the person, Hooper wrote that the act of baptism pleases God because he has commanded its administration. All these thoughts were explained with a topical analogy to the accession and coronation of Edward VI a few months earlier:

> Like as the Kynges maiestie that now is: immediatly a[f]ter the deathe of his father was the trewe and legittym[at]e

---

[179] Ibid., H6r-v.
[180] Ibid., G8r-v.
[181] Ibid., I5v. Hooper mentioned in passing that infants should be examined concerning repentance and faith before baptism.
[182] Ibid., I6r.

> Kyng of Inglond, right heyre unto the crowne and receauid his coronacion not to make hym self there by Kyng, but to manifest that the Kyngdom apperteynid unto hym before, he takith the crowne to confirm his right and title, had all inglond sayd nay and by forse contrary unto godes lawes and manns lawes with an exteriour ceremony and pompe crownid ony other man he shuld haue byn an adulterous and wronge King, with all his solemnites and coronation. Thowgh this ceremony confirm and manifest a King in his Kyngdom yet it makith not a King.[183]

The Christian becomes a brother of Christ and heir to eternal life as soon as he believes, regardless of sacramental ratification. Nevertheless, baptism is the 'lyuerye of god [. . .] which no Christiane shuld neglect.'[184] Just as it was possible for a traitor to be crowned, so an infidel could be baptised invalidly.[185]

The last of Hooper's Zürich treatises, *A declaration of the ten holy commaundementes of allmygthye God* (1548), presented more starkly than before the human promise signified in the sacraments. Hooper warned against failure to perform

> the thing they promes in Godes name by ony othe or vow made according to the law of God, whether it be betwene man and God as in the holie Sacrament of Baptisme and the holie super of the lord where as we swere and promes to lyeue after his will and pleasure.[186]

The sacraments were humanity's oath to God, promising obedience. It was similar to binding oneself 'to ony condicions or

---

[183] Ibid., I6v-7r.
[184] Ibid., I7v.
[185] Ibid., I8r.
[186] John Hooper, *A Declaration of the Ten Holy Commaundementes of Allmygthye God* (Zurich: Augustin Fries, 1548; RSTC 13746), 96.

promeses by the inuocation of Godes name.' Defaulting on such a vow brought down 'not only the law of God but also the law of man' in retribution.[187]

As well as stating this God-ward action, Hooper continued to give priority to the human-ward confirmation and testimony of God's promise. God had given various signs to assure people of his promise to help the good and punish the bad. Hooper cited the Flood and the Ark (Genesis 6–8); the rescue of Lot from the destruction of Sodom and Gomorrah (Genesis 19); the Exodus from Egypt and entry into the Promised Land (Exodus 12; Joshua 3–4), and the preservation of Joshua and Caleb (Numbers 13–14). God's provisions for the flowers of the field and the birds of the air (Matthew 6:26–30) were 'seales and confyrmations of Godes promisis.'[188] These analogies help to clarify Hooper's understanding of the dominical sacraments as tangible representations of God's commitment to humanity.

Just as the Bible contains 'that we ar bound to do the workes that God commaundithe vs to do,' and the addition of human works robs the Scriptures, so, wrote Hooper, 'those that attribute more then is dewe or lesse then is dew vnto the holie Sacramentes institutyd by Christ committithe sacrilege.' Some add too much by asserting the sacraments to be a means of grace; others take too much by reducing them to mere signs differentiating the Church from outsiders, like the gowns of Roman citizens.[189]

In Hooper's view it was plain not only from Scripture but also to reason that the bread of the Eucharist was no more alive than the Golden Calf had been. The Church had no more right to 'change the testament of christ' by claiming a corporal presence than 'to change manes testament nor to add or take ony thing from it but to execute and do euery thing as it is there expressid and none other wice.'[190]

---

[187] Ibid.
[188] Ibid., 28.
[189] Ibid., 186.
[190] Ibid., 64–65.

Since 'all Sacramentes be of one nature' Hooper invoked Paul's exposition of the verb 'to be' in the context of the sacrament of circumcision (Romans 4:11): 'is' meant 'signifythe or confirmithe.' He proceeded to unravel literal interpretations of *hoc est corpus meum*.[191] The corporal presence misled people and 'would mak them be lyue that a phantasie or dreme of a bodie that hathe nether quantite nor qualite to be a trew body.'[192] Hooper appealed to John 6:47–63 to say that to eat Christ's body was to believe in him. Rather than a fleshly distribution, 'this Sacrament was and shuld be a memory of his blessyd passion and paynes suffryd in the fleshe.'[193]

Hooper attacked the authenticity of the Roman Church, arguing that Christ himself was 'minister of this holie sacrament and the churche or people that receauid it to be the elect.' Hence Christ and the apostles were the 'trew old and Catholicke churche.' In denying what Hooper understood to be dominical and apostolic teaching, the Roman Church revealed itself to be neither true, ancient, nor catholic.[194]

On 19 June 1548 Hooper wrote to Bucer about his hopes for a new era of graciousness amongst evangelicals following Luther's death in 1546. He was concerned that Bucer might continue to 'burden the consciences of men' with Luther's opinions. He reflected: 'After the dispute with Zuinglius and Œcolampadius respecting the [Lord's] supper had begun to grow warm, [Luther] did violence to many passages of scripture [. . .] that he might establish the corporal presence of the body of Christ in the bread.'[195] Hooper sought to position himself between Bucer's view, that 'the true and natural body of Christ [is] corporally exhibited to me in any supernatural or heavenly manner,' and what he understood to have been Zwingli's view, that the Eucharist was a 'bare

---

[191] Ibid., 191.
[192] Ibid., 187.
[193] Ibid., 190–91.
[194] Ibid., 66.
[195] Hooper to Bucer, 19 June 1548, *OL*, 46.

sign.' He was particularly keen to exonerate both himself and the Zürichers from this Zwinglian caricature. He explained that he understood the Eucharist as

> a sign of the good-will of God towards me, and an outward testimony of his promise of grace. Not that this promise is applied to me by means of any sacrament, but because the promise previously applied to me by faith is thereby confirmed.[196]

Christ's body was exhibited no differently in the sacrament than in Scripture, continued Hooper, after drawing comparisons with circumcision, and it was eaten by believing, as evidenced by John 6. Indeed, Christ had to be brought to the sacraments by faith because he would not be found in them without it. The sealing of God's promise was the 'chief' among many ends of the sacraments.[197] This was certainly not to reduce them to 'bare signs,' but it was important that the Holy Spirit should not be tied to the administration of the sign. The visible signs prompt recognition of 'things insensible and invisible.'[198]

Although Hooper had once appeared to approach Calvin's understanding of the connection between the sacrament and the work of the Spirit, here he seems to reject Calvin's view. In his concluding remarks to Bucer, Hooper wrote that he had never thought of writing against Calvin, even though Calvin's commentaries on 1 Corinthians 'displeased me exceedingly.'[199] Whether or not this is an allusion to 1 Corinthians 10 on the Eucharist, Hooper clearly did not see himself as a deliberate imitator of Calvin's theology.

En route back to England, Hooper wrote to Bullinger from Antwerp on 26 April 1549. He was comforted that the introduction

[196] Ibid., 47.
[197] Ibid.
[198] Ibid., 48.
[199] Ibid.

of the Interim in East Friesland would mean the return of Jan Łaski to England to counter the influence of Peter Martyr Vermigli, Bernardino Ochino, and Bucer who Hooper erroneously believed 'so stoutly defend Lutheranism.'[200] By 27 December he was more confident, reporting to Bullinger that Cranmer 'entertains right views as to the nature of Christ's presence in the supper' and that 'his sentiments respecting the eucharist are pure, and religious, and similar to yours in Switzerland.' He counted another five or six bishops as being sound, even though he found public practice to be 'very far from the order and institution of our Lord.'[201]

The opportunity for Hooper to articulate his sacramental theology before Edward VI came in Lent 1550, in his fifth Court sermon on Jonah. He chose to concentrate on confuting the corporal presence and correcting sacramental practice, leaving little time for positive theological exposition. He began with the basic point that there were two sacraments and that God used them to confirm with 'visyble woordes' that 'the mercye of God saueth the faithfull and beleuers.' This also occurred inwardly by the Holy Spirit 'who testifieth by his spirite with our spirit.'[202]

---

[200] Hooper to Bullinger, 26 April 1549, Ibid., 61. Hooper failed to distinguish Vermigli and Ochino from Bucer, labelling them all as defenders of 'Lutheranism' because he believed that they were not in agreement with Zürich theology. See Andrew Pettegree, *Foreign Protestant Communities in Sixteenth-Century London* (Oxford: OUP, 1986), 28–29. Vermigli's eucharistic theology was generally mistaken as being Lutheran when he arrived in England. Only on 2 March 1549 did he make his affinity with Bullinger clear: John ab Ulmis to Bullinger, 2 March 1549, *OL*, 388; Philip McNair, "Peter Martyr in England," in *Peter Martyr Vermigli and Italian Reform*, ed. J. McLelland (Waterloo, ON: Wilfred Laurier University Press, 1980), 103–4.

[201] Hooper to Bullinger, 27 December 1549, *OL*, 71–72. Hooper may have contributed to the definition rather than the content of Cranmer's eucharistic theology. See Peter Newman Brooks, *Thomas Cranmer's Doctrine of the Eucharist: an essay in historical development*, 2nd ed. (Basingstoke: Macmillan, 1992), 108; Dalton, "Hooper's Networks," 86.

[202] John Hooper, *An ouersight, and deliberacion vpon the holy prophete Ionas: made, and vttered before the Kynges Maiestie, and his Moost Honorable Councell,*

Hooper offered seven arguments against corporal presence. Firstly, Christ's glorified body is physical.[203] Secondly, the commemorative nature of a sacrament requires that the thing being remembered be absent.[204] Thirdly, the Eucharist commemorates Christ's past and complete sacrifice.[205] Fourthly, the only coming of Christ to be expected from Scripture is at the Last Judgment, not in the elements.[206] Fifthly, the doctrine of the corporal presence had caused the Eucharist to become an occasion of idolatry.[207] Sixthly, that Christ's death is to be proclaimed only until he is present.[208] Finally, the Mass destroys Christ's institution.[209] Hooper preached that the minds of communicants were not to be 'affyxed in the sygnes and elementes of the sacraments, but in heauen.'[210] The sacraments had been named after the thing they represented, 'to confirme, & not to exhibit grace, to helpe, and not to giue faythe: to seale, and not to wynne the promyse of God.' Thus they testify to what is already the case: that we are saved and regenerate.[211]

Hooper's sixth sermon began with a sacramental reading of Christ's words of institution, recognising that this was a 'trope'.[212] Sacramental participation in Christ was symbolic:

> We must therfore lyfte vp oure myndes into heauen when we fele oure selues oppressed with the burden of sinne, and ther by fayth apprehend and receaue the bodye of Christe

---

by Ihon Hoper in Lent last past. Comprehended in seuen sermons (London: Ihon Daye and Wylliam Seres, 1550; RSTC 13763), 116r-v.
[203] Ibid., 118r-19r.
[204] Ibid., 119r-20v.
[205] Ibid., 121r.
[206] Ibid., 121v.
[207] Ibid., 122r-23v.
[208] Ibid., 123v.
[209] Ibid., 124r.
[210] Ibid., 127r.
[211] Ibid., 129v.
[212] Ibid., 133v-34r.

slayne and kylled, & hys precious blud shed for our offences: and so by faith apply the vertue, efficacie, and strength of the merites of Christ to our soules, and by that meanes quit oure selues from the daunger, damnacion, and curse of God. And thus to be partaker of the worthynes and deseruyngs of Christes passion, is to eate the body & to drynke the blud.[213]

It is clear that grace is received spiritually and not by means of the sacrament. Again from John 6, 'the flesh profiteth nothynge.' Christ, said Hooper, used the terms 'believe' and 'eat' interchangeably.[214]

'What auayleth it,' then, 'to haue anye Sacrament?' asked Hooper. The sacraments were designed to combat the devil's schemes. They demonstrated that grace applied to individual believers and not only as a general promise. Those of weak faith who 'dout' because of their afflicted consciences are reassured that God is reliable and are shown, by means of the sacrament, that Christ is their only saviour.[215] This recognition and experience of grace through participation concurred with Bullinger's position:

> the mynde is eleuated and lyfte vp into heauen: perswadyng hym selfe by faythe, that as truly apperteineth vnto hym the promyses and grace of God throughe the merites and death of Christ, as he sensibly, and outwardly receiueth the sacramente and wytnes of gods promyses.[216]

Hooper's pastoral priority in these sermons was clear: he applied baptism as God's promise by insisting that only humans should be baptised; the christening of bells was superstitious, and nothing but water was needed: no 'Oyle, salte, Crosse, lyghtes.' These ought to be abolished because they obscure the simplicity of Christ's

[213] Ibid., 136v.
[214] Ibid., 136v-37r.
[215] Ibid., 137r-v.
[216] Ibid., 146r.

institution, and Hooper facetiously suggested that the king's council should 'prepare a shyp as sone as maye be, to sende them home agayne to theyr mother church.'[217]

A few months later Hooper's *Godly confession and protestacion of the christian fayth* (1550) reiterated the links between circumcision and baptism, the Passover and the Eucharist along covenantal lines. As confirmations of God's promise, 'they hange annexed, as a seale vnto the writynge.'[218] Baptism is the mark of acceptation into God's people and of the 'proper iustice,' that is, righteousness, given to us by God.[219] Hooper rejected, here, baptism as humanity's promise of obedience because this was being used to 'defraud the young chyldren of baptisme.' Infant baptism was justified as a sign of what God had done; it was not a profession of humanity's obedience.[220] However, this did not remove the reciprocal element since circumcision had still meant that Abraham 'was bound to work in a godly life,' even though the sacrament had not confirmed his obedience.[221] This is completely consistent with what he had written in his *Answer* to Gardiner, if slightly more nuanced and adapted for polemical purposes. The Eucharist was described, once again, as a 'remembraunce of Christes death, a seale & confirmation,' the signification of which included an exhortation 'to mutual loue, and godlye lyfe.'[222]

Hooper had rejected the physical presence of Christ in the Eucharist by 1539. When he expounded his sacramental theology in Zürich, relating it to his reciprocal concept of covenant, he exhibited views similar to Bullinger and, occasionally, Calvin, although it seems highly unlikely that Hooper meant to affirm Calvin's position.

---

[217] Ibid., 141v-42r.

[218] John Hooper, *A Godly Confession and Protestacion of the Christian Fayth, made and set furth by Ihon Hooper, wherin is declared what a Christian manne is bound to beleue of God, hys kyng, his neibour, and hymselfe* (London: John Daye, 1550; RSTC 13757), G2r-v.

[219] Ibid., G3r.
[220] Ibid., G3v.
[221] Ibid., G4r.
[222] Ibid., G4v.

John Bradford

The major doctrinal preoccupation of Bradford's writings besides the defence of election was the confutation of Roman eucharistic doctrine. Just as his presentation of the concept of covenant lacked many of the features of a bilateral arrangement, so his understanding of the sacraments concentrated primarily, but not exclusively, on their obsignation of the divine promise. His earliest comments on the Eucharist appear in his preface to Petrus Artopoeus' *Division of the places of the lawe and of the Gospell* (1548). He questioned the possibility that those who say Mass could be trusting in Christ for salvation because the Mass itself is deemed to be 'a Sacryfyce propyciatorye.'[223] In Bradford's view, humanity could make no offering without denigrating the perfection of Christ's historic oblation.[224]

There is no further direct evidence of Bradford's sacramental theology prior to his going up to Cambridge in the summer of 1548, by which time the Zürich position, with its focus on spiritual reception, was ascendant in official circles. In August Bartholomew Traheron wrote to Bullinger about Bradford's most obvious influence at the time, Hugh Latimer: 'As to Latimer, though he does not clearly understand the true doctrine of the eucharist, he is nevertheless more favourable than either Luther or even Bucer.'[225] A few weeks later Traheron reported that 'Latimer has come over to our opinion respecting the true doctrine of the eucharist.'[226] Even allowing for Traheron's biases, it is significant that Bradford was

---

[223] Petrus Artopoeus and John Chrysostome, *The Diuisyon of the Places of the Lawe and of the Gospell, gathered owt of the Hooly Scriptures by Petrum Artopoeum: wher unto is added two orations of prayeng to God made by S. Iohn. Chrisostome*, trans. J. Bradford (London: [S. Mierdman for] Gwalter Lynne, 1548; RSTC 822), A3r.
[224] Ibid., A4r.
[225] Traheron to Bullinger, 1 August 1548, *OL*, 320.
[226] Traheron to Bullinger, 28 September 1548, Ibid., 322.

engaging with people who were considered more favourable than Bucer to the sacramental theology of Zürich.[227]

Philip Johnston has demonstrated Bradford's view that 'no sacrament can be purely symbolical, no sacrament can be only automatic, without due regard to the faith of the believer.'[228] Johnston rightly excludes Catholic or Zwinglian characterisations of Bradford's position, proceeding to draw comparisons with Bucer and Calvin.[229] The undoubted importance of Bucer's teaching to Bradford demands such attention. Bucer understood the sacraments as symbols and tokens of God's covenant, but he saw humanity's part more as a grateful response to God's promise than a reciprocal obligation.

While Bradford was at Cambridge Bucer wrote to Peter Martyr about the recent disputation on the Eucharist held at Oxford between 28 May and 1 June 1549. Bucer explained his desire to avoid 'words which deny the real and substantial presence of Christ in the Sacrament.'[230] In his view the apostles had spoken of the 'presence, not the signification and absence, of the Lord'; Christ's presence was 'not feigned, and verbal only, but real and of the very substance of Christ.'[231] For Bucer, the Eucharist was not designed so that 'faith, excited concerning Christ truly absent, is increased through

---

[227] On connections with Latimer and the Swiss preacher Augustine Bernhere see Susan Wabuda, "Shunamites and Nurses of the English Reformation: the activities of Mary Glover, niece of Hugh Latimer," in *Women in the Church*, eds. W. Sheils and D. Wood (Oxford: Basil Blackwell, 1990), 340–41; Bradford to Bernhere and Mistress Hales, June 1555, in John Bradford, *The Writings of John Bradford, M. A., Martyr, 1555. Containing Letters, Treatises, Remains*, ed. A. Townsend, PS. 2 vols. (Cambridge: CUP, 1853), 2:251.

[228] P. F. Johnston, "The Life of John Bradford, the Manchester Martyr, c.1510–1555," BLitt diss. (University of Oxford, 1963), 126.

[229] Ibid., 123–28. On the Church Fathers and the sacraments in Bradford's thought, see Johnston, "Bradford," 66–72.

[230] Bucer to Martyr, 20 June 1549, George Gorham, ed., *Gleanings of a few scattered ears, during the period of the Reformation in England* (London: Bell and Daldy, 1857), 84.

[231] Ibid., 86.

the Spirit of Christ, by His benefits brought to mind and by meditation.'[232] This was clearly directed against the Zürich position.[233] Bucer wrote to Johannes Brenz in 1550 expressing his extreme disappointment with Martyr's book on the Eucharist. Bucer argued for the physical presence of Christ revealed in spite of 'reason':

> when we reply, that no one supposes a local presence of Christ in the Supper, they again say that the body of Christ cannot be understood to be present anywhere without being locally circumscribed. The sum therefore of their argument is to this effect. Reason does not comprehend what you teach respecting the exhibition and presence of Christ in the Supper; therefore these teachings are not true, and the Scriptures which seem to prove them must be otherwise interpreted. Let us pray for these persons.[234]

In his *Confession on the Eucharist* (1550) Bucer attacked the use of words such as '*ficte et accidentaliter*' (imaginarily and accidentally) to describe reception of the Eucharist and, although he refrained from reiterating his dislike of 'signification,' his preferred formulation was '*reipsa et substantiam eius*' (in his real self and in his substance).[235]

Bradford's sacramental theology clearly allowed more space for signification than Bucer's. Celia Hughes points out that Bradford invented the word 'obsignation'—meaning ratification or confirmation using a seal—to describe the action of the sacrament.[236] It is

---

[232] Ibid., 88.

[233] Vermigli took a similar position to Bullinger on the Eucharist: Peter Martyr Vermigli, *The Oxford Treatise and Disputation on the Eucharist*, ed. J. McLelland (Kirksville, MO: Truman State University Press, 2000), xxv.

[234] Bucer to Brentius, 15 May 1550, *OL*, 544. See the amendments in Porter, *Cambridge*, 66.

[235] Martin Bucer, *Confession on the Eucharist* (1550), in *Commonplaces of Martin Bucer*, ed. D. F. Wright (Abingdon: Sutton Courtenay Press, 1972), 394.

[236] Celia Hughes, "Two Sixteenth-Century Northern Protestants: John

very unlikely that Bradford got this from Bucer because it resembles Jan Łaski's term *'obsignare'* (to affix a seal) rather than Bucer's preferred term *'dare'* (to give).[237] This is not to deny that Bradford attempted to portray a mystical presence of Christ as Bucer desired, but he placed it in a more clearly symbolic context.

In his *Meditation on the Lord's Prayer* Bradford thanked God that he had been born of Christian parents so that he enjoyed the assurance of being 'brought into thy church by baptisme, which is the Sacrament of Adoption.'[238] Baptism signified God's action and, as a sign of initiation, baptism required belief in God's action, both in the remission of sin and in the 'sanctification and holines, to be wrought of thee in me by thy grace and holy spirit.'[239] Baptism testified to what God had done and would do for the believer. Building on this understanding of sacraments, Bradford described our forgiving our neighbour's sins as 'a sacrament vnto vs' because it assures us that God will likewise forgive us.[240] For him the sacraments were not only commemorations of God's grace but also conferred grace. He contemplated the work of the Spirit through the ministry of word and sacrament to propagate, enlarge and govern God's kingdom of grace.[241] Through these ministries 'the holye ghost is and wilbe effectuall.'[242]

Bradford went on to describe baptism in his *Meditation on the*

Bradford and William Turner," *Bulletin of the John Rylands Library* 66, 1 (1983): 113 and the *OED*. For examples of Bradford's usage see Bradford, *Writings*, 1:101, 395; Bradford, *Writings*, 2:289.

[237] Łaski to Bucer, June 1545, Gorham, ed., *Gleanings*, 31.

[238] John Bradford, *Godlie Meditations vpon the Lordes Prayer, the Beleefe, and Ten Commaundementes* [. . .] *a Defence of the Doctrine of Gods Eternall Election and Predestination* (London: Rouland Hall, 1562; RSTC 3484), A8r. See G. W. Bromiley, *Baptism and the Anglican Reformers* (London: Lutterworth Press, 1953), 110–11.

[239] Bradford, *Godlie Meditations* [. . .] *Defence of Election*, A8r.
[240] Ibid., C6r.
[241] Ibid., B7r.
[242] Ibid., B8v.

Ten Commandments as 'the seale of thy couenaunt' that confirms God's commitment to the believer. Bradford claimed that 'thy holye name was not in vaine called vpon me' in baptism,[243] which suggests that he was keen to avoid disconnection of the visible sign from the spiritual signification. He compared baptism to circumcision, which had been called God's covenant, even though it was really 'but the signe of thy couenaunt in dede.' The sacrament could be conflated with the covenant itself because it 'is a most true testimonial and witnes therof.'[244] Similarly, Bradford wrote of the Eucharist as being a spiritual tasting of Christ because tasting referred to faith: 'for confirmation of my faithe, that is, to learne spiritually to taste Christs body broken and his bloude shedde for the remission of my synnes.'[245]

Bradford described Christ's spiritual presence in sensuous terms. He identified the chief function of the sacraments as 'visible and palpable wordes, to the obsignation and confirmacion of the faithe of all suche as vse the same after thy commaundementes.'[246] The sacraments also contributed to the instruction of God's faithful people in his law[247] because the ministries of the word and sacraments were 'meanes wherby thy holye spirite is effectuall to worke in oure hartes sanctification.'[248]

In his apparently private *Meditation on the Lord's Supper* (unpublished until 1848) Bradford called the bread and wine 'signs and symbols [. . .] sanctified in Christ's body and blood, to represent the invisible communion and fellowship of the same.'[249] Christ is 'the food of the soul' which is received for the believer's spiritual refreshment and reception into immortality. Baptism is likewise symbolically credited with God's regeneration and adoption of his

---

[243] Ibid., E8v.
[244] Ibid., F1r; see Johnston, "Bradford," 129.
[245] Bradford, *Godlie Meditations* [. . .] *Defence of Election*, G5r.
[246] Ibid., G4v.
[247] Ibid., G2v.
[248] Ibid., G4r.
[249] Bradford, *Writings*, 1:260.

people, engrafting them into his Church.[250] Bradford wrote of the Eucharist as a 'figure and image [. . .] in visible signs.' In this sense it is a confirmation and 'assured witness' of union with Christ that strengthens faith in the efficacy of Christ's death and 'renews' the 'covenant which thou once hast stricken in thy blood.'[251] The Christian is comforted by the sacrament which witnesses to his mystical communion with Christ who is truly 'exhibited and given' to the believer.[252]

Bradford's emphasis in this meditation was on the 'chiefest and almost the whole pith of the sacrament,' that Christ had been offered for us historically, 'for else it would little help us to have thy body and blood distributed now, except they had been given for our redemption and salvation.'[253] The elements 'represented' the body and blood which were themselves 'the seal of spiritual life.' Communicants should 'stick not in the corporal things, and things which are object to our eyes, hands, taste and feeling, as the papists teach [. . .] but that we may arise to the consideration of spiritual things.' Therefore, Bradford prayed that he would consider the sacrament 'not to exhibit and give the body simply and without further consideration, but rather to obsign and confirm the promise.'[254] His focus was thus not on receiving Christ in the sacrament but on the idea that

> thy sacrament doth send us to thy cross, O Christ, where this promise indeed was performed, and most fully on all sides accomplished: for we cannot to salvation feed on thee or eat thee, O Christ, except thou hadst been crucified; and this we do when with lively sense we apprehend and catch hold on the efficacy of thy death.[255]

---

[250] Ibid.
[251] Ibid., 1:260–261.
[252] Ibid., 1:261.
[253] Ibid., 1:262.
[254] Ibid.
[255] Ibid., 1:263.

This commemorative, historical emphasis on apprehending Christ's Passion in the mind is surprisingly Zwinglian in the scheme of Bradford's theology.

In his *Sermon of Repentance* preached in 1552 Bradford included 'not to communicate hys Sacramentes' as one 'foule spotte' under divine law.[256] He described the clothing made by God for Adam and Eve in Genesis 3:21 as 'a visible sacramente and token of his inuisyble loue & grace, concerning theyr soules' because, Bradford thought, it represented the promise of deliverance by Christ.[257]

In 1553 Bradford wrote his treatise *The Hurt of Hearing Mass* which offered little in the way of constructive eucharistic doctrine. That the commemorative function was at the forefront of his thinking is suggested by his one positive description of the Eucharist as a 'memoriall of hys deathe and passion.'[258] He also claimed that the Catholics' adoration rather than distribution of the elements meant that 'god is not bounde to kepe his promyse thys is my bodie because it is condicyonal, requiryng our obedience of taking and eating.'[259]

Owing to the influx of prisoners following Wyatt's Rebellion in the spring of 1554, Bradford shared a cell in the Tower with Cranmer, Latimer, and Ridley. Latimer recalled that they had searched the Scriptures and 'we could find in the testament of Christ's body and blood no other presence, but a spiritual presence.'[260] It seems very likely that Bradford was significantly influenced by the sacramental theologies of these three divines. Gordon Jeanes argues that Cranmer's mature position, impressed on Bradford through the Book of Common Prayer, was distinct from Bucer's and most closely

---

[256] John Bradford, *A Sermon of Repentaunce* (London: S. Mierdman for Iohn Wight, 1553; RSTC 3496), D1v-2r.

[257] Ibid., F7r.

[258] John Bradford, *The Hurte of Hering Masse* (London: Wyllyam Copland for Wyllyam Martyne, 1561; RSTC 3494), B4r.

[259] Ibid., D6r. This is consistent with Bucer's idea that there are reciprocal responsibilities in ceremonies.

[260] Hugh Latimer, *Sermons and Remains of Hugh Latimer*, ed. G. Corrie, PS (Cambridge: CUP, 1845), 258–59.

resembled Bullinger's.[261] If Bradford had neglected the theology of the *Consensus Tigurinus* up until this point he could hardly have done so now.

Soon afterwards Bradford sent the manuscript of his *Sermon on the Lord's Supper* to Oxford for perusal by Ridley who was imprisoned there.[262] Bradford began by comparing baptism to circumcision, arguing that baptism, as a sealing of entry into Christ's body, is equivalent to engrafting into the 'covenant and league with God':

> christian parents seem to be no less bound to offer their infants and babes to be baptised, that they may be taken and accounted of us as members of Christ's mystical body, wherein they are received and sealed, than were the Hebrews their children to be circumcised and so to be taken as pertaining to the covenant and league with God, wherein they were engraffed, alonely the circumstance of the eighth day, not necessary to be observed, being now abrogate.[263]

Bradford then gave nine reasons against transubstantiation,[264] in the course of which he said that 'as by baptism we are engraffed

---

[261] Gordon Jeanes, *Signs of God's Promise: Thomas Cranmer's sacramental theology and the Book of Common Prayer* (London: T&T Clark, 2008), 163–71. Compare Bradford's position with Cranmer's *Answer to a Crafty and Sophistical Cavillation devised by Stephen Gardiner* (1551): 'I do not say that Christ's body and blood be given to us in signification, and not in deed. But I do as plainly speak as I can, that Christ's body and blood be given to us in deed, yet not corporally and carnally, but spiritually and effectually': Cranmer, *Writings*, 37. Compare also Ridley's allowance of Christ's Real Presence in the sense of 'something that appertaineth to Christ's body': Nicholas Ridley, *The Works of Nicholas Ridley*, ed. H. Christmas, PS (Cambridge: CUP, 1843), 213; see Megan Wheeler, "Protestants, Prisoners and the Marian Persecution," DPhil diss. (University of Oxford, 2006), 96; Hughes, "Two Northern Protestants," 111–12; Gottfried Locher, *Zwingli's Thought: New Perspectives* (Leiden: Brill, 1981), 362–64.

[262] Ridley to Bradford, May 1554, Bradford, *Writings*, 2:93.

[263] Bradford, *Writings*, 1:82–83.

[264] Ibid., 1:84–92.

into Christ, so by the supper we are fed by Christ.'[265] This helps to explain the kind of reception of which Bradford conceived, because his concept of engrafting at baptism was clearly figurative: 'in the Lord's supper is given unto us the communion of Christ's body and blood, that is, grace, forgiveness of sins, innocency, life, immortality, without any transubstantiation or including of the same in the bread.' Engrafting into Christ's natural body is only achieved by virtue of the fact that Christ is simultaneously the head of the mystical body.[266]

Bradford continued to define the Eucharist, not as 'bare bread and a naked sign,'[267] but as a token of God's gracious disposition. He gave an illustration of a 'token' sent by 'a loving friend' and said that one would miss the point of the gift if 'thou considerest not the mind of thy friend that sendeth or giveth thee the thing, and according thereto to esteem and receive it.' Likewise, in the sacrament, one should consider 'the mind of thy lover Christ' and not the elements themselves. The sacrament was to be valued for what it signified about Christ.[268] Bradford warned against reducing the sacrament to 'a sign or a figure of his body; except you will discern betwixt signs which signify only, and signs which also do represent, confirm, and seal up, or (as a man may say) give with their signification.'[269]

In most respects Bradford seems to have been attacking strawmen. The obstacle for Zürichers would have been his suggestion that the sign gives what it signifies. Like Bucer, Bradford wanted to portray signs as 'exhibitive,' 'a declaration of a gift, yea, in a certain manner a giving also,' so that baptism 'is also a very cleansing from

---

[265] Ibid., 1:88. Johnston observes that Bradford 'very frequently links his theories concerning the correct usage of the Lord's Supper, to right observance of the rite of Baptism': Johnston, "Bradford," 125.

[266] Bradford, *Writings*, 1:89. Bradford's understanding of eucharistic reception echoes Cranmer's second Book of Common Prayer wherein 'we spiritually eat the flesh of Christ, and drink his blood, then we dwell in Christ and Christ in us, we be one with Christ, and Christ in us': *Two Liturgies*, 274.

[267] Bradford, *Writings*, 1:92.

[268] Ibid., 1:93.

[269] Ibid., 1:93–94.

sin' and the Eucharist 'a partaking of the Lord's body.'[270] He was not denying that the sacraments were 'sacramental and external signs' nor that the reality was 'tied to the element otherwise than sacramentally and spiritually.' His much less ambitious intention was to ensure 'that they might be discerned from significative and bare signs only, and be taken for signs exhibitive and representative.'[271] In this respect Bradford's view seems concurrent with Calvin's symbolic instrumentalism.

Bradford's reverence for the elements stemmed from their being 'ordained to serve for food of the soul,' which involved a 'spiritual, figurative, sacramental, or mystical' change. He affirmed no other presence of Christ than 'by grace, a presence by faith, a presence spiritually' and used the argument—shunned by Bucer—that 'Christ's body is only in heaven.'[272] Nevertheless, Christ's presence was such that 'reason knoweth not,' one that could be discerned only 'with the ears and eyes of the Spirit and of faith,' which is more reminiscent of Bucer's objection to absence.[273] Bradford compared the spiritual 'coupling' of Christ's body and blood to the sacrament with the proposition that a man's wife is 'with her husband one body and flesh, although he be at London and she at York.'[274]

Among the five benefits of participation listed by Bradford was receiving 'remission of our sins and confirmation of the new Testament.' The Eucharist testified to God's promise. The other benefits were union with Christ; life with God; reception of Christ as both God and man, and 'by faith an increase of incorporation with Christ and among ourselves which be his members.'[275] This final benefit shows

---

[270] Ibid., 1:94. Trueman claims that Bradford says that baptism 'actually *is* such a cleansing'. However Bradford explained that they are 'sacramental and external signs' which are 'exhibitive and representative' of a spiritual action: Trueman, *Luther's Legacy*, 285.

[271] Bradford, *Writings*, 1:94.

[272] Ibid., 1:95.

[273] Ibid., 1:96–97. Locher overstates the 'Zwinglian content' of Bradford's eucharistic theology: Locher, *Zwingli's Thought*, 358–59.

[274] Bradford, *Writings*, 1:99.

[275] Ibid.

that the Eucharist also had a communal purpose as well as declaring God's promise. Bradford went on to deny that weak humanity could receive Christ 'with so much light and by such sensible assurance' through 'only meditation of Christ's death or hearing of his word' as compared to receiving the sacrament. In the sacrament Christ entered the heart by stimulation of all the senses. Since the sacraments were so efficacious in this regard, Bradford considered that 'the apostle full well calleth the sacraments obsignations or "sealings" of God's promise,' with a reference to circumcision in Romans 4.[276] By the calling to mind of Christ's Passion in the Eucharist, Christ is 'beholden with the eyes of faith' and those present are called to repentance and their faith in God's mercy is strengthened.[277] The benefits of this certainty made 'this supper *eucharistiam*, "a thanksgiving."'[278]

Shifting the focus, Bradford asked why the Eucharist had been instituted, answering in terms of commemoration and assurance of the benefits of Christ's death. He concentrated on the latter, with the encouragement that 'you, worthily receiving this sacrament, shall receive remission of all your sins, or rather certainty they are remitted; and that you are even now God's darlings, temples, and fellow-inheritors of all the good that ever he hath.'[279] The testamental signification is particularly clear here, as well as the metaphorical sense in which Bradford sometimes speaks of the sacraments as intrinsically salvific. The worthy reception which he mentions consisted of preparing the conscience in faith and repentance.[280] The joy of sacramental union with Christ included, for Bradford, the attempt to 'live worthy of your profession' and 'have society with the works of light,' and was placed in the context of the unilateral covenant: 'Now God hath renewed his covenant with you: in God's sight now you are as clean and healed from all your sores of sins.' 'Godliness and

---

[276] Ibid., 1:101.
[277] Ibid., 1:102–4.
[278] Ibid., 1:105.
[279] Ibid., 1:107–8.
[280] Ibid., 1:108; see *Two Liturgies*, 274.

virtue' were essentially a response to divine grace but they were not without warning against 'idleness, lest the devil come "with seven spirits worse than himself," and take his lodging; and then your latter end will be worse than the first.'[281]

Bradford's treatise entitled *An Exhortacion to the carienge of Chrystes crosse* (early 1550s) was published by the Marian exiles and identified transubstantiation, propitiatory sacrifice, 'prayers for the dead & to the dead' as the '4. pillours' supporting the Mass.[282] His aim was the pulling down of these pillars. Since a sacrament required that the sign should have 'some similitude' with that signified, transubstantiation, by annihilating the bread and wine, destroyed the sacrament.[283] Instead, the faithful receive, not Christ's body, but 'euen whole Chryste, into whom they are incorporate.'[284] This rather brief statement is Bradford's definition of reception here which 'shall suffyse to the declaracyon of our faith, concerning the Lordes supper, whervnto agreeth the Catholik church and al the fathers.' He referred his readers to Cranmer's *Defence of the true and catholic doctrine of the sacrament* (1550) for more detail,[285] which is a further indication of the archbishop's influence on him. Bradford went on to argue that Christ's sacrifice was applied by believing in it, by preaching and by prayer. The sacrifice could not be reiterated, nor was it applied by the sacraments.[286] Bradford also made an incidental statement on baptism: it is administered on the basis of God's election or, if the child is of age, faith, since he can declare God's promise. The whole purpose of baptism is to declare the divine promise.[287]

---

[281] Bradford, *Writings*, 1:109–10.

[282] John Bradford, *An Exhortacion to the Carienge of Chrystes Crosse wyth a true and brefe confutacion of false and papisticall doctryne* (Wesel?: H. Singleton?, 1555?; RSTC 3480.5), 62–67.

[283] Ibid., 74; see the same argument in Hooper, *Ionas*, 119r-20v.

[284] Bradford, *Chrystes Crosse*, 76.

[285] Ibid., 77. For analysis of Cranmer's *Defence* see Diarmaid MacCulloch, *Thomas Cranmer: a life* (New Haven & London: YUP, 1996), 462–69.

[286] Bradford, *Chrystes Crosse*, 88–89.

[287] Ibid., 126.

In *Another treatise of election and freewill* (1554?) Bradford stated that 'a man regenerate (which we ought to beleue of oure selues, I meane that we are so by our baptisme, the sacrament ther of requiring no lesse faith) a man I say regenerate, that is, borne of god, hath the spirite of god.'[288] Bradford clearly recognised two baptisms: one spiritual, one sacramental. The sacrament demands that we believe that the spiritual event has occurred. Similarly, in *A Treatise against the fear of death* Bradford almost conflated the spiritual and sacramental baptisms when he wrote that the poor Christian conscience 'by baptism is brought into God's church and made a member of the same "through faith".'[289]

The fact that the dates of so many of Bradford's works are unknown makes it difficult to discern development in his sacramental theology. His prison letters, however, are unusual in the scheme of his theology in their understanding of baptism as the Christian's vow, which presumably reflects the pastoral challenges with which he was faced. In September 1554 Bradford urged his friends in Coventry to choose suffering over compromise with Rome:

> you have professed in baptism to fight under the standard of your Captain Christ: and will you now, for peril's sake, leave your Lord? You made a solemn vow that you would forsake the world: and will you be foresworn and run to embrace it now? You sware and promised to "leave all and follow Christ:" and will you now leave him for your "father, your mother, your children, your lands, your life," &c.?[290]

This passage is reminiscent of Zwingli's metaphor for baptism as a soldier's oath of allegiance. A month earlier Bradford had told Humphrey Hales that in baptism we 'have vowed and solemnly sworn to

---

[288] Bradford, *Godlie Meditations* [. . .] *Defence of Election*, N3r.
[289] Bradford, *Writings*, 1:347.
[290] To Hopkins and others, 2 September 1554, Ibid., 1:396.

forsake the world.'[291] In 1555 he encouraged Joyce Hales not to forget 'your profession made in baptism, which Christ requireth of all that will be his disciples, namely to "deny yourself and take up your cross,"'[292] and he described another correspondent as 'a man of God' who 'by profession in baptism have forsaken the world.'[293] Forsaking the world was a recurrent aspect of humanity's baptismal 'vow' for Bradford, a term synonymous with the 'solemn profession' against the 'fancy of the flesh [. . .] as also against the devil and the world, in our baptism.'[294] The Gospel and promise, as well as the sacraments and their 'substance,' Christ, required 'of every one that is baptised, and brought into God's church' that they be 'persuaded' of God's 'new covenant' to forgive and preserve his elect.[295] The only comparable example of reciprocity in baptism outside the prison letters appears in Bradford's undated *Comparison between the old man and the new* (published in 1567) where he wrote that baptism requires 'under paine of damnation' that we be regenerate. That is, having had our regeneration testified to us in the sacrament, we should strive to realise it by trying not to doubt it.[296]

Bradford took a final opportunity in early 1555 to express his understanding of the Real Presence in his 'farewell letters'. He used much the same formula in his *Farewell to the City of London*, *Farewell to Lancashire and Cheshire*, and *Farewell to Walden*: 'in the supper of

---

[291] To Humphrey Hales, 5 August 1554, Bradford, *Writings*, 2:105; see also *Exhortation to the brethren in England* in Bradford, *Writings*, 1:417–18.

[292] To Joyce Hales, 14 March 1555, Bradford, *Writings*, 2:203; see Susan Wabuda, "Henry Bull, Miles Coverdale, and the Making of Foxe's *Book of Martyrs*," in *Martyrs and Martyrologies*, ed. D. Wood (Oxford: Blackwell, 1992), 249.

[293] To Shallcross and his wife, 1555, Bradford, *Writings*, 2:235.

[294] To men who relieved the prisoners, undated, Bradford, *Writings*, 1:384.

[295] To certain free-willers, 1 January 1555, Bradford, *Writings*, 2:166–67.

[296] John Bradford, *Godly Meditations vppon the Ten Commaundementes, the Articles of the Fayth, and the Lords Prayer* [. . .] *a Comparison Betweene the Old Man and the New: the Lawe and the Gosple* (London: William Seres, 1567; RSTC 3493.5), 92.

Christ [. . .] is a true and very presence of whole Christ, God and man, to the faith of the receiver, (but not to the stander by or looker upon,) as it is a true and very presence of bread and wine to the sense of men.'[297] The eating of Christ was 'sacramentally and spiritually' in 'remembrance' of his sacrifice.[298] Bradford had been influenced by Swiss sacramental theology only indirectly. Bucer was responsible for his 'mystical' conception of Christ's presence in the Eucharist, although he understood this to occur by 'obsignation'. Bradford's sacramental theology was related to his unilateral concept of covenant but the connection was not developed extensively.

The Swiss Reformed elements of Bradford's sacramental theology were received second-hand and were not closely related to the covenantal aspects of his understanding, whereas Bucer's major influence may be gathered from Bradford's exhortatory *Farewell to Cambridge*: 'Remember the readings and preachings of God's prophet and true preacher, Martin Bucer.'[299] Bucer's teaching was certainly reflected in Bradford's expression of a 'mystical' presence of Christ in the Eucharist,[300] but it cannot be ignored that he maintained Christ's presence in the bread principally 'by signification.'[301] Bradford denied dependence on Luther, Zwingli or Œcolampadius for his sacramental theology. However, Swiss theology, especially that of Bullinger and the *Consensus Tigurinus*, was mediated to him through his colleagues and Cranmer's publications. This explains Bradford's departures from Bucer's position.

By contrast, the sacramental theologies of Tyndale, Coverdale, and Hooper bore the marks of their concepts of covenant and, although they may have lacked a degree of technical abstraction,

---

[297] *Farewell to the City of London*, Bradford, *Writings*, 1:435–36, see also 450, 456.
[298] To Hopkins and others, 2 September 1554, Ibid., 1:393.
[299] *Farewell to Cambridge*, Ibid., 1:445.
[300] Conference with Weston, Ibid., 1:546.
[301] Conference with Alphonsus a Castro, Ibid., 1:533. See Johnston, "Bradford," 130.

they can be helpfully interpreted according to continental patterns. Tyndale's broadly Lutheran sacramental theology of the 1520s was developed around 1529 by his emphasis on the covenantal significance of the sacraments. Comparisons with Swiss Reformed theology are most easily drawn in 1530–31 when Tyndale enthused over the Zwinglian understanding of sacraments as covenantal memorials and vows (although covenant seals were not emphasised). This was tempered in subsequent years as Tyndale went beyond contemporary Zürichers in allowing that the signs exerted a greater power for the believer than the benefits of historic remembrance only, although he stopped short of ascribing instrumentality to them.

Coverdale's eucharistic position was Sacramentarian by 1528 and there is no reason to suppose he departed from it. During the 1530s his translation of Lutheran texts omitted sacramental theology and there were oblique indications that he maintained Reformed views on the Eucharist. In the early 1540s Coverdale embraced the sacramental theology of Zürich integrated with the concept of covenant. Initially, in 1540, Zwingli's thought was influential, but in 1541 Bullinger was the obvious source. Perhaps as early as 1544, but certainly by 1548, Coverdale's sacramental theology moved towards Calvin's. This would not have entailed any discernible shift in his concept of covenant.

Hooper had abandoned traditional beliefs on the Eucharist by 1539 but it was not until 1546 that he fully expounded his sacramental theology. It is inaccurate to describe it as Zwinglian because he clearly embraced characteristics of Bullinger's, and even Calvin's, views. In 1547 he made the reciprocal elements of the covenant in relation to the sacraments more explicit, but there was no change in his theology.

Where Swiss concepts of covenant were adopted by Englishmen, their sacramental theologies evidence this reception. It is possible to associate Tyndale with a broadly Swiss Reformed position from the time the covenant became the controlling idea in his theology. Coverdale's general Sacramentarianism did not initially depend on a concept of covenant, but covenantal elements of his sacramental understanding were developed in line with his apprehension of Swiss Reformed theology. Hooper's reception of Bullinger's theology is clear in the integration of the covenant to his sacramental thought. Meanwhile it is clear from Bradford's theology that Swiss Reformed ideas about Christ's presence could be received without the more profound sacramental implications of the reciprocal concept of covenant.

7

Imprecisely Reformed

Man, wylt thou lyue ryght vertuously,
And with God reygne eternally,
Then must thou kepe these commaundements ten
That God commaunded to all men.
Kirieleyson.
—Miles Coverdale (c.1535)[1]

Miles Coverdale versified the Decalogue sometime before 1539. The result was not a theological statement of his developing concept of covenant but, for those with eyes to see, it memorably instilled the practical implications of covenant relationship. The *Kyrie eleison* refrain suggested the inability of human beings to fulfil the requirements of divine law. Righteousness according to scriptural precepts and its gracious deliverance through Christ were the leading ideas in Reformed thought during the Reformation. The covenant theology articulated by Huldrych Zwingli, Heinrich Bullinger, and John Calvin was bilateral and conditional. The reciprocal concept of covenant can therefore be said to constitute a characteristic element of Swiss Reformed theology uniting the leading reformers of Zürich and Geneva. It serves as a marker for the proliferation of

---

[1] Miles Coverdale, *Goostly Psalmes and Spirituall Songes drawen out of the Holy Scripture* (London: J. Rastell for Iohan Gough, 1535?; RSTC 5892), B3r.

Swiss theology because it can be distinguished from the unilateral concepts expressed by Martin Luther and Martin Bucer.[2]

Zwingli's christocentric soteriology was structured according to his concept of covenant that emerged in 1523. His point of departure was the socio-political turmoil he witnessed in Switzerland which he interpreted as being the result of anthropocentric worship and unfaithfulness to God. In his opinion the solution was a return to God's law which taught true worship. Through appropriate worship and faithfulness to God humanity would fulfil its covenantal obligations towards him and thereby elicit his promised blessing and salvation. However, fallen humanity was incapable of discharging these obligations; only through union with Christ could humanity become righteous by virtue of the apprehension of Christ's righteousness. Although Zwingli accepted the importance of faith, his emphasis was on union with Christ and Christ's fulfilment of what is demanded, which tended to concern ethical regeneration accomplished and perfected by Christ.

The social aspects of Zwingli's soteriology were maintained and accentuated by Bullinger. He regarded himself in Zwingli's debt for the revived appreciation of the importance of the divine covenant in his day. From the mid-1520s Bullinger articulated a covenant concept and contributed a refinement of its details and a broadening of its communal implications. This he did by defining humanity's obligations as love of God and of neighbour, an ethic which he expounded from the Decalogue. Like Zwingli he emphasised Christ's fulfilment of the conditions on humanity's behalf as the basis for salvation.

Calvin's agreement with the covenant theology articulated by the Zürichers is apparent from the emergence of covenant themes in his theology as early as 1536 and a reciprocally-binding, conditional concept by 1539. Calvin's covenantal soteriology was thoroughly

---

[2] The influence of Philip Melanchthon's concept of covenant is beyond the scope of this study but deserves investigation.

christocentric; he emphasised union with Christ as the means of fulfilling the conditions of the covenant. Further study might usefully illuminate the difference between the Zürichers' consideration of righteousness as being imparted through this union and Calvin's preference for the language of imputation.

The consistency of Swiss concepts of covenant confirms Richard Muller's arguments against Leonard Trinterud's thesis that a Rhineland 'law-covenant' existed which was separate from Calvin's allegedly unilateral notion of 'testament'. It is impossible to sustain a bifurcation of the Swiss Reformed tradition according to different covenant models. As Lyle Bierma, Cornelis Venema and Andrew Woolsey have shown, Wayne Baker's attempt to ground that disjunction in the doctrines of election expressed by Bullinger and Calvin is unpersuasive. In order to distinguish between the variegated positions of Zwingli, Bullinger, and Calvin it is instead necessary to examine their respective applications of the covenant to sacramental theology. They shared an understanding of the sacraments as covenant signs denoting reciprocal obligations, but it has been shown that they assigned varying degrees of importance to those signs for the believer's experience of divine grace.

Zwingli's sacramental theology, like his soteriology, was christocentric in that he refused to grant to the signs themselves anything which he considered to belong to that which was signified. The value of the sacraments was solely derivative from the historic work of Christ. He had strong polemical reasons for denying that the sacraments communicated grace, emphasising instead that the Holy Spirit needed no vehicles and that faith itself—which a person either had or did not have—apprehended Christ. As early as 1523 Zwingli associated the sacraments with the covenant and from the mid-1520s came to see them as rich signs of humanity's allegiance to God as well as commemorations and ratifications of God's promise. Baptism was the sacrament of initiation into the covenant; the Eucharist was the sacrament of faithfulness to the community living under its precepts.

While Zwingli understood the sacraments primarily as human activities, Bullinger saw them as God's proclamation and confirmation of the Spirit's work on the heart. In this sense he was not a Zwinglian but he often chose to defend Zwingli's teaching and concentrated on the reciprocal, covenantal significance of the sacraments. His own view, which became more public in the late 1540s, was that the sacraments testify to grace by analogy, sealing the promise of grace conferred by God. To some extent, Bullinger's position was moulded against Calvin's in that Bullinger carefully denied sacramental instrumentality even if it were credited to the Spirit. He succeeded in enshrining his understanding in the *Consensus Tigurinus* (1549).

Yet another view was taken by Calvin who held that the sacraments were in some sense instruments of grace. In 1536 he defined sacraments as covenantal tokens expressing reciprocal obligations, but went beyond testimonial function to assert that they actually offer what they signify. By 1539 he saw the binding of God and humanity into reciprocal relationship as their primary purpose. He remained hopeful for an agreement with the Lutherans into the early 1540s even though he understood Christ's presence in the Eucharist to be spiritual. The later 1540s witnessed Calvin's willingness to compromise for the sake of agreement with Zürich in the *Consensus Tigurinus*.

A good understanding of covenant theology reinforces the significance of continental influence on the English Reformation. The doctrine of covenant and the theology of the sacraments found in Reformation England not only suggest the reception of continental theology in general but also help to indicate the influence of particular patterns of Reformation on English Reformed theology. William Tyndale, Miles Coverdale, and John Hooper all experienced exile on the continent; all came to exhibit reciprocal concepts of covenant consistent with Swiss Reformed theology. It is highly likely that their exposure to Swiss ideas was the impetus for the development of their concepts. Through examination of their sacramental theologies it has been possible to track the different Swiss influences upon them.

As early as the mid-1520s Tyndale differed from Luther on the ability of the Christian to fulfil the law. The gradual refinement of his ethical concerns through the following decade bears out Carl Trueman's thesis of continuity in Tyndale's thought and confutes William Clebsch's arguments for a radical legalisation of Tyndale's theology around 1530. Initially, however, as far as the concept of covenant was concerned, Tyndale's definition of 'testament' in his Romans Prologue (1526) concurred with Luther's unilateral understanding. Tyndale's reading of Swiss Reformed texts is demonstrable from 1527/28.[3] An early sign of development in that direction in terms of the concept of covenant appeared in May 1528 in a lone reference to a reciprocal testament unilaterally initiated by God in *The Parable of the Wicked Mammon*. Even if the reciprocal concept was at this stage peripheral, it is clear that God's testament had already become central to Tyndale's understanding of the Gospel and, moreover, that he had the principles in place to expand the concept. He had already strayed from Luther's soteriology by teaching the impartation of extrinsic righteousness through union with Christ. A few months later, in *The Obedience of a Christian Man*, there were several examples of a mutual 'testament,' a term used interchangeably with a 'bond' between two parties. Tyndale used 'covenant' explicitly only when describing God's obligation, but there were hints that the concept might apply to humans too.

Clebsch's exaggerated thesis does at least highlight the importance of the development occurring in Tyndale's concept in 1529–31. In January 1530 Tyndale's Pentateuch made it clear that the word 'testament' was to be understood primarily as a bilateral covenant. In the revision of 1534 the word 'covenant' had been adopted throughout. The legalism supposedly detected by Clebsch and Broughton

---

[3] Ryan Reeves, "'Ye Gods': Political Obedience from Tyndale to Cromwell, c.1528–1540," *ARG* 105, 1 (2014): 243.

Knox in Tyndale's mature theology stems from the careful distinction made by Tyndale between the means and basis of justification: the former is faith alone; the latter is imparted righteousness through union with Christ. In *The Practice of Prelates* (1530) Tyndale invoked natural law summarised in the Decalogue as the standard for the true worship required of a believer. His description of the covenant as an indented obligation in his exposition of 1 John (1531) marked the completion of the maturation of his concept since 1529.

Tyndale's exposition of law and covenant in the 1530s encourages inference of the influence of the Swiss reformers on him. Even more evident is that the maturation of Tyndale's concept of covenant around 1529 ended his espousal of Lutheran sacramental theology in favour of a Swiss approach. This emerged as almost Zwinglian in 1531, although his views during the mid-1530s were more positive about the benefits of the sacraments for the believer than those of contemporary Zürichers, including Bullinger.

Coverdale first translated a work by Bullinger in around 1528. This study has contended that he was Tyndale's disciple throughout the years of Tyndale's exposition of the reciprocal concept of covenant, 1529–35. The Coverdale Bible (1535) shows Zürich influences and, in Clebsch's opinion, exhibited Tyndale's concept of covenant. However, the remainder of Coverdale's writings in the 1530s yield no sign of the concept. It has been argued here that this is explicable on political rather than theological grounds. Return into exile revealed Coverdale's high view of the covenant. His *Fruitful Lessons* (1540), modelled on a work by Zwingli, exhibited the concept and, although it was not central to the treatise, its bilateral and conditional nature was unequivocal. The concept was clearly foundational to the argument of his *Confutation of Standish* (1541) published at Zürich. Later that year Coverdale produced the first English translation of a continental covenant text, written by his correspondent Bullinger: *The old faith* was circulated and received to great acclaim by its English readership.

Coverdale's interest in Zürich theology continued into Edward

VI's reign but his sacramental theology reveals shifts in his primary influences. He had held Sacramentarian opinions since 1528 at least and there is no reason to think he renounced them in the 1530s. By 1540–41 his sacramental theology was consistent with the opinions of the Zürichers, apparently moving from Zwinglianism towards Bullinger's strain. This moderating trend continued as Calvin's influence succeeded Bullinger's sometime between 1544 and 1548, but Coverdale never moved so far as to endorse the Lutheran position in which he took cursory interest.

Hooper was strongly influenced by Zürich theology and by Bullinger in particular. His conversion to Swiss reformism occurred in 1538–39 and he studied briefly in Basle in 1545. Evidently he had intended for some time to visit Zürich and finally moved there in 1547 for a period lasting two years. This study has found, contrary to the views of Jens Møller and David Newcombe, that all three of Hooper's Zürich treatises exhibited evidence of a robust concept of the bilateral and conditional covenant. Thus, Morris West was correct to regard it as foundational to Hooper's theology. Trueman, who also made the comparison between Hooper and Bullinger's concepts, underplays its soteriological significance in Hooper's theology.

Hooper's proselytisation on behalf of Zürich theology confirms that his concept of covenant remained stable after his return to England in 1549. His conduct during the Vestment Controversy demonstrated a fervour untempered by Bullinger's sense of diplomacy. Examination of Hooper's sacramental theology likewise suggests that from the late 1530s Zürich theology maintained a constant influence over him. The important figure was Bullinger; Hooper was never a Zwinglian, nor was he consciously attracted to Calvin's opinions.

The case of John Bradford offers a counter-example to Muller's judgment that unilateral concepts of covenant should not be linked with more predestinarian theologies. Indeed it was specifically Bradford's predestinarian emphasis, unusual amongst contemporary English reformers, which prompted his decision not to invoke a reciprocal concept of covenant to support his Reformed emphasis on godliness. The primacy of unconditional election provides the best explanation for his refusal to expound his moral priorities as conditional obligations. In this respect his predestinarian emphasis had a different effect to Calvin's. Bradford's contrasting conclusions further suggest the utility of the concept as an indicator of Swiss influence on the English.

Bradford's evangelical conversion in 1547 brought him under the influence of Hugh Latimer who was, at about that time, won to Zürich's eucharistic doctrine. For perhaps three years Bradford struggled for assurance of his salvation; he perceived his own obstinacy in the face of God's call and felt intense guilt over past misconduct. He was acutely aware that he ought to receive salvation with thankful obedience, and yet he made no link to the covenant. In Cambridge from 1549 until 1551 Bucer exerted a seminal influence on Bradford; it was probably due to Bucer's lectures, coupled with Bradford's personal struggles, that the doctrine of election became axiomatic for Bradford's theology. However, all that Bradford believed to be required for assurance was faith. The limits of his moralism were evident in the controversy with the free-willers, in which he sought to maintain determinism without fatalism. Moreover, his concept of covenant lodged any conditionality with God, thereby excluding effective mutuality.

Although Bucer was responsible to a significant extent for Bradford's unilateral concept of covenant, Bradford's sacramental theology suggests an indirect Swiss influence. The impact of the *Consensus Tigurinus*, even before its publication in England in 1552, and the mediation of Zürich sacramental theology via Cranmer, Latimer, and Ridley, Cranmer's eucharistic treatises, and the Book of Common Prayer appear to explain the peculiarities of Bradford's position where it diverged from Bucer's. Swiss sacramental theology was received more widely into early English Reformed thought than the Swiss concept of covenant. Where the reciprocal covenant was adopted, sacramental theology can be used to determine its specific origin. The unilateral concept articulated by Bradford would seem to confirm its association with Bucer as well as Luther. The concept of covenant can therefore be utilised to measure Swiss influence on English Reformed theology.

The chronological distribution of the reciprocal concept of covenant in early English Reformed theology can be gauged using several additional examples. Predictably, the concept is most evident in the writings of other exiles, namely George Joye, John Bale, and Edmund Allen.[4] In 1534 Joye defined a testament as 'a promyse a [bar]gyn or a couenaunt wherby God hath promysed testifyed and declared his Godly wil and mercyfull plesure vnto vs agreinge with vs vpon certayne condicions.'[5] Bale, who became a sacramentary in 1530,[6] described baptism in 1547 as 'a couenaunt of a good conscience to god' wherein the person being baptised 'bindeth him selfe or maketh a couenaunt with god: that from thens forth he wyll lyue after hys wyll.'[7] When Allen translated a Zürich catechism in 1550, he decided that it was unnecessary to render the German word *bundt* into English:

> if God haue receaued vs into hys bundt & frendship [...] it is conuenient and mete that we kepe the condicion conteined in the bundt namely that we walke godly and verteously in his sight that is to do that he commaundeth & eschew that

---

[4] The exile John Frith did not use the term 'covenant' but employed many conditional ideas to spur Christians to do their duty, e.g., John Frith, *The Work of John Frith*, ed. N. T. Wright, *CLRC*, Vol. 7 (Appleford: Sutton Courtenay Press, 1978), 230–33, 239–41, 269–70, 277. See Leonard Trinterud, "The Origins of Puritanism," *CH* 20, 1 (1951): 40.

[5] Joye, *The Subuersion of Moris*, 52v and ff.

[6] Jesse W. Harris, *John Bale: a study in the minor literature of the Reformation* (Urbana, IL: University of Illinois Press, 1940), 20; Jens Møller, "The Beginnings of Puritan Covenant Theology," *JEH* 14 (1963): 55.

[7] John Bale, *A bryefe and plaine declaracion of certayne sentences in this litle boke folowing to satisfie the consciences of them that haue iudged me therby to be a fauourer of the Anabaptistes* (London: John Day?, 1547; RSTC 1035), A6r.

he forbiddeth. [. . .] For fayth and baptisme bind vs to obey God vnto whom we be bounde as with an othe.[8]

Bundt, which literally meant 'covenant,' had been defined bilaterally by Zwingli and apparently Allen was confident that his Edwardian readership would appreciate its reciprocal quality. The reciprocal covenant was also expressed by some evangelicals who did not experience exile. The equivocal Thomas Becon explained in 1543 that the Abrahamic covenant was made with all the faithful; hence

> God require of vs also, that we walke before hym and be perfecte that we stedfastelye cleaue vnto him by stronge faythe, as the onelye and sole Authore of al goodnes, & so institute oure lyfe, that we maye breath nothynge but purite, innocency, holynes & intergrite, all the tyme of our lyfe in this worlde. Thus doyng, God wyl be our God, yea our almyghty God, our strong defender, and our sufficient great rewarde, no lesse than he was Abrahams. Therfore as Abraham walked before God, so let vs do. By this means shall God be no lesse beneficiall to vs, than he was to Abraham. If ye were the sonnes of Abraham, sayth Christ, ye woulde do the worckes of Abraham.[9]

These cases suggest that Tyndale was not a lone voice at the beginning of the English Reformation. Joye, Coverdale, and Bale also held reciprocal covenant ideas in the 1530s and it is interesting to hypothesise about mutual influences.[10] These ideas were continued

---

[8] Edmund Allen, *A Shorte Cathechisme: a briefe and godly bringinge vp of youth* (Zurich: C. Froschauer, 1550; RSTC 361), E1r-v, see also C7r, D2v, E2r.

[9] Thomas Becon, *A New Yeares gyfte more precious than golde* (London: Iohn Mayler for Iohn Gough, 1543; RSTC 1738), M6v-M7r; see also Thomas Becon, *A Pleasaunt Newe Nosegaye Full of Many Godly and Swete Floures* (London: Iohn Mayler for Iohn Gough, 1543; RSTC 1743), E7r-v, G2v.

[10] John Bale, *A tragedye or enterlude manyfestyng the chefe promyses of God unto*

in the 1540s and 1550s by Becon, Coverdale, Hooper, and Allen, suggesting a relatively consistent distribution of interest in a theology of reciprocal covenant throughout the early English Reformation.

The Swiss-influenced theologians examined in this study were among the most precocious examples of English Reformed theology surveyed in chapter two. The utility of the covenant in analysing Reformed convictions among the theologically-educated élites is not easily reproduced at the popular level. This is not to deny the doctrinal interest of lay people, whom Geoffrey Dickens pictured 'talking of Scripture on the ale bench.'[11] Peter Blickle's study of popular Reformation in upper Germany in the mid-1520s found that peasants took a genuine theological interest in Zwingli's preaching. They were convinced of the close relationship between the Gospel and 'godly law,' but Blickle concludes that the distinction between these concepts was 'undoubtedly beyond the peasants' mental powers of abstraction.'[12] As Felicity Heal and Clive Holmes write of England, 'deep ideological engagement with the new order must have been the prerogative of a small minority in the Reformation years.'[13] While popular Sacramentarianism made significant progress in England and might have owed something to Swiss theology as well as to Lollardy, communication of the abstract concept of covenant was not a priority for educated reformers. Its influence might be observed in the disciplinary themes of pastoral theology,[14] but it

---

man by all ages in the olde lawe from the fall of Adam to the incarnacyon of the Lorde Iesus Christ (Wesel: Dirik van der Straten, 1547; RSTC 1305). The play was first performed in 1538.

[11] A. G. Dickens, *The English Reformation*, 2nd ed. (London: B. T. Batsford, 1989), 375.

[12] Peter Blickle, *Communal Reformation: the quest for salvation in sixteenth-century Germany*, trans. T. Dunlap (London and New Jersey: Humanities Press International, 1992), 47, see also 17, 42–43, 201.

[13] Felicity Heal and Clive Holmes, *The Gentry in England and Wales, 1500–1700* (Basingstoke: Macmillan, 1994), 357.

[14] See Michael McGiffert, "William Tyndale's Conception of Covenant," *JEH* 32 (1981): 182–84; John King, *English Reformation Literature: The Tudor*

would be nearly impossible to trace definitively in the socio-political context until specific appeals were made to it later in the century.

Where continental influence on early English Reformation theology has been considered it has been in Lutheran terms, most notably by Trueman and Alec Ryrie. This study suggests that a new perspective is needed that neither paves the way for Puritanism nor perpetuates the notion of a mild, proto-Anglican *via media*. It is far from clear that Luther's opinions ever gained significant currency in England. The Henrician formularies of faith were eclectic rather than Lutheran. Although Reformed evangelicals were in a minority before 1547, there are good reasons to think they were very significant in both number and conviction. The Reformed label can be applied to individuals in London, both universities, and the Court. Oxford benefitted from an exchange programme with Zürich in the late 1530s sponsored by the Vice-Gerent in Spirituals himself. The dissemination of continental Reformed texts from the 1520s, reports of thriving Sacramentarianism from the early 1530s, spontaneous iconoclasm, and exposures under the Six Articles all suggest that the Swiss-influenced sector of English evangelicalism was at least exerting a significant influence in this period.

The question of the origins of Puritanism and of federal theology has been consciously avoided here but this study has ramifications for that debate. Protestant orthodoxy was indebted to humanist methods and forms but it also undertook a systematisation of early Reformation approaches and drew on scholastic patterns of argument, becoming in Muller's words 'more overtly philosophical'.[15] An important feature of it was the federal concept

---

Origins of the Protestant Tradition (Princeton: Princeton University Press, 1982), 320–22, 352–55; Ralph Houlbrooke, *Church Courts and the People during the English Reformation, 1520–1570* (Oxford: OUP, 1979), 67–68, see also 200–201.

[15] Ulrich Leinsle, "Sources, Methods, and Forms in Early Modern Theology," in *Oxford Handbook of Early Modern Theology*, eds. Lehner, Muller and Roeber, 26–43; Richard Muller, "Reformed Theology between 1600 and 1800," in *The Oxford Handbook of Early Modern Theology, 1600–1800*, eds. U. Lehner,

which was introduced into Reformed thought in 1562 by Zacharias Ursinus (1534–83).[16] The so-called *Doppelbund* included a covenant of works and a covenant of grace. Wayne Baker and Charles McCoy describe this as a Federalist Reformed tradition which acted as an alternative to the Calvinist Reformed tradition. They therefore see Bullinger and Calvin as the originators of two separate but related traditions. Muller has sought to demonstrate the essential unity of these alleged alternatives. According to Michael McGiffert the intention of federal theology was, on the one hand, to define formal limits of covenantal conditionality and, on the other, to bind everyone formally to the moral law. The integrity of the covenant of grace was upheld by confining the law to the parallel covenant of works.[17] The dilemma between legalism and antinomianism was evaded through this conveniently abstract division of human obligation and divine grace into different economies. Consequently 'puritans were freed to be as puritanical as they pleased—to do helpful and holy things, to serve God and love neighbour, without running the risk of a bad conscience.'[18] The relationship between grace and law was clearly defined so as to ensure the integrity of both concepts.

A significantly different attitude to the concept of covenant in the early Reformation has emerged from this study which separates it from later developments. The early reformers who espoused a reciprocal concept of covenant were content to co-ordinate faith and law

---

R. Muller and A. G. Roeber (New York: OUP, 2016), 171–72, 174.

[16] David Weir, *The Origins of the Federal Theology in Sixteenth-Century Reformation Thought* (Oxford: OUP, 1990), 22. Muller claims that the doctrine of covenant in later Reformed theology derived its substance from Bullinger, Wolfgang Musculus, Ursinus, and Caspar Olevian more than Calvin: Richard Muller, *After Calvin: Studies in the Development of a Theological Tradition* (Oxford: OUP, 2003), 86.

[17] Michael McGiffert, "Grace and Works: The Rise and Division of Covenant Divinity in Elizabethan Puritanism," *HTR* 75, 4 (1982): 467, 497–98; Michael McGiffert, "From Moses to Adam: the making of the Covenant of Works," *SCJ* 19, 2 (1988): 137, 145–46.

[18] McGiffert, "Grace and Works," 468.

without any formal theological protection for the principle of *sola gratia*, which they nevertheless still upheld in practice. The difference between early and later attitudes in England can be correlated with different stages of English reception of continental ideas.

Until the 1550s Reformed covenant theology is comparable to, and clearly continuous with, late medieval covenant theology and the social and spiritual culture fostered by it. Berndt Hamm's description of 'this moderate, accommodating, balanced mediation of God's severity and mercy, of threat and consolation [...] typical of everyday pastoral life in the majority of European towns around 1500' can easily be applied to the attitudes of early Reformed covenant theologians.[19] This was a pivotal period. Late medieval *pactum* theology was recast within the radically gracious christocentric economy of the Reformation. Salvation *sola gratia* was comprehensively emphasised and, at the same time, reciprocal human obligation was redefined *sola scriptura*. There was no attempt to regulate the reciprocal economy until the emergence of federal theology. This delicately balanced, imprecisely Reformed position was reflected in the English reception of Swiss theology under Henry VIII and Edward VI.

Early Reformed continental theology imbued late-medieval and humanist moral reform with the striking implications of the sole sufficiency of Christ for salvation.[20] Righteousness could be attained only through union with Christ and was defined according to his law summarised in the Decalogue. Scriptural law displaced the rules

---

[19] Berndt Hamm, *The Reformation of Faith in the Context of Late Medieval Theology and Piety*, trans. H. Heron, G. Wiedermann and J. Frymire (Leiden & Boston: Brill, 2004), 86.

[20] William Bouwsma, "The Two Faces of Humanism: Stoicism and Augustinianism in Renaissance Thought," in H. Oberman, ed., *Itinerarium Italicum: the profile of the Italian Renaissance in the mirror of its European transformations* (Leiden: Brill, 1975), 15–16; J. M. Stayer, "Zwingli before Zurich: Humanist Reformer and Papal Partisan," *ARG* 72 (1981): 55–67; Alister McGrath, "Humanist Elements in the Early Reformed Doctrine of Justification," *ARG* 73 (1982): 5–20; Erika Rummel, *The Confessionalisation of Humanism in Reformation Germany* (Oxford: OUP, 2000), 24–25, 38, 41–42.

of the late-medieval Church and had to be obeyed in response to the gift of grace in order to maintain covenant relationship with God. Potentially passive participation in the patterns of late-medieval devotion gave way to the imperative to strive for personal and communal godliness. Moreover, the external forms of public devotion were reworked to express true worship. This contrasted with Luther's radically solifidian approach which stripped human works of their salvific efficacy altogether, yet was prepared to tolerate those material symbols and patterns of late-medieval devotion which were not perceived to be complicit in works-righteousness.[21]

When English Reformed evangelicals had their moment under Edward they implemented the dogmatic changes modelled by Zürich: salvation *sola gratia, solo Christo, sola scriptura*. However, they retained practices and structures which they did not consider to be contrary to Scripture, like clerical vestments, kneeling at communion, certain holy days, and the ecclesiastical polity, even though these purported adiaphora had been abolished in continental Reformed churches.[22] This judicious approach arose not through default of indolence or any particular yearning for late-medieval custom, but because these symbols and structures were not judged inimical to godliness by leading reformers.

During Mary Tudor's reign numerous English evangelicals, like their Henrician predecessors, sought refuge in Zürich, but by this stage there were other choices. Exile congregations were also founded in Emden, Frankfurt, and Geneva.[23] The exiles were able not only to experiment amongst themselves with alternative

---

[21] On Luther's and Zwingli's different attitudes to the connection between reforming the spiritual and the material, see Lee Wandel, "The Body of Christ at Marburg, 1529," in *Image and Imagination of the Religious Self in Late Medieval and Early Modern Europe*, eds. R. Falkenburg, W. Melion and T. Richardson (Turnhout: Brepols, 2007), 207–11.

[22] Philip Benedict, *Christ's Churches Purely Reformed: a social history of Calvinism* (New Haven & London: YUP, 2002), 240.

[23] See Christina Garrett, *The Marian Exiles: a study in the origins of Elizabethan Puritanism* (Cambridge: CUP, 1938), 47ff.

ecclesiastical structures but to observe the achievements of aggressive reform. Coverdale's radicalisation during this period is a case in point. The effect was to broaden and to intensify the continental influence upon English Reformed identity in the 1550s.

The internal tensions within the Elizabethan Church can be understood in terms of these different periods of continental Reformed influence. The architects of the Elizabethan Settlement were not exiles but evangelicals who had survived in Marian England as Nicodemites. Their experience of reform was still Cranmer's Zürich-influenced programme, not Calvin's Geneva. Elizabeth I herself represented 'old-fashioned evangelicals.'[24] Her establishment enshrined Reformed theology as it had been received under her father and her brother and was built on foundations laid by Thomas Cromwell in the 1530s, making his schemes 'the most successful Nicodemite enterprise of the whole Reformation.'[25] The Act of Uniformity (1559), Book of Common Prayer (1559) and Thirty-nine Articles (1563) essentially restored and did not move beyond the doctrinal and liturgical position of 1552.[26] Adiaphora were retained on the basis that true culpability lay in superstitious intentions rather than traditional practices. It was a sound if somewhat vulnerable position to defend.[27] Bullinger acknowledged, albeit reluctantly, that vestments could be used in good conscience.[28] Erstwhile exiles eager

[24] Alec Ryrie, *The Age of Reformation: the Tudor and Stewart realms 1485–1603* (Abingdon: Routledge, 2017), 180.

[25] Diarmaid MacCulloch, *Thomas Cromwell: A Life* (London: Allen Lane, 2018), 543.

[26] Diarmaid MacCulloch, "Putting the English Reformation on the Map," *TRHS* 15 (2005): 87–89; see also MacCulloch, "Sixteenth-century English Protestantism," in Dorothea Wendebourg, ed., *Sister Reformations: the Reformation in Germany and in England: symposium on the occasion of the 450th anniversary of the Elizabethan Settlement, September 23rd-26th, 2009* (Tübingen: Mohr Siebeck, 2010), 8–9.

[27] See Euan Cameron, *Enchanted Europe: superstition, reason, and religion 1250–1750* (Oxford: OUP, 2010).

[28] Heinrich Bullinger, *The iudgement of the godly and learned father M. Henry Bullinger [. . .] declaring it to be lawfull for the ministers of the Churche of Englande,*

for further reform were confronted with a hierarchy already aspiring to the godly and christocentric maxims of Zürich.[29]

Theodore Bozeman argues that the imperious spirit of these men, who earned the epithets 'precise' and 'Puritan,' was derived from concepts forged in the dialogue between the early English reformers and continental Reformed theologians.[30] This is undoubtedly true, but it is important to recognise that continental Reformed theology itself was an evolving influence and that the Marian exiles, unlike most Elizabethan evangelicals, had seen for themselves how it was being applied abroad. The significance of their direct experience should not be underestimated. The controversies that had dogged the exile congregations were brought home with them. These Puritans 'pushed beyond mid-Tudor precedents to harder values.'[31] From the 1570s they began to see the potential of the concept of covenant as 'a heaven-sent auxiliary to an ethically strenuous programme' for individuals and the nation.[32] By 1600 Puritanism had taken a 'pietistic turn' wherein the moral elements of covenant theology became intimately concerned with behavioural regulation and the 'new science and praxis of piety.'[33]

---

to weare the apparell prescribed by the lawes and orders of the same realme (London: William Seres, 1566; RSTC 4063); see also *ZL*, 2:136–140.

[29] Torrance Kirby, "Peter Martyr Vermigli's Political Theology and the Elizabethan Church," in *The Reception of the Continental Reformation in Britain*, eds. P. Collinson and P. Ha, *PBA*, Vol. 164 (Oxford: OUP, 2007), 85–91, 104–6.

[30] Theodore Bozeman, *The Precisianist Strain: Disciplinary Religion and Antinomian Backlash in Puritanism to 1638* (Chapel Hill, NC and London: University of North Carolina Press, 2004), 60.

[31] Ibid., 30; see also John Craig, "The growth of English Puritanism," in *The Cambridge Companion to Puritanism*, eds. J. Coffey and P. Lim (Cambridge: CUP, 2008), 37.

[32] Bozeman, *Precisianist Strain*, 37; see also Jonathan Willis, "'Moral Arithmetic' or Creative Accounting? (Re-)defining Sin through the Ten Commandments," in *Sin and Salvation in Reformation England*, ed. J. Willis (Farnham: Ashgate, 2015), esp. 73–83; Craig, "Growth of English Puritanism," 34.

[33] Bozeman, *Precisianist Strain*, 85–86; see also Felicity Heal, *Reformation in Britain and Ireland* (Oxford: OUP, 2003), 336–38; Benedict, *Christ's*

Imprecisely Reformed

The early Reformed concept of covenant was not nearly so precise in its definitions. Faith and godliness were the two poles of a carefully balanced soteriology. The covenant had real conditions within a gracious context. It was not locked into particular ecclesiastical structures or customs which varied between England, Zürich, and Geneva. The balance was increasingly upset by the Puritan attempt to define the implications of Christ's law in all areas of life.[34] In the process they struggled to reconcile conditionality with solifidianism in the personal experience of the godly.[35] Federal theology was less an indicator of growing Reformed conviction so much as a different interpretation of what such beliefs implied. Arguably the theological temperament of the Elizabethan establishment owed more than the precisianists did to Zürich's luminaries.

For four decades, from the 1520s to the 1550s, the Swiss Reformed concept of covenant was poised between medieval *pactum* ideas and the emergence of federal theology. A relationship of mutual agreement and conditional obligation between God and humanity formed the basis of a theology in which divine grace and human works were held together. Grace and law were carefully balanced; both were affirmed but their equilibrious relationship was not formally defined. The law of love embraced but did not replace the obligations of fidelity. The reciprocal covenant became a marker of the proliferation of Swiss Reformed theology and left its traces in England. The transmission of the reciprocal concept of covenant encourages further investigation of the links between England and the Alps in the 1520s to 1550s. English Reformed theology grew in significance from the 1520s and between 1547 and 1553 reform of the kingdom was driven by Zürich theology. This reception had a formative influence upon the Elizabethan Settlement. To its Puritan

---

Churches, 246.

[34] See McGiffert, "Grace and Works," 465, 485; Heal and Holmes, *The Gentry*, 360.

[35] See Bozeman, *Precisianist Strain*, 253–54; McGiffert, "Moses to Adam," 148.

critics the Church of England under Elizabeth may have been imprecisely Reformed, but the links established between England and Switzerland in the early Reformation period suggest that it is best understood in league with Zürich.

Bibliography

Manuscripts

Bodleian Library, Oxford
MS. Bodley 53, fos. 48v-61v: John Bradford, A treatyse of predestinacion.

Parker Library, Corpus Christi College, Cambridge
MS. CCCC 128: Documents relating to Archbishop Cranmer.
MS. CCCC 168, fos. 209r-v: Speech of Cromwell, earl of Essex, at his execution.

Printed Primary Sources

Allen, Edmund. *A shorte cathechisme: A briefe and godly bringinge vp of youth.* Zurich: C. Froschauer, 1550; RSTC 361.

Anon. *A glasse for housholders.* London: Richard Grafton, 1542; RSTC 11917.

Artopoeus, Petrus and John Chrysostome. *The diuisyon of the places of the lawe and of the Gospell, gathered owt of the hooly scriptures by Petrum Artopoeum: wher unto is added two orations of prayeng to God made by S. Iohn. Chrisostome.* Translated by J. Bradford, London: [S. Mierdman for] Gwalter Lynne, 1548; RSTC 822.

Articles devised by the kynges highnes maiestie [The Ten Articles]. London: Thomas Berthelet, 1536; RSTC 10033.2.

Bibliography

Bale, John, *Yet a course at the Romyshe foxe*. Antwerp: Olyuer Iacobson [A. Goinus], 1543; RSTC 1309.

———. *A brefe chronycle concernynge the examinacyon and death of the blessed martyr of Christ syr Iohan Oldecastell the lorde Cobham*. Antwerp, 1544; RSTC 1276.

———. *A bryefe and plaine declaracion of certayne sentences in this litle boke folowing to satisfie the consciences of them that haue iudged me therby to be a fauourer of the Anabaptistes*. London: John Day?, 1547; RSTC 1035.

———. *A tragedye or enterlude manyfestyng the chefe promyses of God unto man by all ages in the olde lawe from the fall of Adam to the incarnacyon of the lorde Iesus Christ*. Wesel: Dirik van der Straten, 1547; RSTC 1305.

Barlowe, William, *Dialogue on the Lutheran Factions*, edited by A. McLean. *CLRC*, Vol. 15. Appleford: Sutton Courtenay Press, 1981.

Becon, Thomas, *A new yeares gyfte more precious than golde worthy to be embrased no lesse ioyfully than thankfully of euery true christen man*. London: Iohn Mayler for Iohn Gough, 1543; RSTC 1738.

———. *A pleasaunt newe nosegaye full of many godly and swete floures*. London: Iohn Mayler for Iohn Gough, 1543; RSTC 1743.

Beveridge, Henry, ed. *John Calvin: Tracts and Letters*. Vol. 2. Edinburgh: Banner of Truth, 2009.

The Byble in Englyshe [...] truly translated after the veryte of the Hebrue and Greke textes, by ye dylygent studye of dyuerse excellent learned men, expert in the forsayde tonges [The Great Bible]. Paris: Francis Regnaut; London: Rychard Grafton and Edward Whitchurch, 1539; RSTC 2068.

Bradford, John, *A sermon of repentaunce*. London: S. Mierdman for Iohn Wight, 1553; RSTC 3496.

———. *An exhortacion to the carienge of Chrystes crosse wyth a true and brefe confutacion of false and papisticall doctrine*. Wesel?: H. Singleton?, 1555?; RSTC 3480.5.

———. *The hurte of hering masse.* London: Wyllyam Copland for Wyllyam Martyne, 1561; RSTC 3494.

———. *Godlie meditations vpon the Lordes prayer, the beleefe, and ten commaundementes [. . .] a defence of the doctrine of gods eternall election and predestination.* London: Rouland Hall, 1562; RSTC 3484.

———. *Godly meditations vppon the ten commaundementes, the articles of the fayth, and the Lords prayer [. . .] a comparison betweene the old man and the new: the lawe and the gosple.* London: William Seres, 1567; RSTC 3493.5.

———. *The Writings of John Bradford, M.A., Martyr, 1555*, edited by A. Townsend. 2 vols. PS. Cambridge: CUP, 1848/53.

Bradford, John and Thomas Sampson, *Two notable sermons. Made by that worthy martyr of Christ Maister Iohn Bradford, the one of repentance, and the other of the Lordes supper neuer before imprinted.* London: Iohn Awdely and Iohn Wyght, 1574; RSTC 3500.5.

Bromiley, G. W., ed. *Zwingli and Bullinger: Selected Translations.* LCC, 24; Philadelphia: Westminster Press, 1953.

Bucer, Martin, *A treatise declaring and showing that images are not to be suffered in churches.* Translated by William Marshall. [title page missing], 1535; RSTC 24238.

Bullinger, Heinrich, *De testamento seu foedere dei unico & aeterno Heinrychi Bullingeri brevis exposition.* Elektronische Bibliothek Schweiz. Zurich: Christopher Froschauer, 1534.

———. *Sermonum decades quinque, de potissimis Christianae religionis capitibus.* Zurich: Christopher Froschauer, 1557.

———. *The Christen state of matrimony.* Translated by M. Coverdale. Antwerp: M. Crom, 1541; RSTC 4045.

———. *The olde fayth, an euydent probation out of the holy scripture, that the christen fayth (which is the right true, old & undoubted faith, hath endured sens the beginnyng of the worlde).* Translated by M. Coverdale. Antwerp?: Thomas Vautroullier, 1541; RSTC 4070.5.

———. *The iudgement of the Godly and learned father M. Henry Bullinger [. . .] declaring it to be lawfull for the ministers of the*

Churche of Englande, to weare the apparell prescribed by the lawes and orders of the same realme. London: William Seres, 1566; RSTC 4063.

———. *The Decades of Henry Bullinger*, edited by T. Harding. 5 vols. PS. Cambridge: CUP, 1849–52.

———. *A Brief Exposition of the One and Eternal Testament or Covenant of God, 1534.* Translated by C. S. McCoy and J. W. Baker, in *Fountainhead of Federalism: Heinrich Bullinger and the Covenantal Tradition*, 99–138. Louisville, KY: Westminster John Knox Press, 1991.

Burnet, Gilbert, *The History of the Reformation of the Church of England.* 6 vols. London: Baynes and Son, 1825.

Byrne, Muriel St. Clare, ed. *The Lisle Letters.* 6 vols. Chicago and London: University of Chicago Press, 1981.

Calvin, John, *A faythfull and moost godlye treatyse concernyng the most sacred Sacrament of the blessed body and bloude of our sauioure Chryst.* Translated by Thomas Broke. London: John Day, 1548; RSTC 4411.

———. *Calvinism by Calvin; being the substance of discourses delivered by Calvin and the other ministers of Geneva on the Doctrines of Grace* [c.1551], edited by R. Govett and C. Malan. London: James Nisbet & Co., 1840.

———. *Calvin's Calvinism: a treatise on the eternal predestination of God* [1552]. Translated by H. Cole. 2 vols. London: Wertheim and MacIntosh, 1856.

———. *Ioannis Calvini opera quae supersunt omnia*, edited by G. Baum, E. Cunitz, and E. Reuss. 59 vols. *CR*, 29–87; Brunswick: Schwetchke et Filium, 1863–1900.

———. *Institutes of the Christian Religion*, edited by J. T. McNeill. Translated by F. L. Battles. 2 vols. *LCC*. Louisville and London: Westminster John Knox Press, 1960.

———. *Institution de la Religion Chrestienne* [1541], edited by J. Pannier. 4 vols. Paris: Société d'Edition "Les Belles Lettres," 1961.

———. *The Epistles of Paul the Apostle to the Galatians, Ephesians,*

Philippians and Colossians. Calvin's Commentaries. Vol. 9. Edinburgh and London: Oliver and Boyd, 1965.

———. *Institutes of the Christian Religion* [1536]. Translated by F. L. Battles. Grand Rapids, MI: William Eerdmans, 1986.

———. *Institutes of the Christian Religion: 1541 French Edition*. Translated by E. McKee. Grand Rapids, MI and Cambridge: William Eerdmans, 2009.

Cochrane, Alan, ed. *Reformed Confessions of the Sixteenth Century*. London: SCM, 1966.

Coverdale, Miles, *Biblia the Bible [. . .] faithfully and truly translated out of Douche and Latyn in to Englishe*. Cologne?: E. Cervicornus and J. Soter?, 1535; RSTC 2063.

———. *Biblia the Byble [. . .] faithfully translated in to Englyshe*. Southwark?: J. Nycolson, 1535; RSTC 2063.3.

———. *Goostly psalmes and spirituall songes drawen out of the holy Scripture, for the comforte and consolacyon of soch as loue to reioyse in God and his Worde*. London: J. Rastell for Iohan Gough, 1535?; RSTC 5892.

———. *A goodly treatise of faith, hope, and charite necessary for all Christen men to know and to exercyse themselues therein translated into englyshe*. Southwark: James Nicolson, 1537; RSTC 24219.5.

———. *The original and sprynge of all sectes and orders by whome, whan or were they beganne*. Translated out of hye Dutch in Englysh. Southwarke: James Nicolson for Jhon Gough, 1537; RSTC 18849.

———. *The Psalter or boke of Psalmes both in Latyn and Englyshe*. London: Ricardus Grafton, 1540; RSTC 2368.

———. *A confutacion of that treatise, which one Iohn Standish made agaynst the protestacion of D. Barnes in the yeare. M.D.XL. Wherin, the holy scriptures (peruerted and wrested in his sayd treatise) are restored to their owne true vnderstonding agayne by Myles Couerdale*. Zurich: C. Froschauer, 1541; RSTC 5888.

———. *The defence of a certayne poore Christen man who els shuldhaue bene condemned by the Popes lawe. Written in the hye Allmaynes tonge by a right excellent and noble prynce, and translated into Englishe.* Antwerp: S. Mierdman, 1545; RSTC 5889.

———. *Fruitfull lessons, vpon the passion, buriall, resurrection, ascension, and of the sending of the holy Ghost Gathered out of the foure Euangelists: with a plaine exposition of the same.* London: Thomas Scarlet, 1593; RSTC 5891.

———. *Writings and Translations of Myles Coverdale, Bishop of Exeter*, edited by G. Pearson. PS. Cambridge: CUP, 1844.

———. *Remains of Myles Coverdale, Bishop of Exeter*, edited by G. Pearson. PS. Cambridge: CUP, 1846.

Coverdale, Miles and William Tyndale, *The Byble* [. . .] *truly and purely translated into Englysh by Thomas Matthew*, edited by John Rogers. Antwerp: Matthew Crom for Richard Grafton and Edward Whitchurch, 1537; RSTC 2066.

Cranmer, Thomas, *Certayne sermons, or homelies appoynted by the kynges Maiestie.* London: Rychard Grafton, 1547; RSTC 13640.

———. *The Remains of Thomas Cranmer, D.D.*, edited by H. Jenkyns. 4 vols. Oxford: OUP, 1833.

———. *Writings and Disputations of Thomas Cranmer, Archbishop of Canterbury, Martyr, 1556, Relative to the Sacrament of the Lord's Supper*, edited by J. Cox. PS. Cambridge: CUP, 1844.

———. *Miscellaneous Writings and Letters of Thomas Cranmer, Archbishop of Canterbury, Martyr, 1556.*, edited by J. Cox. PS. Cambridge: CUP, 1846.

Foxe, John, *Acts and Monuments*. The Unabridged Acts and Monuments Online. Sheffield: HRI Online Publications, 2011. http://www.johnfoxe.org.

Frith, John, *The Work of John Frith*, edited by N. T. Wright. *CLRC*. Vol. 7. Appleford: Sutton Courtenay Press, 1978.

Frith, John and William Tyndale, *The testament of master Wylliam Tracie esquier, expounded both by William Tindall and Ihon Frith.* Antwerp: H. Peetersen van Middelburch?, 1535; RSTC 24167.

Gardiner, Stephen, *A detection of the Deuils sophistrie wherwith he robbeth the vnlearned people, of the true byleef, in the most blessed sacrament of the aulter.* London: Ihon Herforde, 1546; RSTC 11591.3.

———. *The Letters of Stephen Gardiner*, edited by J. A. Muller. Cambridge: CUP, 1933.

Gorham, George, ed. *Gleanings of a few scattered ears, during the period of the Reformation in England.* London: Bell and Daldy, 1857.

Gray, William, *A Balade agaynst malycyous sclaunderers.* London: Iohn Gough, 1540; RSTC 1323.5.

Hooper, John, *An answer vnto my lord of wynthesters booke intytlyd a detection of the deuyls sophistrye wherwith he robith the vnlernyd people of the trew byleef in the moost blessyd sacrament of the aulter.* Zurich: Augustyne Fries, 1547; RSTC 13741.

———. *A declaration of Christe and of his office.* Zurich: Augustyne Fries, 1547; RSTC 13745.

———. *A declaration of the ten holy commaundementes of allmygthye God.* Zurich: Augustin Fries, 1548; RSTC 13746.

———. *A funerall oratyon made the xiiij. day of Ianuary [. . .] vpon the texte wrytyne in the Reuelatyone of Sayncte Iohne. Ca. 14.* London: S. Mierdman for Edwarde Whitechurch, 1549 [1550]; RSTC 13753.

———. *A godly confession and protestacion of the christian fayth, made and set furth by Ihon Hooper, wherin is declared what a christian manne is bound to beleue of God, hys Kyng, his neibour, and hymselfe.* London: John Daye, 1550; RSTC 13757.

———. *An ouersight, and deliberacion vpon the holy prophete Ionas: made, and vttered before the kynges maiestie, and his moost honorable councell, by Ihon Hoper in lent last past. Comprehended in seuen sermons.* London: Ihon Daye and Wylliam Seres, 1550; RSTC 13763.

———. *Early Writings of John Hooper, D.D.*, edited by S. Carr. PS. Cambridge: CUP, 1843.

———. *Later Writings of Bishop Hooper*, edited by C. Nevinson. PS. Cambridge: CUP, 1852.

Iniunctions for the clerge. London: Thomas Berthelet, 1538; RSTC 10086.

Iniunctions gyuen by the auctoritie of the kynges highnes to the clergie. London: Thomas Berthelet, 1536; RSTC 10084.7.

The Institution of a Christen Man [The Bishops' Book]. London: Thomas Berthelet, 1537; RSTC 5164.

Janelle, Pierre, ed. *Obedience in Church and State: three political tracts by Stephen Gardiner.* Cambridge: CUP, 1930.

Jewel, John, *The Works of John Jewel, bishop of Salisbury,* edited by J. Ayre. PS. Vol. 1. Cambridge: CUP, 1845.

Jordan, W. K., ed. *The Chronicle and Political Papers of Edward VI.* London: George Allen and Unwin, 1966.

Joye, George, *The souper of the Lorde [. . .] the declaracion of the later parte of the .6. ca. of S. Johan [. . .] wheryn incidently M. Moris letter agenst Johan Frythe is confuted.* Antwerp: Niclas Twonson [N. Hill?], 1533; RSTC 24468.

———. *Dauids Psalter, diligently and faithfully translated by George Ioye, with breif arguments before euery Psalme, declaringe the effecte therof.* Antwerp: Maryne Emperowr, 1534; RSTC 2372.

———. *The subuersion of Moris false foundacion where upon he sweteth to set faste and shove under his shameles shoris, to vnderproppe the popis churche.* Emden [Antwerp]: Jacob Aurick [G. von der Haghen], 1534; RSTC 14829.

———. *An apolgye made by George Ioye to satisfye (if it maye be) w. Tindale to pourge & defende himself ageinst many sclaunderouse lyes fayned vpon him.* London: J. Byddell, 1535; RSTC 14820.

Kidd, B. J., ed. *Documents Illustrative of the Continental Reformation.* Oxford: OUP, 1911.

The King's Book, or A Necessary Doctrine and Erudition for any Christian Man [1543]. Church Historical Society; London: SPCK, 1932.

Łaski, Jan and John Calvin, *Breuis et dilucida de sacramentis ecclesiae Christi tractatio in qua & sons ipse, & ratio, totius sacramentatiae nostri temporis controuersiae paucis exponitur: naturáque ac uis sacramentorum compendio & perspicuè explicatur*. London: Stephanum Myerdmannum, 1552; RSTC 15259.

Latimer, Hugh, *Sermons of Hugh Latimer*, edited by G. Corrie. PS. Cambridge: CUP, 1844.

———. *Sermons and Remains of Hugh Latimer*, edited by G. Corrie. PS. Cambridge: CUP, 1845.

Letters and papers, foreign and domestic, of the reign of Henry VIII, 1509–1547, edited by J. S. Brewer, J. Gairdner, and R. H. Brodie. 21 vols. London: H. M. Stationery Office, 1862–1910.

Lloyd, Charles, ed. *Formularies of faith put forth by authority in the reign of Henry VIII*. Oxford: OUP, 1825.

Luther, Martin, *Luther's Works*, edited by H. Lehmann, J. Pelikan, et al. 55 vols. American ed., St. Louis: Concordia/Philadelphia: Muhlenberg Press/Fortress Press, 1955–86.

———. *De Servo Arbitrio* [1525]. Translated by P. Watson, 100–334. LCC. Vol. 17. Philadelphia: Westminster Press, 1969.

Melanchthon, Philip, *A godlye treatyse of prayer*. Translated by J. Bradford. London: S. Mierdman for Iohn Wight, 1553; RSTC 17791.

———. *Opera quae supersunt omnia*, edited by K. Bretschneider and H. Bindseil. 28 vols. *CR*. Vols 1–28. Brunswick: Schwetchke et Filium, 1834–60.

———. *Loci Communes Theologici* [1535], edited by W. Pauck. LCC. Vol. 19. London: SCM, 1969.

Merriman, R. G., ed. *Life and Letters of Thomas Cromwell*. 2 vols. Oxford: OUP, 1902.

Mueller, Janel, ed. *Katherine Parr: Complete Works and Correspondence*. Chicago and London: University of Chicago Press, 2011.

The Order of the Communion, London: Richard Grafton, 1548; RSTC 16458.3.

Original Letters Relative to the English Reformation, edited by H. Robinson. 2 vols. PS. Cambridge: CUP, 1846/47.

Reid, J. ed. *Calvin: Theological Treatises. LCC*. Vol. 22. London: SCM, 1954.

Reu, J. M., ed., *The Augsburg Confession: a collection of sources*. Chicago, IL: Wartburg Publishing House, 1930.

Ridley, Nicholas, *The Works of Nicholas Ridley*, edited by H. Christmas. PS. Cambridge: CUP, 1843.

Schaff, Philip, ed., *The Creeds of Christendom*. Vol. 3. Grand Rapids, MI: Baker, 1977. http://www.ccel.org/ccel/schaff/creeds3.i.html.

Standish, John, *A lytle treatyse [. . .] against the protestacion of Roberti Barnes at the tyme of his death*. London: Robert Redman, 1540; RSTC 23209.

Strype, John, *Ecclesiastical Memorials, relating chiefly to religion, and the reformation of it*. 3 vols. Oxford: OUP, 1822.

Taverner, Richard, *The most sacred Bible [. . .] translated into English, and newly recognised with great diligence after most faythful exemplars*. London: John Byddell, for Thomas Barthlet, 1539; RSTC 2066.

Tudor Royal Proclamations, edited by P. L. Hughes and J. F. Larkin. 3 vols. New Haven and London: YUP, 1964.

The Two Liturgies, A.D. 1549, and A.D. 1552: with other documents set forth by authority in the reign of King Edward VI, edited by J. Ketley. PS. Cambridge: CUP, 1844.

Tyndale, William, *The New Testament* [Cologne Fragment, 1525]. Cologne: H. Fuchs?, 1525; RSTC 2823.

——. *A compendious introduccion, prologe or preface vnto the pistle off Paul to the Romayns*. Worms: P. Schoeffer, 1526; RSTC 24438.

——. *The Obedience of a Christen Man and How Christen Rulers Ought to Governe*. Antwerp: J. Hoochstraten [Martin de Keyser?], 1528; RSTC 24446.

——. *The Pentateuch*. Antwerp: Johan Hoochstraten, 1530; RSTC 2350.

——. *The practyse of prelates, Whether the Kinges grace maye be separated from hys quene, be cause she was his brothers wyfe*. Antwerp: Joannes Hoochstraten, 1530; RSTC 24465.

——. *The exposition of the fyrst epistle of seynt Jhon with a prologge before it*. Antwerp: M. de Keyser, 1531; RSTC 24443.

———. *The prophete Ionas*. Antwerp: M. de Keyser, 1531; RSTC 2788.

———. *An exposicion vppon the v. vi. vii. chapters of Mathew which thre chaptres are the keye and the dore of the scripture [. . .] before the booke, thou hast a prologe very necessarie, contaynynge the whole somme of the couenaunt made betwene God and vs, vppon which we be baptised to kepe it*. Antwerp?: J. Grapheus?, 1533?; RSTC 24440.

———. *The firste boke of Moses called Genesis newly correctyd and amendyd by W.T.* Antwerp: M. de Keyser, 1534; RSTC 2351.

———. *A Treatyse of the Iustificacyon By Faith Only, otherwise called the Parable of the Wyked Mammon* [1528]. Southwarke: Iames Nycolson, 1536; RSTC 24455.

———. *A briefe declaration of the sacraments*. London: Robert Stoughton, 1548; RSTC 24445.

———. *Doctrinal Treatises and Introductions to Different Portions of the Holy Scriptures*, edited by H. Walter. PS. Cambridge: CUP, 1848.

———. *An Answer to Sir Thomas More's Dialogue*, edited by H. Walter. PS. Cambridge: CUP, 1849.

———. *Expositions and Notes on Sundry Portions of the Holy Scriptures, together with the Practice of Prelates*, edited by H. Walter. PS. Cambridge: CUP, 1849.

———. *The New Testament* [1534], edited by D. Daniell. New Haven and London: YUP, 1995.

Vermigli, Peter Martyr, *The Oxford Treatise and Disputation on the Eucharist*, edited by J. C. McLelland. Kirksville, MO: Truman State University Press, 2000.

Vowell, John, *The Antient History and Description of the City of Exeter [. . .] with a catalogue of all the bishops to the year of our Lord 1578. Collected chiefly by John Vowell, alias Hooker*. Exeter: Andrews and Trewman, 1765.

Werdmüller, Otto, *A spyrytuall and moost precyouse pearle Teachyng all men to loue and imbrace the crosse [. . .] Sett forth by the moste honorable lorde, the duke hys grace of Somerset.* Translated by M. Coverdale. London: S. Mierdman for Gwalter Lynne, 1550; RSTC 25255.

Whitgift, John, *The Works of John Whitgift, D.D.*, edited by J. Ayre. 3 vols. PS. Cambridge: CUP, 1851–53.

Wright, D. F., ed., *Commonplaces of Martin Bucer.* Abingdon: Sutton Courtenay Press, 1972.

The Zurich Letters, comprising the correspondence of several English bishops and others, with some of the Helvetian Reformers, during the early part of the reign of Queen Elizabeth, edited by H. Robinson. 2 vols. PS. Cambridge: CUP, 1842/45.

Zwingli, Huldrych, *The rekening and declaracion of the faith and beleif of Huldrik Zwingly bisshoppe of Ziiryk the cheif town of Heluetia, sent to Charles V.* Translated by G. Joye. Antwerp: Widow of C. Ruremund, 1543; RSTC 26138.

———. *Selected Works of Huldreich Zwingli*, edited by S. M. Jackson. Philadelphia: University of Pennsylvania, 1901.

———. *Huldreich Zwinglis Sämtliche Werke*, edited by E. Egli and G. Finsler. *CR.* Vols. 88–101. Berlin: C. A. Schwetschke; Leipzig: M. Heinsius Nachfolger; Zürich: TVZ, 1905–1991.

———. *The Latin Works of Huldreich Zwingli*, edited by S. M. Jackson. 3 vols. Durham, NC: Labyrinth, 1912–83.

———. *Huldrych Zwingli: Writings*, edited by E. J. Furcha and H. W. Pipkin. 2 vols. Allison Park, PA: Pickwick, 1984.

Secondary Literature

Althaus, Paul, *The Theology of Martin Luther.* Philadelphia: Fortress Press, 1966.

Amos, N. Scott et al., eds., *The Education of a Christian Society: Humanism and the Reformation in Britain and the Netherlands: papers delivered to the Thirteenth Anglo-Dutch Historical Conference, 1997.* Aldershot: Ashgate, 1999.

Arnold, Jonathan, *The Great Humanists: European thought on the eve of the Reformation*. London and New York: I. B. Tauris and Co., 2011.

Aston, Margaret, "Lollardy and the Reformation: Survival or Revival?" *History* 49 (1964): 149–70.

———. *Lollards and Reformers: Images and Literacy in Late Medieval England*. London: Hambledon Press, 1984.

———. *England's Iconoclasts: Laws Against Images*. Vol. 1. Oxford: OUP, 1988.

———. "Iconoclasm at Rickmansworth, 1522: Troubles of Church-wardens." *JEH* 40, 4 (1989): 524–52.

———. *Faith and Fire: Popular and Unpopular Religion 1350–1600*. London and Rio Grande, OH: Hambledon Press, 1993.

Bailey, Sherwin, "Robert Wisdom under Persecution, 1541–43." *JEH* 2 (1951): 180–89.

Bainton, Roland, *Here I Stand: a life of Martin Luther*. New York: Abingdon Press, 1950.

———. *The Age of the Reformation*. Princeton: Van Nostrand, 1956.

Baker, Derek, ed., *Reform and Reformation: England and the continent c.1500–c.1750*. Oxford: Blackwell, 1979.

Baker, J. Wayne, *Heinrich Bullinger and the Covenant: The Other Reformed Tradition*. Athens, OH: Ohio University Press, 1980.

———. "Church, State, and Dissent: The Crisis of the Swiss Reformation, 1531–1536." *CH* 57, 2 (1988): 135–52.

———. "Zwinglianism." In *OER*, edited by H. J. Hillerbrand. Vol. 4. New York and Oxford: OUP, 1996.

———. "Heinrich Bullinger, the Covenant, and the Reformed Tradition in Retrospect." *SCJ* 29, 2 (1998): 359–76.

Baker, J. Wayne and Charles McCoy, *Fountainhead of Federalism: Heinrich Bullinger and the Covenantal Tradition*. Louisville, KY: Westminster John Knox Press, 1991.

Baltzer, Klaus, *The Covenant Formulary in Old Testament, Jewish, and Early Christian Writings*. Translated by D. Green. Oxford: Basil Blackwell, 1971.

Bibliography

Beeke, Joel, *Assurance of Faith: Calvin, English Puritanism, and the Dutch Second Reformation*. New York: Peter Lang, 1991.

Benedict, Philip, *Christ's Churches Purely Reformed: A Social History of Calvinism*. New Haven and London: YUP, 2002.

Bernard, G. W., "The making of religious policy, 1533–1546: Henry VIII and the search for the middle way." *HJ* 41, 2 (1998): 321–49.

———. *The King's Reformation: Henry VIII and the remaking of the English Church*. New Haven and London: YUP, 2005.

Biel, Pamela, *Doorkeepers in the House of Righteousness: Heinrich Bullinger and the Zurich Clergy 1535–1575*. Berne: P. Lang, 1991.

Bierma, Lyle, "Federal Theology in the Sixteenth Century: Two Traditions?" *WTJ* 45 (1983): 304–21.

———. "The Role of Covenant Theology in Early Reformed Orthodoxy." *SCJ* 21, 3 (1990): 453–62.

Blickle, Peter, *Communal Reformation: The Quest for Salvation in Sixteenth-Century Germany*. Translated by T. Dunlap. London and New Jersey: Humanities Press International, 1992.

Bossy, John, "Moral arithmetic: Seven Sins into Ten Commandments." In *Conscience and Casuistry in Early Modern Europe*, edited by E. Leites, 214–34. Cambridge: CUP, 1988.

Bowd, Stephen, *Reform before the Reformation: Vincenzo Querini and the religious renaissance in Italy*. Leiden: Brill, 2002.

Bozeman, Theodore, *The Precisianist Strain: Disciplinary Religion and Antinomian Backlash in Puritanism to 1638*. Chapel Hill, NC and London: University of North Carolina Press, 2004.

Brady, Thomas, "From Revolution to the Long Reformation: Writings in English on the German Reformation, 1970–2005." *ARG* 100 (2009): 48–64.

Brigden, Susan, "Popular disturbance and the fall of Thomas Cromwell and the reformers, 1539–1540." *HJ* 24, 2 (1981): 257–78.

———. "Youth and the English Reformation." *PP* 95 (1982): 37–67.

———. "Thomas Cromwell and the 'brethren'." In *Law and government under the Tudors*, edited by C. Cross, D. Loades, and J. Scarisbrick, 31–49. Cambridge: CUP, 1988.

———. *London and the Reformation*. Oxford: OUP, 1989.

———. "Henry Howard, Earl of Surrey, and the 'Conjured League'." *HJ* 37 (1994): 507–37.

———. "'The shadow that you know': Sir Thomas Wyatt and Sir Francis Bryan at court and in embassy." *HJ* 39 (1996): 1–31.

———. *New Worlds, Lost Worlds: The Rule of the Tudors 1485–1603*. London: Penguin, 2000.

———. *Thomas Wyatt: the Heart's Forest*. London: Faber and Faber, 2012.

Brigden, Susan, and Nigel Wilson, "New Learning and Broken Friendship." *EHR* 112 (1997): 396–411.

Brigden, Susan, and Jonathan Woolfson, "Thomas Wyatt in Italy." *RQ* 58 (2005): 464–511.

Britnell, Jennifer, "John Gough and the *Traité de la Différence des Schismes et des Conciles* of Jean Lemaire de Beiges: Translation as Propaganda in the Henrician Reformation." *JEH* 46, 1 (1995): 62–74.

Bromiley, G. W., *Baptism and the Anglican Reformers*. London: Lutterworth Press, 1953.

Brooks, Peter Newman, *Thomas Cranmer's Doctrine of the Eucharist: An Essay in Historical Development*. 2nd ed. Basingstoke: Macmillan, 1992.

Brown, Andrew, *William Tyndale on priests and preachers: with new light on his early career*. London: Inscriptor Imprints, 1996.

Burnett, Amy Nelson, *The Yoke of Christ: Martin Bucer and Christian Discipline*. Kirksville, MO: SCJ Publishers, 1994.

———. *Teaching the Reformation: Ministers and their Message in Basel, 1529–1629*. Oxford: OUP, 2006.

Buxton, Brian, "William Tyndale in Gloucestershire." *TBGAS* 131 (2013): 189–98.

Cameron, Euan, *The European Reformation*. Oxford: OUP, 1991.

———. "The Search for Luther's Place in the Reformation." *JEH* 45, 3 (1994): 475–85.

———. *Enchanted Europe: Superstition, Reason, and Religion 1250–1750*. Oxford: OUP, 2010.

Campi, Emidio, and Peter Opitz, eds., *Heinrich Bullinger: Life—Thought—Influence: International Congress Heinrich Bullinger (1504–1575), 25–29 August 2004*. 2 vols. Zurich: TVZ, 2007.

Cargill Thompson, W. D. J., "Who wrote 'The Supper of the Lord'?" *HTR* 53 (1960): 77–91.

Carley, James, "'Her moost lovyng and fryndely brother sendeth gretyng': Anne Boleyn's Manuscripts and Their Sources." In *Illuminating the Book: Makers and Interpreters*, edited by M. Brown and S. McKendrick, 261–80. London: British Library, 1998.

Catto, Jeremy, "Theology after Wycliffism." In *The History of the University of Oxford*, edited by J. Catto and R. Evans, 263–80. Vol. 2. Oxford: OUP, 1992.

———. "Oriel in Renaissance Oxford, 1479–1574." In *Oriel College: a history*, edited by J. Catto, 60–93. Oxford: OUP, 2013.

Chadwick, Owen, *The Reformation*. Harmondsworth: Penguin, 1964.

Christ-von Wedel, Christine, *Erasmus of Rotterdam: advocate of a new Christianity*. Toronto and London: University of Toronto Press, 2013.

Clebsch, William, "More evidence that George Joye wrote *The Souper of the Lorde*." *HTR* 55 (1962): 63–66.

———. *England's Earliest Protestants, 1525–1535*. Westport, CT: Greenwood Press, 1964.

Collinson, Patrick, "England." In *The Reformation in National Context*, edited by B. Scribner, R. Porter and M. Teich, 80–94. Cambridge: CUP, 1994.

———. "William Tyndale and the Course of the English Reformation." *Reformation* 1 (1996): 72–97.

———. "The Reformation." In *A Century of Theological and Religious Studies in Britain*, edited by E. Nicholson, 187–213. The British Academy. Oxford: OUP, 2003.

Collinson, Patrick, and Polly Ha, eds., *The Reception of Continental Reformation in Britain*. *PBA* Vol. 164. Oxford: OUP, 2010.

Coolidge, J. S., *The Pauline Renaissance in England: Puritanism and the Bible*. Oxford: OUP, 1970.

Courvoisier, Jaques, *Zwingli: A Reformed Theologian*. London: Epworth, 1964.

Craig, John, "The growth of English Puritanism." In *The Cambridge Companion to Puritanism*, edited by J. Coffey and P. Lim, 34–47. Cambridge: CUP, 2008.

Cross, Richard, "Alloiosis in the Christology of Zwingli." *JTS* 47, 1 (1996): 105–22.

Cummings, Brian, *The Literary Culture of the Reformation: Grammar and Grace*. Oxford: OUP, 2002.

D'Alton, Craig, "The Suppression of Lutheran Heretics in England, 1526–1529." *JEH* 54, 2 (2003): 228–53.

Daniell, David, *William Tyndale: a biography*. New Haven and London: YUP, 1994.

———. "Coverdale, Miles (1488–1569)." In *ODNB*. Oxford: OUP, 2004. http://www.oxforddnb.com/view/article/6486.

———. "Frith, John (1503–1533)." In *ODNB*. Oxford: OUP, 2004. http://www.oxforddnb.com/view/article/10188.

———. "Tyndale, William (*c.*1494–1536)." In *ODNB*. Oxford: OUP, 2004. http://www.oxforddnb.com/view/article/27947.

Davies, Catherine, *A Religion of the Word: the defence of the Reformation in the reign of Edward VI*. Manchester: Manchester University Press, 2002.

Davis, David, *Seeing Faith, Printing Pictures: Religious Identity during the English Reformation*. Leiden and Boston: Brill, 2013.

Davis, John, "The Trials of Thomas Bylney and the English Reformation." *HJ* 24, 4 (1981): 775–90.

———. *Heresy and Reformation in the south-east of England, 1520–1559*. London: Royal Historical Society, 1983.

De Kroon, Marijn, *The Honour of God and Human Salvation: a contribution to an understanding of Calvin's theology according to his Institutes*. Translated by L. Bierma and J. Vriend. Edinburgh and New York: T&T Clark, 2001.

Dembek, Arne, *William Tyndale (1491–1536): Reformatorische Theologie als kontextuelle Schriftauslegung.* Tübingen: Mohr Siebeck, 2010.
Dent, C. M., *Protestant Reformers in Elizabethan Oxford.* Oxford: OUP, 1983.
Dickens, A. G., *Lollards and Protestants in the Diocese of York, 1509–1558.* Oxford: OUP, 1959.
———. *The English Reformation.* 1st ed. London: B. T. Batsford, 1964.
———. "Heresy and the Origins of English Protestantism." In *Britain and The Netherlands: Anglo-Dutch Historical Conference 1962,* edited by J. S. Bromley and E. H. Kossmann, 47–66. Vol. 2. Utrecht and Amsterdam: J. B. Walters, 1964.
———. "Review of 'English Humanists and Reformation Politics under Henry VIII and Edward VI. By James K. McConica'." *History* 52 (1967): 77–78.
———. *The German Nation and Martin Luther.* London: Edward Arnold, 1974.
———. "The Early Expansion of Protestantism in England 1520–1558." *ARG* 78 (1987): 187–222.
———. *The English Reformation.* 2nd ed. London: B.T. Batsford, 1989.
Disley, Emma, "Degrees of glory: Protestant doctrine and the concept of rewards hereafter." *JTS* 42, 1 (1991): 77–105.
Dowling, Maria, "Anne Boleyn and Reform." *JEH* 35, 1 (1984): 30–46.
———. *Humanism in the Age of Henry VIII.* London: Croom Helm, 1986.
———. "The Gospel and the Court: Reformation under Henry VIII." In *Protestantism and the National Church in Sixteenth Century England,* edited by P. Lake and M. Dowling, 36–77. London, New York and Sydney: Croom Helm, 1987.
Duffy, Eamon, *The Stripping of the Altars: Traditional Religion in England c.1400–c.1580.* New Haven and London: YUP, 1992.
Dugmore, Clifford, *The Mass and the English Reformers.* London: Macmillan, 1958.

Duke, Alastair, *Reformation and Revolt in the Low Countries*. London and Ronceverte: Hambledon Press, 1990.

Dunning, Robert, "The last days of Cleeve Abbey." In *The Church in Pre-Reformation Society*, edited by C. Barron and C. Harper-Bill, 58–67. Woodbridge: Boydell Press, 1985.

Ella, George, *Henry Bullinger: Shepherd of the Churches*. Eggleston, Durham: Go Publications, 2007.

Elton, G. R., *The Tudor Revolution in Government*. Cambridge: CUP, 1953.

———. *England under the Tudors*. London: Methuen, 1955.

———. *Reformation Europe 1517–1559*. London: Collins, 1963.

———. *Policy and Police: the Enforcement of the Reformation in the Age of Thomas Cromwell*. Cambridge: CUP, 1972.

———. *Reform and Reformation: England 1509–1558*. London: Edward Arnold, 1977.

Euler, Carrie, *Couriers of the Gospel: England and Zurich 1531–1558*. Zurich: TVZ, 2006.

———. "Does Faith Translate? Tudor Translations of Martin Luther and the Doctrine of Justification by Faith." *ARG* 101 (2010): 80–113.

Farthing, John, *Thomas Aquinas and Gabriel Biel: Interpretations of St. Thomas Aquinas in German Nominalism on the Eve of the Reformation*. Durham, NC and London: Duke University Press, 1988.

Fenlon, Dermot, *Heresy and Obedience in Tridentine Italy: Cardinal Pole and the Counter Reformation*. Cambridge: CUP, 1972.

Ferguson, Jamie, "Miles Coverdale and the Claims of Paraphrase." In *Psalms in the Early Modern World*, edited by L. Austern, K. McBride and D. Orvis, 137–54. Farnham: Ashgate, 2011.

Ferry, Anne, *The "Inward" Language: Sonnets of Wyatt, Sidney, Shakespeare, Donne*. Chicago and London: University of Chicago Press, 1983.

Fines, John, ed., *A Biographical Register of Early English Protestants and others opposed to the Roman Catholic Church, 1525–1558*, 2 vols. Vol. 1. Abingdon: Sutton Courtenay Press, 1981. Vol. 2. [typescript]: West Sussex Institute of Higher Education, 1985.

Gäbler, Ulrich, *Huldrych Zwingli: His Life and Work*. Translated by R. Gritsch. Philadelphia: Fortress Press, 1986.

Gairdner, James, *Lollardy and the Reformation: A Historical Survey*, 4 vols. London: Macmillan, 1908–13.

Ganoczy, Alexandre, *The Young Calvin*. Translated by D. Foxgrover and W. Provo. Edinburgh: T&T Clark, 1987.

Garrett, Christina, *The Marian Exiles: A Study in the Origins of Elizabethan Puritanism*. Cambridge: CUP, 1938.

Gelbert, J. P., *Magister Johann Bader's Leben und Schriften, Nicolaus Thomae und seine Briefe*. Neustadt: A. P. Gottschict-Witter, 1868.

Gerrish, Brian, *The Old Protestantism and the New: Essays on the Reformation Heritage*. Edinburgh: T&T Clark, 1982.

———. *Continuing the Reformation: Essays on Modern Religious Thought*. Chicago and London: University of Chicago Press, 1993.

———. *Grace and Gratitude: The Eucharistic Theology of John Calvin*. Edinburgh: T&T Clark, 1993.

Goeters, J. F. Gerhard, "Föderaltheologie." In *Theologische Realenzyklopädie*, edited by H. Balz et al., 246–52. Vol. 11. Berlin and New York: Walter de Gruyter, 1983.

Gordon, Bruce, "Zurich and the Scottish Reformation: Rudolf Gwalther's *Homilies on Galatians* of 1576." In *Humanism and Reform: the Church in Europe, England, and Scotland, 1400–1643*, edited by J. Kirk, 207–19. Oxford: Blackwell, 1991.

———. ed., *Protestant History and Identity in Sixteenth-Century Europe*. Vol. 1. Aldershot: Scolar Press, 1996.

———. *The Swiss Reformation*. Manchester and New York: Manchester University Press, 2002.

———. *Calvin*. New Haven and London: YUP, 2009.

Gordon, Bruce, with Luca Baschera and Christian Moser, "Emulating the Past and Creating the Present: Reformation and the Use of Historical and Theological Models in Zurich in the

Sixteenth Century." In *Following Zwingli: Applying the Past in Reformation Zurich*, edited by L. Baschera, B. Gordon and C. Moser, 1–40. Farnham: Ashgate, 2014.

Graham, Michael, and Gretchen Minton, "The Word as as an Artifact of Remembrance." *Reformation* 18, 1 (2013): 64–83.

Greaves, Richard, "The origins and early development of English covenant thought." *The Historian* 31, 1 (1968): 21–35.

Green, V. H. H., *Religion at Oxford and Cambridge*. London: SCM Press, 1964.

Greenblatt, Stephen, *Renaissance Self-Fashioning: From More to Shakespeare*. Chicago and London: University of Chicago Press, 1980.

Greenslade, S. L., *The Work of William Tindale*. London and Glasgow: Blackie and Son, 1938.

———. "The Faculty of Theology." In *The History of the University of Oxford*, edited by J. McConica, 295–334. Vol. 3. Oxford: OUP, 1986.

Gregory, Brad, *Salvation at Stake: Christian Martyrdom in Early Modern Europe*. Cambridge, MA and London: HUP, 1999.

Greschat, Martin, "Der Bundesgedanke in der Theologie des späten Mittelalters." *Zeitschrift für Kirchengeschichte* 81 (1970): 44–63.

Gunn, Steven, "The Structures of Politics in Early Tudor England." *TRHS* 6th series, 5 (1995): 59–90.

Gunther, Karl, *Reformation Unbound: Protestant Visions of Reform in England, 1525–1590*. Cambridge: CUP, 2014.

Hagen, Kenneth, "From Testament to Covenant in the Early Sixteenth Century." *SCJ* 3, 1 (1972): 1–24.

Haigh, Christopher, *Reformation and Resistance in Tudor Lancashire*. Cambridge: CUP, 1975.

———. ed., *The English Reformation Revised*. Cambridge: CUP, 1987.

———. *English Reformations: religion, politics, and society under the Tudors*. Oxford: OUP, 1993.

———. "Religion." *TRHS* 6th series, 7 (1997): 281–99.

———. "Henry VIII and the German Reformation." In *Religion und Politik in Deutschland und Grossbritannien*, edited by R. Bonney, F. Bosbach, and T. Brockmann, 31–42. Munich: K. G. Saur, 2001.

Hall, Basil, "Calvin against the Calvinists." In *John Calvin: a collection of distinguished essays*, edited by G. Duffield, 19–37. Grand Rapids, MI: Eerdmans, 1966.

———. "Cranmer, the Eucharist and the Foreign Divines in the Reign of Edward VI." In *Thomas Cranmer: Churchman and Scholar*, edited by P. Ayris and D. Selwyn, 217–58. Woodbridge: Boydell Press, 1993.

———. "Martin Bucer in England." In *Martin Bucer: Reforming church and community*, edited by D. F. Wright, 144–60. Cambridge: CUP, 1994.

Hamm, Berndt, *Promissio, Pactum, Ordinatio: Freiheit und Selbstbinding Gottes in der scholastischen Gnadenlehre*. Tübingen: Mohr, 1977.

———. *The Reformation of Faith in the Context of Late Medieval Theology and Piety*. Translated by H. Heron, G. Wiedermann and J. Frymire. Leiden and Boston: Brill, 2004.

Haran, Menahem, "The *Běrît* 'Covenant': Its Nature and Ceremonial Background." In *Tehillah le-Moshe: Biblical and Judaic Studies in Honour of Moshe Greenberg*, edited by M. Cogan, B. Eichler, and J. Tigay, 203–19. Winona Lake, IN: Eisenbrauns, 1997.

Harris, Jesse W., *John Bale: A Study in the Minor Literature of the Reformation*. Urbana, IL: University of Illinois Press, 1940.

Hazlett, Ian, "Eucharistic communion: impulses and directions in Martin Bucer's thought." In *Martin Bucer: Reforming church and community*, edited by D. F. Wright, 72–82. Cambridge: CUP, 1994.

Heal, Felicity, *Reformation in Britain and Ireland*. Oxford: OUP, 2003.

Heal, Felicity, and Clive Holmes, *The Gentry in England and Wales, 1500–1700*. Basingstoke: Macmillan, 1994.

Hellinga, Lotte, ed., *The Bookshop of the World: the role of the Low Countries in the book-trade 1473–1941*. 't Goy-Houten: Hes and De Graaf, 2001.

Helm, Paul, *John Calvin's Ideas*. Oxford: OUP, 2004.

Hesselink, I. J., *Calvin's Concept of the Law*. Allison Park, PA: Pickwick, 1992.

Hoak, Dale, *The King's Council in the Reign of Edward VI*. Cambridge: CUP, 1976.

Hornbeck, J. Patrick, *What is a Lollard? Dissent and Belief in Late Medieval England*. Oxford: OUP, 2010.

Houlbrooke, Ralph, *Church Courts and the People during the English Reformation, 1520–1570*. Oxford: OUP, 1979.

———. "Parkhurst, John (1511?–1575)." In *ODNB*. Oxford: OUP: 2004. http://www.oxforddnb.com/view/article/21362.

Hudson, Anne, *The Premature Reformation: Wycliffite Texts and Lollard History*. Oxford: OUP, 1988.

Hudson, Winthrop, *The Cambridge Connection and the Elizabethan Settlement of 1559*. Durham, NC: Duke University Press, 1980.

Hughes, Celia, "Coverdale's Alter Ego." *Bulletin of the John Rylands Library* 65, 1 (1982): 100–124.

———. "Two Sixteenth-Century Northern Protestants: John Bradford and William Turner." *Bulletin of the John Rylands Library* 66, 1 (1983): 104–38.

Hume, Anthea, "William Roye's "Brefe Dialogue" (1527): An English Version of a Strassburg Catechism." *HTR* 60 (1967): 307–21.

———. "English Protestant Books Printed Abroad, 1525–35: An Annotated Bibliography." In *The Complete Works of St. Thomas More*, edited by L. Schuster et al., 1063–91. 8 vols. New Haven and London: YUP, 1973.

Hunt, E. W., *The Life and Times of John Hooper (c.1500–1555) Bishop of Gloucester*. Lampeter: Edwin Mellen Press, 1992.

Ives, Eric, *Anne Boleyn*. Oxford: Basil Blackwell, 1986.

———. *Lady Jane Grey: a Tudor mystery*. Oxford: Wiley-Blackwell, 2009.

James, Susan, *Kateryn Parr: The Making of a Queen*. Aldershot: Ashgate, 1999.

Jeanes, Gordon, *Signs of God's Promise: Thomas Cranmer's Sacramental Theology and the Book of Common Prayer*. London: T&T Clark, 2008.

Jones, Whitney, "Turner, William (1509–10–1568)." In *ODNB*. Oxford: OUP, 2004. https://doi.org/10.1093/ref:odnb/27874.

Jones, William, "Uses of Foreigners in the Church of Edward VI." *Numen* 6 (1959): 142–53.

Jordan, W. K., *Edward VI: the Young King*. London: George Allen & Unwin, 1968.

Karlberg, M. W., "Reformed Interpretation of the Mosaic Covenant." *WTJ* 43 (1980): 1–57.

Karpman, Dahlia, "William Tyndale's Response to the Hebraic Tradition." *Studies in the Renaissance* 14 (1967): 110–30.

Kendall, R. T., *Calvin and English Calvinism to 1649*. Oxford: OUP, 1979.

King, John, *English Reformation Literature: The Tudor Origins of the Protestant Tradition*. Princeton: Princeton University Press, 1982.

———. "Thomas More, William Tyndale, and the Printing of Religious Propaganda." In *The Oxford Handbook of Tudor Literature, 1485–1603*, edited by M. Pincombe and C. Shrank, 105–20. Oxford: OUP, 2009.

Kipling, Gordon, "Belmaine, Jean (*fl.*1546–1559)." In *ODNB*. Oxford: OUP, 2004. http://www.oxforddnb.com/view/article/2041.

Kirby, Torrance, "Wholesale or retail? Antoine de Marcourt's *The Boke of Marchauntes* and Tudor political theology." *Renaissance and Reformation* 28, 2 (2004): 37–60.

———. *The Zurich Connection and Tudor Political Theology*. Leiden and Boston: Brill, 2007.

Knappen, Marshall, "William Tyndale—First English Puritan." *CH* 5 (1936): 201–15.

———. *Tudor Puritanism: a chapter in the history of idealism*. Gloucester, MA: Peter Smith, 1963.

Knox, D. Broughton, *The Doctrine of Faith in the reign of Henry VIII*. London: James Clarke & Co., 1961.

Kolb, Robert, *Luther's Heirs Define His Legacy: Studies on Lutheran Confessionalisation*. Aldershot: Variorum, 1996.

Kristeller, Paul O., *Renaissance Thought and its Sources*. New York: Columbia University Press, 1979.

Kümin, Beat, *The Shaping of a Community: the Rise and Reformation of the English Parish c.1400–1560*. Aldershot: Scolar, 1996.

Latré, Guido, "The 1535 Coverdale Bible and its Antwerp Origins." In *The Bible as book: the Reformation*, edited by O. O'Sullivan, 89–102. New Castle and London: Oak Knoll Press, 2000.

Leedham-Green, Elizabeth, *Books in Cambridge Inventories: book lists from Vice-Chancellor's Court probate inventories in the Tudor and Stuart periods*. 2 vols. Cambridge: CUP, 1986.

Lehner, Ulrich, Richard Muller and A. G. Roeber, *The Oxford Handbook of Early Modern Theology, 1600–1800*. New York: OUP, 2016.

Leinsle, Ulrich, *Introduction to Scholastic Theology*. Translated by M. Miller. Washington, DC: The Catholic University of America Press, 2010.

Letham, Robert, "The Foedus Operum: some factors accounting for its development." *SCJ* 14, 4 (1983): 457–67.

Lewis, C. S., *English Literature in the Sixteenth Century excluding drama*. Oxford: OUP, 1954.

Lillback, Peter, *The Binding of God: Calvin's Role in the Development of Covenant Theology*. Grand Rapids, MI: Baker Academic, 2001.

Litzenberger, Caroline, *The English Reformation and the laity: Gloucestershire, 1540–1580*. Cambridge: CUP, 1997.

Lloyd Jones, G., *The Discovery of Hebrew in Tudor England: a third language*. Manchester: Manchester University Press, 1983.

Loach, Jennifer, "Reformation Controversies." In *The History of the University of Oxford*, edited by J. McConica, 363–96. Vol. 3. Oxford: OUP, 1986.

———. *Edward VI*. New Haven and London: YUP, 1999.

Loades, David, *The Reign of King Edward VI*. Bangor: Headstart History, 1994.

———. "Books and the English Reformation prior to 1558." In *The Reformation and the Book*, edited by J. Gilmont, 264–91. Aldershot: Ashgate, 1998.

———. "Hilles, Richard (c.1514–1587)." In *ODNB*. Oxford: OUP, 2004. http://www.oxforddnb.com/view/article/47402.

———. *Henry VIII: court, church and conflict*. Kew: The National Archives, 2007.

———. *Thomas Cromwell: servant to Henry VIII*. Stroud: Amberley, 2013.

Loane, Marcus, *Pioneers of the Reformation in England*. London: The Church Book Room Press, 1964.

———. *Masters of the English Reformation*. 2nd ed. Edinburgh: Banner of Truth, 2005.

Locher, Gottfried, *Zwingli's Thought: New Perspectives*. Leiden: Brill, 1981.

Lohse, Bernhard, *Martin Luther's Theology: Its Historical and Systematic Development*. Translated by R. Harrisville. Edinburgh: T&T Clark, 1999.

MacCulloch, Diarmaid, "The Myth of the English Reformation." *JBS* 30, 1 (1991): 1–19.

———. "The Religion of Henry VIII." In *Henry VIII: A European Court in England*, edited by D. Starkey, 160–62. London: Collins & Brown, 1991.

———. ed., *The Reign of Henry VIII: Politics, Policy and Piety*. Basingstoke: Macmillan, 1995.

———. "Archbishop Cranmer: concord and tolerance in a changing Church." In *Tolerance and intolerance in the European Reformation*, edited by O. Grell and B. Scribner, 199–215. Cambridge: CUP, 1996.

———. *Thomas Cranmer: A Life*. New Haven and London: YUP, 1996.

———. *Tudor Church Militant: Edward VI and the Protestant Reformation.* London: Allen Lane, 1999.

———. *Reformation: Europe's House Divided 1490–1700.* London: Penguin, 2004.

———. "Putting the English Reformation on the Map." *TRHS* 15 (2005): 75–95.

———. "Calvin: Fifth Latin Doctor of the Church?" In *Calvin and His Influence, 1509–2009*, edited by I. Backus and P. Benedict, 34–44. Oxford and New York: OUP, 2011.

———. "Sixteenth-century English Protestantism and the Continent." In *Sister Reformations: the Reformation in Germany and in England: symposium on the occasion of the 450th anniversary of the Elizabethan Settlement, September 23rd-26th, 2009*, edited by D. Wendebourg, 1–14. Tübingen: Mohr Siebeck, 2010.

———. *Thomas Cromwell: A Life.* London: Allen Lane, 2018.

Maitland, S. R., *Essays on Subjects connected with the Reformation in England.* London: Francis and John Rivington, 1849.

Marsh, Christopher, *Popular religion in sixteenth-century England: holding their peace.* Basingstoke: Macmillan, 1998.

Marshall, Peter, "Papist as heretic: the burning of John Forest, 1538." *HJ* 41, 2 (1998): 351–74.

———. "Mumpsimus and Sumpsimus: The Intellectual Origins of a Henrician *Bon Mot*." *JEH* 52, 3 (2001): 512–20.

———. "Is the Pope a Catholic? Henry VIII and the semantics of schism." In *Catholics and the 'Protestant nation': religious politics and identity in early modern England*, edited by E. Shagan, 22–48. Manchester: Manchester University Press, 2005.

———. *Religious Identities in Henry VIII's England.* Aldershot: Ashgate, 2006.

———. "Religious Exiles and the Tudor State." In *Discipline and Diversity*, edited by K. Cooper and J. Gregory, 263–84. Ecclesiastical History Society. Woodbridge: Boydell Press, 2007.

———. "(Re)defining the English Reformation." *JBS* 48, 3 (2009): 564–86.

Marshall, Peter, and Alec Ryrie, eds., *The Beginnings of English Protestantism*. Cambridge: CUP, 2002.

Martin, J. W., "English Protestant Separatism at its Beginnings: Henry Hart and the Free-Will Men." *SCJ* 7, 2 (1976): 55–74.

Mayhew, G. J., "The progress of the Reformation in East Sussex, 1530–1559: the evidence from wills." *Southern History* 5 (1983): 38–67.

McConica, James, *English Humanists and Reformation Politics under Henry VIII and Edward VI*. Oxford: OUP, 1965.

McDiarmid, John, "John Cheke's Preface to *De Superstione*." *JEH* 48, 1 (1997): 100–120.

McEntegart, Rory, *Henry VIII, the League of Schmalkalden and the English Reformation*. Woodbridge: Royal Historical Society, 2002.

———. "Henry VIII and the German Lutherans: a reassessment." In *Sister Reformations: the Reformation in Germany and in England: symposium on the occasion of the 450th anniversary of the Elizabethan Settlement, September 23rd-26th*, 2009, edited by D. Wendebourg, 29–52. Tübingen: Mohr Siebeck, 2010.

McGiffert, Michael, "William Tyndale's Conception of Covenant." *JEH* 32 (1981): 167–84.

———. "Grace and works: the rise and division of covenant divinity in Elizabethan Puritanism." *HTR* 75, 4 (1982): 463–502.

———. "From Moses to Adam: The Making of the Covenant of Works." *SCJ* 19, 2 (1988): 131–55.

McGrath, Alister, "Humanist Elements in the Early Reformed Doctrine of Justification." *ARG* 73 (1982): 5–20.

———. "*Homo Assumptus*? A Study in the Christology of the *Via Moderna* with Particular Reference to William of Ockham." *ETL* 60 (1984): 283–97.

———. *Luther's Theology of the Cross: Martin Luther's Theological Breakthrough*. Oxford: Blackwell, 1985.

———. *The Intellectual Origins of the European Reformation*. Oxford: Basil Blackwell, 1987.

---. "Justification and the Reformation: The Significance of the Doctrine of Justification by Faith to Sixteenth Century Urban Communities." *ARG* 81 (1990): 5–19.

---. *Iustitia Dei: A History of the Christian Doctrine of Justification*. 3rd ed. Cambridge: CUP, 2005.

McNair, Philip, "Peter Martyr in England." In *Peter Martyr Vermigli and Italian Reform*, edited by J. McLelland, 85–106. Waterloo, ON: Wilfred Laurier University Press, 1980.

Methuen, Charlotte, *Kepler's Tübingen: Stimulus to a Theological Mathematics*. Aldershot: Ashgate, 1998.

---. "Oxford: Reading Scripture in the University." In *A Companion to Peter Martyr Vermigli*, edited by T. Kirby, E. Campi and F. James, 71–93. Leiden and Boston: Brill, 2009.

Miller, Gregory, "Huldrych Zwingli." In *The Reformation Theologians: an introduction to theology in the Early Modern period*, edited by C. Lindberg, 157–69. Oxford: Blackwell, 2002.

Miller, Perry, *The New England Mind: The Seventeenth Century*. 2nd ed. New York and London: Macmillan, 1954.

---. *Errand into the Wilderness*. London and Cambridge, MA: HUP, 1956.

Minnis, Alastair, "The Restoration of All Things: John Bradford's Refutation of Aquinas on Animal Resurrection." *Journal of Medieval and Early Modern Studies* 45, 2 (2015): 323–42.

Møller, Jens, "The Beginnings of Puritan Covenant Theology." *JEH* 14 (1963): 46–67.

Mozley, J. F., *William Tyndale*. London: SPCK, 1937.

---. *Coverdale and His Bibles*. London: Lutterworth, 1953.

Muller, Richard, *Christ and the Decree: Christology and Predestination in Reformed Theology from Calvin to Perkins*. Grand Rapids: Baker, 1988.

---. "Review of 'Fountainhead of Federalism'." *Anglican and Episcopal History* 63 (1994): 89–91.

---. *The Unaccommodated Calvin: Studies in the Foundation of a Theological Tradition*. Oxford: OUP, 2000.

———. *After Calvin: Studies in the Development of a Theological Tradition.* Oxford: OUP, 2003.

Murdock, Graeme, "The Importance of Being Josiah: An Image of Calvinist Identity." *SCJ* 29, 4 (1998): 1043–59.

Newcombe, D. G., "Hooper, John (1495x1500–1555)." In *ODNB*. Oxford: OUP, 2004. http://www.oxforddnb.com/view/article/13706.

———. *John Hooper: Tudor Bishop and Martyr.* Oxford: Davenant Press, 2009.

Nicholson, Ernest, *God and His People: Covenant and Theology in the Old Testament.* Oxford: OUP, 1986.

O'Donovan, Joan, *Theology of Law and Authority in the English Reformation.* Grand Rapids: Eerdmans, 2004.

Oberman, Heiko, *The Harvest of Medieval Theology: Gabriel Biel and Late Medieval Nominalism.* Cambridge, MA: HUP, 1963.

———. *Forerunners of the Reformation: The Shape of Late Medieval Thought.* New York: Holt, Rinehart and Winston, 1966.

———. ed., *Itinerarium Italicum: The Profile of the Italian Renaissance in the Mirror of its European Transformations.* Leiden: Brill, 1975.

———. *Masters of the Reformation: the emergence of a new intellectual climate in Europe.* Translated by D. Martin. Cambridge: CUP, 1981.

———. *The Dawn of the Reformation: Essays in Late Medieval and Early Reformation Thought.* Edinburgh: T&T Clark, 1986.

———. *Luther: Man between God and the Devil.* New Haven and London: YUP, 1989.

———. *The Reformation: Roots and Ramifications.* Translated by A. Gow. Edinburgh: T&T Clark, 1994.

Olofsson, Staffan, *The LXX Version: a guide to the translation technique of the Septuagint.* Stockholm: Almqvist & Wiksell, 1990.

Opie, John, "The Anglicising of John Hooper." *ARG* 59, 2 (1968): 150–77.

Opitz, Peter, "The Exegetical and Hermeneutical Work of John

Oecolampadius, Huldrych Zwingli and John Calvin." In *Hebrew Bible/Old Testament: The History of Its Interpretation*, edited by M. Sæbo, 407–51. Vol. 2. Göttingen: Vandenhoeck & Ruprecht, 2008.

———. "Bullinger and Paul." In *A Companion to Paul in the Reformation*, edited by R. Holder, 243–65. Leiden and Boston: Brill, 2009.

Overell, Anne, *Italian Reform and English Reformations, c.1535-c.1585*. Aldershot: Ashgate, 2008.

Overfield, James, "Scholastic Opposition to Humanism in Pre-Reformation Germany." *Viator* 7 (1976): 391–420.

Paisey, G. and G. Bartrum, "Hans Holbein and Miles Coverdale: a new Woodcut." *Print Quarterly* 26 (2009): 227–53.

Pardue, Brad, *Printing, Power, and Piety: appeals to the public during the early years of the English Reformation*. Leiden and Boston: Brill, 2012.

Parker, T. H. L., *John Calvin: a biography*. London: J. M. Dent & Sons, 1975.

Parker, T. M., *The English Reformation to 1558*. London: OUP, 1950.

Pearse, M. T., *Between Known Men and Visible Saints: a study in sixteenth-century English dissent*. London and Toronto: Associated University Press, 1994.

Pelikan, Jaroslav, *Reformation of Church and Dogma (1300–1700)*. The Christian Tradition: A History of the Development of Doctrine. Vol. 4. Chicago and London: University of Chicago Press, 1984.

Penny, D. A., *Freewill or Predestination: the battle over saving grace in mid-Tudor England*. Woodbridge: Royal Historical Society, 1990.

Pettegree, Andrew, *Foreign Protestant Communities in Sixteenth-Century London*. Oxford: OUP, 1986.

———. ed., *The Early Reformation in Europe*. Cambridge: CUP, 1992.

———. *Marian Protestantism: Six Studies*. Aldershot: Scolar Press, 1996.

———. ed., *The Reformation World*. London and New York: Routledge, 2000.

Pettegree, Andrew, et al., eds., *Calvinism in Europe, 1540–1620*. Cambridge: CUP, 1994.

Pineas, Rainer, *Thomas More and Tudor Polemics*. London and Bloomington, IN: Indiana University Press, 1968.

Porter, H. C., *Reformation and Reaction in Tudor Cambridge*. Cambridge: CUP, 1958.

Potter, G. R., *Ulrich Zwingli 1484–1531*. Cambridge: CUP, 1976.

Powicke, F. M., *The Reformation in England*. London: OUP, 1941.

Primus, J. H., "The Role of the Covenant Doctrine in the Puritanism of John Hooper." *Dutch Review of Church History* 48, 2 (1968): 182–96.

Questier, Michael, *Conversion, Politics and Religion in England, 1580–1625*. Cambridge: CUP, 1996.

Raath, Andries, and Shaun de Freitas, "From Heinrich Bullinger to puritanism: John Hooper's theology and the office of magistracy." *SJT* 56, 2 (2003): 208–30.

Racaut, Luc and Alec Ryrie, eds., *Moderate Voices in the European Reformation*. Aldershot: Ashgate, 2005.

Reeves, Ryan, *English Evangelicals and Tudor Obedience, c.1527–1570*. Leiden and Boston: Brill, 2014.

———. "'Ye Gods': Political Obedience from Tyndale to Cromwell, c.1528–1540." *ARG* 105, 1 (2014): 230–56.

Rex, Richard, "The English Campaign against Luther in the 1520s." *TRHS* 5th series, 39 (1989): 85–106.

———. *The Theology of John Fisher*. Cambridge: CUP, 1991.

———. "The New Learning." *JEH* 44, 1 (1993): 26–44.

———. "The crisis of obedience: God's word and Henry's reformation." *HJ* 39, 4 (1996): 863–94.

———. "The Early Impact of Reformation Theology at Cambridge University, 1521–1547." *RRR* 2 (1999): 38–71.

———. *The Lollards*. Basingstoke: Palgrave, 2002.

———. "New Light on Tyndale and Lollardy." *Reformation* 8 (2003): 143–71.

———. *Henry VIII and the English Reformation*. 2nd ed. Basingstoke: Palgrave Macmillan, 2006.

Roper, Lyndal, *Martin Luther: renegade and prophet*. London: Penguin, 2016.

Rorem, Paul, *Calvin and Bullinger on the Lord's Supper*. Alcuin Club. Nottingham: Grove Books, 1989.

Ross, D. S., "Hooper's alleged authorship of *A Brief and Clear Confession of the Christian Faith*." *CH* 39, 1 (1970): 18–29.

Ross, J. B., "Gasparo Contarini and His Friends." *Studies in the Renaissance* 17 (1970): 192–232.

Rummel, Erika, *The Confessionalisation of Humanism in Reformation Germany*. Oxford: OUP, 2000.

Rupp, E. G., *Studies in the Making of the English Protestant Tradition (Mainly in the Reign of Henry VIII)*. Cambridge: CUP, 1949.

———. *The Righteousness of God: Luther Studies*. London: Hodder and Stoughton, 1953.

———. *Six Makers of English Religion 1500–1700*. London: Hodder and Stoughton, 1957.

———. "John Bradford, Martyr. ob. 1 July, 1555." *The London Quarterly and Holborn Review* 6th series, 32 (1963): 50–55.

———. *Patterns of Reformation*. London: Epworth Press, 1969.

———. "The Battle of the Books." In *Reformation in Principle and Practice: Essays in Honour of A.G. Dickens*, edited by P. Brooks, 1–19. London: Scolar Press, 1980.

Ryrie, Alec, "Divine kingship and royal theology in Henry VIII's Reformation." *Reformation* 7 (2002): 49–77.

———. "The Strange Death of Lutheran England." *JEH* 53, 1 (2002): 64–92.

———. *The Gospel and Henry VIII: Evangelicals in the Early English Reformation*. Cambridge: CUP, 2003.

———. "Gough, John (*d.*1543/4)." In *ODNB*. Oxford, OUP, 2004. http://www.oxforddnb.com/view/article/11136.

———. "Paths not taken in the British Reformations." *HJ* 52, 1 (2009): 1–22.

———. *The Age of Reformation: the Tudor and Stewart Realms 1485–1603*. 2nd ed. Abingdon: Routledge, 2017.

Sanders, E. P., "The Covenant as a Soteriological Category in the Nature of Salvation in Palestinian and Hellenistic Judaism." In *Jews, Greeks and Christians: Religious Culture in Late Antiquity*, edited by R. Hamerton-Kelly and R. Scroggs, 11–44. Leiden: Brill, 1976.

Scarisbrick, J. J., *The Reformation and the English People*. Oxford: Basil Blackwell, 1984.

———. *Henry VIII*. 2nd ed. New Haven and London: YUP, 1997.

Schneider-Ludorff, Gury, "Philipp of Hesse as an example of princely Reformation: a contribution to Reformation studies." *RRR* 8, 3 (2006): 301–19.

Schofield, John, *Philip Melanchthon and the English Reformation*. Aldershot: Ashgate, 2006.

Schrenk, Gottlob, *Gottesreich und Bund im glteren Protestantismus vornehmlich bei Johannes Cocceius*. Gütersloh: Bertelsmann, 1923.

Seebohm, Frederic, *The Oxford Reformers: John Colet, Erasmus, and Thomas More*. 3rd ed. London: Longmans, Green & Co., 1911.

Selderhuis, Herman, ed., *The Calvin Handbook*. Grand Rapids and Cambridge: Eerdmans, 2009.

Shagan, Ethan, *Popular Politics and the English Reformation*. Cambridge: CUP, 2003.

Sharpe, Kevin, *Selling the Tudor Monarchy: Authority and Image in Sixteenth-Century England*. New Haven and London: YUP, 2009.

Skinner, Quentin, "Meaning and Understanding in the History of Ideas." *History and Theory* 8, 1 (1969): 3–53.

Smeeton, Donald, *Lollard themes in the Reformation theology of William Tyndale*. Kirksville, MO: SCJ Publishers, 1986.

Smith, H. Maynard, *Henry VIII and the Reformation*. London: Macmillan & Co, 1948.

Smith, Preserved, "Englishmen at Wittenberg in the Sixteenth Century." *EHR* 36 (1921): 422–33.

Smyth, Charles, *Cranmer and the Reformation under Edward VI*. Cambridge: CUP, 1926.

Spaans, Joke, "Reform in the Low Countries." In *A Companion to the Reformation World*, edited by R. Po-chia Hsia, 118–34. Oxford: Blackwell, 2004.

Speight, Helen, "'The Politics of Good Governance': Thomas Cromwell and the government of the south-west of England." *HJ* 37, 3 (1994): 623–38.

Spinks, Bryan, *Early and Medieval Rituals and Theologies of Baptism: from the New Testament to the Council of Trent*. Farnham: Ashgate, 2006.

Spruyt, B. J., "Wessel Gansfort and Cornelis Hoen's *Epistola Christiana*: 'The ring as a pledge of my love'." In *Wessel Gansfort (1419–1489) and Northern Humanism*, edited by F. Akkerman, G. Huisman and A. Vanderjagt, 122–41. Leiden: Brill, 1993.

———. *Cornelius Henrici Hoen (Honius) and his Epistle on the Eucharist (1525)*. Leiden and Boston: Brill, 2006.

Stayer, J. M., "Zwingli before Zurich: Humanist Reformer and Papal Partisan." *ARG* 72 (1981): 55–67.

Steinmetz, David, *Calvin in Context*. Oxford and New York: OUP, 1995.

———. *Reformers in the Wings: From Geiler von Kayserberg to Theodore Beza*. 2nd ed. Oxford: OUP, 2001.

Stephens, W. P., *The Holy Spirit in the Theology of Martin Bucer*. Cambridge: CUP, 1970.

———. *The Theology of Huldrych Zwingli*. Oxford: OUP, 1986.

———. "Huldrych Zwingli: The Swiss Reformer." *SJT* 41, 1 (1988): 27–47.

———. *Zwingli: An Introduction to His Thought*. Oxford: OUP, 1992.

———. "Bullinger and the Anabaptists with reference to his *Von Dem Unverschamten Frevel* (1531) and to Zwingli's writings on the Anabaptists." *RRR* 3 (2001): 96–107.

Strehle, Stephen, "*Fides aut Foedus*: Wittenberg and Zurich in conflict over the Gospel." *SCJ* 23, 1 (1992): 3–20.

Sykes, Norman, *The Crisis of the Reformation*. London: Geoffrey Bles, 1938.

Temple, William, *Readings in St John's Gospel*. London: Macmillan, 1939.

Thompson, Nicholas, *Eucharistic Sacrifice and Patristic Tradition in the Theology of Martin Bucer, 1534–1546*. Leiden and Boston: Brill, 2005.

Thomson, J. A. F., *The Later Lollards 1414–1520*. Oxford: OUP, 1965.

Tjernagel, N. S., *Henry VIII and the Lutherans: a study in Anglo-Lutheran relations from 1521 to 1547*. St Louis, MO: Concordia, 1965.

Tov, Emanuel, *The Greek and Hebrew Bible: collected essays on the Septuagint*. Leiden and Boston: Brill, 1999.

Tracy, James, "Heresy Law and Centralisation under Mary of Hungary: conflict between the Council of Holland and the central government over the enforcement of Charles V's placards." *ARG* 73 (1982): 284–307.

Trinkaus, Charles, *The Scope of Renaissance Humanism*. Ann Arbor: University of Michigan Press, 1983.

Trinterud, Leonard, "The Origins of Puritanism." *CH* 20, 1 (1951): 37–57.

———. "A Reappraisal of William Tyndale's Debt to Martin Luther." *CH* 31 (1962): 24–45.

Trueman, Carl, *Luther's Legacy: Salvation and English Reformers, 1525–1556*. Oxford: OUP, 1994.

———. "Early English Evangelicals: Three Examples." In *Sister Reformations: the Reformation in Germany and in England: symposium on the occasion of the 450th anniversary of the Elizabethan*

Settlement, September 23rd-26th, 2009, edited by D. Wendebourg, 15–28. Tübingen: Mohr Siebeck, 2010.

Tudor-Craig, Pamela, "Henry VIII and King David." In *Early Tudor England: Proceedings of the 1987 Harlaxton Symposium,* edited by D. Williams, 183–205. Woodbridge: Boydell Press, 1989.

Tyacke, Nicholas, *Aspects of English Protestantism c.1530–1700.* Manchester and New York: Manchester University Press, 2001.

Underwood, William, "Thomas Cromwell and William Marshall's Protestant books." *HJ* 47, 3 (2004): 517–39.

Vainio, Olli-Pekka, *Justification and Participation in Christ: The Development of the Lutheran Doctrine of Justification from Luther to the Formula of Concord (1580).* Leiden and Boston: Brill, 2008.

Van den Brink, J. N. Bakhuizen, "Ratramn's Eucharistic Doctrine and its Influence in Sixteenth-Century England." In *Studies in Church History,* edited by G. Cuming, 54–77. Vol. 2. London: Thomas Nelson, 1965.

Venema, Cornelis, "Heinrich Bullinger's Correspondence on Calvin's Doctrine of Predestination, 1551–1553." *SCJ* 17, 4 (1986): 435–50.

———. *Heinrich Bullinger and the doctrine of predestination: author of 'the other reformed tradition'?* Grand Rapids, MI: Baker Academic, 2002.

———. *Accepted and Renewed in Christ: the 'Twofold Grace of God' and the Interpretation of Calvin's Theology.* Gottingen: Vandenhoeck & Ruprecht, 2007.

Visser, Derk, "Covenant." In *OER,* edited by H. J. Hillerbrand, 442–45. Vol. 1. New York and Oxford: OUP, 1996.

Wabuda, Susan, "Shunamites and Nurses of the English Reformation: the Activities of Mary Glover, niece of Hugh Latimer." In *Women in the Church,* edited by W. Sheils and D. Wood, 335–44. Oxford: Basil Blackwell, 1990.

———. "Henry Bull, Miles Coverdale, and the Making of Foxe's *Book of Martyrs.*" In *Martyrs and Martyrologies,* edited by D. Wood, 245–58. Oxford: Blackwell, 1992.

———. "Equivocation and Recantation during the English Reformation: the 'Subtle Shadows' of Dr Edward Crome." *JEH* 44, 2 (1993): 224–42.
Wainwright, Robert, "William Tyndale on Covenant and Justification." *RRR* 13, 3 (2011): 353–72.
———. "I believe in the English Reformation." *Faith and Worship*, 85, Trinity (2019): 38–53.
Wallace, Dewey, *Puritans and Predestination: grace in English Protestant theology, 1525–1695*. Chapel Hill, NC: University of North Carolina Press, 1982.
Wallace, Ronald, *Calvin's Doctrine of Word and Sacrament*. Edinburgh: Oliver & Boyd, 1953.
———. *Calvin, Geneva and the Reformation: a study of Calvin as social reformer, churchman, pastor and theologian*. Edinburgh: Scottish Academic Press, 1988.
Walser, Georg, *The Greek of the Ancient Synagogue: an investigation on the Greek of the Septuagint, Pseudepigrapha and the New Testament*. Stockholm: Almqvist & Wiksell, 2001.
Walton, Robert, *Zwingli's Theocracy*. Toronto: University of Toronto Press, 1967.
Wandel, Lee, *Always Among Us: Images of the Poor in Zwingli's Zurich*. Cambridge: CUP, 1990.
———. *Voracious Idols and Violent Hands: Iconoclasm in Reformation Zurich, Strasbourg, and Basel*. Cambridge: CUP, 1995.
———. *The Eucharist in the Reformation: Incarnation and Liturgy*. Cambridge: CUP, 2006.
———. "The Body of Christ at Marburg, 1529." In *Image and Imagination of the Religious Self in Late Medieval and Early Modern Europe*, edited by R. Falkenburg, W. Melion and T. Richardson, 195–213. Turnhout: Brepols, 2007.
Weir, David, *The Origins of the Federal Theology in Sixteenth-Century Reformation Thought*. Oxford: OUP, 1990.
Wendebourg, Dorothea, ed., *Sister Reformations: the Reformation in Germany and in England: symposium on the occasion of the 450th*

anniversary of the Elizabethan Settlement, September 23rd–26th, 2009. Tübingen: Mohr Siebeck, 2010.

Wendel, François, *Calvin: the origins and development of his religious thought*. Translated by P. Mairet. London: Collins, 1963.

Werrell, Ralph, *The Theology of William Tyndale*. Cambridge: James Clarke & Co., 2006.

———. *The Roots of William Tyndale's Theology*. Cambridge: James Clarke & Co., 2013.

———. *The Blood of Christ in the Theology of William Tyndale*. Cambridge: James Clarke & Co., 2015.

———. "Sin and Salvation in William Tyndale's Theology." In *Sin and Salvation in Reformation England*, edited by J. Willis, 23–38. Farnham: Ashgate, 2015.

West, W. M. S., "John Hooper and the Origins of Puritanism [1]." *BQ* 15, 8 (1954): 346–68.

———. "John Hooper and the Origins of Puritanism [2]." *BQ* 16, 1 (1955): 22–46.

———. "John Hooper and the Origins of Puritanism [3]." *BQ* 16, 2 (1955): 67–88.

White, Hayden, *The Content of the Form: Narrative Discourse and Historical Representation*. London and Baltimore: John Hopkins University Press, 1987.

White, Micheline, "Women's Hymns in Mid-Sixteenth Century England: Elisabeth Cruciger, Miles Coverdale, and Lady Elizabeth Tyrwhit." *ANQ* 24, 1–2 (2011): 21–32.

Wicks, Jared, "Johann von Staupitz under Pauline Inspiration." In *A Companion to Paul in the Reformation*, edited by R. Holder, 319–36. Leiden and Boston: Brill, 2009.

Williams, C. H., *William Tyndale*. London: Thomas Nelson & Sons, 1969.

Willis, Jonathan, "'Moral Arithmetic' or Creative Accounting? (Re-)defining Sin through the Ten Commandments." In *Sin and Salvation in Reformation England*, edited by J. Willis, 69–84. Farnham: Ashgate, 2015.

Wooding, Lucy, *Rethinking Catholicism in Reformation England*. Oxford: OUP, 2000.

——. *Henry VIII*. London and New York: Routledge, 2009.

——. "From Tudor Humanism to Reformation Preaching." In *The Oxford Handbook of the Early Modern Sermon*, edited by P. McCullough, H. Adlington and E. Rhatigan, 329–47. Oxford: OUP, 2011.

Woolsey, Andrew, *Unity and Continuity in Covenantal Thought: A Study of the Reformed Tradition to the Westminster Assembly*. Grand Rapids, MI: Reformation Heritage Books, 2012.

Wright, David, "The Ethical Use of the Old Testament in Luther and Calvin: a comparison." *SJT* 36 (1983): 463–83.

Wright, Jonathan, "Marian Exiles and the Legitimacy of Flight from Persecution." *JEH* 52, 2 (2001): 220–43.

Unpublished Dissertations

Dalton, Alison, "John Hooper and his Networks: a Study of Change in Reformation England." DPhil diss., University of Oxford, 2008.

Dunnan, Stuart, "The Preaching of Hugh Latimer: a reappraisal." DPhil diss., University of Oxford, 1991.

Franke, John, "The Religious Thought of John Hooper." DPhil diss., University of Oxford, 1996.

Hildebrandt, Esther, "A Study of the English Protestant Exiles in Northern Switzerland and Strasbourg 1539–47, and their role in the English Reformation." PhD diss., University of Durham, 1982.

Johnston, P. F., "The Life of John Bradford, the Manchester Martyr, c.1510–1555." BLitt diss., University of Oxford, 1963.

Wheeler, Megan, "Protestants, Prisoners and the Marian Persecution." DPhil diss., University of Oxford, 2006.

Index of Scripture

Genesis
3—218
3:21—320
6–8—307
6:18—155
9—265, 298
9:9—155
9:11–12—155
9:13—155
9:15–17—155
12—301
15—3, 170
15:18—126, 155
17—3, 122, 124, 144, 155, 170, 171n, 299, 301
17:1—156, 188
17:1–14—130
17:7—126, 155, 207n, 263
17:9–11—155
17:12–14—277
17:13–14—155
17:14—251
17:19—155
17:21—155
18:16–33—177
19—192, 307
21:27—155
21:32—155
26:28—155
31:44—155

Exodus
12—307
19—190
20:6—260

Leviticus
18:5—138
18:16—56
20:21—56

Numbers
13–14—307
21:8–9—304

Deuteronomy
6:5—133
6:13—125
10:20—125

Joshua
3–4—307

1 Kings
11:34–39—219

Psalms
1—111
2:9—196
14:2—15
19:10—176
82–89, 152, 170
103:17–18—146

Isaiah
28:15–18—211
54:9—209

Ezekiel
9:4—203n

Jonah
1–4—159, 195
2:9—272
3—193

Index of Scripture

Matthew
4:10—125
5–7—163–64
5:7—166
6:14—166
6:26–30—307
7:7—166
16—182

Luke
11:9—15
23:39–43—18
24:35—252

John
6—281, 309, 312

6:47–63—308
6:55—239
6:63—226
14:23–24—133
17:20–26—215

Acts
2:37–41—284
2:42—285
15—291

Romans
4—324
4:11—308
9–11—185
11—190

1 Corinthians
1:13—255
10—309
11—287

2 Corinthians
3:6—262

Galatians
3:15—144

Colossians
2:11—123

Revelation
3:20–22—203n

Index of Subjects and Names

Act for the Advancement of True Religion (1543), 86
Act of Six Articles (1539), 61, 64, 72, 79, 86, 88, 91, 172, 184, 295, 342
Allen, Edmund (1510s–59), 27, 34, 44, 106, 110, 147, 211, 339–41, 346
Anabaptism, 47, 67, 71, 74, 91, 100, 117–19, 126, 128, 142, 163, 180, 195, 234–35, 259, 288, 339
Antwerp, 47, 50, 68–70, 87, 92–93, 95, 147, 151–52, 154–56, 158, 167–69, 178, 181, 265, 268, 272, 274, 276, 289, 309
Aquinas, Thomas (1225–74), 13, 15, 40
assurance, 6, 18–19, 142, 203, 208, 215–17, 245, 257, 275, 317, 324, 338
Augsburg Confession, 61–62
Augsburg Interim, 2
Aureole, Peter (c.1280–1322), 13

Bale, John (1495–1563), 34, 50, 69, 101, 168, 339–40
Barnes, Robert (1495–1540), 31, 42–43, 81, 168–69, 171, 175–76, 287–88
Basle, 6, 10, 66, 68, 73, 92, 104, 106, 117, 135, 137, 147, 185, 242, 337
Bayfield, Richard (d. 1531), 42–43, 49, 68, 168
Becon, Thomas (1512/13–67), 34, 58, 64–65, 69, 89, 340–41
Bern, 106, 241
Bible, 1, 4, 35, 37, 50, 55, 69–70, 82–83, 86–87, 111, 114, 136, 167, 169, 171, 177, 182–83, 307
  Coverdale Bible, 57, 87, 92, 169, 336
  English Psalter, 70
  Great Bible, 57, 172
  Greek New Testament, 100
  New Testament, 4, 14, 42, 68, 70–71, 73–74, 80, 92–93, 117, 120–21, 128, 136, 138, 140, 148, 156–57, 160, 164–67, 169–70, 179, 196, 210, 229, 242, 247, 269, 290

Index of Subjects and Names

Old Testament, 4, 107, 114, 121, 129, 133–34, 140, 156, 163, 203–4, 226, 242, 247, 268, 286, 296
sola scriptura, 20, 50, 114, 118, 344–45
translation, 35, 37
vernacular, 46, 55, 70, 82, 87
Vulgate, 4
Zürich Bible, 69, 169
Biel, Gabriel (c.1420/25–95), 12, 14–17, 127
Bilney, Thomas (1495–1531), 48, 76, 97
book trade, 65, 74–75, 80, 89, 92–93, 169, 283, 331, 340
censorship, 66, 69, 90
Frankfurt book fair, 70, 92
Bradford, John (1510–55), 34, 39–40, 97, 146, 200–221, 314–28, 330, 337–38
and John Traves, 201
at Cambridge, 205
imprisoned, 219
legal training, 201
preaching tour, 211, 327
Bucer, Martin (1491–1551), 2, 11–12, 29, 40, 51, 66, 68, 75, 77, 81, 84, 95, 106–7, 111, 135, 180, 184, 195, 198, 200, 205, 210, 215, 221, 223, 242, 257, 297, 304, 308–10, 314–17, 320, 322–23, 328, 332, 338
Bullinger, Heinrich (1504–75), 1–2, 7–10, 27, 29, 32, 34, 39, 46–47, 54, 67, 69, 73, 77, 79, 81–82, 84–85, 88, 105–9, 111, 113–14, 122, 124–25, 127–37, 139–40, 144–45, 160, 168, 177–86, 189, 192–95, 198, 200, 206, 220, 224, 226, 234, 239–53, 259, 263, 270, 278, 282–83, 288–89, 291, 295, 297, 300–302, 309–10, 312–14, 316, 321, 328–34, 336–37, 343, 346
and First Helvetic Confession, 242
and Waldensians, 240, 283

Calais, 73, 82, 93
Calvinism, 6–7, 25, 40, 43, 47, 50, 84, 106, 127, 135, 343, 345
Calvin, John (1509–64), 3, 6–10, 13, 26, 34, 40, 45, 51, 68, 76–77, 84, 102, 104, 107, 109, 111, 114, 125, 128–29, 131, 133, 135–45, 172, 183–84, 186, 192, 198, 206–7, 215, 219, 221, 224, 236, 240, 242–43, 247–50, 252–63, 283, 291–94, 297, 300, 302, 309, 313, 315, 323, 329, 331–34, 337–38, 343, 346
education, 135
Institutes of the Christian Religion, 109, 137–44, 172, 247, 253–62, 297, 302
marriage, 172
Worms Colloquy, 253

Index of Subjects and Names

Cambridge, 6, 8–9, 11–12, 14, 19, 21–24, 26–30, 35, 37, 40, 42, 44–45, 47–48, 50, 52, 59, 65–66, 74–77, 83, 88, 97, 99–100, 103, 107, 109, 110, 115, 118, 132, 135, 137, 141, 143–44, 147–48, 157, 160, 164, 167–69, 173, 183–84, 199–202, 205–6, 211, 214–15, 221, 223, 244, 264, 273, 285, 292–93, 297, 314–16, 320–21, 328, 338, 345, 347
catholicity, 51, 56
chantries, 111
Christian brethren, 47, 71–72, 98
Christian III, King of Denmark (1503–59), 291
Christology, 3, 8, 14, 17, 20, 131, 143, 194, 225–26, 238–39, 345
    Christocentrism, 117, 125, 132, 143, 145, 225, 332–33, 344, 347
    Son of God, 125, 225, 237
confessionalisation, 2–3, 9, 29, 47–48, 86, 106–7, 111, 221, 346
continental influence, 2, 6, 20, 22–23, 25, 27–28, 30–31, 33, 37, 41, 54, 66, 70, 91–92, 96, 98, 100–102, 107, 109, 146, 158, 160, 168, 177, 200, 220–21, 264, 283, 288, 329, 334, 336, 338, 342, 344–47
covenant, xii, 1–12, 14–16, 18–20, 30, 32–39, 41, 68–69, 113–14, 116–34, 136–47, 150–51, 153, 155, 160–79, 181, 183, 185, 188–89, 192–94, 196, 199–200, 205–11, 214–16, 218–21, 223–25, 227–29, 233–35, 237–41, 245–48, 251–53, 256–57, 259–61, 263–64, 268, 272, 277, 280–82, 285–86, 288, 295, 298–99, 301, 313–15, 318–19, 321, 324, 327–29, 331–41, 343–45, 347–48
    Abrahamic, 1, 3, 5, 122–24, 128, 130, 132–33, 139–40, 143, 155, 163, 177–79, 188, 207, 234–35, 245, 257, 260, 269, 277, 289, 301, 313, 340
    and Adam, 70, 123–24, 126, 128, 132, 148, 178–79, 186, 191, 203, 218, 267, 320, 341, 343, 348
    and blood, 62, 72, 119, 121, 126, 131–32, 150, 153–54, 158–59, 162, 166–67, 196, 207–8, 222–23, 225, 227, 235, 237–38, 240, 242–43, 245, 255–57, 261–62, 266, 271–75, 277, 279, 281, 285, 292–94, 318–23
    and Eden, 178
    and Egypt, 194, 289, 307
    and Noah, 128, 132, 178–79, 209, 269, 296
    berit, 3, 130, 155–56, 170, 172
    bilateral, xii, 4–5, 7–8, 10–11, 14, 16, 30, 34, 39, 41, 60, 71, 108, 114, 119–20, 122, 126, 128, 131–32, 134, 136, 138,

141–42, 144–46, 150–51, 153, 155–56, 158, 162–63, 168–71, 173, 176–78, 182, 186, 190, 192, 194, 196, 200, 204–5, 207, 211, 215–16, 220–21, 224–25, 237, 245, 252, 256–57, 259–61, 263, 268, 271, 274–75, 278–80, 295, 298, 313–15, 320, 329–31, 333–40, 343–44, 348
circumcision, 123, 155, 179, 227, 229, 234–35, 238, 241, 245, 247, 251, 255, 257, 259, 269–70, 272, 277, 279, 287–88, 296, 301, 308–9, 313, 318, 321, 324
commercium, 117
conditional, 4–7, 11, 14, 16–17, 19, 29, 31, 33, 35–36, 38, 59, 114–15, 119, 122–24, 129–33, 135–36, 138–40, 142, 145, 148, 152, 156, 158–59, 162, 164–67, 169–70, 173, 175, 181–82, 188–90, 192–93, 196, 198, 200–201, 204, 208, 211, 215, 221, 225, 228, 237, 240, 242, 259–61, 272, 279, 296, 331–32, 336–39, 343, 348
contract, 14, 35, 39, 136, 144, 165, 187, 189, 192, 298
Davidic, 119, 219
diathēkē, 3, 130, 144
erbgemächt, 121
foedus, 4, 11–12, 119, 122, 125, 130–31, 133, 137–38, 140, 143, 227–28, 242

friendship, 285
marriage, 168, 246
Near Eastern ritual, 130
pact, 4, 14–16, 18, 119, 122, 130–31, 136–37, 190, 227, 344, 348
pflicht, 120
pundt, 119–21, 128–30
testament, 1, 4–7, 11–12, 15–16, 49, 119–23, 125, 128–30, 133, 136–38, 141, 144, 148, 150–53, 155–56, 158–60, 163, 166–67, 169–72, 179, 181, 188, 193, 196, 204, 223–25, 227–28, 235, 237–38, 240, 251–53, 257, 268, 275, 279–80, 307, 320, 323, 333, 335, 339
unconditional, 4, 6–7, 16, 136, 139, 191, 216, 219, 223, 253, 338
unilateral, 4–5, 7–8, 10, 12, 16, 34, 119–20, 129, 131, 134, 136, 138, 140, 146, 148, 155, 171, 207, 219, 221, 223–24, 253, 269, 324, 328, 332–33, 335, 337–38
verstand, 119–21
Coverdale, Miles (1488–1569), xii, 31, 34, 37–38, 47, 57, 67, 69–70, 81, 87, 92, 146, 154, 167–73, 175–83, 199, 207, 220, 282–89, 291–94, 327–29, 331, 334, 336, 340, 346
at Bergzabern, 180, 183
at Tübingen, 172
in Hamburg, 154

Index of Subjects and Names

Cranmer, Thomas (1489–1556), 21, 27, 31, 34–35, 44, 50–51, 55, 59, 63, 65–66, 70, 75, 78–80, 82, 88, 107–8, 111–12, 195, 200, 223, 292, 297, 310, 320–22, 325, 328, 338, 346

Cromwell, Thomas (1485–1540), 23, 28, 32, 44, 58–59, 63, 69, 73–75, 77, 78–85, 87, 91, 111, 147, 152, 168, 171–72, 335, 346

Deuteronomy, book of, 113, 125, 133, 144

dissimulation, 64, 71, 80, 85, 90–91, 346

ecclesiology, 213, 233, 237

Edward VI, King of England (1537–53), 2, 21, 23, 27, 32, 41, 64, 76–77, 79, 87–88, 102, 106, 108–10, 112, 145, 181, 185, 211, 213, 220, 292, 305, 310, 337, 344

godly Josiah, 109

Eucharist, 223, 293

eucharistic theology, xii, 11, 66–68, 81, 94, 99–100, 107, 122, 223, 235–36, 241, 243, 249, 252, 266, 293, 302, 310, 314, 320, 322–23, 329, 338

federal theology, 5, 7, 10, 33, 38, 118, 126, 129, 137, 342–44, 348

covenant of grace, 129, 219, 343

covenant of works, 10, 343

First Zürich Disputation (1523), 118

forgiveness, 12, 159, 240, 266, 273, 275, 280, 299, 305, 322

Frith, John (1503–33), 66, 72, 73, 100–101, 167, 281, 304, 339, 356, 367

Froschauer, Christoph (1490–1564), 70, 130, 133, 175, 182, 242, 287, 340

Gardiner, Stephen (1483–1555), 30, 56, 59, 64, 89, 184–85, 295, 304, 313, 321

Genesis, book of, 3, 46, 118, 122, 124, 126, 130, 144, 155–56, 170–72, 177, 188, 207, 218, 235, 251, 263, 265, 268, 270, 277, 298–99, 301, 307, 320

Geneva, 2–3, 6, 10, 12, 33, 51, 74, 106, 135, 145, 183, 224, 249, 331, 345–46, 348

grace, 6–7, 9–10, 13–16, 18–19, 40, 46, 49, 57–58, 62, 66, 115, 117–18, 121–22, 126, 131, 133–37, 141, 153, 156, 158, 160, 162, 165–66, 173–75, 177, 182, 187, 191, 193, 197, 199–200, 205–6, 208, 213, 216, 220–22, 224–26, 228–32, 236, 240–41, 243–44, 246–56, 260, 263, 265, 272, 278, 281, 284, 290, 294, 298, 300, 302, 307,

Index of Subjects and Names

309, 311–12, 317, 320, 322–23, 325, 331, 333–34, 343–45, 348
  habitual, 13, 135
  sola gratia, 3, 16–17, 20, 31, 344–45
Grynaeus, Simon (1493–1541), 54, 185
Gwalther, Rudolph (1519–86), 79, 85, 105

Hamburg, 154, 168
Henry VIII, King of England (1491–1547), xii, 2, 22–23, 25, 27–28, 31, 35, 37, 41, 44, 47–49, 51–59, 61–62, 64–65, 76–77, 83, 87–88, 90, 98, 101–2, 106, 109, 112, 145, 149, 152, 157, 171, 344
  Defender of the Faith, 56
  household, 83
  Royal Supremacy, 57, 60, 82, 112
heresy, 21, 51, 54, 58, 72, 82–84, 91, 97, 129, 377
Hilles, Richard (1508–36), 73, 85, 92, 180
historiography, 26, 33, 96
  post-revisionist, 26
  revisionist, 24, 26, 96
Hoen, Cornelisz (1440–1524), 71, 94, 235, 240, 246, 258, 385
Holy Spirit, 12, 140, 157, 162, 167, 203, 210, 212, 217, 220, 224, 226, 229–31, 235–36, 241, 248–50

Hooper, John (1495/1500–1555), 34, 38–39, 85, 108–9, 129, 146, 172, 183–200, 206–7, 210, 213, 220–21, 236, 295–313, 325, 328–30, 334, 337, 341
  at Basle, 185
  at Cleeve, 183–84
  diocesan visitation, 199
  future Zwingli, 195
  marriage, 185
humanism, 2, 22–23, 54–55, 76–79, 83, 85, 90, 94, 99, 101–6, 109, 114, 117, 122, 147, 240, 342, 344
  biblical criticism, 104
  Erasmus of Rotterdam, 3, 45, 49, 54, 80, 103–4, 106, 111, 114, 117, 182, 205

iconoclasm, 74–75, 95, 342
Israel, 107, 116–17, 120–21, 186, 189, 194, 207, 235, 304

Jewel, John (1522–71), 32, 50
Jews, 4, 134, 138, 143, 158, 179, 185, 234, 238, 248, 259–60, 269–71, 274, 289–90
Joye, George (1490/95–1553), 34, 68, 70, 74, 169, 276, 339–40
justice, 19, 28, 58, 77, 101, 104, 106, 123, 140, 181, 196, 206, 231, 234, 237, 241, 256, 270
justification, xii, 13–19, 30–31, 36, 41, 55, 58–59, 62, 86, 90, 95, 105,

Index of Subjects and Names

113, 121–23, 129, 133–34, 139,
147–52, 156–58, 160–61, 164–
67, 176, 178–79, 182, 190, 192,
194, 199, 205, 208, 212, 226,
229, 242, 244, 254–55, 257,
264, 266, 276, 313, 336, 344
and Rahab, 178
by faith, xii, 3, 16, 19–20, 30–31,
35, 45, 55, 58–59, 62, 75, 86,
95, 113, 149–51, 156–57, 188,
336, 345, 348
double justification, 35, 157, 208
facere quod in se est, 14–17, 19
simul iustus et peccator, 165

Karlstädt, Andreas Bodenstein von
(1486–1541), 66–67, 71, 93
Kayserberg, Johannes Geiler von
(1445–1510), 17, 19, 118, 385

Latimer, Hugh (1485–1555), 76, 84,
88, 109, 110, 201, 211, 314–15,
320, 338
law, 6, 20, 31–32, 35, 63, 74, 94,
105, 116, 119, 133, 138–39,
145, 149–51, 157–60, 163–66,
172–73, 179, 182, 186, 189,
193, 201, 204, 208–9, 211–12,
214, 219–20, 273–74, 276, 279,
281, 291, 306–7, 318, 332–33,
335–36, 341, 343–44, 348
antinomianism, 30, 59, 153, 175,
204, 216, 343
Decalogue, 15, 38, 55, 74, 132–33,
158, 188, 194–95, 206, 214,
331–32, 336, 344
divine law, 56, 145, 170, 196, 200,
320, 331
legalism, 7, 36, 158, 165, 335, 343
moral, 132, 139, 343
Mosaic, 138, 157, 186, 196, 290
of love, 20, 133, 139, 152, 178,
274, 348
Pentateuch, 129, 154–57, 163–64,
168, 170, 220, 268, 271, 335
Sermon on the Mount, 163
Lollardy, 23–24, 69, 71, 76, 95–96,
98–101, 104, 282, 341
London, 3, 6, 15, 21–27, 29–31,
35–37, 40, 42–46, 48–53, 55, 57,
59, 62–81, 83–85, 87, 89–93,
96–98, 100–106, 109–11, 114,
118, 124, 127, 134–35, 139, 144,
146–47, 149, 157, 164, 166–73,
175, 182–83, 195, 198–99, 201,
204, 206–8, 211, 213, 223–24,
226, 229, 236–37, 241–43, 247,
249, 256–57, 261, 276, 284, 291,
293, 295, 310–11, 313–15, 317,
320–21, 323, 325, 327–28, 331,
339–42, 345–47
Low Countries, 46, 67, 70, 75,
91–96, 98
Lutheranism, xi, 3, 11, 15, 22, 26,
28–31, 43–47, 49–50, 53–54,
61–62, 69, 72–74, 76–78, 82,
84–87, 90, 93, 99–101, 103,
106, 147, 149, 171–72, 183,

Index of Subjects and Names

204, 223–24, 226, 242, 253, 257, 260, 281–83, 291–92, 294, 305, 310, 329, 334, 336–37, 342
political theory, 87
Luther, Martin (1483–1546), xi–xii, 3–5, 11, 15–18, 20, 22, 24, 26, 28–31, 35–36, 39–40, 42–47, 50, 53, 65–67, 70–72, 76–78, 90, 94–95, 97, 103–4, 106, 113–14, 119, 125, 140, 147–51, 153, 157–58, 161, 165–67, 169, 189, 192, 203, 205, 208, 214–17, 222–25, 230, 240, 242–44, 253, 256, 258, 266–68, 272–73, 282, 292–95, 297, 304, 308, 314, 323, 328, 332, 335, 339, 342, 345

Marburg Colloquy, 47, 95, 169, 173, 222–23, 230–31, 345
Marian Exile, 32, 88, 107, 183, 345
medieval theology, 3, 10, 12, 14–17, 19–20, 23–24, 29, 40, 50, 81, 96, 99, 102, 117, 122, 135, 202, 205, 222, 236, 268, 282, 344–45, 348
Melanchthon, Philip (1497–1560), 60, 66, 104–5, 134, 157, 205, 213, 243–46
merit, 15–17, 19, 30, 62, 126, 134, 156, 190, 211, 271

natural theology, 14
New England, 5–6, 136
nominalism, 52

Ockham, William of (1285–1347), 13, 15, 135
Œcolampadius, Johannes (1482–1531), 10, 36, 42–43, 49, 65–68, 77–78, 91, 93, 95, 101, 114, 118, 205, 226, 293, 308, 328
Oxford, xii, 2–9, 12, 21, 23–26, 28–29, 31, 34, 39–40, 44–46, 49–51, 58–59, 63, 66, 70, 74–81, 84–85, 92–93, 96, 98–108, 110, 115, 118, 122, 128, 133, 141, 146–47, 149, 158, 160, 163, 175, 180, 183–84, 189, 198, 200, 213, 218, 223, 227, 256, 264, 272, 282, 291, 295, 297, 310, 315–16, 321, 327, 342–44, 346–47

Paltz, Johannes von (1445–1511), 18
papacy, xi, 29, 43, 51, 56–57, 59–61, 94, 151, 172, 195, 283, 326, 344
Pelagianism, 16–17
political theory, 87, 113, 118, 136, 152
Pontefract Articles (1536), 66
predestination, 7–10, 31, 40–41, 76, 126, 128, 131, 137, 192, 203, 206–7, 214–19, 229, 233, 247, 301, 314, 317, 325–26, 333, 338
Free-will Controversy, 214–16, 327, 338
Puritanism, 3–6, 9–10, 19, 29, 31, 34–36, 38–39, 49–50, 78, 88, 101, 114, 118, 125, 136–37,

150, 167, 171, 178, 183–84,
194–95, 199, 211, 216, 236,
339, 342–43, 345, 347–48

Reformation
Edwardian, 21, 200
Henrician, 21, 30, 89, 98
Reformed theology, 2–3, 5–6, 8–10,
32–34, 37, 41, 60, 67, 135, 146,
160, 167, 183, 200, 220, 243,
253, 272, 328–29, 331, 333–35,
343, 348
religious identity, xi–xii, 2, 9, 27, 29,
34, 41, 43, 48–52, 57, 59, 63,
65, 69, 76, 80, 112, 115
repentance, 17, 94, 151, 166, 176,
187, 197, 201, 204, 211–12,
218, 248, 259, 275, 280, 288,
305, 320, 324
attrition, 18, 96
confession, 55
penance, 58, 73, 199, 212, 266–67
revelation, 13, 113, 131, 143, 187,
215, 240
righteousness, 5, 18, 20, 26, 121–22,
124, 126–27, 132, 134, 140,
143, 145, 148–49, 151, 157,
160, 164, 170, 188, 191,
208–10, 213, 289, 313, 331–33,
335–36, 344
imparted, 122, 148, 191, 333,
335–36
imputed, 122, 140, 191, 208–10,
333

Sacramentarianism, 43, 46–47, 63,
66–67, 70–74, 81–82, 84,
87–88, 91, 94–96, 99, 253, 304,
329, 337, 339, 341–42
sacraments, 2, 11, 14, 19, 33–34, 39,
41, 46, 55, 63, 71–74, 76, 96,
104, 109, 111, 124–25, 137,
140–41, 163, 178, 186, 194,
206, 221–34, 236–37, 239–59,
261–78, 281–84, 286–88, 290–
91, 293–329, 333–34, 336–38
alloiosis, 239
and Passover, 238, 279, 287–88,
296, 313
baptism, 14, 46, 100, 118, 123,
125, 128, 222, 226–29, 232–35,
238, 242, 247, 251, 254–56,
259, 263, 265–67, 269–70,
272, 274, 277, 279, 283–84,
288, 292, 296, 299–300, 305–6,
312–13, 317–18, 321–23,
325–26, 333, 339
circumcision, 123, 155, 179, 227,
229, 234–35, 238, 241, 245,
247, 251, 255, 257, 259, 269–
70, 272, 277, 279, 287–88, 296,
301, 308–9, 313, 318, 321, 324
Consensus Tigurinus (1549), 106,
111, 224, 244, 248–51, 321,
328, 334, 338
corporal presence, 46, 55, 82, 86,
94, 99, 222–23, 225, 238, 243,
266, 281, 292, 302, 304–5,
307–8, 310–11, 319, 321, 327

401

Index of Subjects and Names

Eucharist, 5, 12, 30, 46–47, 67, 73, 95, 111, 122, 125, 128, 168, 185, 205, 222–26, 228, 230, 232, 235, 237–43, 252, 255–57, 259–61, 263, 267, 275, 278–79, 281–83, 285–87, 288, 292–96, 301, 303–4, 307–11, 313–16, 318–20, 322–24, 328–29, 333–34
eucharistic sacrifice, 11, 266
Golden Calf, 307
marriage, 60, 83, 117, 266, 283
Mass, 23, 55, 74, 78, 82–83, 86, 95, 127, 206, 213–14, 222, 224–26, 236, 241, 311, 314, 320, 325
memorialism, 95, 227–28, 236, 243
military uniform, 270
monastic cowl, 233
paedobaptism, 247, 259–60, 273, 277, 300
pflichtszeichen, 227, 229
rainbow, 265, 268, 296, 298
repentance, 274
ring, 235, 270, 278
seals, 11, 121, 132, 137, 217, 225, 235, 247–50, 253, 257, 260–61, 280, 297, 316, 319, 322
Sodom, 177, 307
sunbeams, 297
symbolic parallelism, 240
tokens, 11, 235, 245, 252–53, 256–57, 269–71, 274, 285, 289, 297, 320, 322
transubstantiation, 55, 91, 205, 222, 281, 292, 295, 301, 304, 321, 325
true absence, 239, 315
unworthy participation, 237, 281
sanctification, 20, 41, 139, 157, 161, 164–65, 173–74, 189, 191, 209, 217, 220, 233, 255, 261, 265, 317–18
Schmalkaldic League, 60, 82, 106
scholasticism, 12–13, 19, 78, 102, 117, 342
Scotus, Duns (c.1266–1308), 13
sin, 15–18, 37, 115, 124, 131, 138, 143, 155, 159, 175, 182, 187, 190–91, 193, 202, 206, 210–11, 226, 233, 240, 255, 272, 275, 288, 305, 317, 323, 347
idolatry, 74, 109, 115, 124, 132, 135, 237, 272, 293, 311
original sin, 67, 76, 124–25, 148, 191, 228–29, 234–35
soteriology, 1, 4–6, 9, 11, 13–14, 16–20, 28, 30–31, 33, 35–37, 44, 52, 59, 95, 99, 115–16, 126, 129, 132–33, 135–36, 140–42, 145, 148–49, 151, 153, 155, 162–63, 165–66, 173, 178–79, 188, 192–95, 198, 200, 202–4, 207–12, 214, 216, 219, 221, 225–26, 230, 233, 236–38, 248, 250, 256–57, 260, 272, 277, 288, 300, 314, 319, 332–33, 335, 337–38, 341, 344–45, 347–48
propitiation, 122, 287

Index of Subjects and Names

Staupitz, Johannes von (c.1460–1524), 17–18
Strassburg, 2, 6, 11, 17, 22, 29–30, 38, 70–71, 73, 75, 79, 85, 92–93, 106, 135, 168, 172, 177, 180, 184–85, 253, 257, 283, 291
Swiss Confederation, 1–2, 38, 79, 88, 113, 168, 240, 291, 310, 332, 349
Swiss Reformation, xii, 1–2, 5, 8, 10, 26, 32–34, 37, 39, 41, 43, 54, 60, 65–67, 69–70, 74–75, 77, 79, 87, 94, 100–101, 104, 106–8, 111–16, 118–19, 127, 129, 135–36, 146–47, 152, 160, 167, 170, 172, 183, 200, 213, 220–24, 242–43, 253, 260, 264, 272, 315, 328–29, 331, 333–38, 341–42, 344, 348

Ten Articles (1536), 55, 62
Tyndale, William (c.1491–1536), xii, 32, 34–37, 42–43, 49, 67–68, 70, 73–74, 82, 84, 87, 92–93, 100, 105–6, 146–72, 183, 189, 196, 207–8, 210, 220–21, 265–82, 284, 304, 328–29, 334–36, 340–41
   and Martin de Keyser, 152, 169, 265

Vadian, Joachim (1484–1551), 81, 160
Vermigli, Peter Martyr (1499–1562), 32, 45, 78, 107, 310, 316, 347

Vestments Controversy, 38, 110, 198, 210, 337
via antiqua, 13, 117
via moderna, 13, 15–16, 117, 135

wills, 75, 101
Wittenberg, 22, 29–31, 46, 51, 53, 61, 67, 81, 131, 147, 172, 192, 224
Wolsey, Thomas (1473–1530), 65, 70, 77, 81, 92
worship, 115–16, 123, 145, 158–59, 161–62, 245, 332, 336, 345
Wyatt, Thomas (d.1542), 48, 65, 82, 85, 90, 320
Wyclif, John (1328–84), 96, 99, 101, 282

Zürich, 1–2, 6, 10, 12, 22, 27, 29–30, 32–33, 44, 46–47, 67–70, 73–76, 78, 80, 83, 85, 88, 104–9, 112–13, 115, 117–18, 120, 127, 130–31, 133, 135–36, 145–47, 150, 152, 168–69, 175, 180, 182–83, 185, 188–90, 192, 194–95, 198–200, 220, 224–25, 234, 239, 241–43, 249, 259, 268, 276, 281–84, 286–87, 291, 293–95, 304, 306, 310, 313–14, 316, 329, 331, 334, 336–40, 342, 344–46, 348
   exchange programme, 78, 80, 88, 342
   sausage-eating, 79
Zwinglianism, 47, 68, 71, 73, 75, 94,

99, 105, 116, 146, 170, 239,
243–44, 246, 249, 253, 258,
263, 270, 291, 293, 295, 302,
309, 315, 320, 323, 329, 334,
336–37

Zwingli, Huldrych (1484–1531), xii,
2, 10, 26, 33–34, 36, 42–44,
46–47, 49, 66–69, 71, 77–78,
81, 84–85, 89, 91, 93, 95, 104,
107–8, 113–28, 130–32, 134–
36, 138–40, 143–45, 148–49,
152, 160, 170, 173, 184, 186,
191, 195, 205, 221–45, 247,
249–56, 258–59, 263, 268–71,
273, 275–77, 282, 284–87, 293,
295–98, 302, 308, 321, 323,
326, 328–29, 331–34, 336,
340–41, 344–45

army chaplain, 115
education, 117
people's priest, 115
Sixty-Seven Articles, 225

Available in the Reformed Academic Dissertation Series

◆

It Has Not Yet Appeared What We Shall Be: A Reconsideration of the Imago Dei *in Light of Those with Severe Cognitive Disabilities*,
by George C. Hammond

How Should We Treat Detainees? An Examination of "Enhanced Interrogation Techniques" under the Light of Scripture and the Just War Tradition,
by J. Porter Harlow

Preaching with Biblical Motivation: How to Incorporate the Motivation Found in the Inspired Preaching of the Apostles into Your Sermons,
by Ray E. Heiple Jr.

The Trinity, Language, and Human Behavior: A Reformed Exposition of the Language Theory of Kenneth L. Pike,
by Pierce Taylor Hibbs

See Dead People: The Function of the Resurrection of the Saints in Matthew 27:51–54,
by Raymond M. Johnson

Marks of Saving Grace: Theological Method and the Doctrine of Assurance in Jonathan Edwards's A Treatise Concerning Religious Affections,
by Eric J. Lehner

The Triune God of Unity in Diversity: An Analysis of Perspectivalism, the Trinitarian Theological Method of John Frame and Vern Poythress,
by Timothy E. Miller

From Inscrutability to Concursus: Benjamin B. Warfield's Theological Construction of Revelation's Mode from 1880 to 1915,
by Jeffrey A. Stivason

The Doctrine of the Spirituality of the Church in the Ecclesiology of Charles Hodge,
by Alan D. Strange

"King of Israel" and "Do Not Fear, Daughter of Zion": The Use of Zephaniah 3 in John 12,
by Christopher S. Tachick

Early Reformation Covenant Theology: English Reception of Swiss Reformed Thought, 1520–1555,
by Robert J. D. Wainwright

I Do Good to All People as You Have Opportunity: A Biblical Theology of the Good Deeds Mission of the New Covenant Community,
by John A. Wind

A Strategy for Incorporating Biblical Counseling in North American Church Plants,
by Rush Witt

A Development, Not a Departure: The Lacunae in the Debate of the Doctrine of the Trinity and Gender Roles,
by Hongyi Yang

Free to Be Sons of God
by Geoffrey M. Ziegler

Robert J. D. Wainwright (M.A., M.St., D.Phil., University of Oxford) is chaplain, fellow, and tutor for admissions and outreach at Oriel College and a member of the theology faculty at the University of Oxford. Before coming to Oriel, he read history at St John's College, Durham, and Christ Church, Oxford, and theology at Wycliffe Hall, Oxford.

Also from P&R Publishing

Christ and Covenant Theology: Essays on Election, Republication, and the Covenants

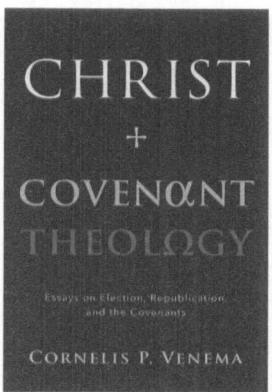

"No one today is better qualified to address the perennially important issues of covenant theology than Cornel Venema. In this volume he considers some of these issues in the context of current discussions and debates, doing so in a particularly instructive and helpful manner."
—**Richard B. Gaffin Jr.**, Professor of Biblical and Systematic Theology, Emeritus, Westminster Theological Seminary

"Cornelis Venema sheds much-needed light on issues ranging from the doctrine of republication to the Federal Vision theology. Regardless of whether one agrees with all of Venema's specific conclusions, his arguments cannot be ignored. A must-read."
—**Keith Mathison**, Professor of Systematic Theology, Reformation Bible College

"Cornel Venema . . . is an expert to whom I have often looked for analysis and assessment of important issues relating to classic covenant theology. . . . Venema is superb in his synopsis of and engagement with these kinds of issues."
—**Ligon Duncan**, Chancellor and CEO, Reformed Theological Seminary

www.ingramcontent.com/pod-product-compliance
Lightning Source LLC
Chambersburg PA
CBHW020544300426
44111CB00008B/787